IMMIGRANT ENGLAND, 1300–1550

D1609822

Manchester University Press

MANCHESTER MEDIEVAL STUDIES

SERIES EDITOR Professor S. H. Rigby

The study of medieval Europe is being transformed as old orthodoxies are challenged, new methods embraced and fresh fields of enquiry opened up. The adoption of interdisciplinary perspectives and the challenge of economic, social and cultural theory are forcing medievalists to ask new questions and to see familiar topics in a fresh light.

The aim of this series is to combine the scholarship traditionally associated with medieval studies with an awareness of more recent issues and approaches in a form accessible to the non-specialist reader.

IMMIGRANT ENGLAND,
1300–1550

W. Mark Ormrod, Bart Lambert and Jonathan Mackman

Manchester University Press

Published by Manchester University Press
Altrincham Street, Manchester M1 7JA
www.manchesteruniversitypress.co.uk

British Library Cataloguing-in-Publication Data
A catalogue record for this book is available from the British Library

ISBN 978 1 5261 0915 6 hardback
ISBN 978 1 5261 0914 9 paperback

First published 2019

Typeset by Out of House Publishing
Printed in Great Britain
by TJ International Ltd, Padstow

CONTENTS

FIGURES

TABLES

PREFACE

This book has its genesis in the research project 'England's Immigrants, 1330–1550' (2012–15), funded by the Arts and Humanities Research Council of the United Kingdom. The database that resulted, 'England's Immigrants, 1330–1550', www.englandsimmigrants.com, provides much of the raw evidence that is analysed in the chapters that follow and offers many further opportunities for development and interpretation.

W. Mark Ormrod was the principal investigator on the 'England's Immigrants' project; Bart Lambert one of the research assistants; and Jonathan Mackman the research fellow. Our primary debts of gratitude go to the other members of the core research team: the co-investigators, Nicola McDonald and Craig Taylor; the other research assistant and impact officer, Jessica Lutkin; the two PhD students, Jenn Bartlett and Christopher Linsley; and the editorial assistant, Jonathan Hanley. We are also appreciative of the invaluable input from the members of the International Board set up to advise the project, comprising James Bolton, Peter Fleming, Francesco Guidi-Bruscoli, Antonio Castro Henriques, Christian Liddy, Serge Lusignan, Maryanne Kowaleski, Sarah Rees Jones, Andrea Ruddick and Len Scales. Alan Bryson and Alan Kissane also contributed to the later stages of the project's academic development.

Judith Bennett was a major supporter of the project throughout, and we acknowledge her willingness to share her own research from the project data in advance of its publication. Nicholas Amor, Michael Bennett, Alan Bryson, David Ditchburn, Jonathan Finch, Judith Frost, Tom Johnson, Robert Kinsey, Ada Mascio, Christine Meek, Milan Pajic, Joshua Ravenhill, Jill Redford and Megan Tidderman have been generous with advice and references from their unpublished research. We are grateful to Cath D'Alton for her expertise in compiling the maps, and to Áine Foley for constructing the index. Michael Pidd and Matthew Groves of the Digital Humanities Institute at the University of Sheffield, who created and continue to host the 'England's Immigrants' database, have provided exemplary professional services throughout. Sean Cunningham, Andrew Payne and other colleagues at the UK National Archives have provided essential liaison, created the local infrastructure for the London-based researchers, and been instrumental in the development of the impact strategy.

A special acknowledgement is due to Nicola McDonald, who was originally going to contribute to the writing of this book but was subsequently prevented by circumstance and other duties. Nicola provided significant creative input to the early planning phases, and her knowledge of the linguistic and literary background of later medieval England helped inform the cultural history contained in chapters 9 and 10.

In the latter phases of the writing of this book, Bart Lambert's work was funded by the HERA Joint Research Programme 3: Uses of the Past (on the project 'CitiGen') and the European Commission through Horizon 2020 (grant agreement 649307).

We are grateful to the series editor, Stephen Rigby, for his close reading and constructive criticism of our work; to the staff of Manchester University Press, especially Meredith Carroll and Alun Richards, for their support and advice in preparing this book for publication; and to the anonymous reader who provided many useful comments on the penultimate version of the text. Finally, we acknowledge with particular gratitude the support provided to our project by the Centre for Medieval Studies, the Department of History and the Humanities Research Centre at the University of York.

W. Mark Ormrod
Bart Lambert
Jonathan Mackman
February 2018

ABBREVIATIONS

CCR	*Calendar of the Close Rolls Preserved in the Public Record Office, Henry III–Henry VII*, 61 vols (London, 1892–1963).
CFR	*Calendar of the Fine Rolls Preserved in the Public Record Office, Edward I–Henry VII*, 22 vols (London, 1911–62).
CIM	*Calendar of Inquisitions Miscellaneous, 1219–1485*, 8 vols (London and Woodbridge, 1916–2003).
CLBL A–L	*Calendar of the Letter Books of the City of London, A–L*, ed. R. R. Sharpe, 11 vols (London, 1899–1912).
Complete Peerage	G. E. Cokayne (ed.), *The Complete Peerage of England, Scotland, Ireland, Great Britain and the United Kingdom*, rev. V. Gibbs et al., 13 vols (London, 1910–59).
CPR	*Calendar of the Patent Rolls Preserved in the Public Record Office, Henry III–Henry VII*, 54 vols (London, 1891–1916).
LMA	London Metropolitan Archives (London).
LP	*Letters and Papers, Foreign and Domestic, of the Reign of Henry VIII*, ed. J. S. Brewer, J. Gairdner and R. H. Brodie, 37 vols (London, 1862–1932).
ODNB	H. C. G. Matthew and B. H. Harrison (eds), *Oxford Dictionary of National Biography*, 61 vols (Oxford, 2004).
POPC	*Proceedings and Ordinances of the Privy Council of England*, ed. N. H. Nicolas, 7 vols (London, 1834–7).
PROME	*The Parliament Rolls of Medieval England*, ed. P. Brand, S. Phillips, W. M. Ormrod, G. Martin, C. Given-Wilson, A. Curry and R. Horrox, 16 vols (Woodbridge, 2005).
SR	*Statutes of the Realm*, 11 vols (London, 1810–28).
TNA	The National Archives of the United Kingdom (Kew).
WAM	Westminster Abbey Muniments (London).

1

Introduction: immigrant England

Between 1300 and 1550, England was a temporary or permanent home to hundreds of thousands of people of foreign birth. These immigrants – male and female, adults and children – came from other parts of the British Isles, from more or less all the regions of continental Europe, and (especially at the end of the period) from the wider world of Africa and Asia. They settled not just in the major cities and towns but also in rural communities, having a documented presence in every county of England. They numbered in their ranks aristocrats, professional people such as scholars, doctors and clergy, prosperous traders and skilled craftspeople, and numerous semi- and unskilled workers involved in commerce, manufacturing and agriculture. Some came as refugees escaping economic, political or religious turmoil in their homelands, and a few may have come as forced labour. Most, though, arrived as a result of self-determination, facilitated by the general openness of borders and encouraged by the perceived opportunities that migration might bring. Their host communities in England occasionally remarked on their difference in terms of language, custom and dress, and gave them identities that either reinforced connections to the homeland (John the Frenchman, Joan Scot) or effectively eradicated it by using occupational surnames (Henry Brewer, William Goldsmith, Alice Spinner). Some were allowed to become subjects of the king and to acquire the status of denizen, equivalent to that of people born in England. Others were subject to severe limitations on their legal rights and ability to work. During periods of national emergency, these incomers could fall under suspicion as infiltrators and spies, and be subjected to head counts, restrictions on movement and repatriation. At other moments of high tension, they could be easy scapegoats for the frustrations both of the elite and of ordinary folk. But they were also acknowledged for their contribution to the economy, to education, culture and religion, to the defence of the realm and to public service. If immigrants were sometimes seen as a potentially disruptive presence, they were also understood to be a natural and permanent part of the social order.

This book sets out to explore and understand the lives and experiences of these people, and thus to address a notable problem in existing understandings of English history. Conventional histories of immigration to Britain sweep briefly across the Middle Ages, noting the waves of conquerors and settlers from the Romans and the Anglo-Saxons to the Vikings and the Normans. Thereafter, virtually nothing is said until the mid-sixteenth century, with the first arrivals of religious refugees in the form of the French Huguenots and 'Dutch' Protestant dissenters.[1] General political and cultural histories have reinforced this notion by treating England as comparatively isolated from the continent of Europe after the loss of Normandy by King John in 1204 and noting its development over the later medieval period as a sovereign state with a keener, more exclusive sense of nationhood.[2] Only London, supposedly, was an exception: as the national centre both for government and for trade, it continued, in every generation, to attract people from all over Europe and beyond.[3] Otherwise, England in the fourteenth and fifteenth centuries is generally perceived as a 'closed' society whose contacts with the outside world were founded not on the presence of immigrants but on a passing acquaintance with foreign envoys, merchants and pilgrims.

Migration involves both 'push' and 'pull' factors: people moved around in medieval Europe because of poor conditions in their natal lands and the perception or reality of better opportunities elsewhere. At first sight, the appalling natural and man-made disasters that hit England during the period look like disincentives to immigration. The onset of a severe famine in 1315–22 and the advent of the Black Death in 1348 took a terrible toll in the fourteenth century, reducing the population from between 4 and 6 million in 1300 to only about 2.75 million in the late 1370s. Plague and other diseases became endemic, so that the population remained virtually static, at around 2 to 2.5 million, until the end of the fifteenth century.[4] From the 1370s, the balance of trade went into long-term deficit, and foreigners coming into England were subjected to higher and higher customs duties and restrictions on their commercial activities and personal movements. In the 1440s, England went into a deep and prolonged economic recession, with a collapse of imports and exports, a major contraction in internal markets and a serious shortage of ready coin; signs of recovery did not become evident until the 1470s.[5]

For much of the period under consideration, furthermore, England was at war. Hostilities with Scotland began in the 1290s as a result of Edward I's attempts to take over the independent northern kingdom as an adjunct of England; although such aims were abandoned under Edward III, war with the Scots continued intermittently into the fifteenth and sixteenth centuries. War with France also began in the 1290s and continued into the early Tudor period: although historians use the term 'Hundred Years War' specifically to refer to the phases of hostility between 1337 and 1453, these were really part of a more prolonged series of conflicts lasting intermittently from the reign of Edward I to that of Henry VIII. Such wars, and disputes with other continental powers, created further significant strains on the economy. They pushed up levels of taxation such as to precipitate regular discontent and occasional open defiance, as in the Peasants' Revolt of 1381 and the resistance to the ironically labelled Amicable Grant in 1525. Endemic warfare intensified suspicions of enemy aliens and led to occasional demands for their expulsion. On a local level at least, there were also occasional threats to social order as a result of noble rebellions and civil war, especially in the so-called Wars of the Roses of the later fifteenth century.[6]

Finally, the later Middle Ages witnessed the introduction in England, as in other parts of Europe, of exclusionary policies designed severely to limit racial and religious diversity.[7] Edward I's decision to expel all Jews from England in 1290, and the official upholding of this ordinance until the seventeenth century, meant that England was marked by deep cultural and institutional discrimination against racial minorities. Muslims from southern Europe, North Africa and the Middle East – usually referred to as 'Saracens' in medieval Christendom – were not subject to an official ban, but the presumption was that they, like the Jews, were only officially acknowledged in England if they accepted conversion to Christianity. Historians have long remarked how, in the sixteenth century, the Tudor state bowed to political concerns over the presence of observable ethnic and racial minorities and began an intermittent programme of minority persecution, first against gypsies and later supposedly against people of colour. Such actions sent the very firm message that minorities were not just unwelcome but also effectively outlawed. Under this combination of environmental, economic, institutional and cultural factors, it is easy to suppose why historians have assumed for so long that there were few 'pull' factors encouraging foreign immigrants into late medieval England.

Such a negative picture is significantly modified, however, when we understand the 'push' factors that induced people to move, and the better conditions and positive attractions that were still available, and understood to prevail, in England.[8] Significant numbers of people from other parts of the British Isles, whether the Plantagenet dominions of Ireland and Wales or the enemy state of Scotland, clearly found that the relatively highly urbanised and commercialised economy of England provided opportunities for advancement that were not available at home. The situation was different for people from southern Europe: for the inhabitants of the kingdom of Castile, for example, which recovered rapidly from the Black Death and whose stable agricultural and commercial economy was buoyed up by the exploration and colonisation of the Atlantic and the Indies, England offered palpably few incentives, at least until Jewish converts to Christianity began fleeing religious persecution in Iberia in the sixteenth century.[9] In many parts of north-west Europe, however, an even greater intensity of natural disasters and political turmoil made England seem, in comparison, a relatively stable and conducive destination.[10] The drop in the rural and urban workforce meant that wages and purchasing capacity in England were attractively high, and certainly higher in real terms than in many parts of the continent: the so-called 'golden age of the English labourer' in the fifteenth century, when goods were cheap and wages were high, provided a strong inducement to the movement of labour over both short and long distances.[11] For all the suspicion that immigrants could arouse, moreover, the English state continued at least until the first half of the fifteenth century to offer them a widening range of fiscal and legal incentives. Laws were passed to make it easier for aliens involved in trade to maintain their commercial interests in England; special measures were taken to draw in people with particular skills; and exemptions were readily granted from the periodic threats to expel enemy aliens during times of war.[12] Facilitating all of this was the fact that England's borders generally remained open, at least to those who were not active enemies of the state. The great majority of people who crossed to England were not required to produce and keep identification papers, and often found it relatively easy to disappear into their new host communities.

The absence of, or lack of access to, detailed records about immigrants in the Middle Ages meant the development of various unsupported traditions and myths in post-medieval popular culture. Particularly powerful in the public imagination was (and to some extent still is) the story of the Flemish weavers. There is good documentary evidence, long available, that Edward III encouraged skilled cloth makers from Flanders into England to help develop what was then still a nascent textile industry.[13] Many of the historic centres of woollen cloth production in East Anglia and Kent have therefore long claimed that Flemish weavers moved there in the fourteenth century, conveniently ignoring the fact that in many cases the real influx came with the much larger numbers of 'Dutch' weavers who arrived among the Protestant refugees reaching England from the 1560s onwards.[14] Not surprisingly given the nineteenth century's interest in all things medieval, the great textile-producing cities of the North that grew to greatness after the Industrial Revolution also began to exercise their historical imagination in claiming the same lineage. In the early 1880s Ford Madox Brown painted a series of historical murals for Manchester Town Hall. One of them, *The Establishment of Flemish Weavers in Manchester, A.D. 1363*, a detail of which appears on the cover of this book, created the attractive fiction that Edward III's wife, Philippa of Hainault, had been patroness of a Flemish settlement in Lancashire and visited its members every springtime.[15] The statue of the Black Prince erected in the centre of Leeds in 1903 made a similar fanciful reference by linking the prince with his father's Flemish ally, James van Artevelde, and thus suggesting that Leeds, too, owed its modern textile industry to the enterprise of fourteenth-century immigrants from Flanders.[16]

In fact, the explosion of record keeping that occurred in England during the thirteenth century allows us, in a way that is not possible before that time, to trace the immigrant presence not just as a general impression or popular tradition but in the highly detailed and personal experiences of named individuals. Two key sources shed light on this matter for the fourteenth and fifteenth centuries: first, grants of special rights by the crown to aliens dwelling within the realm, kept in the records of the royal Chancery; and secondly, the returns to a special series of taxes on foreigners resident in the realm collected at various points between 1440 and 1487, known as the alien subsidies, preserved among the documentation of the king's Exchequer. The archivist Montagu Giuseppi and the economic historian William Cunningham first drew scholarly attention to these records in the 1890s.[17] It was not until after World War II, however, that historians began to make systematic use of these and other records in order to test older notions about the alien presence in later medieval England. In 1954, Clive Parry published an important study that recognised the contribution to the longer history of naturalisation made by the so-called letters of denization: that is, royal grants of denizen equivalence given to aliens in return for their taking oaths of loyalty to the English crown.[18] Legal historians – most notably Keechang Kim – have developed Parry's work into more detailed analyses of the origins of denization and of the status of aliens within the English common law.[19] Meanwhile, in 1957,

Sylvia Thrupp published the first attempt to analyse the alien subsidy material for the first year of the collection of the tax, 1440.[20] She, and later Gervase Rosser and Martha Carlin, made studies of the alien subsidy material as it related to the city of London and its suburbs; and in 1998 J. L. Bolton published a definitive edition of the most complete of the London returns for the tax, those of 1440 and 1483–4.[21] A number of case studies for other regions and towns, including Norfolk, York and Bristol, were also published from the 1960s onwards.[22] However, serious work on both denizations and the alien subsidies was still hampered by the inaccessibility and cumbersome nature of the relevant records. In 2015, W. Mark Ormrod and his research team released the website 'England's Immigrants, 1330–1550', which includes a complete database of the contents of these and certain other relevant archival materials.[23] This resource greatly facilitates further analysis both of the origins of denization and of the immigrant groups who found their way to England in the fourteenth and fifteenth centuries.[24]

Since the alien subsidy records lie at the heart of the present study, a little more should be said here about the circumstances under which this new tax was introduced in 1440 and perpetuated for nearly a half-century thereafter.[25] The tax was granted by the English Parliament at a moment of particularly high tension in Anglo-French relations when, as a result of a series of disastrous diplomatic and military setbacks, there was a very real risk that England would lose all her remaining possessions in France and suffer direct coastal attacks and even full-scale invasion. Suspicion therefore fell not just upon French-born people living in England but on a wide range of others who might be thought to be sympathetic to the Valois monarchy, especially immigrants from the duke of Burgundy's territories in the Low Countries and those from France's oldest ally, Scotland. For this reason, the tax grant was written in very general terms, with very few exemptions allowed. It was to be collected as a poll tax and levied on all adults over the age of twelve at the rate of 1s. 4d. for householders and 6d. for non-householders. There was little perception of the amount that might be raised by this means, and the householder rate was not fixed so high as to suggest a real attempt to exploit alien wealth. Rather, the original intention of the subsidy was probably two-fold: to top up the income the crown derived from taxation of the population at large; and to provide a very crude form of alien registration so as to give an assurance to sections of the political community that 'something was being done' about the potential security risk posed by the presence of foreigners within the realm.

This new form of security measure was considered useful enough to be repeated regularly in the 1440s, and then turned into an annual process for the lifetime of Henry VI in 1453. When Henry was deposed in 1461, the new regime of Edward IV ordered the continuation of the 1453 grant, and the levy became a regular and relatively routine event, referred to colloquially as 'aliens' money' or 'aliens' silver'.[26] After 1471, however, Edward IV chose not to renew it, and it was revived briefly on only two subsequent occasions, in 1483 and 1487. The abandonment of the separate alien subsidy thereafter was an acknowledgement that it had long since outlived its useful purpose. The fiscal category of alien was revived under Henry VIII, and in 1512 became part of a new series of comprehensive direct taxes known as the Tudor subsidies, but was included as a matter of completeness rather than because of any particular effort to track foreigners.

In spite of the challenges involved in their analysis and interpretation, the records of the alien subsidies provide an unparalleled resource for studying the numbers, types and conditions of immigrants to late medieval England. Because it was a poll tax with no lower limit of assessment, the subsidy caught in its net many of the 'little people' who normally go unnoticed in other immigrant records, as well as a very significant number of women. From these basic units of information, we can build quite detailed models, developed in chapters 3–7, about overall numbers, about the social and geographical distribution of the alien population, and about the particular contributions that such people made to the economic life of their localities and regions. We can demonstrate that, far from being a solely urban phenomenon, immigration was a regular reality in the small towns and villages of rural England and, in some cases, a significant component in the agricultural economy. By combining the alien subsidy records with other sources – the documentation of central and local government, literary texts and visual imagery – we can also go further and, in chapters 9 and 10, consider some of the non-material aspects of immigrants' lives. In particular, we address there the issues of inclusion and exclusion and question the typicality of the host community's latent or active hostility to incomers and minorities. We therefore aim to work out from the records of the alien subsidies and analyse, both quantitatively and qualitatively, the immigrant presence and experience in England between the expulsion of the Jews in 1290 and the coming of the Huguenots and the 'Dutch' Protestants in the 1560s, and thus to restore a lost and important element of the wider history of immigration.

This vocabulary of 'immigration' used in this book requires some explanation and justification. The English word 'immigrant' has its roots in classical Latin but was not used in the vernacular until as late as the eighteenth century. It literally means a 'comer-in': someone who leaves one place for another. Although it can apply to local or regional migration, it tends today to denote the crossing of national boundaries, and carries implications of long-term settlement.[27] In the later Middle Ages, the status of immigrant was normally captured by the term 'alien': *alienigenus* in Latin, and hence *alien* in both Anglo-Norman French and, by the later fourteenth century, Middle English usage.[28] In formal terms, an alien was understood as someone who owed no direct allegiance to the sovereign power, the king, and was thus separated off from his direct subjects. It is important to note, however, that 'alien' was just as applicable to visitors as it was to permanent settlers: in general, the law of alienage that emerged from the thirteenth century made no formal distinction between such sub-categories.[29] Consequently, while all immigrants were aliens, not all aliens were immigrants.

The terms 'foreigner' and 'stranger' were also in frequent use in later medieval England: the general Latin forms were *forinsecus* and *extraneus*, while Anglo-Norman used *forein* and *estranger* and Middle English *forein* and *straunger*.[30] Originally, a 'foreigner' was simply an outsider to the town, locality or region concerned: English people were therefore treated as 'foreigners' when they moved to new places within the realm. The term continued to have this meaning through the later Middle Ages and beyond, especially in self-governing cities and towns that distinguished between those who acquired civic freedom by birth and those who had to earn it in other ways.[31] The word 'stranger' originally had much the same sense as 'foreigner', but came more quickly to denote a different nation-ality, and with the development of Middle English as a language of record in the fifteenth and sixteenth centuries it was often preferred over the more legalistic 'alien'.[32]

All three words, 'alien', 'foreigner' and 'stranger', are therefore somewhat problematic for a modern readership considering a medieval topic. For the purposes of this book, we have generally dropped the term 'stranger': as with other words used to describe outsiders in the later Middle Ages, like the Middle English adjective *outlandish*, it now carries other connotations, and can be misleading to a modern readership. However, we freely deploy all three of our other key terms – 'immigrant', 'alien' and 'foreigner' – and do so specifically and solely to denote people born outside the borders of England. Our default for long-term settlers, 'immigrant', is ironically the most useful precisely because it was not in usage during the period concerned. In claiming the term, however, we do not seek necessarily to associate ourselves with any of the modern political, social and cultural meanings that attach to it; rather, we are mindful of the fact that 'alien' and 'foreigner' were also heavily freighted with meanings, both positive and negative, during the later Middle Ages and that anachronistic terminology can sometimes convey meanings more appropriate for a modern audience addressing a given time and place in history.

The word 'immigrant', as we noted above, is often today associated with medium- to long-term settlement. Neither today nor in the Middle Ages, however, is the immigrant to be considered automatically as one seeking permanent residence. Apart from those passing through as part of a longer-distance migration, there are always others who seek to live in the adopted place only for a defined period, or for a part of their life; and there is also the phenomenon of reverse migration to be taken into account, in which the individual returns to his or her homeland out of necessity or choice. As chapter 3 makes clear, then, there is much uncertainty over the length of time that those caught in the tax net of the alien subsidies had actually been resident in England, let alone how much longer they continued to remain after the assessment and collection of the tax. Nevertheless, there are strong indications, explored further in the discussion of national groupings in chapters 4 and 5, that the officials responsible for administering the alien subsidy concentrated their efforts, for good reasons, on the more settled members of the incoming population. Furthermore, as we shall see in chapters 6 and 7, while agricultural labourers in particular may have circulated back and forth across national boundaries on a regular basis, there are good reasons to believe that other people, of low as well as high estate, made the move to England for whole stages of their lives, and in a significant number of cases permanently. In spite of the difficulties of tracking specific individuals across time, then, there is sufficient evidence in samples taken from the alien subsidies to indicate that many of the immigrants identified at various points between 1440 and 1487 were indeed settled for some considerable time within the realm.

Finally, it needs to be stressed that the study that follows focuses almost exclusively on *first*-generation immigrants. In modern usage, the term 'immigrant' is sometimes used to describe self-perpetuating cultures in which subsequent generations, although born within the host country and having full rights there, maintain the traditions of the ancestral homeland and identify strongly with it, especially in terms of their ethnicity or race. As we shall see in chapters 8–10, there is comparatively little evidence, even in those places that had relatively high numbers of immigrants from particular countries or linguistic groupings, that the children and grand-children of incomers to England in the later Middle Ages preserved a coherent sense of foreignness – or indeed had one imposed upon them. Ultimately, this was because the vast majority of England's immigrants up to the time of the Reformation were born, or absorbed, into the one religion sanctioned by Church, state and society: Catholic Christianity. In identifying the apparently high levels of assimilation and toleration of immigrants found in England during the later Middle Ages, we therefore need also to reflect on the wider cultural and legal forces that saw diversity as a threat and regarded conformity as an absolute.

Notes

1 Among more recent such works, see Miles, *Tribes of Britain*; Conway, *A Nation of Immigrants?*; Windsor, *Bloody Foreigners*.

2 See, for example, Prestwich, *English Politics*; Turville-Petre, *England the Nation*; Harriss, *Shaping the Nation*; Clanchy, *England and its Rulers*.

3 *Alien Communities*.

4 Goldberg, *Medieval England*, pp. 71–87; Rigby, 'Introduction', pp. 1–30.

5 For the significance of the 'great slump', see chapters 2 and 6.

6 Grant, *Independence and Nationhood*; Curry, *Hundred Years War*; Cohn, *Popular Protest*.

7 For further discussion of the points raised in this paragraph, see chapter 8.

8 See further discussion in chapter 6.

9 Mackay, *Spain in the Middle Ages*, pp. 121–42, 168–71.

10 See chapter 6.

11 Dyer, 'A golden age rediscovered'; and see further discussion in chapter 7.

12 See chapter 2.

13 One of the first historians properly to document this process was Lipson, *Economic History of England*, *I*, pp. 451–2. The first edition of Lipson's book appeared in 1915.

14 For an indicative antiquarian approach to the local presence of Flemish weavers, see Tarbutt, 'Ancient cloth trade of Cranbrook'.

15 Treuherz, *Ford Madox Brown*, pp. 290–1. For Madox Brown's own explanatory notes on the mural, written in c. 1893, see Bendiner, *Art of Ford Madox Brown*, p. 159.

16 Dimes and Mitchell, *Building Stone Heritage of Leeds*, p. 42. The myth was first dispelled, at least for scholarly circles, by Heaton, *Yorkshire Woollen and Worsted Industries*, pp. 8–21. See also, more generally, Gribling, *Image of Edward the Black Prince*, pp. 1–3.

17 Giuseppi, 'Alien merchants'; Cunningham, *Alien Immigrants*, pp. 65–134. Note that Cunningham remained unaware of the alien subsidies.

18 Parry, *British Nationality Law*.

19 Kim, *Aliens in Medieval Law*; Summerson, 'Foreigners and felony'; Jenks, 'Justice for strangers'.

20 Thrupp, 'Survey'. For an earlier case study, see Redstone, 'Alien settlers in Ipswich'.

21 Thrupp, 'Aliens in and around London'; Rosser, *Medieval Westminster*, pp. 182–96: Carlin, *Medieval Southwark*, pp. 157–62; *Alien Communities*.
22 Kerling, 'Aliens in the county of Norfolk'; Dobson, 'Aliens in the city of York'; Dresser and Fleming, *Bristol*.
23 England's Immigrants 1330–1550, www.englandsimmigrants.com (accessed 11 September 2017).
24 Lambert and Ormrod, 'Friendly foreigners', pp. 5–7.
25 For the remainder of this and the next three paragraphs, see Ormrod and Mackman, 'Resident aliens', pp. 8–11.
26 *PROME*, XIII, 298; *CPR 1467–77*, pp. 95, 110.
27 Oxford English Dictionary, www.oed.com, s.v. 'immigrant' (accessed 10 August 2017).
28 Middle English Dictionary, http://quod.lib.umich.edu/m/med/, s.v. 'alien' (accessed 10 August 2017); and see further discussion in chapter 2. Note also the adoption of the word 'alien' into Welsh by the fifteenth century: Lewis, 'Late medieval Welsh praise poetry', p. 124.
29 Pollock and Maitland, *History of English Law*, I, 458–67.
30 Dictionary of Medieval Latin from British Sources, www.dmlbs.ox.ac.uk, s.vv. (accessed 18 January 2018); Anglo-Norman Dictionary, www.anglo-norman.net, s.vv. (accessed 10 August 2017); Middle English Dictionary, http://quod.lib.umich.edu/m/med/, s.vv. (accessed 10 August 2017).
31 See, for example, Masschaele, *Peasants, Merchants, and Markets*, pp. 149–58.
32 Pearsall, 'Strangers'; Pettegree, 'Stranger community'.

2

Defining and regulating the immigrant

The category of 'alien'

'Alien' is a word that has strong legal connotations today, since it is often used in relation to the non-naturalised immigrant. Until the thirteenth century, however, the term did not have any particularly clear implications in law. This is generally explained by the fact that, for the previous two hundred years and more, England was ruled by people of Scandinavian and French birth or descent. Since many of these had interests outside England, it was impossible to have a legal system limited only to defending the rights of native-born 'English'. Instead of developing a separate code for the Normans, then, the law simply adapted and expanded to take on certain of the northern French customs that the invaders regarded as important to their needs.[1] Nationality showed up most visibly in the period after the Norman Conquest of 1066 in the process known as presentment of Englishry. If it was proved that a murder victim was Norman, then the local community bore collective responsibility and had to pay a penalty (the *murdrum* fine) to the king.[2] In general, though, English law of the twelfth century tended to be inclusive in its approach to English and Normans – and thus, at least implicitly, to other nationalities as well.

After King John lost control of Normandy to Philip Augustus of France in 1204, there was a very significant change of attitude towards people born outside the realm. During Henry III's successive confrontations with the baronage between 1258 and 1265, his opponents picked up the idea that the king's 'natural' (that is, native-born) advisers among the political elite ought to have a greater say than those from other lands.[3] It was partly in response to such sensitivities that, in 1295, Edward I allowed that Sir Elias Daubeney, a Breton nobleman with estates in Somerset and Lincolnshire, be regarded as 'pure English' and treated 'as an Englishman' in the courts.[4] At the same time there was a noticeable sharpening of political and cultural notions of nationality that emphasised English birth as a prerequisite for membership of the political elite.[5] The general antipathy towards Edward II's favourite, Piers Gaveston, was reinforced not just by his foreign (Gascon) birth but also by the allegation that he encouraged the king to favour foreigners.[6]

The advent of long-term war with Scotland and France from the end of the thirteenth to the fifteenth and sixteenth centuries reinforced these trends and enshrined them in law. In the North of England, magnates who had previously managed to hold on to landed interests on both sides of the border were now forced to make choices about their political loyalties and to abandon hopes of recovering estates in Scotland.[7] Similarly, the very few noble and gentry families that still held landed property on both sides of the English Channel found themselves under increasing state surveillance in both kingdoms. The choices they made about which side to support on the outbreak of the Hundred Years War in 1337 determined – permanently, as it turned out – whether they and their descendants would thereafter be 'English' or 'French'.[8] The decision of Edward III in 1340 to declare himself king of France was initially a diplomatic ruse to persuade disaffected people in the French provinces to join his quarrel with Philip VI and John II. The English Parliament understood the wider legal implications, and in the same year required the king to issue a statute declaring a strict constitutional separation between the two kingdoms.[9] This was maintained after Henry V renewed the war in the early fifteenth century and, under the Treaty of Troyes (1420), secured recognition as heir to the throne of France. Parliament promptly insisted on a reissue of the 1340 legislation, which guaranteed that the French would still be treated emphatically as aliens and would have no automatic privileges in England.[10]

The consequences of these shifts in the territorial and constitutional make-up of the Plantagenet Empire were felt in exalted circles. During the Hundred Years War, English military leaders often took their wives with them to France and elsewhere, or married local women, and had children born abroad. In 1351 the English Parliament declared, in the statute known as *de natis ultra mare* ('regarding those born overseas'), that persons born outside the realm to English parents could themselves be considered fully English.[11] The legislation meant that, for high-status people at least, Englishness was not confined to those born within the kingdom. It also meant that members of the royal family were formally protected from discrimination. Edward III's son John of Gaunt was born at Ghent in Flanders, Richard II at Bordeaux in Gascony and Edward IV at Rouen in Normandy. All three of these men suffered popular prejudices to the effect that being born abroad somehow compromised the legitimacy of their royal power. No one, however, seriously proposed that their having been born outside England barred any of these men from the royal succession.[12]

The wars – and especially the hostilities with France – that prevailed between the reigns of Edward I and Henry VI therefore had a profound impact on the distinction between denizen and alien status. Whereas the Norman Conquest had resulted in French people having arguably greater rights at law than their English subjects, the Hundred Years War resulted in a much more precise notion of denizen status, one that formally excluded the vast majority of people born in France. The same Parliament that enacted the separation of powers between Edward III's titles to England and France in 1340 also agreed to the formal annulment of presentment of Englishry. Historians have generally assumed that this was a simple admission of the fact that the process was already outdated and redundant.[13] But it also closed a loophole and sent a powerful symbolic message that Edward III's new French-born subjects could expect no preferential treatment in England. Ironically, though, this apparently powerful polarisation also raised many questions about the treatment of the significant numbers of French-born people who lived within England; as we shall see below, it was members of this immigrant group that were the foci and beneficiaries of the important mechanisms found by public authorities in England to allow protection and rights to aliens dwelling within the realm.

English nationality and the Plantagenet dominions

The increasingly exclusive notion of English denizenship that emerged as a result of the Hundred Years War also affected the status of people living in the wider dominions of the Plantagenets in the British Isles and in France. In particular, the treatment of people from the dependencies who travelled to England can tell us much about the confusions – and resentment – that could arise as a result of the firmer application of 'denizen' and 'alien' status.

From the twelfth century, Ireland was a lordship of the English crown, with a delegated system of administration, justice, taxation and finance. Within the island, a crucial distinction was drawn between the 'English of Ireland' (the descendants of Anglo-Norman settlers and other more recent

14

arrivals from England) and the native Irish: only the former group had access to 'English' law.[14] In Wales, the position was still more complicated. The east and the south of the country, the so-called Marches, were under the private jurisdiction of the successors of the Norman lords who had conquered the area after 1066. Persons living in the principality itself – that is, the west and the north, beyond the Marches – were assimilated into English law under the terms of Edward I's conquest of that land in the 1280s. After 1295, however, Welsh-born persons were excluded from the new system of English law operating in the boroughs of the principality.[15] The status of people born on the Isle of Man, meanwhile, was difficult even for contemporaries to fathom. With the transfer from Scottish to English control in the fourteenth century, the island was ruled by a series of English magnates who enjoyed virtual autonomy as 'kings of Man'. Their subjects were answerable directly to them, and only indirectly to the crown of England.[16]

These complexities meant that it was extremely difficult for English authorities to define and regulate Irish, Welsh and Manx people who came into their midst during the later Middle Ages.[17] Sometimes these incomers had their loyalty tested by being required, in moments of emergency, to return to their native lands and assist in defending the English regime against local insurgency.[18] They were also subject to some significant surveillance. On multiple occasions under Henry V and Henry VI, the unruliness of Irish residents in England was taken as a pretext for threats of mass deportation that were only mitigated for certain groups – in particular, students at Oxford and Cambridge – by the taking of appropriate oaths.[19] By far the most serious of the English crown's attacks on the rights of its subject peoples, however, came in the aftermath of the revolt of Owain Glyn Dŵr in Wales in 1400. While much of the resulting welter of legislation in the English Parliament was directed against those who remained in Wales, Welsh residents in England were also subjected to severe discrimination. 'Full-blooded' Welshmen (those of Welsh parentage on both sides) were formally banned from purchasing any new lands in England, and those already in possession of interests in the kingdom would only be allowed security of tenure by finding pledges for their good conduct. Welshmen could not become burgesses in a specified list of boroughs along the Welsh border from Gloucester to Chester or (though this point was less clear) elsewhere in the realm, and were thereby effectively debarred from holding civic office.[20] The message of the new legislation was, as the historian R. R. Davies put it, that 'the Welsh (like the native Irish) could not be part of the political nation of England'.[21]

In assessing the practical consequences of such policies we need to understand that Welsh-born people of special and privileged status seem rarely to have suffered any significant prejudice in England. For example, Welsh clerics who studied at Oxford (and, more rarely, at Cambridge) continued to be appointed to cathedral posts and archdeaconries in England throughout the fourteenth and fifteenth centuries – and a total of eight became bishops of English dioceses.[22] Lower down in the social hierarchy, we need also to stress that a very significant number of ordinary labourers and servants from Wales, as from Ireland, who made their way into England in the fifteenth century remained 'beneath the radar' both of the state and of lesser jurisdictions in the towns and in manor courts. The people most at risk were those who already held property or wished to pursue particular trades in the commercial economies of English urban centres. In 1283 there was a conspiracy at Alveston in Staffordshire to prevent the locally born Thomas Wade from having access to the law because, it was claimed, he was 'a mere Irishman' from Carlow.[23] And at Henry V's first Parliament, in May 1413, Rhys ap Thomas, describing himself as 'a Welshman, born and engendered of a father and mother born in Wales', pointed out the iniquities of the legislative programme of 1401–2 for Welsh émigrés in England, and asked that he and his heirs be treated as 'true English lieges of our lord the king'. Although the king supported Rhys, the very act made on his behalf sent a message that the civil liberties of Welsh-born people in England were now a matter of royal whim.[24]

Dependency upon the king's grace also determined the status of people from the Plantagenet-controlled regions of France. In strict constitutional terms, the Channel Islands continued to be ruled by the king of England after 1204 under his residual title as duke of Normandy. Successive royal charters issued in the later Middle Ages did not actually allow the Islanders to *be* English; rather, when in England, they could simply have access to the broad range of legal and commercial rights enjoyed by natives.[25] The county of Ponthieu, held by the English crown from 1279, though effectively lost to France during periods of war and never recovered after 1369, was a similar case: merchants from the region had to work out their own pragmatic arrangements with civic and royal authorities in order to ensure their safekeeping while in England.[26] Calais, conquered by Edward III in 1347, was at first treated as being under the direct jurisdiction of the English crown, so that its established residents, whatever their place of birth, were technically 'English'. With Henry VI's inheritance of the title of king of France in 1422, however, some ambiguity emerged.[27] Inhabitants of Calais – especially those of mixed parentage or who had not been born there – could be subjected to significant scrutiny when they crossed to England. Ingelram Slumpart, who had been born in Calais to a Picard father and a Flemish mother, realised the precariousness of his position on moving across the Channel, and swore allegiance to the English crown in 1432.[28] In 1512 Henry VIII's government attempted to make sense of the complicated position by ordaining that the children of English-born men and women who were married to native Calesians would be considered fully English. This, however, held only as long as they continued to reside under the king's allegiance: leaving Calais for other parts of France would result in automatic loss of rights and property.[29]

Similar complexities surrounded the status of the people of Gascony. They were ruled by the Plantagenets in their capacity as dukes of Aquitaine, and were always quick to make this point in order to preserve the distinctive customs of their land. It was this tradition of independence that drove the campaign by Edward I and his successors to have Gascony recognised by the French crown as an allod, a sovereign territory in its own right.[30] All of this had important consequences for Gascons operating in England. In 1389, Edmund Arnold, a wine merchant from Aquitaine who had been living at Dartmouth (Devon) for twenty years, secured letters of denization: that is, a royal grant allowing a legal status roughly equivalent to that of English-born people.[31] Others, however, were less sure of the wisdom of a move that might be construed as giving up on the independent traditions of their duchy. In 1411, the Gascons living in England petitioned the Westminster Parliament about their desire to live freely as Henry IV's 'faithful and loyal lieges'. This, they argued, was confounded by the English, who 'make and speak many injuries and evils to them … such as calling them aliens, and many other undesirable names'. They requested a general charter defining the status of all Gascon-born residents of the realm.[32] The crown would only yield, however, by allowing individuals to come forward and seek special protection. Behind this decision lay an obvious nervousness about having to create a legal enclave for Gascons living in England, outside the normal operations of the common law. It was only after the final loss of all remaining English possessions in Aquitaine in 1453 that the Gascon-born community in England finally came to terms with the reality that their allegiance was no longer to the duke of Aquitaine, but to the king of England.

Finally, there is the case of Normandy, conquered by Henry V and run as territory under English occupation until the final withdrawal of the Plantagenet regime from northern France in 1450. In a constitutional sense, Normandy was one of the least colonised of all the dominions: law and governance were still determined almost entirely by the charters previously granted to the duchy by Capetian and Valois monarchs, duly confirmed by the English regime in 1423.[33] However, the conquest of Normandy also did much to promote a two-way, cross-Channel exchange of people, goods and services and thus to point up the particularly large number of people from northern France who moved to England to settle and work.[34] Consequently, while Norman incomers to England were 'aliens' in the strict sense that applied to all French-born people, both national politics and local circumstance encouraged pragmatic accommodation for persons seeking residence in England.[35]

The various engagements with the king's subjects from the wider dominions who made their way to England were therefore, in large measure, a function and consequence of the constitutional deals that the crown made with those dependencies over the course of the Middle Ages. Whether people from these areas could be treated as denizens or aliens within England remained both a complicated and an uncertain issue. Nor did a 'third way' evolve that allowed such people rights that fell short of those provided to denizens but were more extensive than those allowed to most aliens. If anything, there was something of a trend towards exclusion, as English law became increasingly disinclined simply to accept people from the dominions as having the same rights as those born in England. In chapter 3 we shall see the consequences as played out in the initial categorization of all people from the dependencies (with the exception of the Welsh) as being liable to the alien subsidy of 1440. For the present, however, we need to consider further the various legal processes devised across the later Middle Ages that sought to mitigate the denizen–alien divide both for people from the dominions and for those from other foreign lands.

Commercialisation, common law and royal protections

Passports, in the modern sense of the term as defining documentation of national status, were effectively unknown in medieval Europe. What did exist, in considerable numbers and diversity, were letters of safe conduct, which granted the protection of a given state to foreign visitors.[36] Rulers supplied letters of safe conduct to their own subjects as well as to aliens; importantly, though, the letters were valid only within the jurisdiction of the issuing authority, so people who felt in need of such protection needed multiple safe conducts as they traversed political boundaries. During times of war these safe conducts could sometimes take on the modern sense of a special visa application, by seeking to exempt the recipients from the suspension of rights that might fall upon them as 'aliens in enmity'. In the negotiations that followed the attempted Franco-Burgundian siege of English Calais in 1436, for example, the authorities of Holland and Zeeland, although recently brought under the jurisdiction of the duke of Burgundy, attempted to distinguish themselves from people from the Burgundian heartlands in Flanders with whom they were often confused; they suggested that Hollanders and Zeelanders travelling abroad might carry letters testimonial issued by their towns of origin, and thus seek to escape any disabilities applied upon the Flemings.[37] Importantly, however, both letters of safe conduct and letters testimonial were designed for high- and relatively high-status people temporarily residing in another jurisdiction: mainly diplomats, members of the military elite and merchants providing goods and financial services.[38] Consequently, we need to dispel the notion that the generality of aliens required identification papers in order to enter England in the later Middle Ages.

Nor was there the bureaucratic capacity to provide much formal regulation of incomers at the point of entry. By the early fourteenth century the English crown was appointing 'searchers' in the head customs ports intended, in part, to watch the flow of people. The searchers' principal task, however, was to provide a check on the smuggling of goods and to help regulate the flow of bullion.[39] Although there were very occasional general bans on the entry of subjects of hostile foreign rulers, the searchers were actually much more frequently charged to prevent certain English people – notably soldiers, monks and pilgrims – from leaving the country at moments of national emergency.[40] During such wartime embargos, English people wishing to go abroad therefore had to apply to the crown for licences, and (in theory) to present these letters at the port of departure. In general, however, the flow of people into England was remarkably unregulated, and the vast majority of those entering the realm in search of work as traders, craftspeople and labourers did so completely 'under the radar'.

Until the time of Henry III and Edward I, aliens from outside the Plantagenet dominions who were resident in England were effectively ignored by the law, and had no observable rights within the realm. However, the general quickening of the English economy during the so-called commercial revolution of the thirteenth century put special pressure upon the crown to provide foreign merchants with a clearer sense of the rights they enjoyed while they remained within England's borders. Magna Carta (1215) acknowledged that such men were an integral part of the English economy, gave them security and freedom to trade within the realm, and provided guarantees as to what might happen to foreign nationals detained as a result of the outbreak of war.[41] The city of London approached the matter rather differently, seeking to ban foreign merchants from holding real estate in the city, requiring that they lodge with citizens and setting a limit of forty days on their visits. A tension therefore quickly emerged between the *laissez-faire* approach of the central government and the more restrictive instincts of the capital and certain other English towns. This was often played out in relation to those groups – the German and Scandinavian members of the Hanse, the merchants of Gascony and those representing the great Italian banking companies – to whom the crown gave specially privileged status and rights.[42]

At first, therefore, government policy regarding aliens was all about creating discreet but effective means by which foreigners involved in trade, whether resident or not, could uphold their interests in England.[43] An important feature of this process was the provision made in the royal courts to allow aliens to recover outstanding debts. Statutes of 1283 and 1285 created a framework for the registration of debts and an effective legal process for their recovery. The most wide-ranging statement of the rights of alien merchants, Edward I's *Carta Mercatoria* of 1303, established the principle that aliens had the right to remedy on civil actions in the courts, with the additional guarantee that half the jurors sitting in cases involving merchants should also be aliens (the so-called 'half-tongue' jury). In 1353, as part of a package of measures intended to encourage foreigners into the country to handle wool exports, those entering into debt agreements were allowed to register their transactions at the English staples (the depots through which all wool exports had to be processed), and a speedier and cheaper procedure for recovery was set up in cases of default. In the following year, the provision of 1303 was extended so that aliens were allowed to have half-foreign juries in any cases to which they were party in the king's courts, whether civil or criminal actions. This covered the interests of a much wider group than just visiting merchants. The general extension of aliens' access to the royal courts also meant that it was not necessary to create separate tribunals for the hearing of foreigners' legal grievances in England. Those who felt that they could not get a hearing were, like their denizen neighbours, free to petition the crown directly in Parliament or, from the later fourteenth century, to appeal to the equity court of the Chancery.[44]

To this general story of access there was one very important exception. The official position of the common law was that aliens were not allowed to hold land, houses and other buildings in their own right, or therefore to instigate litigation about such property. In fact, a variety of solutions emerged to deal with this problem. The earliest of these were provided by the public authorities of cities and towns. From at least the thirteenth century, various self-governing urban jurisdictions allowed aliens to enter the franchise and become 'freemen' or 'citizens' of the relevant place. They were treated in this regard simply as part of a wider group of 'foreigners': that is, persons born outside the designated town, whether from other parts of England or from abroad. 'Foreigners' paid more than those admitted on the basis of birth or apprenticeship in the relevant town, but had equal rights. Vitally, the admission to the freedom of the town meant that enfranchised aliens were able to buy and sell property there, to sue freely in the relevant urban courts, to participate in civic politics and government and even to hold office.[45]

The newly found legal security that aliens thus enjoyed could, however, be threatened by the penalties that the crown applied on resident foreigners during periods of international conflict. In 1270–1 a diplomatic dispute between Henry III and the countess of Flanders led to mutual reprisals, in which all Flemish merchants in England, along with their property and belongings, were subject to arrest.[46] To mitigate the effects, a number of Flemings were granted royal letters of protection from the Chancery, and larger numbers of men from other parts of the continent were issued with licences guaranteeing their right to continue trading. In addition, the crown stated that Peter Bonyn, a prominent citizen of Bruges, and Poncius de la More, from Cahors in France, should each be 'reputed as a denizen': that is, to have the equivalent status and rights of those born inside England.[47]

On the outbreak of hostilities with Philip IV in 1294, Edward I ordered the arrest of all the subjects of the king of France found in the realm, together with their material and financial assets. Similar general sanctions were applied during the so-called War of Saint-Sardos of 1323–4 and on the outbreak of the Hundred Years War in 1337.[48] The best-known victims of these successive reprisals were the so-called alien priories, English monasteries that were dependencies of mother houses located in France, and principally in Normandy. Successive English kings and their subjects were eager to take advantage of the landed and moveable assets of the alien priories, and for the rest of the fourteenth century their resources were regularly seized during periods of war. In 1378 many of the foreign-born monks in these houses left the realm forever, and in 1413–14 Henry V permanently confiscated the estates of many of the remaining alien priories. Some were able to continue as autonomous religious houses, but the general atmosphere of distrust now severely limited the opportunities for foreigners to join monastic institutions in England.[49] It has often been assumed that the policy with regard to the alien priories set the tone for the treatment of all French-born people resident in England during the Hundred Years War. In fact, when it came to merchants, secular clergy and other professional groups, the crown was increasingly disposed to soften the effects of war by issuing a range of licences that guaranteed the right to operate as normal in England.

In choosing which individuals should have such special privileges, the royal Chancery put considerable store on evidence of their trustworthiness. In 1324 and 1326, for example, it exempted the Frenchman Nicholas Chamberleyn from confiscation of his goods on the grounds that, as a freeman of Bath (Somerset), he paid local taxes and had a fixed domicile in the town.[50] After 1337, the crown was relatively generous in granting such licences to remain. For those who were not in the commercial economy or the urban elite, there were also ways of proving good faith, such as the production of named guarantors, the swearing of oaths, and the personal recommendation of members of the English nobility and gentry. In the process, too, the government was prepared to consider whether the birthplace of the individual justified protection. Under Edward III, a number of people produced evidence that they hailed from the king's dominions in Ponthieu and Aquitaine, or from the lands of his ally, the duke of Brittany, and even further afield from Italy and elsewhere, and should therefore be exempt from measures intended only for those born in the lands of the king's enemy of France.[51] Herein lay the beginnings of a distinction that, by the early modern period, clearly differentiated the legal rights of the 'alien friend' from those of the 'alien enemy'.[52]

It is important to stress that neither the civic franchise nor royal letters of protection made any formal difference to the nationality of the individuals. For some of the people who received them, any such inference would indeed be disadvantageous. Drew Malherbe, the son of a French father and an English mother, was described as a 'burgess of Amiens and Northampton' in a petition for the release of his property following the confiscations of 1294, denoting his determination to retain rights on both sides of the Channel.[53] Similarly, Walter de Bardi, who was a member of the great Florentine family of bankers and ran the king's mint in London from the 1360s to the 1390s, took out citizenship of London and royal letters of protection in order to be able to go about his business unencumbered by restrictions on aliens.[54] Any notion that he intended thereby to become more 'English' is, however, clearly inappropriate and deeply anachronistic.

There are, however, cases from the mid-fourteenth century in which the crown was prepared to accept the notion of denizen equivalence. In 1340 and 1346 the prominent citizen of Wells Peter le Monnier, who came originally from Amiens in Picardy, secured letters patent that he should be considered 'as a denizen' in England. In 1347, Edward III went further and declared Peter to be 'both a denizen and an inhabitant' of the realm.[55] The initiative seems to have been influenced by a Roman law principle, known as *incola*, which had been deployed in France since the 1310s to apply the franchise of a single city at the level of the entire kingdom.[56] This idea was not, in fact, to take off in England, where the notion of fealty to the king ultimately prevailed over a more abstract idea of citizenship. Its most significant application came in 1349, when Edward III accorded *incola* status to eight named weavers 'and others' who had fled to England from Flanders as a result of the threat of reprisals from their count, Louis de Male, and had taken up residence in London, Canterbury, Norwich, Lynn and Salisbury.[57]

These developments represented real rights for the recipients that extended significantly further than those that had been accorded to Peter Bonyn and Poncius de la More three quarters of a century earlier. High on the list of benefits was fiscal advantage. Beginning in 1303, foreign merchants participating in England's overseas trade were required to pay progressively higher rates of duty than their denizen counterparts; even the most privileged of trading groups, the Hansards from the Baltic ports, had to pay at least some of these supplementary levies.[58] To declare residency in England and to hold royal protections during times of war were no protections in themselves from such duties. Being considered 'as a denizen and inhabitant', however, changed this. In 1348 the Chancery informed the London customs collectors that Peter le Monnier should be entirely quit of the alien surcharges on imports and exports.[59] For some years thereafter, the equation between the freedom of a city or town and the right to be taxed at the denizen rates seems to have persisted. When concerns arose over the proving of such rights, high-ranking merchants could feel confident about gaining the support of the crown. In the 1360s, for example, the merchants Simon Bochel and Benedict Zakarie, who originated from Lucca and Genoa respectively but lived permanently in London, secured letters patent confirming their exemptions from the extra alien rates of custom.[60] Fiscal status would therefore become one of the key issues for aliens contemplating a formal transfer of allegiance under the new process of denization that developed after 1377.

Denization

The periodic rhetoric about the repatriation of enemy aliens continued into the middle of the fifteenth century, though with increasingly less sense of real threat. In 1406, for example, Henry IV's government intervened in London to avoid overreaction to a recent order for a selective confiscation of goods held by resident Frenchmen.[61] It also took payments of between 1s. 10d. and £33 from over a hundred artisans and merchants wishing to be exempt from the measure, without requiring them to pay the additional fees needed for formal documentation.[62] Government was also now a good deal more chary about blanket expulsions: in 1410 the royal council reminded Parliament that those foreigners already living in the realm could generally be trusted to be loyal, with some taking an active part in the war on the English side and those involved in manufacturing continuing at their crafts.[63]

The one group notably absent from the system of Chancery protections until the late fifteenth century were the subjects of the king of Scotland. This may have been the consequence of the official English policy between 1296 and 1328 to treat the Scots as rebels against the sovereignty claimed by Edward I, II and III over the northern kingdom.[64] This legacy was evident in the 1330s and 1340s, when the English crown made repeated efforts to reduce the traffic of unreliable Scots over the northern border.[65] Those Scottish immigrants prepared to live at peace with their neighbours were allowed to remain so long as they swore oaths to the officials of the English March. By the fifteenth century, the wardens of the March were issuing formal written confirmations of these oaths.[66] These documents could be used to 'trump' local discrimination: in the city of York, where Scots were excluded from the franchise in 1419 for reasons of national security, it was agreed that an exception would be made for those who could produce letters issued by the wardens of the March or who swore suitable oaths in the guildhall.[67] From the 1460s, a new general spirit of amity in Anglo-Scottish relations also facilitated access to the English Chancery for a small number of Scots seeking formal licences to remain.[68] This precedent meant that, when a state of war resumed between 1480 and 1484, some 115 Scots living in England were allowed to sue out letters of protection from the Chancery and remain at peace within the realm.[69] In 1490, responding to anti-Scottish sentiment in the North, Parliament declared that all Scots living in England and Wales without the appropriate papers were to be expelled. Once again, however, the government softened this act with the prospect that the taking of oaths of loyalty would allow Scottish persons to remain in the kingdom unharmed.[70]

Alongside the continued use of protections, there also developed the formal process known as denization. The special grants of 1271 and 1347 may have allowed the recipients the *equivalence* of denizenship, but they had not included the notion of exclusive nationality. Denization, by contrast, required the recipient to swear an oath of fealty to the king of England, which implied or required the renunciation of previous loyalties. In return, recipients were confirmed to have the same legal rights as English-born subjects of the crown, which meant that they could prosecute freely in the royal courts and – vitally – hold both personal property and real estate. Women (both single and married) could receive denization in their own right. Denization was conditional: it was not retrospective, was sometimes only granted for a defined period, and did not automatically include the foreign-born children of the individual. It was, however, the only process before the sixteenth century by which aliens could formally enshrine their rights to hold property throughout the realm and to operate more or less without restriction in the king's courts, and its development marks a very important stage in the longer history of immigrant status in England.[71]

Denization came about as a direct result of the decision of the crown, pressed on by Parliament, to expel all French aliens from the realm and confiscate their property over the winter of 1377–8.[72] Although there is scant evidence of mass eviction, numerous foreign-born monks from the alien priories are known to have left the realm, and relatively stringent conditions were set on all classes of foreigners who wished to remain.[73] In particular, they were required to provide proofs and surety of their loyalty to Richard II. It was generally assumed that this evidence- and oath-taking would be undertaken locally. In Leicester, for example, Michael Brabançon (likely a Brabanter) paid 2s. 'for suit taken from aliens sworn to the king to conduct themselves with fealty'.[74] But in a few cases, the Chancery was asked to intervene. In December 1377, just as the proclamations for the new measure were going out, John le Monnier, a French merchant who had lived in the realm for twelve years (and was almost certainly a relative of the Peter le Monnier noted above) was given letters patent stating that he had sworn to act as a 'faithful liege' of the king of England, and should have a permanent right to denizen status. A few months later, John Reynold, a French-born inhabitant of Upavon (Wiltshire), was presented by his guarantors as a 'faithful Englishman' and swore an oath of allegiance and fealty to the crown in return for denizen status.[75] Once the panic of 1377–8 was over, the Chancery decided that it should continue to respond to requests for denizen equivalence by setting the oath of fealty as a regular condition on beneficiaries, and thus effectively enshrined the new legal status of the adopted denizen.[76]

Denization was a process specifically designed for those who had made the conscious decision to remain permanently in England. Herman Steynford, a German merchant residing at Boston who married a local heiress and became a prominent member of the town's fashionable Corpus Christi guild, was recorded in his letters patent of denization of 1390 as having made a commitment 'to live there as long as he lives'.[77] It is important to emphasise, however, that those who petitioned for the new status did so for reasons of self-interest rather than out of a simple emotional attachment to their new homeland. The alien priories are a case in point. In order to avoid the expulsion ordinance of 1378 and to continue to function after Henry V's general confiscation, the remaining French-born inmates of these houses were allowed to petition the Chancery to have their houses granted corporate denizen status.[78] In addition, the foreign-born heads of these priories would very occasionally seek additional safeguards by applying for personal letters of protection and denizations.[79] In similar vein, the very small numbers of Irish and Welsh who took out denizations in the late fourteenth and fifteenth centuries may have done so to immunise themselves against the periodic orders to return to their homelands and more particularly, in the case of the Welsh, against the legislation preventing their holding property in England.[80] These and other practical considerations, however, served to persuade other foreigners that they too should press for denization. Over the fifteenth century at large, people from a wide geographical range – Scotland, Scandinavia, the Low Countries, France, the Iberian Peninsula, Italy and Greece – sought the benefits of changed allegiance that came with the new process.

This is not to say that large numbers of people rushed to gain such privileges. Between the 1380s and the 1430s, there were never more than thirty denizations recorded in the Chancery per decade. Some denizations were apparently granted without being recorded in the central registers, the patent rolls, but these appear to account only for a handful of additional instances.[81] We can therefore assume that the number of completed denization processes in this period was very small. One reason for the slow take-up was cost. General letters of protection were expensive enough, usually costing somewhere between 6s. 8d. and £2.[82] Applicants for denizenship, however, could expect to pay anything between £2 and £30.[83] These were large sums of money to find at a time when skilled labourers might earn 4d. a day and persons aspiring to gentry status might have a net income from landed property of as little as £5 a year. Denizations were therefore effectively only within the reach of people of high status, including foreign women married to members of the royal family and titled nobility, merchants and artisans with the necessary liquid capital, and professionals such as clergy, physicians and soldiers whose patrons might help foot the bill.

One reason why denization did not take off more quickly during the fifteenth century was that the crown itself seems to have been reluctant to dilute the particular force of this process. In 1436-7, for example, it devised a special hybrid between routine protections and formal denizations for the subjects of the duke of Burgundy living in England. Following the breakdown of the Anglo-Burgundian alliance against France and the rapprochement between the duke of Burgundy and the king of France in the Treaty of Arras of 1435, people from the Burgundian dominions were seen as a particularly serious threat to national security. In a heightened state of public anxiety, the council probably felt some pressure to apply an expulsion ordinance along the lines of that of 1377-8. To avoid the disruptions that would result, but to appease concerns about resident Burgundians being allowed too many rights, the crown therefore allowed the subjects of the duke who were living in England to take an oath of fealty in Chancery guaranteeing their support for Henry VI's cause. In return, they were to be granted licences to remain and to have uninterrupted rights to their own possessions.[84] The names of 1,839 people in receipt of such protections were enrolled in the Chancery in the following month, with a further nineteen stragglers entered in batches over the course of 1437.[85] This set of records is especially useful to the history of immigration because of the precise information it contains about the places of origin of the recipients, and it is used extensively in chapters 4-7.

A further reason why denization did not take off more quickly than it did was that the rules about exemption from the customs duties changed significantly in the mid-fifteenth century. From the time of Henry IV, Parliament began to set the alien rates significantly higher than the denizen ones; and by the 1450s, aliens usually paid twice as much as denizens on exports of wool, representing well over 50 per cent of the price of the commodity on the domestic market.[86] The piling up of the alien duties was the consequence of the development, by the end of the fourteenth century, of the English Company of the Staple, a commercial organisation run by denizen merchants that controlled the export of wool to the continent through the English-controlled entrepôt of Calais. The only major exception to this monopoly was for the Italians, who were permitted to continue to export high-quality ranges of English wool directly to the textile-producing centres of their homeland. Given the very large amounts of money that the staplers generated for the crown, both in customs revenues and in loans, it was deemed only reasonable that the Italians should pay significantly higher duties for the special privilege of exemption from the Calais staple.[87] However, the existence of these new differentiated rates served to highlight the special privileges allowed to aliens holding letters of denization. From 1430, the Chancery began to differentiate between denizations that allowed the payment of the lower, denizen rate of customs duties and those whose recipients still had to pay the higher, alien ones. Then, in 1442, Parliament began to limit the category of those paying the denizen rate to persons '*born* [the king's] liegeman'.[88] This new wording needs to be interpreted in the context of the specific debates around 1440 over the need for aliens to make a greater contribution to the public purse.[89] The decline in the customs revenues during the later fifteenth century resulted in further political pressure to address questions of entitlement and fraud. At Henry VII's first Parliament, in 1485-6, it was decided that all aliens holding letters of denization should henceforth pay the duties at the alien rate.[90] The consequence of this new dispensation was, perversely, that letters of denization were now rather less useful – at least for merchants involved in international trade – than they had been in the half-century before 1430.

It was only at the very end of our period, in the 1540s, that denization briefly became a kind of mass movement. In 1540 and 1544, as part of Henry VIII's campaign of sanctions against Francis I of France, the English government threatened significantly to curtail the rights of French-born aliens dwelling within the realm, including those who already held letters of denization. As a result, in the latter year particularly, the Chancery processed an unprecedentedly large number of applications for the new denizations that were made available to those wishing to claim the right to remain. A large roll was compiled to record the grants made in the middle years of the decade, bearing 1,179 denizations, and a further document, now in Westminster Abbey, lists 2,665 recipients of denizen status granted letters patent dated 1 July 1544.[91] It is difficult to tell the precise number of individuals represented in these two documents, because there is some overlap of entries between, and even within, them. A total of 2,500 can probably stand as a rough minimum figure for 1544. The Westminster Abbey document is also useful in that it contains a great deal of information about the places of origin, occupation and marital status of those French-born (and indeed other) aliens granted denization in the mid-1540s, and is used in some of the analyses of alien numbers in the chapters that follow. The surge was, however, exceptional, and denization long remained the preserve of a privileged minority. There were fewer than a hundred denizations issued in 1546–9; and although the figure increased again in 1550, to 485, the long reign of Elizabeth I produced fewer than 2,000 denizations in total.[92]

Political campaigns against aliens: absentee clergy

There was a lively and multi-valenced debate on aliens in late medieval England. In this and the next two sections we will examine the criticisms levelled in Parliament and elsewhere about three particular groups: absentee clergy, brokers and merchants, and artisans.

One of the earliest political controversies concerned absentee foreign clergy: those who held ecclesiastical offices in England but turned up in person only occasionally, if at all, to fulfil their duties, put in substitutes to do the work for them and took the associated revenues for themselves. This group of clergy increased significantly in size and visibility as a result of the development, during the first half of the fourteenth century, of the system of papal provisions, by which the pope claimed the right of appointment to a wide range of higher-level ecclesiastical positions throughout Western Christendom. Parliament became especially incensed that the supposedly pro-French popes were using the wealth of the English Church to support the Valois cause during the early stages of the Hundred Years War.[93]

In the immediate aftermath of Edward III's victory at the Battle of Crécy in 1346, the Commons made a typically assertive statement about this situation. They demanded that both resident and absentee alien clergy should be expelled from their benefices, outlawed and replaced by suitably qualified Englishmen. Many prejudices were exposed: vicars put in by papal provisors and others, the Commons said, were mere 'tailors, shoe makers and chamberlains to cardinals', incapable of preaching the faith to their flocks, so that 'our faith is in danger of destruction'.[94] Nothing much had changed, it seemed, in 1425, when the Commons again complained that rich benefices were being taken over by 'divers persons of other tongues, and of foreign lands and races', including the king's enemies. As a result, they claimed, 'the wealth of the realm [is] taken away into the hands of aliens, and the whole estate of Holy Church [is] brought into less reverence than used to be the case in the past'.[95]

The official remedy came in the Statute of Provisors (1351) and subsequent extensions and amendments to this legislation, which aimed to limit the number of papal provisions (whether for English or foreign clergy) to English benefices. It was in the interests of the crown to adopt a selective approach to the enforcement of this legislation, with the result that the political community often remained dissatisfied.[96] While Parliament was prepared to sanction a more moderate policy towards papal provisions at the beginning of Henry IV's reign, it still insisted in 1401 that the full rigour of the legislation be applied specifically against *alien* provisors.[97] The controversy became closely linked to anxieties about the draining of silver and gold bullion out of the realm, and thus merged with wider debates about the economy discussed below. In 1337, those appointed to seize the property of the enemy French across England took advantage of the moment to proceed against both absentee and resident alien clergy from other parts of the continent, too.[98] In fact, as we shall see in chapter 7, the alien subsidy returns of the fifteenth century reveal that there was a continued influx of foreign clergy into England to staff the lower reaches of the ecclesiastical hierarchy. The debate on papal provisions can therefore be seen less as an attack on alien-born parish clergy duly going about their duties in England, and much more as part of the wider criticism of diplomacy and economic policy during the era of the Hundred Years War.

Political campaigns against aliens: brokers and merchants

The political discussions of the role of aliens in the economy took off particularly with the decline in the balance of trade that set in from the 1370s. Whereas England had previously had a significant surplus of exports over imports, the falling away of the overseas market for English wool and the increasing demand within the realm for foreign-made luxuries resulted, it was claimed, in the decline of the native agricultural and manufacturing economy and the exhaustion of England's bullion reserves.[99] A particular focus of animosity in this context was alien brokers: traders who derived their livelihood from setting up business transactions between suppliers of goods and wholesale purchasers, often on credit, and taking a cut from the profits of the deal. In the so-called Good Parliament of 1376 there was an extraordinarily vitriolic attack on the northern Italian brokers operating in England:

> There is in the land a greater multitude of Lombard brokers than merchants, who help with nothing except doing wrong; those who are held as Lombards are really Jews and Saracens and secret spies; and recently they have brought into the land a most horrible vice that should not be named.[100]

Earlier in 1376, the civic authorities in the capital had already taken the initiative to ban aliens from serving as brokers and to prosecute those who had negotiated loans on high rates of interest, and the crown now affirmed this measure, though without extending it to the rest of the realm.[101] The supposition that foreign brokers were Jews, or had the instincts of Jews, also reflects a general cultural nervousness about the enforcement of the 1290 expulsion of the Jews and the constant anxiety about the Christian prohibition on unreasonable interest: in the 1376 petition, the 'unmentionable vice' was not (as was more usually the case) the sin of sodomy, but that of usury.[102]

A regular flow of parliamentary petitions against alien brokers continued through the first half of the fifteenth century. The last of them, in 1442, made explicit the point that the ban operative in London since 1376 should be extended for the 'benefit of both the merchants and the common people of this land'.[103] It seems likely that the Londoners were behind much of this campaign, and the lack of obvious support from elsewhere in the realm made it easier for the crown to ignore the demand for blanket legislation. As a result, the strategy changed: rather than trying to force alien brokers to leave, Parliament now attempted to make them the focus of more punitive fiscal measures, with the alien subsidy of 1453 imposing a new, higher rate of taxation on the fiscal category of Italian merchants and brokers.[104]

There was much more general support over the same period for the idea of imposing a range of restrictions on alien merchants' involvement in the internal wholesale and retail trades. The prevailing policy of the early fourteenth century, summed up in the *Carta Mercatoria* of 1303 and the Statute of York of 1335, was that foreigners should be free to operate in internal markets. In 1376, however, the city of London challenged this position, complaining that aliens' ability to buy and sell in retail and to sell on to other foreigners for resale was driving up prices for English consumers.[105] In 1393, the crown was persuaded to modify the Statute of York and to place a ban on alien involvement in retail and in wholesale transactions where both parties were foreigners.[106] The measure did not survive beyond the deposition of Richard II of 1399, but it reflected what was now perceived to be a chronic problem in the political economy.

There now developed a new set of rules about the activities of non-resident alien merchants. From the last decade of the fourteenth century, foreign importers were required to use the money they made from sales to purchase English goods. This package of measures, beginning in 1390, is sometimes called the Employment Acts because sales of imports had to be 'employed' in the purchase of exports. These laws, however, were only very erratically enforced, as repeated complaints and reissues in Parliament made clear.[107] At the same time, the Bullion Ordinances, which began in 1397 and continued to be issued into the 1430s, required that the few aliens who were still purchasing English wool for export had to make deposits of gold coin and/or bullion at the royal mints.[108] Finally, the hosting laws proposed in 1420 and eventually enacted in 1440 – an extension, to the national level, of the existing civic and borough customs on the lodging of merchant strangers – stated that non-resident aliens should register with a denizen host or supervisor and provide surety that they would undertake their transactions in timely fashion.[109] None of these initiatives served the economy very well: indeed, the so-called Bullion and Partition Ordinances issued in the Parliament of 1429–30 proved one of the greatest disasters of English monetary and diplomatic policy in the later Middle Ages.[110] Nor, crucially, were they well enforced – and certainly did not result in the withdrawal of aliens from involvement in English trade.

The most revealing measures in this respect are the hosting regulations put in place in the Parliament of 1439–40, in parallel with the introduction of the new alien subsidy. The surviving views of hosts (records kept by the English hosts itemising the activities of the aliens who lodged with them) show that the new rules were initially implemented with some determination, at least in the major ports of London, Southampton and Hull. Soon, however, the impetus was lost, and by 1444 the new system was already considered to be in abeyance.[111] Again, it is arguable that the 1440 hosting laws were really the initiative of the Londoners, and were of much less interest or perceived advantage in provincial ports, whose own existing arrangements for hosting were much better suited to the needs of the local economy. In Great Yarmouth, for example, which had a very significant temporary resident alien population, the civic records are replete with offences against the hosting regulations set out in the town's common ordinances of 1300. Yet they yield only a single example, from 1472, where explicit reference was made to the statute of 1440 as the basis on which a foreign-born householder was prosecuted for lodging other aliens in his hostel.[112] The hosting laws therefore stand as a revealing example of the gap that seems often to have existed between a strongly anti-alien political rhetoric and the more pragmatic solutions that central, local and civic governments found to deal with the 'alien problem'.

Political campaigns against aliens: artisans

The perceived decline in England's economic fortunes also had an impact on attitudes to those aliens who, as we shall detail in chapter 6, had set themselves up in the manufacturing and retailing trades in many English towns. From the early fifteenth century, civic governors in London and some provincial centres responded to the competition from such alien artisans by issuing their own protectionist legislation. Immigrants were sometimes excluded from civic office: in Norwich in 1415, for example, it was ordained that aliens could no longer hold positions of public authority in the city.[113] Later, London and Ipswich also denied immigrants entry to the franchise, a step that not only barred them from civic office but also, at least officially, prevented them from engaging in skilled occupations.[114] In some places, town governors introduced stricter regulations for the occupations in which aliens specialised. In Ipswich, for example, the urban authorities became extremely vigilant in enforcing quality controls on the 'Dutch' brewers of beer (as distinct from the predominantly English brewers of ale), imposing higher fines on them than on native-born masters in other trades.[115]

From the 1440s onwards, a significant economic recession, sometimes referred to as the 'great slump', reduced the general opportunities for craftspeople.[116] The result was two-fold. Firstly, the restrictions imposed earlier on alien artisans were extended to other 'outsiders'. In places such as Norwich, Coventry and Bristol, even male incomers from else-where in England were subordinated to the economic interests of men born in the relevant place; while all women in such towns, whether natives or incomers from other parts of the realm, were subject to significant controls and limits on their right to work.[117] Secondly, the hostility against alien artisans gained greater traction in Parliament. English craft guilds had petitioned the crown about the privileges of immigrant craftspeople before 1450, but their complaints had met, on the whole, with only a luke-warm response.[118] In the second half of the fifteenth century the position changed, and successful parliamentary lobbying, especially by the London livery companies, led to more frequent national legislation confirming and extending the existing civic initiatives.[119]

A comparatively early indication of this new dispensation is provided by a sequence of petitions made in Parliament from 1455 by the silkwomen of London.[120] They argued that their trade – and by extension that of all silk workers in England – was being materially damaged by a conspiracy among the Italian merchants, who allegedly refused to import unworked silk and were instead introducing inferior goods for immediate sale. The solution proposed, and adopted, was to ban the importation of the rele-vant manufactured goods. This was not altogether a new device: as far back as 1336, Edward III had placed an embargo on imports of foreign cloth and other commodities in order to promote manufacture at home.[121] The later fifteenth century, however, saw a rush of so-called sumptuary laws, which – usually, it must be said, with little real effect – sought to limit the importation or purchase of foreign luxury items in order to encourage domestic industries and internal commerce.[122]

Fired by these precedents, a variety of manufacturing trades set out bolder allegations about aliens and further proposals for protectionist measures. In 1463, a common petition in Parliament, sponsored by the Londoners, proposed that production in a wide range of crafts was imperilled by 'the great number and multitude of aliens and strangers of various nations who are craftsmen and householders and dwellers in various cities, towns, boroughs and villages within the realm ... and employ and give work in their houses to a great number of people of their own nations, and to no others'. The crown acceded to the demand for a ban on the importation of a long list of items including wares of woollen cloth, leather, metal, pottery and wood, though it did insist that such goods produced in Wales and Ireland should be freely sold in England.[123] Twenty years later, in Richard III's Parliament of 1484, the campaign reached fever pitch. Aliens, it was claimed, were coming into the realm with their wives, children and servants; they refused to take up honest occupations as carters or ploughmen, but instead were pursuing cloth making and other crafts, and took into their employment only people born in their own homelands. Meanwhile honest Englishmen and women were forced into penury, crime, begging and vagabondage. Once more the remedy was sought, and found, in the tightening of regulations on imports of manufactured goods.[124] On this occasion, moreover, the crown went rather further and countenanced a formal prohibition on aliens residing in England to 'exercise or occupy any craft or manual occupation' unless they took out denization or were in service to native citizens.[125] This legislation was reissued on a number of occasions in the early Tudor period. The very repetition of such measures, however, strongly suggests that they were poorly enforced. It is significant, moreover, that the later iterations included a large number of exceptions for people with skills considered to be in short supply within the realm, ranging from bakers and brewers to scriveners and surgeons.[126]

The 'alien problem'

We must be very cautious about assuming that such protectionist policies, directed predominantly at artisans, amounted to a more systematic form of nationwide discrimination against foreigners. In many respects, indeed, the 'alien problem' that we can identify gathering force during the second half of the fifteenth century was invented and managed by the Londoners. Partly because of the crown's very heavy dependency on the London financial markets for loans, the capital city and its craft organisations now had a uniquely powerful influence over parliamentary legislation. To read the statutes discriminating against aliens as national in their relevance and application is therefore to forget that the agenda of the Londoners had a quite disproportionate impact on a range of social and economic policies in the late medieval and early Tudor state.[127] Bolton has recently argued, for example, that the proposals in the Parliament of 1439–40 for the new hosting laws, and for the alien subsidy itself, were led by the London MPs John Carpenter, Geoffrey Feldying, Robert Clopton and William Estfield, who between them had a formidable range of contacts both in the city and across the commercial sector. It was the London interest, Bolton suggests, that forced through the anti-alien legislation; the MPs for other English cities and towns were prepared to accept it because they knew perfectly well that their own constituencies would find ways of managing the new rules that suited local conditions.[128]

A similar London emphasis is evident in the 1463 and 1484 legislation limiting alien imports and crafts. The central government's willingness to bow to pressure from the livery companies of the capital in these two Parliaments arguably reflected its continuing need to draw bullion into the country rather than any general policy to protect the rights of English craftspeople through stringent protectionism.[129] It was also well aware that many civic administrations would enforce the laws only very selectively, if at all. Moreover, the records of the customs service indicate that, following the recovery from the great slump, the overall value of goods imported to England – including many officially on the 'forbidden' lists of 1463 and 1484 – actually increased significantly between the 1470s and the 1510s.[130] As we shall see in chapter 6, this upward trend reflected a longer-term demand in the English marketplace for foreign-made goods, and therefore shows that English consumers, as distinct from English manufacturers, continued to favour open borders.

Similar caveats need to be registered about the typicality of the instances where London and certain provincial towns restricted aliens' access to office holding, the urban franchise and the freedom to participate in skilled trades. In spite of the examples outlined above, civic office was still at least theoretically open to aliens in a majority of English towns. Among the larger urban centres, for example, Southampton continued quite conspicuously to include the Italians in its civic elite: Gabriel Corbizzi, a Venetian master mariner who was awarded letters of denization in 1431 for his services in the Hundred Years War, acted as steward and as water bailiff for the town in the 1440s; and the Florentine Cristoforo Ambruogi, denized in 1472, was elected mayor of Southampton twice, in 1486 and 1497.[131] Admission to the civic franchise was also still available to aliens in many places. At Exeter, for example, which had no restrictions on admission, over a third of alien householders in a sample taken from the period 1436-41 joined the freedom, compared with half of denizen householders – and this in spite of the fact that, as was customary in most urban jurisdictions, the process was more expensive for aliens.[132] Even in London, where aliens were formally prohibited from entering the franchise in 1427, exceptions and loopholes continued to be made. For example, John Evynger, a beer brewer from the Low Countries, was active in the capital during the second half of the fifteenth century and described himself in his 1496 will as a citizen of London.[133] In many other medium-sized and smaller towns, the anti-alien lobby was at most muted, and in some cases simply irrelevant. In Great Yarmouth, for example, where most denizens and all aliens avoided joining the franchise, immigrants (mainly from the Low Countries) were able to participate freely in a range of economic activities so long as they paid the necessary fines for acting 'as if they were burgesses'.[134] In spite of the tight regulation of overseas trade and the increasingly restrictive controls placed on guild-based manufactures in some larger towns, aliens continued throughout the fifteenth century to have a range of commercial and employment opportunities both in those cities that chose not to enforce the Londoners' programme and in many other small, unincorporated towns. Finally, if their economic freedoms were infringed, the formal legal rights that foreigners had acquired in the thirteenth and fourteenth centuries remained remarkably secure, and if anything were reinforced towards the end of the fifteenth century: in the 1480s, it was even specified in the opening formalities of two Parliaments that aliens were freely able to sue there.[135]

The later Middle Ages had therefore witnessed both the invention of the alien as a legal entity and the development of a recognisable 'alien problem' in urban and national politics. However, although foreigners were the object of increasing scrutiny from the middle of the fifteenth century, it does not follow that the greater polemic about aliens that sometimes characterised local and parliamentary politics either reflected, or was translated into, a wider and more organised animosity on the ground. The crown occasionally found it necessary to engage in gesture politics that pandered to the prejudices and perceived interests of a small number of manufacturers and financiers, mainly in the city of London. Even if a larger number of people across the country genuinely believed that economic ills could be addressed simply by excluding aliens, however, they were clearly thwarted: for, as we shall see in the next five chapters, there is abundant evidence that foreigners found England a viable – and in many cases a positively attractive – place to move to in the fifteenth and early sixteenth centuries.

Notes

1   Thomas, *The English and the Normans*, pp. 277–9.
2   In practice, these arrangements were often renegotiated at a local level in recognition of the fact that the vast majority of murdered persons were English: Hunnisett, *Medieval Coroner*, pp. 27–8.
3   Treharne, *Baronial Plan of Reform*, pp. 33–4; Ridgeway, 'King Henry III and the "aliens"'.
4   *PROME*, I, 9; *Complete Peerage*, IV, 95.
5   Ruddick, *English Identity*, pp. 100–31.
6   Burgtorf, ' "With my life, his joyes began and ended" ', p. 44.
7   Tuck, 'Emergence of a northern nobility'.
8   Lambert and Ormrod, 'A matter of trust', pp. 210–11, 221.
9   *PROME*, IV, 268; *SR*, I, 292; Curry, *Hundred Years War*, pp. 46–50.
10 *PROME*, IX, 258–9; Curry, *Hundred Years War*, pp. 86–90. See also, more broadly, Watts, 'Plantagenet Empire and the continent'.
11 *SR*, I, 310.
12 Ormrod, 'DNA of Richard III'.
13 Hamil, 'Presentment of Englishry'.
14 Crooks, 'State of the union'.
15 Davies, 'Twilight of Welsh law'. See also, more generally, Davies, 'Peoples of Britain and Ireland, 1100–1400: III'.
16 Dickinson and Sharpe, 'Courts, crime and litigation', pp. 142–4.
17 Davies, 'Peoples of Britain and Ireland, 1100–1400: II', p. 20.
18 Bolton, 'Irish migration'; Bennett, 'Late medieval Ireland', p. 381.
19 *PROME*, IX, 28; X, 57–8, 63, 188–9, 424–5; Griffiths, *Reign of King Henry VI*, p. 135. See also Brand, 'Irish law students'.
20 *PROME*, VIII, 136–7, 144–6, 211–13; *SR*, II, 124, 128–9, 140–1.
21 Davies, *Revolt of Owain Glyn Dŵr*, p. 284.
22 Emlyn, 'Serving Church and state'.
23 *CIM*, I, nos 1303, 2260.
24 *PROME*, IX, 10–11; *CPR 1413–16*, p. 31.
25 Griffiths, *King and Country*, p. 39; Thornton, *Channel Islands*.
26 Sheely, 'Persistence of particularism'.
27 Grummitt, *Calais Garrison*, pp. 8–9.
28 *CPR 1429–36*, p. 214.
29 *Tudor Royal Proclamations I*, no. 64.

30 Chaplais, 'English arguments'.
31 SC 8/253/12631; *CPR 1388–92*, p. 23. For further details of Arnold's career, see chapter 10.
32 *PROME*, VIII, 536–7.
33 Allmand, *Lancastrian Normandy*; Contamine, 'The Norman "nation" and the French "nation"', pp. 224–5.
34 Murphy, 'War, government and commerce'.
35 See chapter 5.
36 For the system as it operated in its most refined form, see Chaplais, *English Diplomatic Practice*, pp. 91–3, 140–3, 244.
37 *Bronnen tot de Geschiedenis van den Handel met Engeland*, II, 706; Thielemans, *Bourgogne et Angleterre*, pp. 115–17.
38 Safe conducts for soldiers are itemised in the online database, The Soldier in Later Medieval England, research.reading.ac.uk/medievalsoldier (accessed 19 January 2018).
39 Baker, *English Customs Service*, p. 36.
40 See, for example, *CCR 1343–6*, pp. 351, 362, 544, 545–6; *CCR 1346–9*, pp. 403, 518; *CCR 1349–54*, pp. 206–7, 233, 375, 399, 496–7, 621.
41 Holt, *Magna Carta*, pp. 460–3.
42 Miller and Hatcher, *Medieval England: Towns, Commerce and Crafts*, pp. 379–81; Davis, *Medieval Market Morality*, pp. 141–2.
43 For the remainder of this paragraph, see Jenks, 'Justice for strangers'.
44 In 1453, the chancellor was given specific jurisdiction to deal with 'aliens in amity' who were molested by the king's subjects: *SR*, II, 363–4. There are considerable numbers of late medieval petitions to the chancellor in the TNA series C 1.
45 Beardwood, 'Mercantile antecedents', p. 69.
46 Lloyd, *English Wool Trade*, pp. 28–30.
47 *CPR 1266–72*, pp. 553, 555, 557–8; Lambert and Ormrod, 'Friendly foreigners', pp. 5–7.
48 Lambert and Ormrod, 'A matter of trust', pp. 208–26.
49 Morgan, 'Suppression of the alien priories'; Matthew, *Norman Monasteries*, pp. 81–107; Thompson, 'The laity, the alien priories and the redistribution of ecclesiastical property'.
50 *CPR 1324–7*, pp. 38, 299.
51 Lambert and Ormrod, 'A matter of trust', pp. 219–21.
52 *Returns of Strangers in the Metropolis*, pp. 1–16.
53 SC 8/312/E3. For his parentage, see *CIM*, II, no. 306.
54 *CPR 1361–4*, p. 247; *CPR 1364–7*, p. 234; Allen, *Mints and Money*, pp. 85–6.
55 Lambert and Ormrod, 'Friendly foreigners', pp. 8–14.
56 d'Alteroche, *De l'étranger à la seigneurie à l'étranger au royaume*, pp. 62–7, 82–5.
57 LMA, CLA/023/DW/93/19, cited (but misdated), with context, by Lambert and Pajic, 'Immigration and the common profit', pp. 637–8. See further discussion in chapter 6.
58 Lloyd, *England and the German Hanse*, pp. 153–4.
59 *CCR 1346–9*, p. 455.

60 *CPR 1361–4*, p. 42; *CPR 1364–7*, p. 103.
61 *CIM*, VII, no. 319.
62 Given-Wilson, *Henry IV*, p. 334 n. 8.
63 *PROME*, VIII, 465–6.
64 Prestwich, 'England and Scotland'.
65 Summerson, *Medieval Carlisle*, I, 267.
66 Neville, 'Local sentiment and the "national" enemy'; Summerson, 'Responses to war', p. 171.
67 Rees Jones, 'Scots in the North of England', p. 62.
68 *CPR 1461–7*, pp. 50, 56, 57, 64, 93, 152, 164, 191, 210, 212, 221, 230, 263, 271, 322, 333, 459, 468, 538; *CPR 1467–77*, pp. 447, 448; *CPR 1476–85*, pp. 46, 177, 154. For the background, see Neville, *Violence, Custom and Law*, pp. 152–60.
69 *CPR 1476–85*, pp. 189–310, passim; Galloway and Murray, 'Scottish migration', p. 31.
70 Neville, *Violence, Custom and Law*, pp. 152, 168–9.
71 Beardwood, 'Mercantile antecedents', pp. 72–3.
72 *PROME*, V, 407; VI, 48–50.
73 McHardy, 'Alien priories'.
74 *Records of the Borough of Leicester, II*, p. 163.
75 C 76/60, m. 2; C 76/61, m. 1.
76 Lambert and Ormrod, 'Friendly foreigners', pp. 15–23.
77 *CPR 1389–92*, p. 367; Thompson, *History and Antiquities of Boston*, p. 126.
78 Knowles and Hadcock, *Medieval Religious Houses*, esp. pp. 96–101.
79 *CPR 1405–8*, p. 221; *CPR 1416–22*, p. 66; *CPR 1422–9*, p. 356.
80 For Welsh and Irish denizations, see chapter 4.
81 Petitions for denization that do not have corresponding entries in the patent rolls may in some cases have been rejected, or in others have led to letters whose recipients did not have them enrolled. For examples of such petitions, see C 81/1445/19; C 81/1512/37; SC 8/121/6010; SC 8/130/6465; SC 8/198/9873; SC 8/198/9875; SC 8/198/9880. Such instances appear to be quite few.
82 *CPR 1413–16*, pp. 122–5.
83 See, for example, *CPR 1416–22*, p. 311; *CPR 1422–9*, p. 358; *CPR 1466–77*, p. 65.
84 *CCR 1436–41*, p. 58; *CLBL K*, p. 204.
85 *CPR 1429–36*, pp. 537–88; *CPR 1436–41*, pp. 36–7, 94–5; Thielemans, *Bourgogne et Angleterre*, pp. 283–343.
86 Carus-Wilson and Coleman, *England's Export Trade*, pp. 194–5.
87 Power, 'Wool trade', pp. 39–46.
88 *PROME*, XI, 329–30 (emphasis added); *SR*, II, 501–2, 579.
89 The 1442 Parliament also decreed that *all* denizens exporting goods in Italian galleys should pay the alien rate, even if they did so in their own names: *SR*, II, 318–19.
90 *PROME*, XV, 88, 227–8; *SR*, II, 501–2; Cavill, *English Parliaments of Henry VII*, p. 58. The legislation was confirmed in 1531: *SR*, III, 325–6. Note also the decision in 1524 that English-born merchants who had declared fealty to foreign princes should pay the alien rates: *SR*, III, 212.

91 C 67/73; WAM 12261; Wyatt, 'Aliens in England', pp. 77, 80–1.
92 Selwood, *Diversity and Difference*, pp. 49–50.
93 Cheyette, 'Kings, courts, cures and sinecures'.
94 *PROME*, IV, 398–401; Barrell, 'The Ordinance of Provisors of 1343'.
95 *PROME*, X, 304–5.
96 Helmholz, *Oxford History*, pp. 176–81; Martin, 'Prosecution of the Statutes of Provisors and Premunire'.
97 *PROME*, VIII, 108; Heath, *Church and Realm*, p. 262.
98 Lambert and Ormrod, 'Friendly foreigners', p. 220.
99 Lloyd, 'Overseas trade'.
100 *PROME*, V, 318.
101 *CLBL H*, pp. 21–2, 27; *PROME*, V, 354–5; Nightingale, *Medieval Mercantile Community*, p. 243.
102 See the very similar (though less obviously racial) preoccupation with the 'horrible and damnable sin of usury' in a related petition from 1404: *PROME*, VIII, 269–70.
103 *PROME*, IX, 465; X, 10; XI, 135, 366–7.
104 *PROME*, XII, 235–6; and see chapter 3.
105 *PROME*, V, 354–5.
106 *PROME*, VII, 241–2.
107 Munro, *Wool, Cloth, and Gold*, pp. 46, 60–1, 72, 90, 139, 178.
108 Munro, *Wool, Cloth, and Gold*, pp. 54–7, 62, 63, 70, 72, 84–96, 99–100, 103–5, 118–27.
109 Munro, *Wool, Cloth, and Gold*, p. 72.
110 Bolton, *Medieval English Economy*, pp. 294–301.
111 Ruddock, 'Alien hosting in Southampton'; *Views of the Hosts*.
112 Liddy and Lambert, 'Civic franchise', p. 134.
113 Liddy, *Contesting the City*, p. 198.
114 In London, this was ordained in 1427: LMA, COL/CC/01/01/002. In Ipswich, aliens were prohibited from entering the freedom in 1483, and again in 1485: Amor, *Late Medieval Ipswich*, p. 16.
115 Amor, *Late Medieval Ipswich*, pp. 154–5.
116 Hatcher, 'Great slump'.
117 Goldberg, 'Coventry's "Lollard" programme', pp. 97–101; Davis, *Medieval Market Morality*, pp. 172–3.
118 See, for example, the 1404 petition by London's cordwainers, discussed in chapter 6.
119 Davies, 'London lobbying'.
120 Dale, 'London silkwomen'.
121 *SR*, I, 280–1.
122 Baldwin, *Sumptuary Legislation*.
123 *PROME*, XIII, 113–15; *SR*, II, 396–8. The list was extended in 1464 and 1465: Munro, *Wool, Cloth, and Gold*, p. 100 n. 15.
124 *PROME*, XV, 71–6.
125 *SR*, II, 495–6.

126 Baker, *Oxford History*, pp. 614–15.

127 Pearl, 'Social policy', pp. 117–19.

128 Bolton, 'London and the anti-alien legislation of 1439–40'.

129 Munro, *Wool, Cloth, and Gold*, pp. 160–1.

130 Goddard, *Credit and Trade*, p. 126.

131 Corbizzi: SC 8/25/1249; *CPR 1429–36*, p. 117; Ruddock, *Italian Merchants*, pp. 160, 170–1. Ambruogi: *CPR 1467–77*, p. 359; Ruddock, *Italian Merchants*, pp. 183–5. For Ambruogi's assessments towards the alien subsidies, see E 179/173/133, m. 1; E 179/235/54.

132 Kowaleski, 'Assimilation of foreigners', p. 170.

133 *Alien Communities*, p. 51. See also chapters 6 and 10.

134 Liddy and Lambert, 'Civic franchise', pp. 134–40 (quote at p. 136).

135 *PROME*, XIV, 409; XV, 8. See, more generally, Baker, *Oxford History*, pp. 611–14.

3

Numbers and distribution

The fiscal alien: who paid the alien subsidy?

Before we discuss in detail what the alien subsidy returns can tell us about the overall numbers and distribution of the alien population in late medieval England, we need to consider the detailed specifications of the tax grants, the ways in which those charged with administering the tax went about identifying their target population, and how this affected the quantity and quality of the information that they returned to the central government.

Aliens had long paid taxes in England before 1440. The main type of direct tax employed in the later Middle Ages, the subsidy on moveable property (after 1332 called the 'fifteenth and tenth'), was certainly no respecter of nationality, and every householder in England who had the appropriate value of goods was deemed liable. For this reason, ironically, the records of direct taxation are generally blind to questions of nationality, and even where we find extensive nominal lists of taxpayers, as with the poll taxes of 1377–81, it is difficult to do anything more than infer national status from surnames.[1] Sometimes context and annotation help us a little more: in York in 1327, for example, taxpayers in the parish of St Martin, Coney Street included Arnold 'de Almaigne' (suggesting German origins, either of himself or of his ancestors), Godfrey and John Braban (relating to Brabant in the Low Countries), Adam Picard (probably from Picardy in northern France) and Peter Lespicer, who, unusually, was specified as a 'stranger' (*extraneus*).[2] It is rare, however, to find a case like that of Octavian Francisse, a merchant of Florence resident in London, who was assessed for a tax to pay for the military contingent that the capital owed for the king's armies in 1356. The London civic authorities were adamant that being an alien did not exempt Francisse from liability to the levy, and pressed their case even when the crown attempted to order that he be let off.[3]

Prior to the reign of Henry VI, there seems to have been no suggestion that aliens should pay more than denizens towards direct taxation. In 1440, however, this is precisely what happened. Parliament granted the king one and a half fifteenths and tenths, but topped this up with what was in effect a moderated poll tax on alien residents.[4] The two taxes were kept strictly separate, and the system for assessing and collecting those subject to the alien subsidy differed significantly from that used for the fifteenth and tenth. Since 1334, the administration of the fifteenths and tenths had been a matter of local initiative, with each tax district charged a fixed lump sum and its inhabitants left to decide how to redistribute the burden across the community; the county-level collectors of the tax were then held personally responsible in the Exchequer for ensuring that the pre-agreed sums were actually levied in each locality.[5] By comparison with this well-honed system, the challenge of enumerating all first-generation immigrants, including non-householders, was an administrative nightmare. Primary responsibility was given to the justices of the peace (and later the sheriffs) of the relevant counties and of those cities, such as London, Bristol and York, which had separate county status.[6] They used what was essentially the same system that had created Domesday Book and many other information-collecting exercises during the Middle Ages: that is, the taking of sworn evidence from juries of local (English-born) men. The inquests were meant to take place at the level of the individual vill (in the countryside) or of the ward or parish (in urban areas). In fact, the rural divisions were not infrequently aggregated up to the level of the hundred, in which case the juries often comprised the constables of the relevant vills; and in some cases, a single inquisition was held for the entire county.

Residents and transients

One of the first difficulties to be encountered by the presiding officials was the question of residency. Before 1453 there was no definition as to how long a person had to have lived in England in order to be liable to the alien subsidies. In theory, this means that the people who appear in returns were not just permanent immigrants into England, but could also include alien merchants trading in the ports, the associated crews of their ships, a range of foreign travellers, visitors and pilgrims, and a host of skilled and unskilled labourers moving on a cyclical basis from one country to another. The most extreme example of such inclusivity is the unfortunate Malise Graham, the Scottish earl of Menteith, who was assessed in Pontefract in the West Riding of Yorkshire in 1440. Graham was a long-term political hostage, held in Pontefract Castle as guarantor for the ransom of King James I of Scotland.[7] It is significant, though, that while he remained in captivity in England until 1453, the earl was never again made subject to the alien subsidy. In practice, it seems unlikely that many forced or unforced 'visitors' of high and middling social status were included in the alien subsidy returns.

On the other hand, the assessors also had to deal with a much larger group of people of lesser status among the alien population. The only differentiation made in the setting of the tax was between 'householders' (those who owned or rented their own home and usually maintained their own familial and/or household dependants, and sometimes ran their own businesses) and 'non-householders' (those who 'lived in' with their employers or others and made their money from wages). No lower limit was set on liability to the subsidy, so that foreigners of extremely modest means were suddenly caught up in the tax net. These people were often highly mobile. In the East Riding of Yorkshire and in Westmorland during the 1440s and 1450s, a few were recorded as 'vagabonds', casual workers who moved back and forth across the northern border as the seasons and circumstances dictated.[8] Consequently, although all those returned in the subsidies of 1440 and later are treated here as 'immigrants', we need to acknowledge that an undefined proportion of them were really continuing migrants, entering and leaving England as they moved in search of short-term contracts of employment.

In light of the existence of a transient population of foreigners, especially in the category of non-householder, a key question arises as to how the inquest juries of 1440 actually knew who were the aliens in their midst. The decision to classify someone as an alien must have started from the fact that the individual in question either could not speak English or spoke it with a discernibly 'foreign' accent. Importantly, it was enough for the jurors to declare an individual to be an alien. They were not required to note specific nationalities – although, fortunately for us, they actually did so in a significant number of cases. Sometimes their evidence came from direct knowledge. At an inquest in High Wycombe (Buckinghamshire) in 1441, one of the jurors, Thomas Fyssher of Langley Marsh, was presumably responsible for reporting both his own servant, Gelam, and his next-door neighbour, whose occupation he gave as tailor but whose name he failed to remember.[9] Given the numbers of living-in servants and workers reported in 1440 and later, it is also likely that the English jurors called in known employers (both denizen and alien) in the area to provide additional evidence on their families and other dependants. We can imagine that there must have been a degree of informal co-operation and goodwill with English nobles and gentry, such as the earl of Oxford (around his home at Castle Hedingham in Essex) and Lady Elizabeth Bowes (at Newington in Surrey), whose household staffs were subject to scrutiny.[10]

Occasionally, there are signs of over-zealousness. In London in 1441 the assessors compiled an extensive list of people who had been assessed for the tax but, for various reasons, were now excused; they included twenty-seven individuals who had been found to be natives or were included in the formally exempt categories.[11] There were also isolated attempts to include second-generation immigrants. At Barling in Essex, the brothers John and Thomas Janyn were enumerated in 1440, even though they were specified as being born in England. In this case the jurors who provided the necessary evidence had a clear memory of the two men's deceased father, identified as Janyn Frensheman. At nearby Great Wakering, the householder Thomas Hervy and his two sons, Robert and William, were all noted as having been born in England, but were made liable on the pretext that Thomas's parents (unidentified in this case) had been aliens.[12]

Exemptions from the alien subsidies

Similar dynamics are evident in the way that the jurors in the alien subsidy assessments navigated the question of formal exemptions. At the beginning of the alien subsidies, in 1440, the only categories officially exempt were the Welsh, those holding letters of denization, the regular clergy (that is monks, nuns and friars – but not parish clergy), the alien wives of English and Welsh-born men and, by extension, the English wives of aliens.[13] The privilege of explicit immunity accorded to the Welsh may seem ironic given the emphasis placed in chapter 2 on the formal discrimination applied against this group after the Glyn Dŵr rebellion. The blanket protection in 1440 was not, however, charitable in its purpose. Rather, it reflected the fact that Wales was the only one of the dominions that was joined to England by land and existed as a parcel of the crown solely by right of conquest.

There were also some categories of aliens who were not specified in the tax grant but who were treated, from the outset, as being immune from the subsidy. Alien women married to alien men were not officially excluded, but the general treatment of married women as 'covered' by their husbands

45

meant that, although sometimes noted in the returns, they were not usually charged for the tax.[14] The merchants of the Hanse, who were normally immune from most forms of direct and indirect taxation in England under the terms of their charters from the king, quickly reminded the government of their privileged status and were also treated, more or less from the start, as exempt.[15] (Occasionally, however, Hansards do appear in some later assessments for the alien subsidies.)[16] Members of the universities in Oxford and Cambridge also seem to have been treated as exempt from the outset, though a few students and academics got caught up in the initial assessment process in Cambridge.[17]

One of the most remarkable features of the alien subsidy of 1440 was that it included, by implication at least, all those other than the Welsh who were from the dominions of the English crown. Whether this was accidental or purposeful, it seems to have been applied with some rigour. In imposing liability on those born in Ireland, for example, the assessors appear to have made no distinction between persons who had privileged 'English' status in their homelands and those assumed to be part of the native 'Irishry'. The earl of Ormond, the head of the administration in Ireland, quickly complained that the 'English born in Ireland' should be outside the remit of the tax. In fact, the English Parliament and government chose to take the point more expansively, and the 1442 subsidy grant explicitly exempted all Irish people – implicitly both English and Gaelic – from the tax.[18] People from the Isle of Man seem to have been treated in the same way, since the label 'Manx' was not used by the assessors after the first collection of the alien subsidy. If, as has been suggested, there was an element of spite involved in the initial inclusion of the Irish (and Manx) in the 1440 tax, it must have dissipated rapidly in the face of the difficulties and opposition encountered.[19]

The decision to tax immigrants from the Channel Islands, Calais, Normandy and Gascony was equally controversial. The Channel Islanders were furious about their inclusion, and rapidly secured an exemption, issued on 22 November 1440.[20] A handful of people specified as coming from Calais were subjected to the tax in 1440–1; one of them, Adrian Grenebough, sought both letters of denization and a confirmation by the Exchequer of his resulting fiscal immunity in 1441.[21] Such detail disappears thereafter, suggesting that Calesians may have been treated as exempt. In the case of the Normans and the Gascons, English officialdom showed more persistence about pressing the case for their inclusion as fiscal aliens, and it was not until 1449 that persons from these two duchies were released from liability.[22] This suggests that the decision to include those from the overseas dominions in the early alien subsidies in 1440 cannot be dismissed entirely as a mistake or an oversight, but reflected the particular vehemence with which Parliament had pressed for the new anti-alien measure in 1439–40.[23]

The alien subsidies also threw up interesting issues over the rights of those alien-born residents of the realm who held letters of denization. In general, the blanket exemption of this group in the form of the tax in 1440 seems to have held. The increase in the number of letters of denization issued in the 1440s (seventy-five over the decade, compared with only thirty in the 1430s) could be seen as a form of self-protection on the part of some more substantial aliens who would otherwise be liable to assessment.[24] In some cases the investment paid off. Thomas Gryntell, born at Caen in Normandy, a resident at Hammersmith (Middlesex), who had been in England since he was five years of age, was taxed as an alien householder in 1440; he promptly sued out letters patent of denization and does not appear in the records of any subsequent assessment for the sub-sidy.[25] But there were some cases in London where the assessors insisted on continued liability. Thus Joyce Hals the younger (likely a Brabanter, from 's-Hertogenbosch) and the Venetian Jacopo Falleron were both assessed for later collections of the alien subsidy, in spite of receiving formal denizations.[26]

In 1453, Parliament made an additional grant alongside the alien sub-sidy, whereby merchants from Italy, Germany and other places outside the Plantagenet dominions who were in receipt of denizations should pay 10 marks (£6 13s. 4d.) a year for life. The crown ordered that this special levy be raised, though in practice it seems rarely to have been collected.[27] Nevertheless, the pressure to categorise at least a few holders of denizations as continuing fiscal aliens may have sent the message that exemption from the subsidy was a matter of grace rather than of right, and thus to have reinforced the sense of conditionality that attached to the pro-cess of denization.

The excusing of those who had been born in the Plantagenet dominions was part of a larger process of disengagement from the alien subsidies over the second half of the fifteenth century. The attitude to the fiscal status of foreign merchants changed significantly over the period. The tax grant of 1453 included the threat of higher rates on foreign merchants and brokers: £2 for those who were resident in the realm and £1 for those who, though not householders in England, resided there for at least six weeks.[28] This, along with the punitive levy on merchants and factors who had taken out denization, clearly indicates Parliament's intention of using the alien subsidies to apply fiscal and political pressure on prosperous foreigners coming into the country to trade. In reality, however, significant numbers of such merchants now began to negotiate directly with the Exchequer to secure personal exemptions from the additional levies.[29] In 1483, the crown provided a more realistic residence requirement of three months on those who were to pay the tax, and extended immunity to merchants from places beyond the bounds of its own dominions in order to reflect the more general pattern of diplomacy and trading privileges. As a result, Spanish, Breton and German merchants were specifically exempt, and the crown intervened to specify that four groups – those from Venice, Genoa, Florence and Lucca – should be immune from the higher rates chargeable on other merchants and factors from Italy.[30]

Defaulters from the tax

The principal reason why the alien subsidy did not cause more consternation and resistance among those required to pay it was the decision made within the administration of the first levy, and applied always thereafter, that the collectors would not be pursued for non-payment by individuals. There was (at least in theory) a time lag, sometimes up to several months, between the drawing up and submission to the Exchequer of the assessment lists of people declared liable to the tax and the actual collection (in one or two instalments) of the moneys thus owed. Whereas other forms of direct taxation made the county-level collectors personally accountable for receiving the total assessed amount within their jurisdictions, the formal grant of the first alien subsidy specified that, to avoid undue pressure on officials, the collectors would not be liable for the sums charged on those who could not be found in the villages and towns where they had been assessed.[31]

The result was an extraordinary level of non-payment. In the first year of the 1440 subsidy, the default rate was 46 per cent, and was roughly the same for both householders and non-householders. The reason generally provided in the nominal rolls was that individuals assessed for the tax had 'moved' and therefore did not pay, though in London and a few of its Middlesex suburbs no fewer than 128 people were also recorded as 'deceased'.[32] The latter figure may seem suspiciously high and could suggest attempts at evading the tax. 'Moved', meanwhile, may have meant many things: that the persons in question were simply not available on the day the collectors arrived, or had reached a secret deal with them to avoid payment; that they had gone to live temporarily or permanently in another part of the town, or the county, or elsewhere in England; or that they had returned, temporarily or permanently, to their places of origin. That it did not necessarily mean permanent removal from the realm is demonstrated vividly by evidence from London. Rent-payers in the capital, denizen as well as alien, moved on a very frequent basis in the fifteenth century: even among the relatively prosperous, about 70 per cent relocated, often within a relatively small area, every two years or less.[33] It should therefore come as no surprise that at least 20 per cent of those aliens recorded in London as 'moved' for the collection of the 1440 subsidy can be shown to occur again in later records of the tax for the same collection districts of the city.[34] Because of the difficulties involved in identifying taxpayers between one subsidy payment and another, this percentage should also be treated very much as a minimum. What the label 'moved' emphatically *did* mean, how-ever, was that the persons thus identified were not to be pursued for their contributions to the tax: and both the taxpayer and the tax collector seem to have been highly aware of the advantages of this unusual loophole.

The very high levels of default experienced in the first of the alien sub-sidies had a major impact on perceptions of the levy and on the way the assessors went about their task in later grants. The comparatively low level at which the subsidy was charged before the 1480s means that it was prob-ably never intended to raise significant amounts of money. The default rate, however, meant that it was hardly worth the effort in strictly fiscal terms: the yield of the first year seems to have been only in the region of £400, at a time when a single fifteenth and tenth could be expected to gen-erate £31,000.[35] The increasing number of formal exemptions noted above inevitably meant that the numbers of persons enumerated tended to drop away with each successive grant. In 1468 and 1470, the collection of the tax in the northernmost counties of Cumberland and Northumberland was farmed out, meaning that the officials were responsible for returning a set fee for the tax, rather than an amount based on a real headcount.[36] Other county officials began to realise that central government had no inten-tion of following up on even quite blatant negligence in the administra-tion of the subsidies. The records of the later grants of the alien subsidies reveal the ruses used to avoid having to run the system over anew on each occasion: not infrequently, the clerks simply copied out the details from previous years, or even made *nil* returns. In Kent in 1467 the man respon-sible for the return of assessed aliens recorded (consecutively) the names 'William Heryng' (Herring), 'John Salmon' and 'Nicholas Sturgyon' (Sturgeon) – a fishy theme that looks suspiciously like the work of an over-active imagination.[37]

49

Interestingly, however, the dropout rate also fell in later collections of the tax: only 8 per cent of persons assessed between 1453 and 1471 were noted as 'moved'. This suggests that, where they were still interested in running the process with some degree of accuracy, the county officials tended to concentrate on those people who were most likely to pay, and probably collected the money immediately upon assessment. The general understanding that it was fruitless to pursue many of the middling and lesser sort of people for the alien subsidy resulted in a major change in policy during the final two grants of the tax, in 1483 and 1487. These were quite different in range and purpose from the previous levies.[38] They abandoned the earlier sums of 1s. 4d. per householder and 6d. per non-householder, and instead introduced the higher rates of 6s. 8d. for every 'craftsman' (*artificer*) who was a householder or living in shared lodgings with other aliens, and 2s. for non-householders, as well as a special charge of £1 on alien beer brewers. At the same time, and very significantly, employees in the agricultural sector (*servauntez of husbondrie*) were declared exempt, indicating that there was now no intention of making a general levy across the kingdom.[39] This new scheme chimed with the more general strategy of Parliament around this time, discussed in chapters 2, 6 and 8, to restrict the rights of alien artisans coming into English towns and to promote the labour market in the countryside. The new rates on householders and non-householders were significantly higher than the payments that their English-born counterparts would have made towards a fifteenth and tenth, and suggest a serious intention of applying fiscal pressure on those involved in the manufacturing economy. Ironically, then, the last levies actually raised more than the 'mass' tax of 1440: the 1487 subsidy resulted in a total receipt of some £774.[40]

In London, whose representatives in Parliament may have pressed particularly hard for the schemes of 1483 and 1487, we know that these later taxes on aliens were also applied with some rigour. In 1483, 1,595 people were charged for the subsidy in the city – though only a dozen of these were assessed at the higher rates established for merchants, suggesting again that the real focus was now on the artisan class.[41] The rate of attrition in the rest of the country was, however, much higher. In Bristol, whereas 648 alien taxpayers had been reported in 1440, the number fell to fifty-one in 1483.[42] In Warwickshire, where there had been 165 reported alien taxpayers in 1440, just six householders and seven non-householders were assessed in 1487 – and none of them paid anything at all.[43] An attempt in 1487 to make landlords liable for the tax due from aliens who fled after they were assessed was not enforced, and the Exchequer exonerated both the landlords and the collectors of any responsibility.[44]

The overall effect of these various trends in the administration of the alien subsidies was a dramatic change over time in the number of people actually assessed and paying the taxes. As we shall see below, for the first year of the subsidy, in 1440, there were around 17,000 people assessed. Already in 1441, however, the number dropped to about half of this, and by 1442 it was probably no more than 4,000. By 1456 it was as low as 2,200, with almost half of that number living in London and Middlesex.[45] The history of the alien subsidies is therefore very largely the story of how the anti-alien feeling of the 1439–40 Parliament rapidly gave way to disillusionment, indifference and collusion as more and more of the aliens living within the realm were formally or informally released from liability to the tax.

Measuring the alien population

How many people in late medieval England had been born abroad, and what proportion of the total population did they represent? In attempting to address these questions, we must remember that there are no absolute figures available. The records on which we chiefly rely for the population as a whole comprise national tax registers, especially the records of the poll taxes of 1377–81 and of the Tudor subsidies of the early sixteenth century. These are among the richest demographic data available for the whole of Europe at this time; but they are not foolproof. The most intractable issue relates to the multipliers that need to be used to express those not included in the taxes, especially wives, those under the age limit for liability (which was usually set between twelve and fifteen) and those who were too poor to pay. Depending on which estimates we use for these groups, calculations of the overall population can differ quite significantly.[46]

As part of her study of the first year of the alien subsidy, Thrupp used the nominal assessment returns to estimate the total number of alien *taxpayers* (rather than the total alien population) within England in 1440, supplementing gaps in those figures by using the equivalent records for the nearest surviving year of the subsidy. This analysis produced a figure of around 16,000, but Thrupp herself conceded that this was a conservative minimum.[47] More realistic – and larger – figures can now be suggested, both for the numbers of alien taxpayers in 1440 and for the overall number of aliens living in England at that time. For those shires where detailed returns no longer survive or are incomplete and damaged, the total numbers of householders and non-householders can still be recovered from a source not used by Thrupp: namely, the so-called enrolled accounts of the subsidy, where the county-level details were recorded in summary form.[48] The effect of supplementing the nominal returns with this evidence is shown in Table 1, where we demonstrate that a total of 16,878 people were recorded as assessed towards the first two payments of this tax.

This figure, however, does not tell the whole story. The apparent fullness of many of the returns disguises some serious omissions and deficiencies. For instance, except for the city of Lincoln itself, no accounts were ever enrolled for Lincolnshire, and although an assessment document survives for one of the three main subdivisions of the county – the Parts of Holland (including the port of Boston) – there is no direct evidence that any money was ever collected there.[49] Even Lincoln city looks suspect: the curious dating of the various stages of accounting suggests that significant administrative problems had occurred there.[50] The enrolled accounts for Yorkshire and Warwickshire omit the substantial towns of Hull and Coventry, while the assessment for Lancashire, noting just five taxpayers, cannot conceivably have been an accurate reflection of the reality on the ground.[51] The surviving documentation for Norfolk also hints at major problems with the assessment, with large areas of the county entirely omitted.[52]

Fortunately it is generally possible to extract figures from later assessments for those counties and towns whose records for 1440 prove particularly problematic, and to use these to compensate for such deficiencies. Thrupp used the nominal accounts for the second year of the first alien subsidy, due in 1441, to address such lacunae. However, her method ignored the fact that there was a very considerable drop in the overall number of persons assessed between the first and second years of the levy.[53] Our approach is to take the available figure for 1441 and inflate it by the average difference between the 1440 and 1441 assessments in other parts of the country. By this method, we may add to the running headline figure of 16,878 assessed taxpayers in 1440 a further 375 entries for the remaining areas of Lincolnshire, a notional 160 for Coventry and 100 for Hull, a very conservative additional 100 for Norfolk and another 250 for Lancashire.[54] There must also have been immigrants living in the palatines of Cheshire and County Durham, where the subsidy did not run at all. A figure of 150 liable persons in each county is probably reasonable. Both were of similar geographical area to Derbyshire, which returned just sixty-eight alien taxpayers, but were much closer to points of entry for Irish and Scottish immigrants.[55] Adding all of these estimates to the running total produces a potential taxpaying alien population of 18,163, which we may round to 18,200.

Still, of course, this only takes into account the known omissions and issues. The adjusted total makes no allowance for those considered too poor to pay the tax, or for those who completely escaped the purview of the assessors. In mainstream taxation, it was common to observe a formal or informal 'taxable minimum', a threshold of wealth below which people were not usually charged.[56] The fact that the 'non-householder' category in the alien subsidy of 1440 had no lower level of liability meant that, in theory at least, all resident foreigners were liable, regardless of their means. The very high default rate on the first payment of the subsidy speaks, in some senses, to the remarkable thoroughness of the initial assessment: we can imagine that at least some of the non-householders who failed to pay the tax would genuinely have found it difficult to pay the 6d. required. Direct evidence for remissions from the tax on account of poverty comes only from the capital, where a system operated for pardoning those too poor to make their contributions.[57] It seems appropriate, however, to assume some level of evasion by householders as well as non-householders, as well as a degree of complicity in the non-enumeration of the poorer sort. A cautious estimate of a 5 per cent evasion rate would yield an additional 900 persons, taking our running total of alien taxpayers to 19,100.

We also have to take into account the national, professional and social groupings that were allowed exemption in the form of the tax. Some of the numbers involved were too low to make much difference to our overall figures: foreign-born monks and nuns, for example, and the Hansards operating in England in 1440, are likely to have been counted in tens rather than hundreds.[58] But a potentially larger category is encountered if we seek to compensate for immigrants from Wales. Some attempt can be made to assess the size of this group on the basis of what is known about the Scots. Approximately 1,000 Scots were identified as such in the surviving nominal returns for the alien subsidy of 1440, but since the assessors were not obliged to give national labels, and did so overall in only 30 per cent of surviving cases, we can suggest that the total figure was at least 3,000, and likely rather more. Scotland's population at this time was perhaps 600,000, indicating that, on the most conservative estimate, the 3,000 alien taxpayers from Scotland represented one in every two hundred people in their homeland. The best guesses suggest that Wales had about 200,000 inhabitants at this time.[59] The detailed 'push' and 'pull' factors that determined the level of migration to England may well have been different for those from Wales. Assuming for present purposes that

Table 1: Total assessed taxpayers for the first year of the 1440 alien subsidy

	Householders	Non-householders	Total
Bedfordshire[a]	121	111	232
Berkshire	153	198	351
Buckinghamshire[a]	118	157	275
Cambridgeshire	81	77	158
Cheshire[b]	–	–	–
Cinque Ports[c]	258	390	648
Cornwall	162	156	318
Cumberland	96	213	309
Derbyshire	19	49	68
Devon	342	333	675
Dorset	243	515	758
Durham[b]	–	–	–
Essex	188	234	422
Gloucestershire	356	602	958
Hampshire	289	832	1,121
Herefordshire	34	24	58
Hertfordshire	168	151	319
Huntingdonshire	37	40	77
Kent	446	683	1,129
Lancashire	3	2	5
Leicestershire	38	59	97
Lincolnshire[d]	80	50	130
London	751	1,084	1,835
Middlesex	256	405	661
Norfolk	149	133	282
Northamptonshire	179	170	349
Northumberland	203	481	684
Nottinghamshire	57	51	108
Oxfordshire	173	186	359
Rutland	15	11	26
Shropshire	30	42	72
Somerset	180	197	377
Staffordshire	72	106	178
Suffolk	248	249	497
Surrey	190	405	595
Sussex	281	596	877
Warwickshire[e]	65	100	165
Westmorland	15	90	105
Wiltshire	204	273	477
Worcestershire	57	67	124

(*continued*)

Table 1: (cont.)

	Householders	Non-householders	Total
Yorkshire[f]	356	643	999
Totals	6,713	10,165	16,878

a Bedfordshire and Buckinghamshire were accounted together. The precise figures for each county are tentative due to damage to the returns, but the combined totals correspond to those in the account for the two counties.

b The palatine counties of Cheshire and Durham were not liable to this or other parliamentary taxation.

c The Cinque Ports were taxed separately from the rest of Kent and Sussex.

d Data survives for the city of Lincoln and the Parts of Holland only.

e Does not include the city of Coventry, for which no information is known.

f Does not include the town of Kingston upon Hull, for which no information is known.

the proportions moving were roughly equivalent, we can posit that there were around 1,000 Welsh-born people in England in 1440 who would otherwise have been made liable to the alien subsidy. Our running total therefore adjusts to 20,100.

The final – and likely the largest – categories that were excluded from the alien subsidy of 1440 were alien women married to alien men, children under the age of twelve born abroad and alien women married to English-born men. Because alien wives of alien husbands had no formal exemption, the assessors of the taxes occasionally listed them, but did not tax them. As a result, the nominal returns for 1440 provide details on a total of 844 named wives, and two further cases in which we know a man to have been married. The clearest overall trend that emerges from these admittedly very incomplete data is that male alien householders were much more likely to be married to alien women than were alien non-householders. In 90 per cent of the 846 known instances of marriage to alien wives in 1440, the husbands were householders. This accords with what demographers have identified as a distinctive marriage pattern prevailing in northern Europe after the Black Death, in which both partners married relatively late (in their mid-twenties) and only once they had established their economic independence.[60] If male householders recorded in 1440 had become established in their occupations while still in their natal lands, it also follows that they would be more likely to have married before they moved to England. The very small number of non-householders (82) declared as married in 1440 is undoubtedly an under-representation. However, a low marriage rate in this group would also fit the northern European demographic pattern, in which young single persons undertook some form of dependent service as part of a pre-marital stage of the life cycle. If and when those aliens who appear as non-householders in England in 1440 did marry, then, it follows that they were more likely, in purely statistical terms, to marry English people than they were to take other foreigners as their life partners.

In trying to estimate the number of alien wives not included in the tax returns of 1440, we should therefore err very much on the side of caution. In London and Southwark in 1483, the assessors for the alien subsidy routinely (though not necessarily always) listed alien wives of alien men. The records show that 46 per cent of alien householders in London and a remarkable 71 per cent in Southwark were married to alien women.[61] There are reasons to believe, however, that endogamy (marriage to people of one's own nationality, either in the birthplace or after removal to another location) was more frequent among the larger, more concentrated and more settled immigrant populations found in the capital and other towns in the South than was the case elsewhere. We might therefore suggest, as rather lower national estimates, that 35 per cent of all alien householders and perhaps 15 per cent of all non-householders in 1440 were married to alien wives. If we take our running total of 20,100 taxpayers, express it in terms of the 40:60 ratio of householders to non-householders shown in Table 1, and then calculate the appropriate percentages for alien-born wives, we reach figures of around 2,800 alien wives for householders and approximately 1,800 alien wives for non-householders – 4,600 in all.

Quantifying the presence of alien-born children under the age of twelve is a highly problematic task. In making his calculations for London, Bolton suggested that it was plausible to assume two alien-born children per married couple.[62] Given that birth rates were generally low in the fifteenth century as a result of women marrying relatively late, this assumes that most if not all of the children of every alien–alien marriage had been born abroad. Caution must again prevail. If we assume a more modest *one* child under the age of twelve born abroad for each of the householder and non-householder marriages modelled above, then we would add a further 4,600 people to our total.

Finally, a number has to be conjured for the foreign-born wives of English men, as well as of Welsh men resident in England. International marriages of this type were certainly not the preserve of the royal family and aristocracy.[63] During the 1440s, when the enumeration of liable women in the alien subsidy returns was conducted with relative thoroughness, there were 2,677 instances of unmarried females made subject to the tax.[64] All of these, whether spinsters or widows, were theoretically available on the

English marriage market. We have no way of telling, of course, whether this was a typical figure that can be straightforwardly projected back in time to imagine the number of women from previous generations of immigrants who had married local men. As an informed guess, we may hazard that approximately 1,000 women from previous generations of incomers may have been living as the wives or widows of English and Welsh-born husbands in 1440, and were therefore invisible in the tax returns of that year. Their children (even if born abroad) would, of course, inherit their fathers' denizen and immune status, and are not therefore to be included in our calculations.

Taking all of these suggestions into account, we have added to our adjusted base figure of 20,100 taxpayers in 1440 a further 4,600 for the alien-born wives of alien taxpayers, 4,600 for alien-born children under twelve and 1,000 for the alien wives of English men. This gives a total of 30,300, which we may round to 30,000. It must be stressed that the margin of error is inevitably very wide. If a larger number of people than we have assumed evaded the tax altogether, and if the numbers that we model for alien–alien marriage and for alien-born children were adjusted upwards, then the overall figure could rapidly approach 40,000. Contrarily, if the marriage rates were reduced, the numbers of wives and children would drop, and we might end up with an overall estimate rather lower – perhaps significantly lower – than 30,000.

Net migration and population trends

What percentage of the overall population of England might, then, have been made up of first-generation immigrants in 1440? As we noted in chapter 1, modern calculations suggest that the total population in the mid-fifteenth century was between 2 and 2.5 million. Taking the middle of that range, at 2.25 million, then an immigrant population of 30,000 would equate to roughly 1.3 per cent of England's inhabitants. Even if it was as much as 2.5 million, at the upper end of modern estimates, this would still give an alien population of 1.2 per cent, while at the lower end, 30,000 aliens could represent 1.5 per cent of a population of 2 million. These figures are obviously open to criticism. If the logic of the preceding discussion is followed, however, it seems that between 1.0 and 1.5 per cent of people living in England in 1440 either had been, or were considered to have been, born outside the bounds of the kingdom.

It is testimony to the extraordinary nature of the 1440 subsidy and the extant records of its assessment and collection that no equivalent data with which to compare this figure exist until the nineteenth century. Censuses of aliens were compiled in the sixteenth century in order to address the perceived and/or actual increase in numbers resulting from the influx of Protestant refugees to England. However, these processes were only conducted at the level of individual cities and towns, and no statistics have ever been posited for the overall size of the alien population of Elizabethan England.[65] The mists only begin to lift with the introduction of the regular ten-year national census in the United Kingdom from 1801.[66] In 1881 and 1891, first-generation immigrants born in the British colonies and in foreign countries were approximately 1.0 per cent of the total population of the United Kingdom; by 1901 there was a slight increase to 1.5 per cent.[67] The comparison with the medieval position is not like-for-like: the 1440 data relate to England alone, and include migrants from other parts of the British Isles, whereas in the late nineteenth century those born in Wales, Scotland and Ireland were full subjects of the British crown. Nevertheless, the similarity of the available percentages for 1440 and 1901 serves as an important reminder that the history of migration to (and within) the British Isles is to be considered not simply in terms of intermittent and arguably untypical 'waves', but also of constant ripples.

Modern governments prefer to express immigration figures in terms of 'net migration': that is, the difference, in a defined period, between people coming into the given country and the number leaving. The hypotheses presented here about the numbers of aliens found in England in 1440 therefore raise the question as to whether any significant number of people *left* the kingdom in this or other generations of the later Middle Ages. There are no systematic records of this process that can yield data akin to those for alien incomers, so our judgements have to be impressionistic. Among those groups that we can identify as leaving England for medium-term or permanent settlement elsewhere in the British Isles and in continental Europe were: minority groups and alien residents who were deported and repatriated, such as the English Jewish community expelled in 1290 and the French-born monks who left England under the expulsion order of 1377-8; English students and advanced scholars going to study and teach at foreign universities; English clergy taking up benefices in alien lands or moving to positions in the papal administration at Rome and, for a time, Avignon; English clerics, soldiers and merchants who got caught up in the running of the outposts of the Plantagenet dominions; and exiles – those English people forced to leave the realm because of their involvement in serious crimes or their disloyalty to the crown.

It is likely that the largest exodus of people from England at a single moment across our period was that of the 2,000 or more Jews who are believed to have left the country (mainly for France) in 1290–1.[68] This, however, was a one-off, and is therefore significantly smaller than the cumulative figures in some other categories listed above. William Chester Jordan has suggested, for example, that around 500 men and women a year (in other words, approximately 10,000 people in a generation of twenty years) left England in the thirteenth and first half of the fourteenth centuries under the judicial process known as abjuration: that is, an agreement reached with the courts to go into exile rather than being tried and sentenced to death for serious crimes.[69] Other continental states also operated various forms of judicial exile, of course, but on a more limited scale, and it is highly doubtful that people expelled from those lands entered England in such large numbers as those who were compelled by the law to leave it.[70] In this particular case, therefore, the net migration figure for England was very probably negative.

Other changes in patterns of migration during the later Middle Ages suggest, however, that the overall numbers of English people leaving the kingdom for the medium to long term was in decline by the time the first alien subsidy was imposed in 1440, and probably not of the same scale as those entering. For example, the small numbers of English students who still attended continental universities (mostly in Italy) by the fifteenth century does not compare with the 6 per cent of the alumni of the University of Oxford – or even the smaller 1 per cent at Cambridge – drawn in this period from Wales, Ireland and Scotland alone.[71] Crucially, too, the collapse of most of the remaining English possessions in France at the end of the Hundred Years War resulted, as we shall see in chapter 5, in the return migration of English colonialists – and, in all likelihood, an influx of northern French émigrés.[72] Even abjuration from England was in decline in the fifteenth century, before it was finally abolished under Henry VIII.[73]

Consequently, while there may well have been moments, and generations, over the course of the fourteenth and fifteenth centuries in which the number of emigrants from England exceeded the number of immigrants arriving into the realm, it seems likely that at most points, and almost certainly by 1440, there were rather more incomers than leavers. The most important and reasonably decisive point, however, is that immigration, whether judged gross or net, was not of a scale in the mid-fifteenth century as to make any demonstrable impact on the overall size of the population of England. The fifteenth century witnessed a remarkably sustained period of demographic stagnation. As a result of a high mortality rate linked to plague and other epidemic diseases and a low birth rate consequential upon the comparatively late age of marriage for women, the population barely replenished itself, and showed no sign of increasing until at least the 1480s, and probably not until the 1520s.[74] In the empty England of the mid-fifteenth century, alien immigrants may well have helped to 'top up' a given generation – especially if we take into account the cumulative effect of the descendants of immigrants born within the realm. There are also clear signs, as we shall see in later chapters, that the qualitative impact of aliens' presence was sometimes greater than the quantitative. In strictly statistical terms, however, the first-generation immigrant presence was simply not sufficient, in a manner now observable, to drive up the overall numbers of people living in the kingdom. When the population did rise again in the early sixteenth century, it did so because both indigenous people and their immigrant neighbours were simply more likely to survive epidemic diseases and now began to produce more children who survived to maturity.

The geographical distribution of the alien population: town and countryside

The headline figure for the alien presence in England in 1440 undoubtedly hides significant differences in the relative density of that population across the country as a whole, and between urban and rural contexts. In investigating how aliens mapped onto the landscape of England, we are greatly assisted by the fact that the assessors in almost all counties registered those assessed at the level of the individual town or, in the countryside, the vill (the administrative 'township' that was the basic unit of administration before the sixteenth century). In most cases, then, it is possible to locate those liable to the alien subsidies very precisely by their English place of residence at the time the taxes were assessed. To demonstrate the power of this evidence, we begin with some examples of distribution patterns in individual towns and at the level of the shire, before moving on in the next section to consider overall distribution at a national level.

We begin with London, which must clearly be recognised as having a major immigrant presence in this period. The London enrolled return for 1440 lists 1,835 taxed aliens in the city (see Table 1). However, because the 1483 return (totalling 1,595 assessed persons) includes much more detailed information on the origins, occupations, marriages and households of the people enumerated, Bolton preferred to use it as his base for calculating the overall size of the alien population of the city in the later fifteenth century.

Including data for the London suburbs in various Middlesex vills and across the Thames in Southwark, and making estimates for those omitted from the tax (exempt aliens, dependent children and so on), he reached an overall figure of 3,400. On the basis of an estimated overall population for London and its suburbs of about 50,000 people, Bolton therefore calculated that around 6 per cent of those living in the capital in the later fifteenth century were first-generation immigrants. (Strictly speaking, the calculation delivers a figure of 6.8 per cent.)[75] Drawing on Bolton's work but making more generous allowance for under-enumeration and exempt groups, Derek Keene subsequently ventured to suggest that immigrants from abroad represented as much as 10 per cent of the capital's population in the late Middle Ages.[76]

How usual or unusual was the London experience? Table 2 provides two sets of data by which to judge the scale of first-generation alien immigration in a range of provincial cities and towns in this period. First, the table expresses the actual number of persons assessed for the alien subsidy in the given urban area as a percentage of that place's tax population in the poll tax of 1377. The 1377 data here act as a surrogate for the overall population of the given place in the aftermath of the major plague epidemics of the fourteenth century. The table then takes adjusted totals for the alien subsidy of 1440 (using the family multipliers adopted above, but no other compensations) and expresses these figures as percentages of rounded estimates, based on the evidence of the Tudor subsidy, for the total population of the given places in 1524/5. We must always bear in mind the fallibilities of these data. In some cases, indeed, local sources can provide important correctives. For example, Christian D. Liddy and Bart Lambert have used the urban archive of Great Yarmouth to calculate that the town may have had as many as 180 foreign immigrants in the mid-fifteenth century. This would raise the proportions significantly higher than they appear in our table, to 4.8 per cent of the 1377 poll tax total and 6.0 per cent of the town's estimated population for 1524/5.[77]

These caveats notwithstanding, we can say that the major trend demonstrated by Table 2 is for major urban centres to exceed the proportion of aliens suggested above for the population at large (that is, between 1.0 and 1.5 per cent). More especially, the percentages tend to be largest for towns south of a line drawn from the Severn to the Wash. By far the most significant cases are Bristol, where both the 1377 and the 1524–5 measures suggest a potential alien population of over 10 per cent, and Southampton, where the 1377 index suggests a figure over 12 per cent and the 1524/5 index a lower but still appreciable figure of nearly 7 per cent.

Table 2: Estimated alien presence in English provincial cities and towns, 1377–1524/5

Town	Taxpayers in 1377[a]	Taxed aliens in 1440	Taxed aliens as % of 1377 taxpayers	Estimated total population in 1524/5[b]	Estimated alien population in 1440[c]	Aliens as % of population
Boston	2,871	78	2.72	–[d]	122	–
Bristol	6,345	648	10.21	8,000[e]	931	11.64
Cambridge	1,902	67	3.53	4,000	108	2.70
Canterbury	2,574	99	3.85	5,000	165	3.30
Carlisle	678	23	3.39	1,700	33	1.94
Colchester	2,955	51	1.73	5,000	75	1.50
Exeter	1,560	92	5.89	7,000	135	1.93
Great Yarmouth	1,941	48	2.47	3,000	72	2.40
Ipswich	1,507	63	4.18	3,000	92	3.07
Leicester	2,101	23	1.09	3,000	34	1.13
Lincoln	2,871	31	1.08	4,000	47	1.18
Newcastle upon Tyne	2,647	107	4.04	6,000	163	2.72
Norwich	3,952	84	2.13	9,000	123	1.37
Salisbury	3,226	99	3.07	6,000	146	2.43
Southampton	1,152	145	12.59	3,000	204	6.80
Winchester	1,440	81[f]	5.63	4,000	113	2.83
York	7,248	83	1.15	8,000	126	1.58

a Figures taken from *The Poll Taxes of 1377, 1379 and 1381*.
b Figures taken from Slack, 'Great and good towns', p. 352.
c Calculated using the methodology employed in chapter 3 (adding a wife and one child for 35% of householders and 15% of non-householders). However, no additions have been made for other exempt categories, Welsh or Hanseatic people, etc.
d Returns for the 1523 lay subsidy, on which these estimates are based, do not survive for Boston.
e Estimated at 10,000 in *The Pre-Reformation Records of All Saints' Church, Bristol, II*, p. 2.
f Does not include a further thirty-seven aliens (fourteen householders, twenty-three non-householders) taxed in the soke of Winchester.

These two cases come as no particular surprise, given the status of Bristol and Southampton as major ports, their close trading links with other parts of the British Isles and the continent, and the general resilience of their economies during the fifteenth century. The quantification does, how-ever, indicate that alien immigrants were at least as significant a presence in relation to the rest of the population in these two towns as they were in London; for Bristol, the proportion would indeed rise appreciably higher were we able to include specific numbers for Welsh immigrants to the town.[78] Other ports – Exeter, Ipswich and Newcastle upon Tyne – also yield proportions of aliens in excess of 4 per cent on the 1377 and/or the 1524/5 measures. Although complete data are lacking for both Boston and Hull, their proportions seem likely to have been slightly smaller but still appreciable: Boston's 1440 population represented 2.72 per cent of a 1377 figure of 2,871, while the notional figure of 100 aliens suggested above for Hull in 1440 would represent 3.33 per cent of a total population in 1524/5 of 3,000.[79] Inland towns exhibit rather lower proportions of aliens in their populations. Even so, Cambridge, Canterbury, Carlisle, Salisbury and Winchester all deliver an alien population in excess of 3 per cent on the 1377 and/or the 1524/5 indices.[80] In fact, with the exception of Colchester, Leicester, Lincoln and York, all the towns listed in Table 2 yield alien proportions in excess of the overall national figures.[81] The 1440 return for York probably seriously underrated the total number of aliens in the city, especially women and servants. However, given the relatively large population of the city at this date, even a doubling of the number would not have a major impact on the *proportion* of aliens within the total population.[82] We can therefore say with certainty that major towns, especially in the South and along the coasts, were natural magnets for incomers to England in the fifteenth century.

The comparatively strong representation of foreigners in the populations of certain major cities and towns is, however, only a relatively small part of the immigrant story of this period. It is possible, in the majority of counties, to pinpoint the exact location of almost all of the alien population assessed for the tax of 1440 and its subsequent manifestations. This evidence vividly illustrates the presence of aliens not just in large and small towns but also in rural areas. So far, the detailed work on such geographical distribution has been done mainly in relation to the North, where recent studies by David Ditchburn, Judith M. Bennett and Sarah Rees Jones reveal three important features. First, there was (as we have already seen) an undoubted clustering in the major urban centres. Secondly, a significant number of aliens were found in the countryside. Thirdly, and most strikingly, the latter group were much less inclined to gather in certain villages but tended to spread out, often very thinly, over the rural areas of the relevant counties, and particularly along some of the main transport routes of the region.[83] The rural phenomenon can be seen especially well in the 1440 alien subsidy return for Cumberland. The nominal assessment for this county in 1440 contains details of 319 taxed individuals, though only 309 were accounted for, presumably as a result of an arithmetical error at the Exchequer. Only twenty-three of those people lived in the major local town of Carlisle, with the remaining 296 found in no fewer than eighty-eight different settlements across the county. Not all such immigrants were isolated. Sixteen were reported as living in Holme (now Abbeytown), probably brought there through links with Holmcultram Abbey. There were also eleven aliens each in Ainstable, Greystoke and Kirkoswald. We need to note, however, that all of these administrative units were reasonably large settlements with significant hinterlands, and the locations of individual aliens within them could still have been disparate rather than concentrated. Most remarkably, of the eighty-eight settlements named within the return for Cumberland, twenty contained only two alien taxpayers, and twenty-six just one each.[84]

The alien population of Cumberland, like that of the rest of the North, was predominantly Scottish in origin. The ready availability of routes by land and sea into England as well as the casual and short-term nature of much of the work undertaken in the predominantly rural economy of the region meant that there was a very high level of mobility among a mainly low-status immigrant population. We therefore need to ask whether the distribution pattern of the North was really typical of the country as a whole. In Midland counties, we might expect to see more evidence of clustering into certain communities, especially given the comparatively large number of small towns in this region. Yet here, too, there was still a considerable diversity of distribution. Of the seventy-six people reported in Shropshire in 1440, twenty-nine were in the county town of Shrewsbury; but the remainder were found in groups of four, three or two, and mainly as single individuals, in no fewer than twenty-seven smaller towns and villages across the shire.[85] The situation was similar in Leicestershire. Of the ninety-seven people assessed in 1440, twenty-three lived in Leicester and its suburbs. No other settlement, however, was home to more than four individual taxpayers: only Thurlaston, Lutterworth and Queniborough had more than two, and a remarkable fifty-eight places returned the name of one alien each.[86] The higher the number of small towns and rural settlements there were in a given area of the Midlands, the more the alien population seems to have spread itself out over the area.

The biggest test comes necessarily with the South and East Anglia, where there was the highest level of urbanisation and where there was an alien presence made up predominantly of people who had travelled from overseas and who were more likely to remain for longer. Here, we certainly find a concentration of aliens in towns. Among Wiltshire's 477 alien taxpayers in 1440, a hundred lived in Salisbury, twenty-seven in Marlborough and twenty-five in Devizes; and there were a further six places (Bradford on Avon,

Chippenham, Heytesbury, Malmesbury, Mere and Warminster) that housed alien taxpaying populations of between ten and sixteen people. Nonetheless, a remarkable eighty aliens reported in this county were the only persons assessed in their village.[87] The pattern also seems to hold in other parts of the South and East Anglia. A high proportion of Devon's 675 assessed alien taxpayers in 1440 lived on the south coast and its estuaries, clustering in the port towns and their immediate rural hinterlands. Elsewhere in the county, however, immigrants were found scattered on the north coast and (thinly) in the rural interior, with no fewer than ninety-two settlements recording the presence of just one or two aliens in their midst.[88] The data for Essex are equally remarkable, with seven towns having between ten and fifty-one alien taxpayers (Barking, Brentwood, Castle Hedingham, Chelmsford, Colchester, Harwich and Maldon), but a further 128 places returning fewer than ten alien inhabitants, a remarkable ninety-six of these being home to only one or two foreigners.[89] It therefore appears that, notwithstanding the 'pull' effect of the major towns for immigrants from outside England, part of the alien population was widely, and thinly, distributed across the small towns and the rural landscape in all parts of England.

The density of the alien population: the national picture

There are several possible ways of expressing and mapping the relative density of the alien presence in England in 1440, and two measures are employed here. Figure 1 represents *demographic* density (aliens per head of population) by expressing the number of aliens assessed in each reportable county as a proportion of the poll tax data of 1377 for the relevant area. The results can then be checked and moderated by representing the 1440 data in terms of the relative *geographical* density (aliens per square mile) of the alien population. Figure 2 uses the unmodified data for alien taxpayers assessed in 1440 and expresses it in terms of numbers of aliens per square mile in each reportable county. The boundaries in both maps are those of the historical counties of England, with Yorkshire divided into its three ridings. It is important to note that the alien populations of London, York and Bristol have all been omitted from both maps. This is partly because these cities were all independent jurisdictions, divorced from the surrounding counties, but it is also because the inclusion of London and Bristol would skew the scaling applied, at county level, across the country at large. In both maps, Lincolnshire, Lancashire, Cheshire and County Durham have been left blank owing (in the first two cases) to the problems of the 1440 data and (in the latter two cases) to their immunity from the alien subsidy.

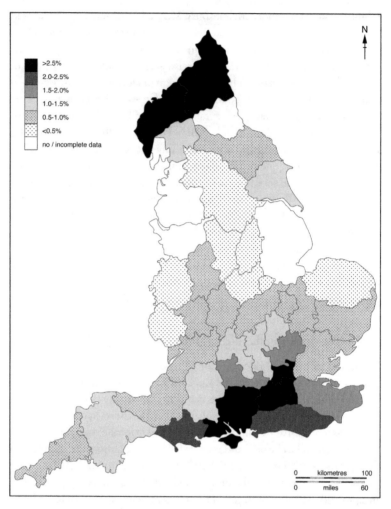

Figure 1 Alien taxpayers in 1440 as a proportion of 1377 poll tax payers, by county

The two maps show a broadly similar pattern. In relation to the total population, the alien presence was strongest in the southern counties of Hampshire, Surrey and Middlesex (the latter two in part at least representing the diaspora from London) and in the most northerly counties of Cumberland and Northumberland. Expressed in geographical density, however, the preponderance of aliens pulls more sharply to the South-East, with Kent and Sussex joining Hampshire, Surrey and Middlesex as

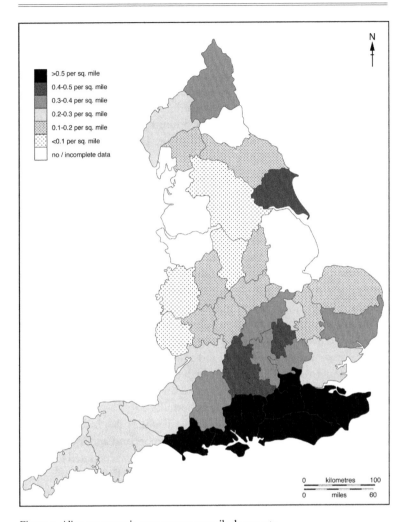

Figure 2 Alien taxpayers in 1440 per square mile, by county

the bloc of highest concentration in the country. In fact, these five counties, along with the Cinque Ports (specially privileged towns in Kent and Sussex that were taxed separately) and the city of London, which together covered 12.9 per cent of the square mileage of the counties covered on the maps, accounted for a remarkable 41.2 per cent of the national figure for taxpayers. The sheer predominance of the South-East as a home for aliens in the later Middle Ages is the most striking and important feature of this mapping exercise.

Second in order of density were the northern Home Counties and the South Midlands. Berkshire, Oxfordshire, Buckinghamshire, Bedfordshire, Hertfordshire, Huntingdonshire and Northamptonshire accounted for 10.7 per cent of the national square mileage covered in the maps, and 11.7 per cent of the total number of foreigners in these areas. This made aliens a statistically more significant presence in these seven counties than in any other part of the country save the South-East. The next most intensively occupied region was the South-West. Dorset's alien population falls into the highest category on each of the measures of density, while Gloucestershire, Wiltshire, Somerset, Devon and Cornwall all had comparatively large concentrations of immigrant population. If we add back in the figures for the city of Bristol, then these six shires, which covered 21.0 per cent of the square mileage of the counties included in the maps, account for 21.2 per cent of the population of those same areas.

The picture in East Anglia is rather less certain. Taken together, the four counties of Essex, Cambridgeshire, Suffolk and Norfolk accounted for 13.6 per cent of the square mileage of the counties included for the purposes of mapping, but only some 8.1 per cent of the total number of persons assessed for the alien subsidy in 1440. The data for Norfolk (unadjusted in the way they are deployed in Figures 1 and 2) are problematic for reasons discussed above, and almost certainly underrate the true alien presence there. The relatively high geographical (though not, interestingly, demographic) density recorded for aliens in Essex and Suffolk may therefore have been replicated in Norfolk.

In the far North, the immediate border counties also had a significant alien presence in 1440. Northumberland, Cumberland and Westmorland represent 9.9 per cent of the national square mileage accounted for in the maps, and 6.5 per cent of the total numbers assessed for the alien subsidy in the relevant counties. All three counties had higher immigrant numbers in proportion to their square mileages and, especially in Cumberland and Northumberland, to their populations than did any other shires north of the Severn–Wash line for which full data survive.

In the Central and West Midlands, and in Yorkshire, however, numbers and densities of aliens were smaller. Herefordshire, Worcestershire, Shropshire and Staffordshire represented 9.2 per cent of square mileage, but only 2.6 per cent of the total number of alien taxpayers, for the whole of the country as covered in the maps. We need to remember that the data exclude the Welsh, who were probably the largest immigrant presence in this region. Nevertheless, it may be instructive that the counties of the West Midlands were among the first to make *nil* returns to the Exchequer for later grants of the alien subsidies.[90] The numbers were, if anything, even thinner in Leicestershire, Warwickshire, Rutland, Derbyshire and Nottinghamshire, which covered 8.6 per cent of the land mass included in the maps but had only 2.8 per cent of the relevant population of alien taxpayers. Further north, only the coastal East Riding of Yorkshire registers a higher demographic and geographical density of aliens. Here it should be remembered that we lack data for Hull in 1440, and that the riding would stand out still more strongly on the density maps if that town's alien population were also included. The alien presence in the West and North Ridings was, however, much more sparse. As a whole, Yorkshire (including the city of York) accounted for 14.0 per cent of the square mileage of the English counties covered in Figures 1 and 2, but only 5.9 per cent of the aliens assessed for taxation in the relevant areas in 1440.

A widely dispersed immigrant population

The above analyses reveal two important features of the alien presence in late medieval England. First, while the greatest concentrations of immigrants were to be found in the towns and cities, and especially the major ports, aliens also penetrated a very significant number of rural communities and spread themselves out remarkably widely over the countryside. Secondly, there were significant variations in the relative density of the alien population, with the South-East, the South-West, the northern Home Counties, the South Midlands and East Anglia as the areas of greatest presence, the rest of the Midlands and Yorkshire being comparatively 'thin', and the far North representing a level of penetration somewhere between those of the South and the Midlands.

It follows that, while the degree of interaction may have varied considerably, virtually all the indigenous population of England had some degree of personal knowledge of foreigners. For the inhabitants of London, Bristol or Southampton, this was a settled, daily reality, while for rural dwellers in the Midlands, it was a matter of very occasional novelty. The degree of clustering or isolation must also have significantly coloured the attitude and behaviour of the aliens themselves. Whereas groups of immigrants in towns and cities conducted business together, intermarried and kept the memories and cultures of their homelands alive, those in isolated rural settlements had no such hope of socialisation with their own kind. For someone like Elgan, a woman taxed in Ossett in the West Riding of Yorkshire in 1440 and described as having been born in Iceland, there could have been little chance to interact with anyone from her native land: the nearest recorded Icelanders in that year lived in Beverley and Cottingham in the East Riding, both around fifty miles away.[91]

This is, of course, an extreme example chosen for effect, and certainly does not tell the entire story of the Icelandic presence in England, any more than that of other national groupings. However, it points usefully and deliberately to the next major question that we need to ask of such material. 'Alien' was an entirely constructed category created by the legal and fiscal framework of royal and urban governments. Meaningful social identities *within* the category were much more likely to be expressed in terms of the membership of a specific national grouping. In the next two chapters, we will therefore explore what the alien subsidy materials, letters of denization and other sources have to tell us about the nationalities of immigrants, and their relative presence, in order to get a better understanding of the ethnic make-up of the alien population of later medieval England.

Notes

1   *Poll Taxes of 1377, 1379 and 1381*, II, 61 records the release of twenty-eight named German merchants from liability to payment of the third poll tax in London: this clearly arose because the merchants of the Hanse were not liable to direct taxation, and the officials of the city were over-zealous in their assumption of the absence of exemptions.
2   E 179/149/126.
3   *CLBL G*, 46–7, 54.
4   *PROME*, XI, 250–5.
5   Dyer, 'Taxation and communities', pp. 173–4.
6   *CPR 1436–41*, pp. 409–11, 576–7.
7   E 179/270/31, m. 12; *Complete Peerage*, VIII, 668–70.
8   See chapter 7.
9   E 179/235/11, rot. 3.
10 E 179/108/113, m. 6; E 179/184/12, rot. 13d.
11 E 179/236/85. For further discussion of this document, see chapter 4.
12 E 179/108/113, m. 4. There is no further nominal list for Great Wakering until 1484, but it is interesting that another Hervy, this time Peter, was then assessed: E 179/108/130, m. 2.
13 Jurkowski, Smith and Crook, *Lay Taxes*, pp. 94–5.
14 Ruddick, 'Immigrants and intermarriage', pp. 182–3.
15 Lloyd, *England and the German Hanse*, p. 174.
16 See chapter 6.
17 See chapter 5. For the general exemption of the universities from other forms of direct taxation, see Lee, *Cambridge and its Economic Region*, pp. 28–9. The chancellors of the two universities were included in the process of assessment in 1440, presumably to ensure that the exemption was upheld: *CPR 1436–41*, p. 410. In general, alien

masters at the universities did not seek denization, though the letters patent granted to John Tregurre (otherwise Joan Tregurrà) in 1442 could conceivably have been prompted by concern over the reach of the subsidy: *CPR 1441-6*, p. 101.

18 Bolton, 'Irish migration', pp. 1–2; Bennett, 'Late medieval Ireland', pp. 383–4; *PROME*, XI, 330–1.

19 Griffiths, 'Crossing the frontiers of the English realm', p. 216.

20 E 159/217, Brevia directa baronibus, Michaelmas, rot. 61d.

21 *CPR 1436-41*, p. 528; E 159/218, Brevia directa baronibus, Michaelmas, rot. 1.

22 *PROME*, XII, 47–8.

23 Ormrod and Mackman, 'Resident aliens', p. 10.

24 *CPR 1429-36*, passim; *CPR 1436-41*, passim; *CPR 1441-6*, passim; *CPR 1446-52*, passim.

25 E 179/141/69, m. 1; *CPR 1436-41*, p. 485.

26 Hals (alternatively Halse): *CPR 1446-52*, p. 53; E 179/235/23, m. 2; E 179/144/64, m. 8; E 179/144/72; E 179/236/74; E 179/144/69; E 179/236/96, m. 2. Falleron (alternatively Faldron/Faleron): *CPR 1446-52*, p. 552; E 179/236/111; E 179/144/67; *Views of Hosts*, pp. 283–4.

27 *PROME*, XII, 236; *CPR 1461-7*, pp. 276–7.

28 *PROME*, XII, 235–6.

29 Giuseppi, 'Alien merchants', p. 93.

30 *PROME*, XIV, 412–13; Jurkowski, Smith and Crook, *Lay Taxes*, pp. 120–1. During the lapse in the collection of the alien subsidies in the 1470s the Italians had been exempted from liability, presumably meaning their non-payment of arrears: *CPR 1476-85*, pp. 2, 342. The formal record of the 1487 grant does not include the special immunity for the merchants of the four Italian cities allowed in 1483: *PROME*, XIV, 412–13. However, it seems that this group was informally exempted. See also Guidi-Bruscoli and Lutkin, 'Perception, identity and culture', p. 89 n. 3.

31 *PROME*, XI, 253.

32 E 179/141/69; E 179/236/85.

33 Keene, 'Metropolitan values', pp. 110–11.

34 Lutkin, 'Settled or fleeting?', pp. 154–5.

35 E 359/28, rots 1–4, 6–9.

36 *CFR 1461-71*, pp. 219, 259.

37 E 179/124/122, m. 2.

38 As signalled by the appointment of separate commissions to assess and collect the tax, rather than relying, as previously, on the justices of the peace and the sheriffs: *CPR 1476-85*, pp. 353–5, 393–7, 425, 447; *CPR 1485-94*, pp. 239–43.

39 *PROME*, XIV, 412; XV, 370–1.

40 Jurkowski, Smith and Crook, *Lay Taxes*, p. 121.

41 *Alien Communities*, pp. 47–105.

42 E 359/28, rot. 1d; E 179/270/54.

43 E 359/28, rot. 1; E 179/291/11.

44 Schofield, *Taxation under the Early Tudors*, pp. 73–7.

45 These estimates are based on the enrolled accounts rather than the nominal returns, which are very patchy for later grants of the alien subsidy.

46 Rigby, 'Urban population'.

47 Thrupp, 'Survey', pp. 270–2.

48 E 359/28, rots 1–4, 6–9. Enrolled accounts for subsequent alien subsidies are detailed in Jurkowski, Smith and Crook, *Lay Taxes*, pp. 96, 100, 107, 122.

49 E 179/136/206.

50 E 179/270/32, Part 1; E 359/28, rot. 2.

51 E 359/28, rots 1–2d; E 179/132/367, m. 2. The omission of Hull was almost certainly a consequence of the town's elevation to county status at precisely this time, but the reason for Coventry's omission is unknown.

52 E 179/149/126.

53 For example, Thrupp's estimate included just fifty-seven people in Bedfordshire (the number assessed in 1441), whereas the enrolled accounts show an actual figure in 1440 of 232: Thrupp, 'Survey', p. 271; E 359/28, rot. 2.

54 Ormrod and Mackman, 'Resident aliens', p. 28 n. 104. There are no worthwhile later figures for Lancashire that can be used to extrapolate the possible number of taxpayers in 1440, and the figure of 250 has been estimated by using data from neighbouring counties and population ratios drawn from the poll tax of 1377.

55 Compare the sixteenth-century data for aliens in County Durham discussed in chapter 4.

56 Dyer, 'Taxation and communities'; Ormrod, 'Poverty and privilege'.

57 See chapter 7.

58 In spite of the exemption of regular clergy, the French-born priors of the alien priories of Modbury and Cowick, both in Devon, paid the first collection of the alien subsidy: E 179/95/100, rots 3d, 5. For further evidence of French monks at Modbury in this period, see McHardy and Orme, 'Defence of an alien priory'; and for Cowick, see chapter 7.

59 For the populations of Scotland and Wales in 1440 we have taken early fourteenth-century figures of one million and 300,000 respectively, as cited in Dyer, *Making a Living*, p. 101, and reduced them by a third to take account of the presumed effects of the Black Death. For the population trend in Wales, see also Carr, 'Wales: economy and society', pp. 126, 133–4.

60 See the reviews of this debate by Goldberg, *Women, Work and Life Cycle*, pp. 8–9, 20, 203–32, 272–9, and Fleming, *Family and Household*, pp. 19–31.

61 *Alien Communities*, p. 8.

62 *Alien Communities*, p. 8.

63 See further discussion in chapter 10.

64 See chapter 7.

65 Yungblut, *Strangers Settled Here Amongst Us*, pp. 9–35.

66 Higgs, *Making Sense of the Census Revisited*, pp. 88–9, 91–2.

67 A Vision of Britain through Time, www.visionofbritain.org.uk/census/1901 (accessed 7 September 2017).

68 Mundill, *England's Jewish Solution*, p. 26.

69 Jordan, *From England to France*, pp. 25–6.

70 For the practice in Flanders, see Dumolyn and Pajic, 'Enemies of the count and of the city'; and further discussion in chapter 6.

71 Leader, *History of the University of Cambridge, I*, pp. 38–9; Warneke, *Images of the Educational Traveller*, pp. 27–8.

72 See also the wider discussion of the decline of opportunity in the colonies by Bennett, 'Plantagenet Empire as "enterprise zone"'.

73 Freeman, '"And he abjured the realm of England"', pp. 301–3.

74 Clay, *Economic Expansion and Social Change*, pp. 12–15; Bolton, '"The world upside down"', pp. 28–40.

75 *Alien Communities*, pp. 8–9.

76 Keene, 'Metropolitan values', p. 109. Compare Pettegree, 'Foreign population of London'.

77 Liddy and Lambert, 'Civic franchise', pp. 128–9.

78 Fleming, 'Identity and belonging'.

79 Kermode, *Medieval Merchants*, p. 10.

80 For a previous estimate of 3 per cent for Winchester's alien population in the period, see Keene, *Survey of Medieval Winchester*, I, 381.

81 For Colchester, where the earlier influx of Flemish weavers had already largely passed by 1440, see chapter 7.

82 Dobson, 'Aliens in the city of York', p. 253.

83 Ditchburn, 'Anglo-Scottish relations'; Rees Jones, 'Scots in the North of England'; Bennett, 'Women (and men) on the move'.

84 E 179/90/27.

85 E 179/269/53.

86 E 179/133/71.

87 E 179/196/100.

88 E 179/95/100; Kowaleski, 'French immigrants'.

89 E 179/108/113.

90 For example, despite returning 250 taxpayers between them in 1440, the sheriffs of Shropshire and Staffordshire reported not a single alien taxpayer in either of their counties in 1455: E 179/166/104; E 179/177/74.

91 E 179/270/31, m. 11; E 179/270/31, mm. 23, 31.

4

Immigrants from the British Isles

One of the most notable aspects of later medieval immigration is the sheer range of different nationalities entering England, and the differing patterns of their distribution across the various parts of the country. The alien subsidy returns are by far our most abundant and significant source in this respect. As noted in chapter 3, the assessors of these taxes were not actually required to provide a nationality label for the people enumerated, but merely to vouch that they were indeed aliens. The recording of nationality was therefore an 'optional extra' for these officials, and varied greatly from place to place and over time. Sometimes we can also ascribe a nationality on the basis of toponymic surname evidence: in the analyses that follow, people with names such as 'Irish', 'Scot', 'Frenchman' and so on have all been assumed to have come from the relevant countries. In the fullest returns, those for the first collection of the 1440 subsidy, it is possible to read or ascribe a nationality in 33 per cent of entries in the nominal returns (that is, 5,106 out of a total of 15,901 entries). In some later subsidies the proportion actually increases, though the size of the sample drops considerably. In the returns for 1483, for example, 67 per cent of the nominal entries have stated or ascribed nationalities (2,195 out of 3,269 entries); and this year delivers the highest proportion of nationalities for London-based aliens over the whole life of the alien subsidies. For those counties and those tax collections where no nominal rolls exist in a given year, nationalities are lost to us entirely, since the enrolled accounts give only summary headcounts and do not break them down into categories. A good deal, however, can still be achieved from analysis of the surviving data. Furthermore, we can usefully supplement this material with information contained in letters of protection and denization, which often stated the national origins of recipients. The remarkable list of people taking the oath of fealty to the English crown in

1436–7 also includes (in the vast majority of cases) details not just about their country of birth but the precise city, town or village from which the individual originally came.

The list of nationality labels used both by tax assessors and the royal Chancery remained fairly static and consistent over the period covered by this study. However, the interpretation of these labels can provide a significant challenge. Latin, French and Middle English terms were all used in official documents to describe people's places of origin, and the distinctive cultural resonances of these different linguistic labels are not always clear.[1] Particular problems emerge in the overlap or conflict between generic and specific terms. For example, many people were noted as 'French'; but in some places within England, regional identifiers were also used, so that immigrants could be named as 'Normans', 'Bretons', 'Gascons' and so on. Similarly the term 'Dutch' denoted a linguistic rather than a political status, and might cover people who in other tax returns were labelled as originating in the many principalities of the Low Countries and western Germany. These ambiguities help to explain some of the cases of inconsistent identity found in successive returns to the alien subsidies. In Lincolnshire, for example, John Browne of Bourne was recorded with no nationality in 1449, as a Zeelander in 1455, as a Fleming in 1456 and as 'Dutch' in 1458.[2] More eccentrically, in the city of Lincoln, John Michell was assessed between 1458 and 1464 variously as French, Norman and Genoese, and may even have been the man of that name who had been taxed as a Gascon in the 1440s.[3]

It is possible to spot certain patterns of behaviour on the part of English officialdom with regard to the use of nationality labels. In a broad sense, for example, the use of differentiating labels to denote the various regions of France in the 1440s was confined to the South of England, where the French were most numerous and where understanding of the cultural and political significance of more specific labels seems to have been highest.[4] But we must also be aware of marked disparities in practice even within neighbouring areas of England and at particular moments in time. For instance, the raw data from the 1440 alien subsidy returns would suggest that a hundred people from Normandy lived in Wiltshire, but that none lived in neighbouring Gloucestershire.[5] However, this really only tells us that the Wiltshire assessors used that term, while the Gloucestershire ones did not: it is entirely possible, and more than likely, that people originally from Normandy were also to be found in the latter county, but were there recorded as French. In Leicestershire in 1440, ninety-nine of the 102 people named in the return had a nationality or country of origin noted. In neighbouring Warwickshire, by contrast, 107 named individuals were given no nationality label, and only John Martyn was described as French, probably to differentiate him from an English neighbour of the same name.[6]

For all these problems, the available sources can still tell us a huge amount about the origins of those who made up England's alien population. This chapter considers those from other parts of the British Isles and the Channel Islands, before we move in chapter 5 to look at incomers from continental Europe.

The Welsh

The numbers and distribution of the Welsh within medieval England is the most difficult to judge, since people from Wales were specifically excluded from the scope of the alien subsidies. Only six obviously Welsh people can be found in the 1440 subsidy records, all in London, with another one taxed in Kent in 1455.[7] All were presumably included by mistake. The numbers of Welsh who appear in the other main sources used for this study are also very small. In 1413, when all Irish and Welsh people living in England were ordered to return home, thirty-nine Welsh people received royal letters exempting them from the injunction.[8] This was clearly a token gesture; only those wealthy enough and with most to lose from forced repatriation would have taken the trouble to secure such letters, and these must have formed a tiny fraction of the Welsh people living in England at that time. Only twenty-two of these noted places of residence. Twelve, not surprisingly, lived in Gloucestershire and Shropshire. The rest were further afield: three in London and two each in Warwickshire and Buckinghamshire, with single individuals in Berkshire, Wiltshire and Lincolnshire. No fewer than nine of these were clerics, one of the groups specifically and regularly targeted by such repatriation orders.

Similarly, only eleven Welsh people are known to have secured letters of denization in the fifteenth century, and one Welsh woman in 1544, though that was probably because she was married to a Breton, rather than any attempt to disavow her Welsh heritage.[9] John Butte alias Hore, originally from Carmarthen, had supposedly been living in Bridport in Dorset for over thirty years when he was granted denization in 1437; as with most such instances, it is not known what prompted his request.[10] David Middelton, given denizenship in 1462, was a yeoman of the crown to Edward IV, while Richard ap Robert ap Jevan Vaghan was also a servant of the king, Richard III, in 1484. Both were possibly recruited from the duchy of York's Welsh estates.[11] Perhaps surprisingly given the Tudor dynasty's connections with Wales, only four Welshmen were granted denization by Henry VII. One, Owen Tydur, was an esquire of the king's body and quite possibly a member of the extended network of legitimate and illegitimate relatives of Owen Tudor (d. 1461), second husband of Henry V's widow, Katherine of Valois, and grandfather of Henry VII.[12]

Denizations are clearly very imperfect measures by which to estimate the numbers and distribution of the Welsh-born people who resided in England in the later Middle Ages. Fortunately, much fuller evidence comes in the form of characteristically Welsh names that appear in the returns of late thirteenth- and early fourteenth-century royal taxes on moveable property, the later fourteenth-century poll taxes and the Tudor subsidies. Among those anglicised names that are regarded as firm evidence of Welsh ancestry where they appear in medieval records from England are Gogh (from *coch*, meaning red [-haired]), Morgan, Owen, Rees, Wallis and Welch/Welsh; the characteristic Welsh patronymic using the prefix 'ab' or 'ap' (Madog ab Owain, etc.) is also often quite readily evident.[13] These instances provide some sense of settlement patterns over a number of generations. Not surprisingly, the highest densities of Welsh surnames in the later Middle Ages are found in the English West Midlands, especially in Shropshire and Herefordshire.[14] Urban archives also reveal a very significant presence of the Welsh in certain towns of the West and North-West of England: in particular, detailed studies by Peter Fleming and Jane Laughton have revealed numerous Welsh-born people in the immigrant populations of Bristol and Chester. In both instances, moreover, such immigrants overcame the formal disabilities that applied to them after the Glyn Dŵr rebellion, and some of their number rose to the highest levels, joining the franchise and achieving high civic office. For Bristol, it has been calculated that some 10 per cent of the city's office-holders across the fifteenth century had Welsh origins.[15]

The Welsh may not have been quite as rare in other parts of England as tax returns alone suggest. Legal records can also be deployed to detect people from Wales who made their way eastwards in the later Middle Ages. In the counties closest to the Welsh border, English law tended simply to treat Welsh immigrants as a given: in the surviving Shropshire coroners' rolls from the reign of Henry IV, for example, none of the people with Welsh patronymic names were explicitly described as being Welsh.[16] In the East Midlands, however, the position was different. In the fourteenth-century judicial records from Lincolnshire, Welsh people were seemingly always identified as such. Moreover, they actually form the largest such national grouping recorded in Lincolnshire cases outside the major towns.[17] It may be that host communities further away from the border were less inclined to preserve characteristically Welsh names, and that the Welsh may yet be demonstrated to have spread further, at least in small numbers, into many of the more prosperous regions of southern and Midland England.

The Irish

Ireland was a dominion of the English crown, with a sophisticated administration operating from a devolved government and parliament in Dublin. In fact, much of Ireland was beyond the practical reach of such bureaucratic and political structures, with Gaelic tribal leaders holding effective control over many parts of the lordship. The tensions within the Anglo-Irish elite over how to maintain charge filtered into English politics too, and resulted in a rhetorical conflict between the crown and the Irish living in England. On numerous occasions throughout the fourteenth and fifteenth centuries, Anglo-Irish people resident in England were ordered to return to their homeland and resume their responsibilities in governing it to the satisfaction of both Dublin and Westminster.[18] As with the Welsh expulsion orders, however, these instructions were little more than window dressing; there were no forced deportations, and such measures again provided an opportunity for the crown to raise money by selling licences to remain in the realm. Over 640 Irish people are known to have taken out such licences between 1394 and 1439, and although these were presumably only the richer and more prominent, the resulting evidence provides significant information about the Irish presence in England at this time. Unfortunately, because the Irish were quickly exempted from the alien subsidy, only the records of the first collection provide us with information about their presence. English-speaking Irishmen may have had more luck in avoiding the tax officials than more obvious immigrants from the continent. Even so, the returns from the 1440 alien subsidy probably give a fairly clear idea of the extent and distribution of the Irish in England.

In total, over 2,000 instances of Irish immigrants into England appear within the records of the alien subsidies, the licences to remain after expulsion orders, and letters of protection and denization between 1300 and 1550. Many of the thousands of other alien people of unspecified and unknown nationality must also have been Irish. Detailed research into the assessments for specific towns or regions may well uncover far more Irish amongst those taxed, though this is far from easy; Fleming has speculated that many of the people taxed in 1440 and 1441 in Bristol (a town for which the returns were especially uninformative) were almost certainly Irish, but has only been able to identify a small number with any certainty.[19]

The subsidy evidence reveals approximately 817 explicitly Irish taxpayers in England in 1440, with a distinct bias to the South-West (see Table 3).[20] Large numbers were recorded in Cornwall, Devon, Gloucestershire and Wiltshire, with further significant populations in the West and Central Midlands, in Northamptonshire, Bedfordshire, Leicestershire, Warwickshire and Buckinghamshire. Relatively few Irish were found further afield, with only five being recorded in Norfolk, Suffolk and Essex combined, and only eight north of the Humber. The evidence from licences, protections and denizations suggests a similar dispersal, though in this case the largest numbers were resident in the counties of the Cotswolds and the South Midlands, as well as in London and Kent. Again, very few Irish appear in the North or in East Anglia. Only a very small number of aliens of any nationality living in Yorkshire, Lancashire and the counties bordering Scotland took the trouble to go to Westminster and purchase such letters, though it is worth pointing out that, of the twelve of those who did so between 1390 and 1490, seven were Irish. The same was true of other extremities of the realm: despite seventy-six Irish taxpayers being recorded in Cornwall in 1440, only one Irishman from that county is known to have been issued with a licence to remain across the entire fifteenth century: Edmund Hope of Lostwithiel in 1413.[21]

The numbers, distribution and economic status of the Irish within England have attracted a certain amount of discussion from historians. Kevin Down and Art Cosgrove have noted the concerns expressed in the Irish Parliament during the later Middle Ages about the effects of the emigration of labourers and servants to England in denuding the lordship of the necessary people to work the land.[22] Thrupp claimed that Scots and Irish immigrants, 'familiar at home with cattle and sheep, had reason to stay mostly in the North and West, as this was pastoral country'.[23] However, Bolton has questioned this, suggesting instead a strong system of 'chain migration' for skilled Irish people entering England through Chester, Bristol and other ports of the South-West.[24] While some stayed in those port towns, many would have migrated eastwards, probably using the same much-travelled routes used by Welsh and Irish migrants for decades: along the Dee and Severn valleys, and the tracks and roads through the Midlands towards Coventry, Northampton and as far east as Cambridge, Leicester and Lincoln. The settlement patterns for Irish immigrants identifiable in the alien subsidy data would certainly bear this out; but the lack of evidence of northward migration from Chester would

Table 3: Identifiable nationalities of taxpayers assessed towards the first year of the 1440 alien subsidy

	Total no. of taxpayers[a]	Taxpayers with known nationality[b]	Irish		Scots[c]		French[d]		'Dutch' etc[e]		Others[f]
			no.	%	no.	%	no.	%[g]	no.	%	no.
Bedfordshire	232	55	21	38%	0	–	23	42%	10	18%	1
Berkshire	351	88	17	19%	1	1%	61	69%	8	9%	1
Buckinghamshire	275	82	19	23%	0	–	46	56%	17	21%	0
Cambridgeshire	158	132	14	11%	4	3%	44	33%	68	52%	2
Cinque Ports	648	23	0	–	1	4%	10	43%	10	43%	2
Cornwall	318	174	76	44%	3	2%	69	40%	20	11%	6
Cumberland	309	142	0	–	142	100%	0	–	0	–	0
Derbyshire	68	0[h]	–	–	–	–	–	–	–	–	–
Devon	675	633	92	15%	1	0%	450	71%	62	10%	28
Dorset	758	110	2	2%	0	–	69	63%	6	5%	33
Essex	422	112	3	3%	2	2%	57	51%	50	45%	0
Gloucestershire	958	75	34	45%	2	3%	15	20%	22	29%	2
Hampshire	1121	93	10	11%	1	1%	48	52%	17	18%	17
Herefordshire	58	58	9	16%	0	–	43	74%	6	10%	0
Hertfordshire	319	73	8	11%	0	–	44	60%	20	27%	1
Huntingdonshire	77	57	6	11%	1	2%	37	65%	13	23%	0
Kent	1,129	296	34	11%	3	1%	173	58%	85	29%	1
Lancashire	5	1	0	–	1	100%	0	–	0	–	0
Leicestershire	97	95	21	22%	6	6%	48	51%	20	21%	0
Lincolnshire	130	51	7	14%	7	14%	18	35%	17	33%	2
London	1,835	131	21	16%	6	5%	34	26%	52	40%	18

County											
Middlesex	661	70	7%	5	1	1%	35	50%	29	41%	0
Norfolk	282	55	2%	1	1	2%	10	18%	41	75%	2
Northamptonshire	349	323	46%	148	1	0%	122	38%	48	15%	4
Northumberland	684	570	0%	2	566	99%	0	–	2	0%	0
Nottinghamshire	108	35	11%	4	4	11%	24	69%	3	9%	0
Oxfordshire	359	0^h	–	–	–	–	–	–	–	–	–
Rutland	26	16	6%	1	1	6%	7	44%	7	44%	0
Shropshire	72	16	19%	3	0	–	10	63%	3	19%	0
Somerset	377	89	17%	15	0	–	57	64%	13	15%	4
Staffordshire	178	50	20%	10	1	2%	38	76%	1	2%	0
Suffolk	497	247	0%	1	7	3%	71	29%	166	67%	2
Surrey	595	47	15%	7	0	–	28	60%	12	26%	0
Sussex	877	104	2%	2	1	1%	87	84%	14	13%	0
Warwickshire	165	38	47%	18	0	–	17	45%	2	5%	1
Westmorland	105	73	4%	3	68	93%	2	3%	0	–	0
Wiltshire	477	448	35%	156	1	0%	252	56%	39	9%	0
Worcestershire	124	41	27%	11	0	–	26	63%	4	10%	0
Yorkshire	999	403	1%	4	234	58%	123	31%	27	7%	15
Totals	16,878	5,106	15%	785	1,067	21%	2,198	43%	914	18%	142

a Numbers taken from Table 1. The notes given there relating to individual county totals also apply to these figures.

b Taxpayers with a stated or readily identifiable nationality or place of origin, or a 'surname' clearly indicative of national origins, e.g. 'Scot'.

c Does not include people specified as Orcadians.

d Includes people identifiable as French, Norman, Breton, Picard and Gascon.

e Includes all people originating from the Low Countries (including Flanders) and medieval Germany, and everyone identified as 'Dutch' or 'Easterling'.

f Includes all people originating from the Channel Islands, Orkney Islands, Wales and the Isle of Man, the Iberian, Italian and Scandinavian peninsulas, Iceland and Greece.

g Taxpayers of this nationality as a percentage of those with known nationality.

h Details for Derbyshire and Oxfordshire are known only from the enrolled accounts, which do not specify nationalities.

seem incongruous if, as Thrupp suggested, the majority of Irish incomers were indeed agricultural labourers and herdsmen. The hill country of the northern counties would surely have been just as attractive to such Irishmen as it was to their Scottish neighbours. Instead, the evidence suggests that the majority headed south-eastwards, into Staffordshire, Warwickshire and the rest of the English Midlands, where they would no doubt have met other Irish people moving up from the South-West.

Although many of the Irish immigrants noted in the alien subsidy returns of 1440 may indeed have been agricultural workers, the proportion of householders within this national group was actually relatively high, with around 55 per cent paying at householder rates compared to a national average of around 40 per cent. As Bolton has noted, these figures are more akin to the proportions associated with immigrants from the Low Countries (traditionally seen as urban artisans), rather than for groups such as the Scots, over three quarters of whom were non-householders in 1440. Comparison with details from the fourteenth- and fifteenth-century licences to remain also suggest that evidence of urban Irish migration in the tax returns may have been partially obscured by the vagaries of record survival. Of the 255 Irish recipients of such letters whose place of residence was stated, twenty lived in Bristol, twelve in Oxford, and nine in Coventry – all places for which little or no evidence survives from 1440. There was also almost certainly a significant Irish population in the capital. Only fourteen of the 255 Irish recipients of licences to remain were noted as living in London, and Ralph Griffiths has suggested that 'the Irish, unlike the Scots, rarely settled in London'.[25] Yet in the sole surviving London tax document from the 1440 payment, a now-incomplete schedule of defaulters drawn up the following year, twenty-one of the 133 people with known origins were identifiably Irish, compared to just six Scots.[26]

Furthermore, Bolton's analysis has shown considerable numbers of Irish artisans assessed in various other parts of England in 1440, as tailors, carpenters, butchers and parchment makers. There were also significant numbers of Irish-born clergy working in England.[27] Many of the Irish recorded as 'servants' in 1440 (155 of the 817 people identified) may well have been workers, assistants or apprentices to artisans or tradesmen, rather than simply domestic servants or agricultural labourers. For instance, Patrick 'Glover', an Irishman taxed in Marlborough in Wiltshire in 1440, was listed along with two Irish 'servants', Maurice and Richard.[28] This may have been the same Patrick later taxed in the same town by the surname Rede; if so, we can propose that he was a glove maker by trade, and that his two 'servants' in 1440 may themselves have been skilled workers in his business. Similarly, in nearby Chippenham, an Irish shoe maker, John Alyn, had four servants, three of whom were also Irish. Two were listed by their forenames only, but the other, named as John Coryer (i.e. 'currier'), was probably a leather worker employed in Alyn's business.[29] Thrupp's description of Irish agricultural workers finding jobs in the rural Midlands was no doubt true for some, but far more seem to have been skilled or semi-skilled workers drawn into England by the prospect of successful careers, and settling predominantly in the South-West and the Midlands. In this context, the lack of penetration of the Irish into eastern England, which would have not only involved longer journeys but also brought them into greater competition with continental rivals coming the other way, is perhaps more understandable.

It would also seem that the majority of Irish people living in England were 'Anglo-Irish', rather than Gaelic Irish. Towns of origin are only rarely identifiable for the Irish people included in our main sources, but those that are known were mainly within areas of stronger English rule. John de Swerdes, taxed in Hereford throughout the early 1440s, was presumably from Swords, near Dublin, while three Waterford natives secured licences to remain in 1394, as did the vicar of Skryne in County Meath in 1401 and a man from Cork in 1430.[30] Very few people with obviously Gaelic names appear in the subsidy records, but it is perhaps no coincidence that one of only two Irishmen known to have secured letters of denization in this period was named as 'Magouin Macdouchide', probably not a member of the Anglo-Irish community.[31] The Anglo-Irish themselves, despite briefly being caught by the subsidy in 1440, were probably secure enough in their status as subjects of the English crown that they found such letters unnecessary.

The Islanders

The Irish were far from the only crown subjects to find themselves caught up in the alien subsidy. The Channel Islanders were even more vociferous about their inclusion in the tax, and rapidly secured an exemption, issued on 22 November 1440.[32] The Channel Islanders in England were clearly far fewer in number than the Irish, and only sixty-seven Channel Islanders were named as such on the surviving 1440 returns, almost all of whom, not surprisingly, lived in southern counties. Most appeared in Dorset and Devon, though the lower numbers in nearby Hampshire, Somerset and Cornwall may simply reflect less conscientious record-keeping and document loss. The only exceptions to this were Emma Gerneseye, assessed in London, and John Gerneseye, who had found his way as far north as

Hitchin in Hertfordshire.[33] Channel Islanders must have been a common if small presence in England throughout this period, particularly in the port towns of the south coast; and on the whole, there is little to suggest that they were treated differently from their English neighbours. In April 1524, two Channel Islanders were assessed for the Tudor subsidy in Lowestoft in Suffolk, but were charged not at the alien rate but at that set for English people.[34] No doubt elsewhere in the 1520s, Channel Islanders were simply not noted as such by the tax assessors, as there was no fiscal reason to do so; for instance, the Cornish returns for the 1523 subsidy explicitly noted dozens of Bretons, but no Channel Islanders.[35] In the 1540s, nine Channel Islanders secured letters of denization, though this was probably just to remove any possible ambiguity over their status at a time of national tension. Two, the unnamed wives of Richard Trybet, a Norman ship-wright in Southampton, and John Mickell, a French cook employed by Lord Cobham, presumably took out the letters alongside their husbands. Some may have followed the example of the carver Michael Tharon, who had lived in England for thirty years but bought letters specifically because he was unsure whether he had actually been born in Jersey or in France.[36]

Other islanders also made their way into England across our period. The Orkney and Shetland Isles remained under nominal Norwegian lordship until 1472, after which they passed into the control of the Scottish monarchy.[37] A small number of people from the Orkneys appear in the alien subsidy returns before and after 1472, described as such or identifiable from their surnames. The same label may have included people from the Shetlands, since no identifiable Shetlanders appear in any of the surviving returns. The Orcadians were predominantly found along the east coast, from Northumberland down to Norfolk, although two intrepid individuals made it as far as the Cinque Ports of Sandwich and Hastings.[38] One Orcadian, Phillip Jonson, clearly described as being from Stronsay in Orkney and living in Brancaster in Norfolk, even swore the oath of allegiance in 1436, presumably to insure himself against any potential hostility from his East Anglian neighbours.[39] In 1542, three Orcadians sought letters of denization. All claimed to have English wives, though where they lived is not recorded.[40] It is likely that other Orcadians and Shetlanders were simply identified as Scots.

A small number of people from the Isle of Man were assessed for the first collection of the alien subsidy, though not thereafter. Three Manxmen and one woman were recorded in 1440, two in Yorkshire and two, per-haps surprisingly, as householders in Brixham in Devon.[41] No Manxmen are known to have taken out letters of denization. The very low numbers suggest that the labelling was rather exceptional; as suggested in chapter 2, the absence of references to Manx people after 1440 may denote their *de facto* exemption from the later alien subsidies. We know that there was a recognisable community of Manx people in late medieval Chester, and it is reasonable to suppose that some other places in the North-West of England also had immigrants born on Man.[42] People from the island may well have been recorded as Scots or Irish, or given no nationalities at all, and are thus hidden from our view.

The Scots

The Scots were most definitely aliens within England, the subjects of a foreign and often hostile monarch. It has often been assumed that Scottish migration to England in the period before the Reformation was insignificant, and that many Scots were deterred from moving south by the constant tensions between the two nations. Thomson, for example, acknowledged how disaffected members of the Scottish ruling classes often found a safe haven in England, but noted that these were few and far between.[43] However, recent research has made it very clear that considerable numbers of Scots did in fact move to England in the later Middle Ages.[44] The vast majority of such migrants were clearly people of relatively low social status, men and women who moved in search of employment or trading opportunities, or were drawn by familial ties. Many were just temporary visitors, seasonal workers taking advantage of labour needs at certain times in the rural calendar; but others were doubtless seeking a more permanent move. In 1587 the English warden of the East March, Lord Hunsdon, claimed that some northern English towns contained more Scots than Englishmen: an exaggerated position, no doubt, but one intended to send a clear message about the level of settlement and its economic and political implications.[45] Neither the phenomenon that Hunsdon described nor the potential threat that it posed was new in the sixteenth century.

The evidence of Scottish migration into later medieval England provided by the surviving sources is, however, surprisingly contradictory. The 1440 alien subsidy returns show that the overwhelming majority of Scottish immigrants were to be found in the northern counties, where they formed the vast bulk of the people assessed towards the tax (see Table 3). As with other groups, Scottish origins were not always noted in the returns. In Cumberland, for example, the assessors failed to record the nationality of any of the 317 taxpayers.[46] However, it is a reasonably safe assumption that the 142 residents of this county given the surname 'Scot' were from north of the border, and names such as Alexander Lidale (Liddel), Thomas

Mewerose (Melrose), Thomas Murray and Gilbert Makecoye (McCoy) suggest that most of the others were also Scots. Of the 539 alien residents of rural Northumberland in 1440 whose names survive, all but five were described as Scots, the only exceptions being one Fleming, one Irishman and three others whose nationalities were not recorded. (One of those uniden-tified, John Galuay of Bywell, is more likely to have come from Galloway in Scotland than Galway in Ireland.)[47] The assessors in Newcastle upon Tyne also did not trouble themselves with national origins, but despite the presence of Henry Ducheman and Margaret Iryssh, the majority were again almost certainly Scots; and in 1451, when the town did note nationalities systematically, the thirty-three taxpayers comprised twenty-seven Scots and six 'Dutch'.[48] In Westmorland, sixty-one of the 105 recorded taxpayers were given the surname Scot, at least thirty-seven of them being women. Five others were explicitly described as Scots, and of the remainder, all but the two recorded Frenchmen were probably either Scots or Irish.[49]

The Scottish reach into northern England also extended beyond the immediate border counties. In 1440, 239 Scots are readily identifiable in the alien subsidy returns for Yorkshire, easily the largest single grouping in the county; and while 60 per cent of the taxpayers there had no stated nationality or origin, it is likely that large numbers of those were also Scots. Of the handful of people who were actually taxed in Lancashire, Thomas Oliver of Bolton-le-Moors, assessed throughout the early years of the tax, was consistently given the alias 'Thomas Scot'.[50] County Durham did not pay the fifteenth-century subsidies, but the Tudor subsidies were levied on the county's alien population from the 1540s, and in 1542 some 187 aliens were assessed to pay there, at least 180 of whom were Scots (the others comprising four 'Dutch', one French, one Irish and a cleric of unspecified origins). In the same year, fifty-three aliens were assessed in Westmorland, and fifty-nine in Newcastle upon Tyne, most almost certainly Scots despite no national-ities being given.[51] In 1549, sixty-seven aliens, all Scots, were taxed in County Durham, and in 1550, 134 aliens were assessed there, all but one being Scots. 128 of this latter group were recorded as living in the bishop's border liberties of Norhamshire and Islandshire rather than in the main county.[52]

Outside these northern counties, Scots were relatively sparsely represented in 1440, and particularly away from the east coast. No single county south of the Humber returned more than seven readily identifiable Scots, though Lincolnshire and possibly Derbyshire may well have done so had records survived, and the Nottinghamshire return does not supply nationalities. There certainly were Scots in the East Midlands, and they become more readily identifiable in documentation for the later alien subsidies. Of the forty-three people assessed in Lincolnshire in 1455 who were given nationalities, for example, twenty-seven were Scots.[53] Similarly thirteen of the seventeen taxpayers in Nottinghamshire in 1465 were Scots.[54] Yet only slightly further south, just six of the ninety-seven Leicestershire taxpayers with known origins in 1440 were Scots, and only one of the 349 in Northamptonshire.[55] In East Anglia, the recording of nationalities was poor, but only around 2 per cent of all taxpayers in Norfolk between 1440 and 1470 were identifiably Scots. In Suffolk the proportion was less than 1 per cent. Only two Scots were recorded in the county of Essex across the whole period during which the alien subsidies ran. Four Scots were identified in Kent in 1440, and three even made their way as far as Truro in Cornwall. So, although individual Scots appeared in many counties, very few were recorded south of a line running from the Mersey to the Wash. Even in the capital, only six Scots were noted in the list of over 1,200 defaulters surviving from 1440 (though the nationalities of only 131 of those are clearly identifiable).[56]

The evidence from the 1440 subsidy therefore suggests that Scottish migration was largely confined to the North of England, with a few making their way into the East Midlands, fewer still to coastal parts of southern England and almost none to the inland counties of the West and South Midlands. Yet by the time of the 1483 alien subsidy, this picture seems to have altered. The situation in the border counties presumably remained much the same, although the numbers of taxpayers being assessed dropped sharply after 1440, in line with the rest of the country, and no details survive at all from after the 1460s. In London, Scots remained almost invisible throughout the life of the earlier alien subsidies – though it has to be noted that only a minority of taxpayers were given a stated nationality by the assessors in the capital down to the 1460s. In 1483, however, when nationalities were recorded relatively comprehensively, no fewer than 163 Scots were noted, forming just over 10 per cent of the taxed alien population of the city.[57] In Kent, just three Scots were taxed in 1440, but ten were named in the first assessment of Edward IV's reign, made in 1463, out of a total of just sixty-six recorded aliens. In 1487, twenty of the eighty aliens taxed in Canterbury were Scots, and twelve Scots were taxed in the city in 1524.[58] Meanwhile in Suffolk, just seven Scots were identified in 1440, out of the 497 taxpayers (1 per cent). In 1483, by contrast, thirty-seven of the 275 taxpayers (13 per cent) with a recorded nationality in this county were Scots; and in 1524, ten of the sixty-four identifiable aliens in the general subsidy returns for Suffolk (that is, 16 per cent) were Scots.[59] In Norfolk, no Scots were recorded in 1440; yet thirteen of the ninety-five taxpayers in the county in 1483 were Scots, seven of them living in Lynn.[60]

How are we to account for this apparent change of pattern in Scottish settlement in England in the 1480s? England and Scotland were at peace for most of the period after the early 1460s, and this may have acted as an inducement to Scots who consciously sought to make a permanent move to southern and eastern England. However, a state of war temporarily prevailed between 1480 and 1484. The English, having lost control of Berwick upon Tweed in 1461, took the town back again in 1482, though the costs of the campaign and the continued anxieties over border security produced a rather critical response from the political community at home that manifested itself in the anti-Scots legislation of 1490, discussed in chapter 2.[61] It is possible, therefore, that there was a rather greater vigilance on the part of tax assessors in the South during the assessment of the 1483 and 1487 alien subsidies about spotting and reporting Scottish people in their midst. Certainly, it is in the 1480s that we encounter a number of cases where English men were effectively 'suspected' as Scots and listed as liable to the alien subsidy. In 1488, the king's attorney, James Hobart, delivered a sworn statement to the Exchequer on behalf of Robert Radclyff, who had been assessed towards the alien subsidy in Southwark. Radclyff had been named as a Scot, but successfully claimed that he had in fact been born in Colwich in Staffordshire.[62] Similarly, Oliver North, taxed as a Scot in Essex in 1483, appeared at the Exchequer in Trinity term 1488 to confirm that he had been born at Whittington in Lancashire.[63] Unless we believe that the assessors in the South of England between the 1440s and the 1460s had consistently avoided the use of the label 'Scottish', however, it would be difficult to put the entire phenomenon of increased numbers in the 1480s down to a fluke of record keeping.

An important clue as to what may have happened to change the pattern of Scottish diaspora over England comes in the letters of protection and denization. As we saw in chapter 2, letters of protection were made available to Scots from the 1460s onwards. Denizations were in fact taken up rather earlier, though in very small numbers: of the twenty-four denizations of Scots that are recorded on the patent rolls before 1500, the majority were issued between 1431 and 1451, before the cessation of hostilities, with another spike during the years of war in the early 1480s.[64] Of the 172 letters of denization and licences to remain issued to known Scots during the fifteenth century, 127 record the new homes of the recipients. Only six of these were north of the Humber, and none were in the immediate border counties. The vast majority of licences and denizations were granted to people living in the South-East and East Anglia, with forty-two in London and Middlesex, twenty-six in Kent and fourteen in both Norfolk and

Essex. Also, with the exception of John Petygrewe, living in Pensford in Somerset, no Scot receiving such letters lived further west than Oxford.[65] It is, perhaps, not surprising that letters of denization were issued more commonly to residents of the South-East, given the need to secure them at Westminster. Nonetheless, the obvious differences between this pattern of distribution and the 1440 alien subsidy material, and the similarities with the later alien subsidy records, are striking.

The occupations of the recipients of these letters were not regularly recorded; but of those that were, the vast majority were clerics, predominantly chaplains or simple 'clerks'. The remainder were mainly artisans, such as smiths, tailors and brewers; very few (as we would expect in such records) were labourers or servants. Further examination of the data from the 1440 alien subsidy suggests that the difference between the social composition of the Scottish population in the North and South of England was already evident. North of the Humber, over 1,000 Scots were assessed to pay the 1440 tax, almost four-fifths of them categorised as non-householders. However, south of the Humber, the fifty-seven identifiable Scots were split almost equally between householders and non-householders, proportions much more akin to other national groups settling in this region, including the Irish discussed above.

The letters of denization and licences to remain also have the advantage of recording the recipients' towns and regions of origin in Scotland. Many came from the eastern Border region, from towns such as Berwick, Melrose and Jedburgh, but also from small border villages such as Mordington and Upsettlington (now Ladykirk) in Berwickshire, and Makerstoun in Roxburghshire. Denization seems initially to have been sought particularly by people from places where the English and Scots regularly vied for control and sovereignty, such as John Erthe, a chaplain from Roxburgh, who received English denization in 1431, and John Grey, doctor of canon and civil law, who originated from Jedburgh and was given letters patent of denization in 1441.[66] More generally, the majority of Scots in receipt of protections and denizations were from the eastern parts of the Lowlands, a region bounded by Montrose and Brechin in the north, Stirling in the west and Jedburgh in the south. Away from the immediate Border region, almost all were from larger settlements on or near the east coast, suggesting either that local inhabitants were being tempted by the seaborne transportation opportunities on offer or that they gave their point of embarkation as their origin when securing their later letters in the English Chancery. Nevertheless, most of the major Scottish cities were represented. Aberdeen provided the largest single number, with twelve of its inhabitants seeking leave to remain in England, all between 1461 and 1480. People also left from Edinburgh, St Andrews, Arbroath, Dundee and Perth.

By contrast, there were very few recorded individuals from the Western Lowlands, and none from Highland Scotland. The most north-westerly recorded places of origin named in the letters of denization and protection were Glasgow, Dunblane and the central district of Atholl.[67] It seems inconceivable that many of the Scots taxed in Cumberland and Westmorland in 1440 did not come from Galloway in south-western Scotland, but there is no explicit evidence that anyone from this region took out letters from the Chancery. There is, however, evidence that some individuals may have travelled together, or been drawn down by friends or acquaintances who had already made the journey, in a pattern of chain migration. John Nicoll and Henry Lilburn, two chaplains from Aberdeen, both took out licences to remain dated 21 June 1474, and lived only around five miles apart, in Rodmersham and Otterden in Kent.[68] Meanwhile, in rural Norfolk, two more Aberdonians, John Mychelson and Alexander Willyamson, took out licences in 1463, and again lived similarly close to each other in Sculthorpe and Little Walsingham.[69] By contrast, the three known people from Dundee settled well away from each other, in London, Reading and East Malling in Kent, and presumably had no connection beyond their shared home town.[70]

Yet it is also abundantly clear that many, or most, Scots living south of the border, even in the southern counties, saw no need to seek any formalisation of their status within their new homeland. In 1440 John Kyllyngworthe successfully sought letters of pardon 'as his liegeman' from Henry VI for himself and his English-born son, having already lived in England for fifty-eight years; and John Graa, a native of Dunblane, received his letters of denization in 1451 after living in London for over fourteen years, having already been apprenticed in the city and admitted to the franchise.[71] Of course, Scots may have been tempted to exaggerate their time in England in order to appear less of a security concern. If, however, such people could live in England for so long before taking out such letters, there must have been many more who never saw any need to do so, or simply did not live long enough or have sufficient money. This was evidently the case on the border, where none of the hundreds of people taxed in the mid-fifteenth century ever received letters of protection or denization (or at least not while living there). While we know that 163 Scots were taxed in London in 1483, only thirty Scots in the city are recorded as taking out licences to remain between 1440 and 1500.

Taken together, this evidence strongly suggests two conclusions about the process of migration from the northern kingdom in the second half of the fifteenth century: that the *numbers* of Scots living in the South of England may have increased somewhat, both in absolute terms and in proportion to those in the North; and that the proportion of the Scots living in the South who were of higher *status* was also greater than was the case in the North of England. Establishing the reasons for this pattern is no easy task, but two factors seem especially germane. First is the marked decline in the duration and intensity of the hostilities between the two realms after 1464. In spite of the war of 1480–4 and evidence of an increase in English suspicion of the Scots towards the close of the fifteenth century, the ending of perpetual campaigns of attrition undoubtedly facilitated cross-border interactions.[72] Even the temporary breakdown of diplomacy and the drama surrounding the Battle of Flodden in 1513 seems to have had remarkably little adverse effect on Scottish people operating in England, though a slightly larger number certainly sought the security of denization in the immediate aftermath of this English victory.[73] The second factor was economic. In spite of the great slump and the campaign against the involvement of aliens in skilled trades, the much higher levels of urbanisation and commercialisation in the South and East of England provided precisely the range of inducements that would have encouraged Scottish people of greater means to venture further southwards. As the sixteenth-century commentators would later complain, these were, of course, precisely the sort of people whom Scotland could least afford to lose.[74]

Notes

1 See, for example, the vernacular and Latin terms used for 'Germans', discussed in chapter 5.

2 E 179/136/234, m. 4; E 179/136/243, mm. 2–3; E 179/136/244, m. 1.

3 E 179/136/248, m. 2; E 179/136/251, m. 1; E 179/136/252, m. 3; E 179/136/261; E 179/270/32 Part 1, m. 2; E 179/269/28, m. 2; E 179/136/216, m. 2; E 179/136/210, m. 2.

4 Linsley, 'The French in fifteenth-century England'.

5 E 179/196/100; E 179/113/130.

6 E 179/133/71; E 179/192/66, m. 8.

7 The six Londoners explicitly did not pay because they were Welsh, but why David Crakowe was taxed in Kent is unknown. See E 179/236/85, rot. 5; E 179/124/120, m. 2.

8 *CPR 1413–16*, pp. 122–5.

9 WAM 12261, m. 9.

10 *CPR 1436–41*, p. 62; SC 8/93/4630.

11 *CPR 1461–7*, p. 198; *CPR 1476–85*, p. 389.

12 *CPR 1494–1509*, p. 43.

13 Oxford Dictionary of Family Names in Britain and Ireland, www.oxfordreference.com, Introduction, section 7 (accessed 14 November 2017).

14 *Wealth of Shrewsbury in the Early Fourteenth Century*; *Poll Taxes of 1377, 1379 and 1381*; *Lay Subsidy for Shropshire, 1524–7*; Hey, *Family Names and Family History*, pp. 57–8.

15 Fleming, 'Identity and belonging', pp. 184–92; Laughton, 'Mapping the migrants'.

16 JUST 2/148–50.

17 Kissane and Mackman, 'Aliens and the law', pp. 111–14.

18 Bolton, 'Irish migration', p. 2.

19 Fleming, 'Identity and belonging', pp. 180–1. Fleming's comparison of the 1440–1 figures with later returns does not appear to allow for the huge nationwide fall in the numbers being assessed, and thus there may have been more continental natives in Bristol than he allows. Nevertheless, his assertion (p. 181) that the 'vast majority' of aliens taxed in Bristol in 1440–1 were Irish-born is still probably correct. On the likely under-assessment of the Irish, see also Bennett, 'Late medieval Ireland', pp. 384–5.

20 Thrupp identified 846 Irish people in the surviving 1440 returns, whereas Bolton found only 706, highlighting issues with Thrupp's identifications. Our total of 817 at least partially reflects the discovery of additional documents since the publication of Bolton's research: Thrupp, 'Survey', pp. 270–2; Bolton, 'Irish migration', p. 5.

21 *CPR 1413–16*, p. 125.

22 Down, 'Colonial society and economy', p. 449; Cosgrove, 'Emergence of the Pale', p. 553.

23 Thrupp, 'Survey', p. 267.

24 Bolton, 'Irish migration', pp. 11–13.

25 Griffiths, 'Crossing the frontiers of the English realm', p. 216; E 179/242/25.

26 This list has been reconstructed from four fragments: E 179/144/73; E 176/236/85; E 176/236/86; E 179/241/327 Part 2.

27 Bolton, 'Irish migration', pp. 14–17. For details of Irish clergy in England, see Davis, 'Material relating to Irish clergy'; and further details in chapter 7.

28 E 179/196/100, rot. 1.

29 E 179/196/100, rot. 2.

30 *CPR 1391–6*, pp. 451, 458, 464; *CPR 1399–1401*, p. 532; *CPR 1429–36*, p. 64.

31 *CPR 1436–41*, p. 384.

32 E 159/217, Brevia directa baronibus, Michaelmas, rot. 61d.

33 E 179/241/327 Part 2, rot. 1d; E 179/120/83, m. 2d.

34 E 179/180/184, rot. 3.

35 For example, E 179/87/136.

36 WAM 12261, mm. 8, 23, 26.

37 Dawson, 'Gaidhealtachd', p. 290.

38 For the cases in Sandwich and Hastings, see E 179/242/9, rots 2, 2d.

39 *CPR 1429–36*, p. 585.

40 *LP*, XVII, no. 283 (50); *Letters of Denization, 1509–1603*, p. 153.

41 E 179/270/31, mm. 18, 42; E 179/95/100, rot. 3d.

42 Laughton, 'Mapping the migrants', pp. 174–7.

43 Thomson, 'Scots in England', pp. 2–3.

44 Galloway and Murray, 'Scottish migration', pp. 29–30; Ditchburn, 'Anglo-Scottish relations'; Rees Jones, 'Scots in the North of England'; Bennett, 'Women (and men) on the move'.

45 Galloway and Murray, 'Scottish migration', pp. 30, 35.
46 E 179/90/27.
47 E 179/158/41.
48 E 179/269/45, m. 2.
49 E 179/195/33.
50 E 179/132/367; E 179/130/57; E 179/130/64; E 179/130/56.
51 E 179/195/48. The native English population was exempt from these taxes across the border counties. No data are available for Cumberland and the rest of Northumberland.
52 E 179/106/4; E 179/106/5. See also other data for County Durham discussed by Ditchburn, 'Anglo-Scottish relations', p. 323.
53 E 179/136/243 (excluding the city of Lincoln); Kissane and Mackman, 'Aliens and the law', p. 109.
54 E 179/159/88.
55 E 179/133/71; E 179/155/80. The Leicestershire return also includes one untaxed Scottish wife.
56 See above, n. 30.
57 E 179/242/25. The Irish, Gascons and Channel Islanders, and various groups of merchants, were by then exempt.
58 E 179/124/107; E 179/242/9; E 179/124/123; E 179/124/129; E 179/124/154; E 179/124/188.
59 E 179/180/92 Part 2; E 179/180/111; E 179/180/126, 134, 136, 182, 184.
60 E 179/149/177; E 179/369/26; E 179/149/126.
61 Ross, *Richard III*, p. 47; Neville, *Violence, Custom and Law*, pp. 160–4.
62 E 207/22/9.
63 E 159/264, Recorda, Trinity term, rot. 14.
64 This is probably an incomplete picture, as a number of privy seal warrants ordering that letters be issued (to aliens of various nationalities) have no corresponding enrolments, such as that for the Scot William Holme, parson of Layham in Suffolk, in 1446: Thomson, 'Scots in England', p. 5; *Calendar of Documents Relating to Scotland*, IV, no. 1192.
65 Thomson mentions a Scot living in Wiltshire, but his details have not been discovered: Thomson, 'Scots in England', p. 8.
66 *CPR 1429–36*, p. 188; *CPR 1436–41*, p. 564; Thomson, 'Scots in England', p. 5.
67 *LP*, II, pt 2, no. 2933; *CPR 1446–52*, p. 505; *LP*, XVI, no. 779 (23).
68 *CPR 1467–77*, p. 447.
69 *CPR 1461–7*, p. 271.
70 *CPR 1476–85*, p. 196; *CPR 1461–7*, pp. 191, 221.
71 *Calendar of Documents Relating to Scotland*, IV, no. 1130; *CPR 1446–52*, p. 505.
72 Ditchburn, 'Anglo-Scottish relations', pp. 332–4.
73 There were eighteen denizations for Scots issued in the 1510s, in comparison with only one in the 1500s and eleven in the 1520s. See also Ditchburn, 'Anglo-Scottish relations', p. 332.
74 Galloway and Murray, 'Scottish migration', p. 30.

5

Immigrants from overseas

Whilst the arrival of people from the constituent parts of the British Isles was clearly a considerable feature of life across medieval and early modern England, it was only part of the wider process of migration into England across this period. Of the 5,106 aliens taxed in 1440 whose nationalities can be readily identified, some 38 per cent (1,936) came from elsewhere within the British Isles and the Channel Islands. However, this leaves almost two thirds of immigrants taxed in 1440 originating from further afield – and some *considerably* further. The varieties of places of origin, and the distances involved, are just two of the remarkable aspects highlighted by this study. Some Scots may only have moved a few miles across the border, but other immigrants to England had clearly travelled many hundreds of miles, from the Mediterranean, the furthest reaches of the Baltic or the far north of Scandinavia. The fact that people arrived from such a wide range of places shows not only the attractiveness of England to people on the move, but also the resulting diversity of its population.

The French

Of all the places from which immigrants came to England across our period, the largest recorded single source was undoubtedly England's closest continental neighbour, France. The French in England have traditionally attracted surprisingly little attention from historians, perhaps because it has been assumed that the frequent animosity between the two kingdoms over the later Middle Ages provided a bar to migration. Certainly, most French immigrants seem to have kept a relatively low profile, and England does not seem to have attracted rich, influential or professional French people to the extent that it did (as we shall see) for groups such as the Italians or the Iberians. However, a number of recent studies have demonstrated that the sources used in this book, especially the alien subsidy returns, prove that French migration to England was a significant phenomenon in the later Middle Ages, and we can now go some way to detailing the size, distribution and profile of this group.[1]

The best single set of data for analysing the French presence remains that of the first alien subsidy, in 1440 (see Table 3). Of the 5,106 taxpayers in 1440 with a stated or readily identifiable nationality, 1,563 people were explicitly recorded, or can be inferred, as 'French'. By itself this was the single largest national designation in this year. As we noted at the beginning of chapter 4, however, it was quite common for English jurors and assessors to use terms denoting provinces and regions within France as the 'national' labels for identified aliens. We can therefore add to this figure those described as Normans (466), Bretons (eighty-seven), Picards (forty-two) and Gascons (forty) in 1440. The overall figure for the French then increases to 2,198, a remarkable 43 per cent of the total number of nationalities given or inferred in the first assessment of the alien subsidy. The erratic nature of the labelling in different counties means, furthermore, that both the number of French and the overall proportion of French within the alien population may have been higher still.

Unfortunately, there are no other figures available to determine with any precision whether the size of the French taxpaying population recorded in 1440 was typical of the fourteenth and fifteenth centuries in general. The letters of denization yield a very different picture, since of the 306 letters issued before 1500 for which the recipients' nationalities are known, only eighty-three, or 27 per cent, were for French people. This lower proportion is likely to be the consequence of the fact that only a small number of French immigrants were of the necessary status to aspire to denizenship. Of the people listed in the alien subsidy returns of 1440 as French (including those with regional identifiers), only about a third were householders, a significantly lower proportion than already identified in chapter 4 for the Irish and found for certain other immigrant groups from the continent discussed below. The 1440 tax assessments, which reveal a quite large number of French non-householders in humble occupations, therefore undoubtedly provide a more comprehensive and realistic sense of the overall numbers than do the letters of denization.

One of the most striking features of French settlement as depicted by the 1440 evidence is the dispersal of that population into almost all parts of England. The only counties where no French people were explicitly recorded in 1440 were Cumberland, Lancashire and Northumberland.

The largest numbers were very definitely in the South. 450 of the 675 taxpayers in Devon were identifiably French (71 per cent of those with recorded origins). In Kent and Wiltshire the proportions were broadly similar, at 58 per cent and 56 per cent of those with known nationalities.[2] In very few counties, moreover, were less than a third of alien taxpayers from French lands, and in nineteen counties more than half were French. It is no surprise that 84 per cent of identifiable Sussex alien taxpayers were French; but so were 74 per cent of those in Herefordshire, 76 per cent in Staffordshire and 69 per cent in Nottinghamshire. Only in the far North were things significantly different.

Yet these basic figures mask a degree of variation in the precise origins of these individuals. Perhaps the most distinctive group in the 1440 records were the Bretons. Brittany had long been a semi-autonomous duchy with its own language and cultural identity; it also had particularly close political, economic and cultural ties to England.[3] Its inhabitants may therefore have been easier to differentiate from other French people – and were perhaps more likely to differentiate themselves. In 1440, eighty-seven known Bretons were taxed, mostly in south-western England, with thirty-one in Cornwall, thirty in Devon and fourteen in the highly detailed Wiltshire return.[4] The South-West was, of course, the closest region to Brittany, with a degree of common heritage, and thus was probably not only the area to which Bretons were most likely to travel, but also where they were most likely to be recognised.[5] Elsewhere, Bretons were mainly recorded near the coast, with two each in Kent and Essex and one in Sussex, although two other individuals did venture further inland. Guy Breton, taxed in Middlesex, was a servant to Nicholas Dixon, a prebendary of St Paul's Cathedral in London.[6] Similarly, Joan Breton was taxed at Eldersfield in Worcestershire as the servant of one Nicholas Breton. A family named Breton had lived at Eldersfield for over a century, and since Nicholas was not taxed, he was presumably English-born.[7] Joan was evidently born overseas, and although her origins can only be assumed from her surname, it seems likely that she was a native Breton who had entered the family's service through its continuing links with the duchy.

Normans were also regularly differentiated in the records. 466 individuals were taxed specifically as Normans in 1440. The overwhelming majority of those were in two counties, Devon (297) and Wiltshire (98). Of the rest, most were in the South-West, Hampshire and Kent, with only very small numbers elsewhere. Again, it is not surprising to find the largest numbers of Normans in these southern counties, but the huge variations in the proportions of people being described as 'French' and 'Norman' across this region highlights the perils of taking descriptions at face value. In Devon, 297 'Normans' were taxed, but only 115 'French', whereas in neighbouring Dorset (where nationalities were less regularly recorded), fifty-six people were described as 'French' and only eleven as 'Norman'. In Wiltshire, ninety-eight Normans and 132 French were recorded. Clearly the assessors all made some kind of distinction between the two categories, but either the demographics or, more likely, the methodologies were quite different. The Devon assessors may just have been more familiar with the term 'Norman', using it to denote many people of French ancestry regardless of their actual origins. However, the Devon assessors' use of many other national labels not common in other parts of the country, including Portuguese, Saxon and Prussian, suggests that they were particularly assiduous in identifying origins, and thus that their evidence should be taken seriously. The Devon material therefore helps us to extrapolate in those cases where assessors were much less scrupulous in their listings. In Hampshire, only ninety-eight out of a total of 1,120 recorded alien taxpayers in 1440 can be ascribed a nationality; of these, forty-four were 'French' and four 'Norman'. In reality, it would seem likely that Hampshire's French-born population was similar to that of Devon, and perhaps even greater, and that the 1,028 undifferentiated aliens in Hampshire actually covered a specifically Norman population of several hundred.

Only forty Gascons can be positively identified in the surviving alien subsidy returns for 1440. Some others may simply have been described as 'French', but it does seem that relatively few Gascons made their way to England. The majority of those assessed were again found in the South-West, with eight taxed in Devon (along with one untaxed Gascon woman), five in Cornwall, three each in Somerset, Gloucestershire and Worcestershire, and two each in Dorset and Wiltshire. This is not surprising given the long-standing maritime links between the two regions; the figures would undoubtedly have been higher if the Bristol return was more informative.[8] However, other Gascons were identified right across England, from Kent and Sussex in the South-East to Lincolnshire and Yorkshire in the North, even though none of these counties recorded more than two individuals. Only two Gascons appear in the surviving list of London defaulters for the 1440 payment, and few in later assessments for the capital, though trading links between London and Bordeaux undoubtedly brought more transitory visitors from Gascony into the city.[9] The precise origins of most assessed Gascons are unrecorded. Some, inevitably, were from Bordeaux. Margaret, the wife of the Brabanter Stephen James taxed in Exeter in 1440, was from Bayonne; and

John de Leybourne, taxed in Lincoln throughout the early 1440s, was from Libourne.[10]

Few Gascons sought denization before the sixteenth century. Four were granted such letters between 1389 and 1400, but there was then a long gap until 1461, and only under Henry VIII did numbers start to increase. This is another measure of the small number of Gascons living permanently in England, though it may also reflect the particular preoccupation among this group, noted in chapter 2, about being treated as the subjects of the duke of Aquitaine rather than of the king of England. The final loss of control over Gascony to the Valois monarchy in 1453 forced some harder realities. Fleming has identified several merchants operating in later fifteenth-century Bristol who were probably refugees from the duchy and who had been forced by the French incursions to decide once and for all whether they would continue their lives and their business in Gascony or in England.[11] The trickle must have continued in the first half of the sixteenth century, for thirty-seven people listed in the Westminster Abbey denization roll of the 1540s were specified as coming from the duchy, most from Bordeaux but others from places such as Agen, Saint-Macaire and Bayonne. The settlement patterns within England also remained much the same, with almost all the recorded sixteenth-century Gascons appearing in the South-West of England or in London. Many were in the kingdom for trade. Angerot Noge, who originated from Bayonne, secured denization in September 1522, though was still taxed at alien rates for the Tudor subsidy at his house in Small Street in Bristol in January 1524, on a not insignificant £12 in goods.[12] Others, however, were clearly not merchants. John Lavaux from Bordeaux, a servant to the dean of York, took out denization in July 1544 after living in England for thirty-one years, while Thomas Gytton had supposedly lived in England for eighteen years when he secured his letters in the same year, having spent the previous twelve years as a gardener to Lord St John.[13] A century after the loss of English Gascony, there was no obviously significant difference between the profile of those from the duchy and that of the hundreds of other French people seeking to make their livelihoods in England.

We may finally note the remaining groups defined in the records as coming from specific parts of France. In 1440, forty-two alien taxpayers were described as coming from the region of Picardy in northern France. The marking out of this territory reflected the older connections of England with the county of Ponthieu and the strategic importance of the region for the occupying forces in Lancastrian France. As with the Normans, many other Picards were probably recorded as French, or given no nationality. In this case, however, there is little discernible pattern of settlement. The recorded Picards were scattered across England, from Yorkshire in the North to Somerset in the South-West, and although there was a slight bias towards the South-East, the numbers are too small to suggest anything particularly significant. The other labels found in later records of the alien subsidy and the letters of protection and denization are very much exceptions. Janyn de Valer, taxed in Hertingfordbury in Hertfordshire in 1443, was the only person ever specified in these sources as coming from Armagnac.[14] Only two people described as coming from Artois appear in the alien subsidy records: the tailor John Boleyn and his servant, Newell, taxed in Lavenham in 1483.[15] Five people from Saint-Omer and Thérouanne swore oaths of fealty in 1436–7, reflecting the position of the county of Artois within the lands of the duke of Burgundy. It was only in later years, after the conquest of the county by Louis XI, that the designation began to be used a little more regularly, with nine Artesians explicitly granted denization between 1480 and 1544.

In only a few cases can more precise points of origin for French immigrants be identified before 1500. We have already seen that a few Gascons had identifiable towns of origin. Two individuals, taxed in Sussex and Surrey in 1440, were described as coming from Calais.[16] It seems highly unlikely that they were the only two Calesians living in England, and the general absence of the detail may reflect the continued uncertainty, discussed in chapter 2, over whether the inhabitants of this town ought to be considered as English. In other cases, we can deduce origins from surnames. The three individuals recorded in tax records of 1440–1 with the surname 'de Parys' were probably natives of the French capital.[17] Perryn de Bolowne, assessed in the Cinque Ports in 1441, was presumably from Boulogne-sur-Mer or the surrounding county, and Andrew Bayou, taxed in Landulph in Cornwall in 1440, hailed from Bayeux.[18] The pre-1500 letters of denization give little more information, though most were issued to people from similar locations across northern France, in Normandy, Brittany, Picardy and the town and pale of Calais. Just three Parisians received letters: Raymond Wacher in 1435, Anthony Vilate in 1457 and George Lovekyn in 1476.[19] Further afield, Peter Gitton of Blois received letters in 1449, and John Tregurre, from Narbonne in distant Roussillon, took out letters in 1442, described as being of the University of Oxford.[20]

A marked feature of the assessment process for the alien subsidies is the very swift decline, after the 1440s, of the use of 'French' or of French regional labels in the identifications of taxpayers. As we noted in chapter 3, the Normans and the Gascons were exempt from the alien subsidy after 1449, so it is no surprise that such labels ceased to be used in this fiscal context. However, the identifiers 'French' and 'Breton' also went into very marked decline after the 1450s; and very significantly, they disappeared at a much faster rate than did other nationality markers. Of the 2,195 people with a given or inferred nationality in the surviving nominal returns of 1483, for example, there were only ninety-three (4 per cent) 'French' (including those with French regional labels), compared with 225 Flemings (10 per cent) and 268 Scots (12 per cent).[21] The mists only dissipate again when we reach the campaign by Henry VIII's government in the early 1540s to get all French people living in England to take out new letters patent of denization. Of the 2,665 people listed in the Westminster Abbey denization roll, 2,123 had identifiable national origins. 1,976 of these were French: more precisely, 1,040 described as Normans, 639 as French, 176 as Bretons, eighty-five as Picards and thirty-six as Gascons.[22] Given that this sample is largely restricted to aliens living in the southern, coastal counties of England, and that persons of lower social status were relatively under-represented, it is clear that the number of first-generation French immigrants to England in the 1540s was higher, and possibly considerably higher, than it had been in 1440.

Do these figures represent a genuine fluctuation in numbers between the mid-fifteenth and the mid-sixteenth centuries, or are they simply a function of erratic record keeping? The fact that the numbers of 'French' recorded in the later alien subsidy rolls fall away so markedly, and more than for other national categories, certainly seems to suggest that there may have been a more casual approach to the identification of erstwhile 'enemy aliens' after the end of major hostilities between England and France in 1453. On the other hand, the numbers of French residents within the realm may always have been subject to quite dramatic fluctuations. There was considerable economic hardship in late medieval Normandy, intensified by the invasion and occupation of the duchy by English armies in the 1410s and 1420s. Historians have remarked the resulting displacement of people to other parts of France, but have not previously considered whether those prepared to declare themselves loyal to the Plantagenet cause also moved, in potentially significant numbers, across the Channel.[23] Prior to the 1430s, no grants of denization were issued to people specified as coming from Normandy; but in the 1440s and 1450s, nineteen were made. Following the end of the French war in 1453, there was a long period of diplomatic stand-off, but very little by way of active warfare: apart from Edward IV's brief campaign in France in 1475, there were no other significant hostilities until Henry VIII reopened the French wars in the 1510s. The number of denizations for French émigrés during this period remained small, and there is little sense of a stimulus to migration akin to that which we hypothesised in chapter 4 for Scottish clergy and artisans moving south during the period of Anglo-Scottish peace in the 1460s and 1470s. Ironically enough, it was the development of the ordnance industry in England to service Henry VIII's plans for renewed war with France that most clearly prompted migration from northern France to southern England during this period.[24] Much still remains to be discovered, then, about cross-Channel movement in the decades around 1500. For the present, at least, it may be suggested that the particularly good transportation systems between England and the northern coast of France, and the fact that a high proportion of French immigrants to England were of lower social-economic status, made the French presence in England an especially mobile one, and that the twists and turns of diplomatic policy could have a particularly direct impact on perceptions of opportunity for French people moving north of the Channel.

The one thing that is reasonably clear is that the recruitment grounds for migrants to England remained solidly in northern and north-western France. Of the sixty-seven denizations granted to known French-born people between the 1470s and the 1530s, sixty-one (79 per cent) specified that the recipients had been born in places within Normandy, Brittany, Picardy and the Pas de Calais. By the end of our period, denizations also began more frequently to specify a particular town of origin. Of the 1,978 people of French background recorded on the Westminster Abbey denization roll of the 1540s, 505 have identifiable towns or cities of origin, the vast majority in Normandy, Picardy, Brittany and elsewhere along the northern coast.[25] No fewer than 116 were from the Norman capital of Rouen, with other concentrations in the Cotentin peninsula, the Pays de Bray along the Normandy–Picardy border and the region around Caen and the Seine estuary. While the major towns of these regions were almost all represented, many other people came from rural villages across northern France. A smaller number originated from further afield. Olivier de Tremount, a resident in England for twelve years by 1544, had come all the way from Avignon, while Antoine Pouse, from Toulouse, had travelled almost as far, and Fraunces Gabbewe, a servant of the courtier Sir John Brydges, was originally from Lyon.[26] Others came from central and western France's major cities, such as Poitiers, Tours, Orléans, La Rochelle and Bordeaux. Twenty-two of those named on the Westminster Abbey denization roll were explicitly from Paris. However, while many from northern France gave their origins as small towns or villages, none from further south proffered such information. Overall, this diverse pattern of origins, combined with statements that many of those receiving denization had lived in England for decades, reinforces the general impression of this section, that French migration to England was a significant, if numerically volatile, phenomenon throughout the later Middle Ages and early sixteenth century.

The 'Dutch'

After the French, the next largest group of continental immigrants to England during our period were those from the Low Countries and Germany. During the later Middle Ages, the area of the Low Countries was divided into a multitude of different principalities, most of which, though largely autonomous, fell under the token suzerainty of the German emperor. The main exception to this was the county of Flanders, the majority of which was technically a fief of the French crown. At the end of the fourteenth century, the dukes of Burgundy, originally junior princes of the French royal house of Valois, acquired Flanders, and in the following decades they added many of the neighbouring principalities to their territories through marriage, purchase and conquest. During the 1430s, Brabant, Holland, Zeeland and Hainaut were all incorporated into these dominions, and the Burgundian Low Countries emerged as a major continental power alongside, and effectively independent from, both France and the Empire. Then, following the death of the last Burgundian duke in 1477 and the marriage of his daughter to the future Emperor Maximilian I, the region came under the control of the house of Habsburg, and thus, in the sixteenth century, became part of the Spanish empire.[27] Further east, the political arrangement of the German lands was even more complicated. While theoretically united under the emperor, they were in reality a patchwork of duchies, counties, ecclesiastical lordships and free cities, all with autonomous jurisdictions and their own identities.[28]

As a result of this fragmentation, people from these regions appear in the English records described in many different ways. Some were given 'national' or regional labels, such as Brabanter or Westphalian, while others were noted as coming from particular principalities or cities. Many were described generically, sometimes by vernacular words such as 'Almain' (which carry the general connotation of 'German') and 'Easterling' (which often denoted people from the Hanseatic cities, whether in Germany or in other parts of the Baltic shore). Most common of all was the catch-all term 'Dutch'. 'Dutch', which is a modern rendering of the Middle English (and Anglo-Norman) word 'Duche' or 'Doche', was primarily a linguistic descriptor, referring to the dialects now known as Middle Dutch and Middle Low German. It was thus also widely used to describe the languages and people of the whole of the Low Countries and the west and north of Germany.[29] In 1483, the alien subsidy returns for London and Berkshire used another term, 'Teutonic', but this may have been just the Latin equivalent of 'Dutch', without any exclusively 'German' connotations.[30] We preserve the distinction between 'Dutch' and 'Teutonic' in this book, but only to remain faithful to the sources; both words are consistently used in inverted commas in order to emphasise that they had no precise territorial connotations.

Table 3 indicates that the 'Dutch' (all jurisdictions within the Low Countries and the Empire, together with those described as 'Dutch', 'German' and 'Easterling') comprised some 18 per cent of the identifiable alien taxpayers in England in 1440. Unlike the French, who settled in the largest numbers along the south coast, the 'Dutch' tended to favour East Anglia and the South-East. In Norfolk, 75 per cent of identifiable taxpayers in 1440 were 'Dutch', as were 66 per cent of those in Suffolk and 45 per cent in Essex.[31] In Kent, despite a larger French presence, 29 per cent of identifiable immigrants were 'Dutch'.[32] The Home Counties also had significant 'Dutch' populations in 1440, comprising 41 per cent of identifiable taxpayers in Middlesex and 27 per cent in Hertfordshire.[33]

It is evident from other tax returns, especially those of 1483, that there was a very significant group of 'Dutch' (in 1483, 'Teutonics') living in the capital. The 1440 data fail to demonstrate this as no nominal returns survive for the first collection of the alien subsidy. The best way to compensate for this is by reference to the licences issued to those who undertook the oath of fealty to the English crown in 1436–7. 97 per cent of the 1,858 recipients of these licences had a recorded place of origin, with around 1,780 coming from within the Low Countries or the Empire (see Table 4).[34] A very significant number of these people lived in London, with at least 309 of the 324 known London-based oath-takers identifiably falling into our constructed category of 'Dutch'. So too were 204 people in Surrey and 110 in Middlesex, most of these living in Southwark and Westminster respectively. This means that over 600 people, roughly a third of all those who swore the oath, were 'Dutch' residents of London and its suburbs. Elsewhere the picture very much parallels the data from the alien subsidy, with East Anglia featuring prominently. No fewer than 161 'Dutch' swore the oath in Norfolk, with 113 in Suffolk and 103 in Essex.

Table 4: Origins of individuals swearing the oath of fealty, 1436–7

County	Burgundian territories						Non-Burgundian territories				Unknown[b]	Total
	Holland	Brabant	Zeeland	Flanders	Hainaut	Frisia	Guelders	Liège	Utrecht	Others[a]		
Bedfordshire	8	10	1	0	0	0	3	1	0	0	0	23
Berkshire	6	2	6	0	0	0	0	0	0	5	0	19
Buckinghamshire	1	21	2	2	0	0	2	3	0	3	2	36
Cambridgeshire	14	13	0	2	0	0	4	2	2	6	1	44
Cheshire	0	0	0	0	0	0	0	0	0	1	0	1
Cornwall	0	0	0	0	0	0	0	0	0	0	0	0
Cumberland	0	0	0	0	0	0	0	0	0	0	0	0
Derbyshire	0	0	0	0	0	0	0	0	0	0	0	0
Devon	6	13	6	0	0	1	4	0	0	12	0	42
Dorset	12	2	1	1	0	0	0	0	1	3	0	20
Durham	0	0	0	0	0	0	1	0	0	0	0	1
Essex	29	30	11	4	1	0	4	6	4	17	0	106
Gloucestershire	11	4	4	0	0	0	0	0	1	10	0	30
Hampshire	16	7	9	1	0	0	3	1	1	2	0	40
Herefordshire	2	0	1	0	0	0	0	0	0	0	0	3
Hertfordshire	15	16	5	0	0	0	6	2	3	6	1	54
Huntingdonshire	3	2	2	2	0	0	0	1	0	4	0	14
Kent	45	29	14	11	1	2	13	8	10	18	0	151
Lancashire	0	0	0	0	0	0	0	0	0	0	0	0
Leicestershire	1	4	0	0	0	0	3	1	0	0	0	9
Lincolnshire	15	12	3	1	0	0	3	3	0	6	1	44
London	93	71	25	38	4	0	27	12	12	41	1	324

Middlesex	39	19	5	7	1	0	1	9	7	4	19	3	113
Norfolk	55	48	17	6	2	1	2	8	3	8	16	2	166
Northamptonshire	5	18	1	1	2	0	0	3	8	1	3	0	42
Northumberland	0	1	0	0	0	0	0	0	0	0	0	0	1
Nottinghamshire	0	5	0	0	0	0	0	0	0	0	0	0	5
Oxfordshire	2	8	0	0	0	0	0	2	1	0	3	0	16
Rutland	1	2	0	0	0	0	0	0	0	0	1	0	4
Shropshire	0	0	0	0	0	0	0	1	0	0	1	0	2
Somerset	8	4	2	0	0	0	0	1	0	1	5	0	21
Staffordshire	0	0	0	0	0	0	0	0	0	0	0	0	0
Suffolk	33	28	14	4	1	1	1	9	13	1	13	0	117
Surrey	61	44	15	11	3	1	3	13	13	8	47	1	217
Sussex	27	17	6	2	0	0	0	5	1	1	6	0	65
Warwickshire	0	1	0	0	0	0	0	0	0	0	0	0	1
Westmorland	0	0	0	0	0	0	0	0	0	0	0	0	0
Wiltshire	12	4	0	1	0	0	0	3	0	0	7	0	27
Worcestershire	0	0	0	0	0	0	0	0	0	0	0	0	0
Yorkshire	1	0	0	0	0	0	0	0	0	0	0	0	1
Wales[c]	1	0	0	0	1	0	1	1	0	0	1	0	3
Unknown[d]	21	30	8	5	1	0	0	12	6	1	12	0	96
Total	543	465	158	99	16	6	16	140	92	59	268	12	1,858

a Includes people explicitly described as from Alsace, Artois, Austria, Bavaria, Calais, Cleves, Ferrara, Florence, Gascony, Iceland, Normandy, Norway, Picardy, Pomerania, Prussia, Saxony, Swabia, Sweden and Westphalia, or places within those lands, as well as those described as French, German, Italian and 'Easterling', and from unidentified places in 'Almain' (i.e. Germany).
b Place of origin not specified or unidentified.
c Two in Pembrokeshire, one in Monmouthshire.
d County of residence not specified or unidentified.

This pattern is not surprising. The South-East and East Anglia were closest to the Low Countries, with strong trading contacts, and the hugely important port of London was clearly a major magnet.[35] But coastal trade and transport also provided easy access along the whole stretch of England's south and east coasts.[36] Thus, forty 'Dutch' people from Lincolnshire swore the oath of 1436, and a few 'Dutch' were taxed as aliens in places along the Yorkshire coast. Although no data exist for Hull for the alien subsidy of 1440, twenty-one of that town's sixty-six alien taxpayers in 1458 were described as 'Dutch'.[37] One man, Henry Ducheman, found service in Newcastle upon Tyne, while another, Walter Brabaner, set up his own household as far north as Alnwick in Northumberland.[38] A similar pattern appears along the south coast. Although no one living in Cornwall swore the oath of fealty in 1436–7, twenty men from the Low Countries were taxed there in 1440, mostly in Truro and Fowey, and one Utrechter made his way as far inland as Lostwithiel.[39] In Devon, forty-two 'Dutch' people swore the oath, and sixty-two were assessed for the tax, though they formed only 10 per cent of the total number of aliens recorded in the county.[40] Twenty-one 'Dutch' residents of Somerset swore the oath, alongside twenty-six from Wiltshire, forty from Hampshire, twenty-seven from Gloucestershire and eighteen from Berkshire. Taken together, the records of the 1436–7 oath and the 1440 alien subsidy therefore reveal a relatively consistent 'Dutch' presence across much of southern and south-western England. These numbers were clearly far lower than in eastern counties, but are nevertheless notable.

Some intrepid 'Dutch' individuals also travelled inland and found new homes throughout much of southern England. The area to the north of the Home Counties was a popular destination: sixty-eight 'Dutch' were taxed in Cambridgeshire in 1440 (52 per cent of the identifiable alien population of that county) and forty-eight in Northamptonshire.[41] The records of the oath of fealty again show a similar picture, with significant populations across the South and East Midlands from Buckinghamshire to Lincolnshire. However, only a few 'Dutch' seem to have crossed the Severn–Trent axis to reside in inland counties or towns. In 1440, a Brabanter weaver was taxed in Staffordshire, two Brabanters and a Hollander in Wem in Shropshire, and six Flemings across Herefordshire, while in 1437, Nicholas Goldsmyth from Frankfurt swore the oath of fealty as living in Nantwich in Cheshire.[42] Two 'Dutch' immigrants found new homes in the Yorkshire Dales, and another in Bishop Auckland.[43] Otherwise, the inland picture was the same as that of the coast, and the 'Dutch' presence north of the Humber was very sparse.

The 'Dutch' immigrants who worked as skilled artisans in English towns will be discussed in much more detail in chapter 6. Here, though, we need to note that not all 'Dutch' immigrants were independent masters of their trades or living in major urban centres. The alien subsidy returns actually suggest a relatively even split between householders and non-householders, with the latter slightly more numerous overall (though this figure would, of course, include many artisan workers and apprentices). As noted, a third of all 'Dutch' people swearing the oath of fealty lived in or around the capital; and there were significant populations in most of the large towns and cities of southern England. Forty-six of the sixty-eight 'Dutch' taxed in Cambridgeshire in 1440 lived in Cambridge, and in the records of the oath of 1436–7, forty-four were living in Canterbury, forty-three in Norwich, twenty-seven in Ipswich, twenty-seven in Lynn and twenty-six in Northampton – far higher numbers, incidentally, than were taxed in those places four years later.[44] However, not all 'Dutch' settlers headed for the larger towns. Of the six Flemings taxed in Herefordshire in 1440, two lived in Hereford, two in the small towns of Leominster and Weobley and two in the villages of Tarrington and Newton.[45] In Leicestershire, eighteen Flemings and Brabanters were recorded in the same year, and while ten were in Leicester, the other eight were in small villages across the county.[46] In both shires, almost all these rural inhabitants were the only recorded people from their homeland in those villages. In Suffolk, twenty-seven of the 113 'Dutch' oath-swearers of 1436–7 were resident in Ipswich, but the other eighty-six lived in forty-seven different towns and villages. This is not to say that the rural dwellers were significantly different from their urban cousins: many undoubtedly came from the same places, and may have pursued the same trades. Nevertheless, many 'Dutch' people evidently saw exploitable opportunities outside the urban sphere.

Most tellingly, the lists of those swearing the oath of fealty in 1436–7 provide valuable information about the precise origins of those individuals, allowing a far more detailed analysis of the 'Dutch' population than is possible for most other groups. As can be seen in Table 4, the largest numbers were unsurprisingly from the Low Countries: 543 were specified as coming from Holland, 465 from Brabant, 158 from Zeeland, 140 from Guelders, and ninety-nine from Flanders. Ninety-two people taking the 1436–7 oath hailed from the prince-bishopric of Liège, and fifty-nine from the diocese of Utrecht, with smaller numbers from the principalities of Cleves (thirty-one) and Hainaut (sixteen). Beyond these political labels, the licences issued to those oath-takers from principalities relatively close to England named very precisely the towns, and even the small villages, from which such people were said to spring. Forty-five of the Zeelanders were recorded as coming from Zierikzee and thirty-one from Middelburg, but the rest were from twenty-nine different towns and villages across that small county. Similarly, the 465 Brabanters came from at least eighty-two different places. Forty-three of these people were the sole recorded representatives of their villages in England; and only 's-Hertogenbosch, Mechlin, Brussels, Antwerp and Maastricht provided more than twenty-five people each.[47]

A number of people who did not come from within the Burgundian dominions also swore the oath of 1436–7, presumably as a kind of insurance policy. Again, the records provide interesting specifics on their origins. Most originated from the Empire, especially the west of Germany, the Rhine valley and Westphalia, and cities such as Cologne, Aachen, Münster and Dortmund. A few were also from the great ports of the Baltic and North Seas, including Hamburg, Lübeck and Rostock, while six men had travelled from the Hanse city of Danzig (now Gdansk in Poland) to settle in places as far apart as Bristol and Norwich. Michael Dumbar from Sussex and Laurence van Oyell, a Bristol goldsmith, both arrived from Reval, now the Estonian capital of Tallinn.[48] Others made even longer journeys. Paul Meykesner and John Vallare, two Southwark embroiderers, travelled from 'Austria'; Hans Coltman and Henry Riter moved from Ulm in Swabia to London and Norwich respectively; and Nicholas Sely forsook Magdeburg in Saxony for a new life at Arundel in Sussex.[49] Perhaps most remarkable were John Skunbek of Ramsey in Huntingdonshire, and John Wynge, who lived around fifteen miles away in Buckden. Skunbek came all the way from Königsberg in Prussia (now the Russian city of Kaliningrad), while Wynge, described as a painter in a later subsidy assessment, was from Eylau (now Bagrationovsk), just twenty-five miles south of Königsberg.[50] The similarities in their movements may be coincidental, but it remains possible that these two men had moved together and found new opportunities a few miles apart in England.

One distinctive subgroup within the general category here labelled as 'Dutch' requires particular attention: the Flemish. As we saw in chapter 1, conventional historiography tends to represent people from Flanders as a very conspicuous element within England's late medieval alien population.[51] We face some particularly significant difficulties, however, in determining the numerical size of this group. As we shall see in chapter 6, the influx of skilled people from the Low Countries in the mid-fourteenth century is certainly to be counted in hundreds, and was all the more apparent because these émigrés naturally clustered in existing and emerging centres of English cloth production. Not all of these, however, were Flemish in the strict sense of the term. From the 1370s, the labels 'Fleming' and 'Flemish' were often used in England as a shorthand for all of the duke of Burgundy's subjects, rather as 'English' is sometimes casually employed today to cover everyone living in the United Kingdom.[52] Conversely, there were times, especially after the defection of the duke from the English cause against France in 1435, when people born in Flanders seem deliberately to have attempted to disguise their origins and when the group as a whole may therefore have been under-represented in English government documents.

As a consequence, it may be that the data from both the oaths of fealty of 1436–7 and the alien subsidy of 1440 are especially skewed in relation to the Flemish. Table 4 reveals that only ninety-nine men identified themselves as coming specifically from the county of Flanders in the licences to remain issued in 1436–7, less than 8 per cent of those from within the jurisdiction of the duke of Burgundy. The number of Flemish people identified for the first collection of the alien subsidy, in 1440, was a little higher, representing some 37 per cent (337 out of 914) of those categorised as 'Dutch' in Table 3, but was still surprisingly small given the general prominence of the Flemish in English political and popular rhetoric at the time. It is possible, indeed, that the especially vehement anti-Flemish feeling in England in the late 1430s persuaded a proportion of erstwhile settlers from Flanders to return, either permanently or temporarily, to their homeland. So, just as there are reasons to argue that the numbers of French residents tracked in the early alien subsidy returns may have been high in comparison with those in the generations that immediately followed, so too is it possible that the evidence from the oaths of fealty of 1436–7 and the first alien subsidy of 1440 marked something of a low point in Flemish settlement in England. A firmer understanding of the position could undoubtedly be gained if we had better evidence from London, for which little nationality information is available from 1440. Unfortunately, even when nominal data survives for the capital, it is disappointingly vague on the issue: as we have noted, the most detailed of the London alien subsidy returns, that of 1483, simply lumps everyone from the Low Countries together as part of the group described as 'Teutonic'.

Ultimately, therefore, only a very impressionistic picture of the Flemish presence in fifteenth-century England can be built up. As we shall see in chapter 6, there are reasons to suppose that the influx of textile workers from Flanders, which was undoubtedly an important feature of the fourteenth century, was already on the wane by the time that the oaths of fealty were taken and the alien subsidy records compiled. There were still strong inducements for a variety of skilled and unskilled people from Flanders to move to England in the fifteenth century, but by this stage numbers may have been relatively small. Ironically, the Flemings – the one national grouping which, as we shall see in chapter 10, was repeatedly targeted in anti-alien protests over the course of the late Middle Ages – remains perhaps the most difficult of all to quantify from the available records.

Scandinavians and Icelanders

Not all continental immigrants to England came from France, the Low Countries and the Empire. England also had long-standing connections with Scandinavia and Iceland, with many parts of eastern England sharing a Viking heritage and enjoying lucrative trading links spanning the North Atlantic.[53] It is therefore perhaps surprising that more people from Scandinavia do not appear in the surviving records. Perhaps the most famous Danish immigrant to England in this period was Sir Andrew Ogard, the noted Lancastrian military commander who started life as Anders Pedersen Gyldenstjerne in Aagaard and took out letters of denization in 1433. A prominent soldier in the Hundred Years War, he was knighted in 1441, and even sat as MP for Norfolk in 1453.[54] Ogard's denization meant that he escaped assessment for the subsidies, and only three other Danes can be identified with any certainty from the returns, all appearing in 1483. Alan Johnson lived in Watling Street in London, while John Dewson was a servant in Walbrook ward for Agnes, widow of the fish-monger Stephen Forster, mayor of London in 1454.[55] John Longe, living in Lynn, was described as a 'servant with a merchant', suggesting that he may have come to England via his master's commercial links.[56] However, other Danes spread further into England. In July 1442, John Holte of Wheatley in Oxfordshire secured denization and a pardon shortly after the county escheator found that he had illegally acquired land despite his Danish birth. Henry Hayward of Royston swore the oath of fealty to the crown in 1437, presumably just in case anyone mistook him for a Burgundian.[57] Only three Danes took out denization during Henry VIII's reign, along with William Wolofer of Beeston Regis in Norfolk, who originated from the Faroe Islands. In his letters, Wolofer was described as a mariner, but he was evidently a wealthy one, having been taxed at the alien rate in 1525 on goods worth £18, an expense that may have prompted his decision to take out denization.[58]

Other Scandinavians are equally scarce in the records. Two Norwegians were taxed in Lincolnshire in 1440, both from the Hanseatic port of Bergen; others may have been recorded in that county had the remaining assessments survived.[59] A London resident, Peter Johnson, felt obliged to swear the oath of fealty in April 1436, when he specified that he came from Finmark, in the extreme north of Norway; and a man named only as 'Beerne' was assessed in 1440 at Stokesley in the North Riding of Yorkshire, again described as coming from Finmark.[60] In 1456, the Norwegian Perkyn Wever was living at Snettisham on the Norfolk coast.[61] Swedes were no more common. Three, one from London and two from Southwark, swore the oath of 1436–7, while Master Benedict Nicoll was assessed for the alien subsidy in Cambridge in 1440. He was described specifically as 'staying in the University', and was part of a group which included a Gascon named Gwyllam Carer, Alexander Scot (presumed to be Scottish), and three further masters: Olavus Guthe, Magnus Daghr and Laurence Arbogh.[62] Given their forenames, the first two of the latter group, if not all three, were probably from Scandinavia.

Only one Swede took out denization across our period, a chaplain named Magnus Hemmingi, who received his letters patent in February 1414. Unlike the Cambridge men, the reasons for Hemmingi's presence in England are at least partly documented. In 1415 Hemmingi, along with other representatives from the mother house of the Bridgettine Order at Vadstena near Linköping, was sent to England to assist in the foundation of Henry V's new monastery at Syon. Hemmingi may have secured his letters in order to help him in this work.[63] Links between the Lancastrian and Swedish courts were strong following the marriage in 1406 of the Swedish King Eric to Henry IV's daughter, Philippa, and Hemmingi may have been a regular visitor to England. Philippa spent much of her time at Vadstena, and Hemmingi may have had connections with her and been involved in earlier planning for the foundation of Syon, which had been under way since Henry FitzHugh, a member of Philippa's retinue in 1406, visited Vadstena and promised to help found a house in England.[64]

The one northern European group that can be found in larger numbers in late medieval England are the Icelanders.[65] Problems remain with identifying Icelanders in the English records. Icelandic patronymic surnames are easily lost in the hundreds described as 'Johnson', 'Derykson', etc, and even the slightly more distinctive female forms are no more secure, as were used across the Scandinavian world at this time. The surnames of Joan and Mariota Robdogthir, living in Irthington and Bothel in Cumberland respectively, might suggest Icelandic origins;

but the two women could equally have come from Sweden or Norway, or even from the Orkney or Shetland Islands.[66] Unusually, too, the 1440 alien subsidy returns are a poor source of information about people from Iceland. Only eleven Icelanders were identified as such in the surviving assessments for 1440: seven in Yorkshire and one each in Norfolk, Suffolk, Northamptonshire and Warwickshire. However, this is partly a result of the uneven survival of nominal records. The assessments for the 1453 tax, collected throughout the 1450s and 1460s, contain far fewer names overall, but include many more Icelanders, most significantly in two towns for which the 1440 returns are missing or uninformative: Hull and Bristol.

A number of assessments for the alien subsidy in Hull survive after 1453, but the number of identifiable Icelanders in them varies considerably and no particularly coherent picture can be gained. The mists lift somewhat in 1458, when all sixty-six assessed aliens in the city had their origins recorded and nineteen (29 per cent) were noted as Icelanders.[67] No identifiable Icelanders were taxed in Bristol before 1455, and even in that year only four were listed, despite twenty of the twenty-one taxpayers having their nationality recorded. In 1459, however, fourteen of the twenty-seven taxpayers in the city (51 per cent) were Icelanders.[68] The vagaries of these documents mean that the following year only three of the eleven identifiable taxpayers in Bristol were Icelandic, and none by the later 1460s; but in 1483, at least thirty of the fifty-one people assessed there (59 per cent) were explicitly Icelanders.[69] All of these were servants to Bristol men; as we shall see in chapter 7, it is possible that at least some of them were subject to a form of forced labour, abducted from their homeland and brought to England effectively as slaves.[70]

Icelanders were not limited to Bristol and Hull, but these two ports probably formed the entry points for most. Five of the seven Icelanders taxed in Yorkshire in 1440 lived in Beverley and Cottingham, both just a short distance from Hull.[71] There was an Icelandic presence in Nottingham throughout the 1450s and 1460s, although no more than four were ever taxed in one year; these people possibly entered via Hull or its environs and then moved down the Humber and the Trent.[72] Coventry's Icelandic residents, and a handful of others in the East Midlands, probably followed the same well-trodden paths from Bristol as the Irish population, but as in Nottingham they were few in number: the twenty-nine known instances of Icelanders paying the alien subsidy in Coventry between 1449 and 1471 represent no more than six different individuals. Some were long-standing residents. John Glassen, a servant in Cross Street, was taxed repeatedly between 1452 and 1471, as was John Gunner between 1450 and 1457.[73] It is perhaps surprising that more Icelanders did not reach London; only thir-teen or fourteen different Icelanders paid the subsidy there between 1449 and 1483, eight of those in 1483 itself.[74] If most Icelanders entered England through Hull and Bristol, perhaps most saw no benefit in moving to the capital, or had no opportunities to do so.

The Italians

While the majority of immigrants to England during our period came from various parts of northern Europe, travel from the Mediterranean world was far from unknown. The distances involved no doubt dissuaded many southern Europeans from making such a journey. As we shall see in later chapters, there were also economic and cultural factors that mitigated against mass movement from the Mediterranean. Yet English trade with southern Europe was strong and well established, and religious links remained significant right up to the Reformation, meaning a constant interaction between England and the Mediterranean world.[75] Travellers to England from that region, while a much smaller group than their northern counterparts, were often richer and more prominent individuals, making journeys for very specific and identifiable reasons, and their stories add greatly to our understanding of late medieval migration.

The largest distinct group of people from the Mediterranean to move to England across our period were the Italians: more correctly, people from the various different states into which the Italian peninsula was then divided. They were also one of the most distinctive immigrant groups, since the majority were from the upper and richer echelons of society, including representatives of the great Italian banking firms that had bases across much of Europe.[76] Members of prominent families such as the Bardi, Aldobrandi and Borromei certainly had names and reputations that they were determined to preserve and exploit. The same was evidently the case for many of the Italian immigrants to England. It is noticeable that most Italians managed to retain their distinctive names, albeit that these were often garbled by English scribes: only a few were identified in the alien taxation records by surrogate surnames denoting their home towns, such as the merchants Grestolde and Valentino de Florencia, taxed in London in 1467.[77] Even the few recorded just by forenames, or without names at all, may well have been junior members of the wealthy families enumerated, learning their trade from their relatives.[78] The six associates of the Venetian Leonardo Contarini taxed as merchant householders in London's Billingsgate ward in 1443 were clearly not menial servants, but apparently people of significant means.[79] The contrast between the Italians and groups such as the Scots or the Icelanders could hardly be more pronounced.

Unlike most other major groups, the vast majority of Italian immigrants to England were also found in one particular place: London. Large numbers of Italians were recorded in the detailed returns for the capital submitted in response to the hosting legislation of 1439–40, although these returns give little indication as to who could be considered 'resident' in a particular place and who was simply passing through.[80] By contrast, the lack of documentation from London for the first payment of the 1440 tax is extremely unfortunate, and only seven Italians appeared on the list of defaulters. However, in the following years the assessors detailed a steady and substantial Italian presence in the city. Seventy-three known Italians were taxed in 1441, and sixty-nine in 1443, and these numbers remained at reasonably consistent levels thereafter; some of the Italians revealed by this evidence can also be found in the hosting returns.[81] The fullness and high survival rate of the later London returns also allow us to track individuals over a longer period of time in a way largely impossible for other national groupings, and show the taxed Italian community fluctuating between the 102 assessed in 1457 and the thirty-four taxed in 1465, with the overall average over the life of the alien subsidies being around sixty-five in any given year.[82]

London's Italians were drawn from a variety of places. Around 700 of the roughly 1,150 instances of Italians taxed in London between 1440 and 1483 specify places of origin.[83] The largest groups were from the great trading cities of Genoa (236), Venice (199) and Florence (152), with another substantial group from Lucca (sixty-one), and other smaller numbers from cities such as Milan, Ferrara and Rome. This close identification with the trading cities of Italy hints at the fact that London's Italian community was very mobile. At least nine members of the Florentine Bardi family were taxed in London between 1440 and 1470, as well as eleven members of the Centurione family and nine Lomellini, all from Genoa. Differentiating individuals can be difficult, but most seem to have resided over a period of a few years before disappearing entirely from the records. For instance, amongst the Lomellini family, Antonio, Bartolomeo and Filippo appear in the early 1440s, Filippo and Cristoforo in the late 1440s and early 1450s, Francesco, Uberto and Giovanni in the late 1450s, and Stefano, Niccolò and presumably a different Filippo in the later 1460s. Very few names appear for longer than a five-year period, suggesting that many Italians fulfilled appointments at their London offices before moving on, to be replaced by others. Some certainly did remain for longer, with a few marrying and being buried in the capital, though whether or not they arrived with that intention is another matter.[84]

London's Italians also congregated in very specific parts of the capital. Bolton noted that in 1483 the majority of London's immigrants lived in the less salubrious outer wards, around the walls and along the Thames.[85] By contrast, most Italians in the 1440s could be found in the prosperous central wards of Broad Street and Langbourn, with smaller groupings in Walbrook, Bishopsgate, Billingsgate and Candlewick Street.[86] Even in 1483, when most Italian merchants were exempt from the alien subsidy, seventeen of the twenty-one assessed Italians lived in the central wards of Langbourn, Candlewick Street and Cornhill. Some did live in the eastern riverside wards, such as Peter Sewall, a comb set maker, who may not have been amongst the wealthiest Italians but was still successful enough to employ an Italian servant.[87] Clearly the members of London's Italian community enjoyed considerably greater affluence than most of their Irish, French or Dutch neighbours, a situation that continued until the Reformation. In 1524, Sir Thomas More sold Crosby Place, his massive town house in Bishopsgate Street, to his friend, the wealthy Lucchese merchant Antonio Buonvisi. Balthasar Guercy, the Milanese surgeon to Katherine of Aragon (amongst others), lived nearby, building a huge new house befitting his status; and members of the Lomellini and Spinola families also lived in the area. As Catholics, Buonvisi and Guercy were later forced to flee abroad; while Guercy, who had married an Englishwoman, later returned and died in England in 1557, Buonvisi, who had fled to his family's other base in Leuven, did not.[88]

Not all England's resident Italians lived in London. The second largest concentration, as represented in the views of hosts and the alien subsidy returns, was in Southampton. This town had strong and long-established trading links with many parts of Italy, not least Genoa, whose merchant fleet was a regular visitor to the port; Southampton was the main point of export for wool brought overland from the Cotswolds and used in northern Italian cloth production.[89] Thirteen Italians were taxed in Southampton in 1440, and this number remained remarkably consistent thereafter, with ten in 1458, fourteen in 1463 and eighteen in 1468. Again, some of these people were long-term residents: the Genoese Edoardo Cattaneo was taxed regularly in the town between 1440 and 1468.[90] More often, the family presence was maintained by new members arriving to replace those who left. Alongside at least five other members of the Cattaneo family, ten members of the Genoese Spinola family were taxed in Southampton across the period of the alien subsidies, and five from the di Negro family, again from Genoa. The Genoese were by far the largest group in Southampton. In 1468, eleven of the town's eighteen Italians were Genoese, alongside four Venetians and two Florentines.[91] Although the Florentine Cristoforo Ambruogi was prominent for many years, and families such as the Florentine Aldobrandi and the Cini and Priuli from Venice were represented, the Genoese were clearly in the majority. Yet, despite these long-standing connections, the Italians showed no interest in moving inland. Just one potential Italian was taxed elsewhere in Hampshire, a 'John Lumbard', assessed in 1440; but with only his surname to identify him, his origins remain uncertain.[92]

In addition to these two large and relatively well-known urban groupings, the alien subsidy returns also reveal other Italians living elsewhere in England. The only other significant cluster of Italians recorded in the tax documents was that based at Sandwich in Kent, which was a convenient place to unload cargoes from larger vessels onto smaller boats for transport to London.[93] The early assessments give few details, but Piero Fiesco and Amone Pinelli, taxed in 1441, can be identified as Genoese through later appearances, and both were clearly wealthy, with Fiesco being taxed alongside two alien servants, and Pinelli no fewer than four.[94] In March 1456, fourteen Italians were taxed in Sandwich, all Genoese, though surnames suggest that these represented just six or seven separate families. Ten were members of the Cattaneo, di Negro and Pinelli families, and the others may have been employees or associates. Unfortunately few later returns survive for Sandwich, but Tommaso Cattaneo and Pietro Pinelli were assessed in 1467 and 1468, indicating that their families still had interests there. However, they were the only two people in the town assessed that year.[95]

Italians elsewhere in England were few and far between. In 1483, three were taxed in Abingdon in Berkshire, being described as servants and weavers.[96] Although these were unusual occupations for Italians in England, the descriptors used for the relevant people – James and Michael 'of Milan' and George 'of Genoa' – suggest that they or their employers supplied specifically accurate information on their origins.[97] 'John de Rome', taxed in Bedfordshire in 1440, and 'Martin Florence', assessed in Buckinghamshire in 1443, may have been from those cities, while William Erle was described as Genoese when taxed in Walberswick in Suffolk in 1483.[98] The social and occupational status of these people is unknown, but some of the Italians living in the English provinces were clearly much like their London-based fellow countrymen. In 1524, for instance, Francesco

Borsa, an Italian living in Gloucester, was taxed on goods worth the signifi-cant sum of £30, and employed at least two servants.[99] Similarly Giorgio Pouncez, living in Canterbury in the same year with his two servants (one Flemish, one 'Dutch'), had goods worth £25, and the Genoese John de Salvo was taxed in Witham in Essex on the not inconsiderable sum of ten marks.[100]

The marked differences in the social composition and geographical distribution of the Italian residents of England, as against those from other areas examined above, are also evident from the records of denization and other royal grants. Altogether, fifty-six Italians are known to have secured letters before 1500, and 104 between 1500 and 1550. Given the relatively low number of Italians in England, the participation rate in denization was very high, even compared to the French for whom it was first devised and to whom it was chiefly applied in the 1540s. Few of the letters patent of denization specify an English place of residence, but tracking the recipients through other sources allows us to say that many of the Italians who received such grants did so while living in London or Southampton. A number were specified as merchants, such as the Venetian Girolamo Dandolo in 1442, the Lucchese Ludovico Buonvisi in 1484 and the Florentine Francesco de Bardi in 1512.[101] Few were quite as socially emi-nent as Lucia Visconti, daughter of the lord of Milan, granted denization by Henry IV in 1408 shortly after her marriage to Edmund Holland, earl of Kent.[102] Many others, however, were skilled or noted individuals in high-status occupations, such as the medical practitioners Ludovico Recouches and Davino Nigarelli, Lucchese doctors to Henry IV, who were granted denization in 1405 and 1412, Agostino degli Agostini, Cardinal Wolsey's Venetian doctor, and Giovanni Signorelli, Ferrarese physician to Humphrey, duke of Gloucester, who was made denizen in 1433.[103] Others were involved in artistic fields. As well as his doctor, Humphrey of Gloucester secured denization for his own poet, the Ferrarese Tito Livio Frulovisi. In 1545, Henry VIII granted denization to ten members of the Venetian Bassano family, all court musicians, as well as three trumpeters and three painters.[104]

The Iberians

Migrants to England from the south-western Mediterranean across our period were rare. Only eighteen people from the Iberian peninsula are known to have been assessed towards the alien subsidy in 1440, and these were scattered across southern England, from Devon and Cornwall in the

South-West to Cambridgeshire and Suffolk in the East. Most such individuals are identifiable only from distinctive surnames, such as 'Portyngale' or 'Spaynard', the latter term, 'Spaniard', being mainly used at this time for people from the kingdom of Castile. Four Portuguese individuals lived in Cornwall, three in the port town of Fowey, where they must have formed a small but noticeable Portuguese community, presumably generated through trading links between that port and their homeland.[105] The Portuguese man named only as Gonzales, taxed in Plymouth, and 'Ferandus Spaynard', a householder in Brixham, may also have been drawn to those places by trade and shipping, as may Edmund Cok, taxed as a 'Spaniard' in the now-lost Suffolk port of Easton Bavents.[106] Others probably arrived through service, such as Hugh, the Aragonese servant of John Zouche of Harringworth in Northamptonshire, while the only Iberian woman taxed in 1440, Maria Portyngale, was in the service of John Asshwell in Cambridge, and John Portyngale, employed by John Helier in Spettisbury in rural Dorset, was assessed in both 1440 and 1443.[107] However, quite how 'Fons Domyngus' reached Bridgwater in Somerset, or the sawyer Andrew Lyon reached the small village of Ashton in Northamptonshire, is unknown.[108] The town of Northampton was also home to the one person described in the tax records of 1440 as Navarrese, a cook named John Fraunce. The reliability of such labels is thrown into question by this last case, since John appeared twice more in the alien subsidy assessments over the next three years, both times described simply as French.[109] Since effective control of Navarre was in the process of shifting from the kings of France to the crown of Aragon in the middle of the fifteenth century, the confusion seems understandable; on balance it seems likely that John's place of birth was in Lower Navarre, in the 'French' region north of the Pyrenees.

Around thirty-four separate individuals who were listed or can be identified as Iberians were assessed for the alien subsidies over the remainder of the tax's life, though most appeared only once, and others no doubt remain in the unidentifiable majority. Most were found, again, across the south coast and East Anglia, though Matthew Trustrem from Aragon was taxed in the Herefordshire town of Leominster throughout the 1450s.[110] Two of Trustrem's countrymen, unnamed but described as doctors of medicine, were taxed in the Suffolk town of Long Melford in 1483.[111] Only one Iberian, Oliver Spaynard, appeared on the London list of defaulters from 1440, but eight others were recorded in subsequent years, such as John Portyngaler, taxed as a householder in the affluent Langbourn ward in 1443, and Augustine Grace, a Catalan goldsmith working in Aldgate with three 'Teutonic' servants in 1483.[112] The 1483 data also contain evidence about the capital's most prominent Portuguese resident, Edward Brampton. Born in Lisbon of Jewish heritage around 1440 as Duarte Brandão, Brampton made his name as a military commander for Edward IV, receiving lavish rewards of property, especially in London.[113] He was granted denization in 1472, and thus did not pay the 1483 alien subsidy himself, although five servants in his house in Broad Street were required to pay, three from his homeland and two from Scotland.[114] As a prominent Yorkist, Brampton returned to Portugal in 1487, receiving re-naturalisation from Alfonso V. His spectacular career showed that foreign and even non-Christian birth was no bar to success in fifteenth-century England.

Unlike the other national groups discussed thus far, almost as many Iberians received letters of denization across our period as appeared in the tax returns: around forty in total. One of the earliest known, receiving letters in 1420, was the Portuguese Pedro de Alcobaça, a royal physician and canon of St George's Chapel, Windsor. Another member of the medical profession was the surgeon Pedro Fernandez, originally from Cordoba and granted letters of denization in 1488.[115] Skilled professionals and merchants were common, such as Gonsalvo Ferdinandi, precentor of St Paul's Cathedral, who received letters in 1508; John de Gerona from Aragon, a doctor of decrees (that is, a qualified canon lawyer) on his denization in 1475; and the merchants Francisco Lopes from Tarazona and Alvarez de Medina of Burgos, both denizened in the 1530s.[116] Many of those who were not obviously important themselves often had powerful connections. As well as Edward Brampton's three Portuguese servants, William Carowe from 'Biscay', granted denization in 1544, was a servant of Thomas Runcorn, archdeacon of Bangor, while Elizabeth Vergus, a denizen in 1517, was a gentlewoman to the queen, Katherine of Aragon.[117] Francisco Philippo, made denizen in 1522, was another servant of the queen; no doubt Katherine secured similar letters for other servants from her homeland.[118] As with the Italians, most Iberians coming to England were clearly people of wealth and connections, drawn by a variety of professional reasons rather than by need or compulsion. Compared to those from northern Europe, however, they arrived in very small numbers.

The 'Greeks' and people from the eastern Mediterranean

Perhaps not surprisingly given the distances involved, evidence of migration to England from the eastern Mediterranean is scant. As will be shown in chapter 8, any potential immigrants from the Muslim world are often very difficult to identify with assurance in the surviving records.

For example, one Luke de la Ark was granted denization in 1541 as a native of Cappadocia in modern Turkey. Given early sixteenth-century understandings of the political and racial geography of this area, however, Ark's precise origins and background have to remain a matter of speculation.[119] Similarly, although there is no direct evidence in our sources of people arriving from the Balkans, the proliferation of Italian (and particularly Venetian) colonies along the Adriatic coast makes it quite likely that anyone coming from that region could have been identified with the Italian city state that controlled their place of origin.[120]

One group that can be seen quite clearly in the surviving records are those recorded as 'Greeks'. Their presence in England is to be explained largely in terms of the advance of the Ottoman Turks during the fifteenth century. The taking of the Christian city of Constantinople by the Muslim Ottomans in 1453 was part of a wider process of conquest that saw the Turks move up the Adriatic and Aegean coasts and directly challenge the previous dominance of the Italians in the region. While accommodations were reached, notably in the treaty between the Sultan Mehmet and the Venetian Republic in 1478, significant numbers of Christians from the eastern Mediterranean became displaced, and moved into central and western Europe.[121] England was obviously at the very edge of this diaspora, so that identifiable numbers were very small and seem to have been confined to the capital. The alien subsidy assessments include around a dozen different Londoners of Greek origin, and another nine appear in the denizations enrolled on the patent roll across the fifteenth and sixteenth centuries. The erratic rendering of names often makes it difficult to isolate specific individuals. Many were simply recorded with the surname 'Greek', such as 'Michael Greke' and 'Jacobus Greke', taxed in Broad Street and Farringdon Without wards in the capital during the early 1440s.[122]

The best-known Greeks in London at this time were probably the Effomatos family of goldwire drawers (that is, metal workers who made fine threads of gold).[123] The two brothers, Alexius and Andronicus (though given various anglicised names in the records), clearly reached London before 1440, probably from Constantinople, and appear consistently in the capital throughout the alien subsidy records.[124] In the 1440s, both brothers lived in Cripplegate ward, but in 1455 Andronicus appeared in Westminster, and by 1483 Alexius had moved to Lime Street ward in the city.[125] They may not have been the only members of their family in the capital. A John 'Effemato' was taxed in 1467 (and probably also as 'John, a Greke' in 1468), and a Carant (or Karant) 'Effemathi' appears in the alien subsidy return in 1457.[126]

Carant Effemathi highlights a wider issue surrounding many of the 'Greeks' recorded in London at this time. Given the profession of the Effomatoi, it seems possible that Carant was also the man taxed in 1465 as 'Corand Goldwyredrawer'.[127] However, that man was specifically described as an Italian, from Venice. Given that many parts of what is now known as Greece were then Italian colonies, predominantly of Venice and Genoa, Carant may therefore have been a relative or adopted associate of the Effomatos brothers who had spent some time in a Venetian colony, had broader Venetian connections and/or had been born in Venice.[128] We must therefore recognise that some 'Greeks' may have been ethnically Italian. The records of 'Greeks' receiving denization show very clearly that places of birth and 'Greek' status were not necessarily one and the same thing. One of the earliest known people from 'Greece' to receive letters of denization was the master of medicine, Thomas Franc. Other evidence (including his surname) suggests, however, that this man was probably a Venetian subject, from the colony of Corone in the southern Peloponnese.[129] A century later, Peter de Mellan, an embroiderer described as coming from 'Candia' (the medieval name for both Crete and its capital Heraklion), may also have been from Venice, which was the colonial master of Crete.[130] Edward Castelyn was born on the island of Chios in the early sixteenth century, the son of a London mercer, William Castelyn. His mother, Angeleca Villacho, may have been 'Greek'; but Chios, then an Ottoman protectorate, had been another Genoese colony, and Angeleca may well have been descended from the island's Genoese ruling class. Rather than using the protection afforded to such offspring of English parentage by the statute *de natis ultra mare* of 1351, Edward followed a new route described further in chapter 8 and, in 1542, had a private act of naturalisation passed on his behalf in the Westminster parliament.[131]

Even so, there were at least a few actual Greeks amongst England's late medieval immigrants. Apart from Alexius and Andronicus Effomatos, the other recorded person with a surname clearly denoting 'Greek' ethnicity is Manuel Sophianos, who was granted denization in 1467 and was probably a member of the once-powerful Sophianos family from the Byzantine Morea.[132] No one of a similar name appears in the surviving records of the alien subsidies, suggesting that Manuel either received his letters shortly after his arrival or simply avoided assessment.

The Effomatoi undoubtedly made a success of their move to England. Whether they set out for London with that intent can only be speculated; they clearly left Constantinople well before its fall in 1453, but they probably knew that collapse was imminent, and there seems little doubt that the majority of 'Greek' immigrants to England, whatever their ethnicity, arrived after fleeing the advancing Ottoman Turks. Among various others, two 'Greek' noblewomen, Isabetta and Helene Lascarina, arrived in England around 1510 to raise ransoms for their children, captured by the Turks during the fall of the castle of Navarino in 1500.[133] Their travels almost certainly ended badly, with Isabetta being arrested for begging in Lincoln in 1512 and petitioning the king from her cell.[134] Their stories were just two of many heard in western Europe, ranging from lowly artisans to members of the Byzantine imperial family. Some, like Isabetta and Helene, ended up in England by accident, as part of an increasingly desperate search for refuge or assistance. The story of the Effomatoi suggests that others made deliberate and purposeful decisions about their future, and chose England because of the perceived opportunities it offered for employment and a new life.

Taken together, the evidence of the alien subsidies and of letters of protection and denization provide uniquely detailed information on the place of origin of those people from foreign lands who made their way to England between the 1430s and the 1540s. The purpose of chapters 4 and 5 has been to explore both the quantity and the quality of that evidence, in order to produce the most accurate picture possible of the various nationalities and ethnicities represented among the immigrant population of the kingdom. One of the most important discoveries especially from the alien subsidy material, however, relates to the different social profiles, and the resulting diversity of economic and professional functions, fulfilled by the various national groupings. In the next two chapters, we will explore this evidence in more detail in order to make a comprehensive evaluation of the place of immigrants in the economy of late medieval and early Tudor England.

Notes

1 Lambert and Ormrod, 'A matter of trust', pp. 208–26; Kowaleski, 'French immigrants', pp. 206–24; Linsley, 'The French in fifteenth-century England', pp. 147–62.

2 E 179/95/100; E 179/196/100; E 179/124/107. The Kent total excludes nine people taxed in the Kentish Cinque Ports, who are included in the separate entry in Table 3 for the Cinque Ports.

3 Jones, *Creation of Brittany*.

4 E 179/87/78; E 179/95/100; E 179/196/100. Only three were noted in Somerset, and none in Dorset, but those returns are poor and/or incomplete: E 179/169/92; E 179/103/83.

5 For Cornish–Breton links, see Berresford Ellis, *Cornish Language*; Wakelin, *Language and History*.

6 E 179/141/69, m. 3d; Le Neve, *Fasti Ecclesiae Anglicanae 1300–1541*, V, p. 31.

7 E 179/200/75, m. 2d; Page and Willis-Bund (eds), *Victoria History of the County of Worcester*, IV, p. 80.

8 See the case of Moses Contarini discussed in chapter 6. For Anglo-Gascon trading links, see Lavaud, *Bordeaux et le vin*.

9 E 179/144/73, E 179/241/327 Part 2. For details of this document, see chapter 4.

10 E 179/95/100, rot 4d; E 179/270/32 Part 1, m. 2. Stephen James was specified as a Brabanter in 1436: *CPR 1429–36*, p. 566.

11 Fleming, 'Bristol and the end of empire', pp. 374–5.

12 *LP*, III, pt 2, no. 2587 (6); E 179/113/192, m. 12d.

13 WAM 12261, mm. 25–6, 21.

14 E 179/120/86, m. 7. He had previously been assessed as 'Janyn Valew' and 'John Valewe', with no recorded nationality: E 179/120/83, m. 2d; E 179/120/87, m. 1.

15 E 179/180/111, rot. 4.

16 E 179/184/212, rots 3–4.

17 Gelemot de Parys in London, 1441 (E 179/144/73, rot. 1 m. 2d); Janyn de Parys in Patrixbourne, Kent, 1440 (E 179/124/107, rot. 9d); and Richard de Parys in Newcastle under Lyme, Staffordshire, 1440 and 1441 (E 179/177/56, m. 5; E 179/369/8, m. 5).

18 E 179/242/9, rot. 4d; E 179/87/78, m. 3.

19 *CPR 1429–36*, p. 462; *CPR 1452–61*, p. 343; *CPR 1467–77*, p. 594. For Lovekyn, see also chapter 6.

20 *CPR 1446–52*, p. 249; *CPR 1441–6*, p. 101.

21 Here, 'French' includes seventy-one French, nineteen Picards, two Artesians and one Norman.

22 WAM 12261. A solitary individual specified as from Artois is included in the subset 'French'.

23 Bois, *Crisis of Feudalism*, pp. 65, 316–27.

24 See chapter 8.

25 WAM 12261.

26 WAM 12261, mm. 19, 26, 3.

27 Blockmans and Prevenier, *The Promised Lands*.

28 Arnold, *Princes and Territories*.

29 For a wider discussion, see Bergs and Brinton (eds), *English Historical Linguistics*, II, pp. 1659–70.

30 E 179/242/25; E 179/73/109.

31 E 179/149/126; E 179/180/92; E 179/108/113.

32 E 179/124/107.

33 E 179/141/69; E 179/120/83.

34 These and other unreferenced statistics relating to those taking this oath have been calculated from the lists published in *CPR 1429–36*, pp. 537–88; *CPR 1436–41*, pp. 36–7, 94–5.

35 Harding, 'Cross-Channel trade'.

36 Kerling, *Commercial Relations*, pp. 89–133, 154–72, 176–80.

37 E 179/202/133.

38 E 179/158/115, m. 3; E 179/158/41, m. 13.

39 E 179/87/78.

40 E 179/95/100.

41 E 179/235/4; E 179/155/80. Fourteen untaxed 'Dutch' wives were also listed in Cambridgeshire, and six in Northamptonshire.

42 E 179/177/56, m. 3; E 179/269/53, m. 3; E 179/117/52; *CPR 1436–41*, p. 37.

43 E 179/270/31, mm. 37, 41; *CPR 1436–41*, p. 94.

44 E 179/235/4; E 179/124/107; E 179/149/130; E 179/235/6; E 179/180/92 Part 2; E 179/149/126.

45 E 179/117/52.

46 E 179/133/71.

47 For further details, see Thielemans, *Bourgogne et Angleterre*, pp. 283–343.

48 *CPR 1429–36*, pp. 556, 545.

49 *CPR 1429–36*, pp. 555, 567, 545.

50 *CPR 1429–36*, pp. 567, 574; E 179/235/4, m. 5.

51 See also Barron, 'Introduction: England and the Low Countries', pp. 11–12.

52 *Alien Communities*, p. 1.

53 Childs, 'The *George* of Beverley and Olav Olavesson'.

54 SC 8/26/1276–7; *CPR 1429–36*, p. 288; Wedgwood (ed.), *History of Parliament*, pp. 644–5.

55 *Alien Communities*, p. 62 n. 67.

56 E 179/149/177, m. 2d.

57 *CPR 1441–6*, p. 63; *CPR 1436–41*, p. 37.

58 *LP*, IV, pt 3, no. 5243 (20); E 179/150/222 Part 2, rot. 4.

59 E 179/270/32 Part 1, m. 3; E 179/136/206, m. 3.

60 *CPR 1429–36*, p. 547; E 179/270/31, m. 39.

61 E 235/67, m. 1.

62 E 179/235/4, m. 4.

63 Lambert, 'Scandinavian immigrants', pp. 111–12; *Responsiones Vadstenenses*, p. 23.

64 For FitzHugh, see www.oxforddnb.com/view/article/50151 (accessed 26 July 2017).

65 For a recent review of this topic, see Fleming, 'Icelanders in England', pp. 77–88.

66 E 179/90/27, m. 2. Many of the nuns sent over to Syon from Vadstena in Sweden had surnames ending in the patronymic '-dotter': *Responsiones Vadstenenses*, p. 22.

67 E 179/202/133.

68 E 179/113/137; E 179/25/175 Part 2, m. 2.

69 E 179/270/54.

70 Fleming, 'Icelanders in England', pp. 79–81; and see further discussion in chapter 7.

71 E 179/270/31, mm. 23, 31.

72 For example, E 179/159/94 (1455).

73 For example, E 179/192/82A (1456); E 179/192/89 (1460).

74 E 179/242/25.

75 See above, chapter 2.

76 For further discussion, see chapter 6.

77 E 179/236/107, m. 2.

78 See chapter 6.

79 E 179/144/53, m. 1.

80 *Views of the Hosts*, pp. 1–121.

81 E 179/144/42; E 179/144/52. Only 186 of the 1,500 taxpayers in 1441 had a readily identifiable nationality in the records, but surname evidence would suggest these included most of the Italians.

82 E 179/144/72; E 179/236/96. The 1465 list was one of the shortest returned for the city.

83 Guidi-Bruscoli and Lutkin, 'Perception, identity and culture', have identified many of the people described in the records only as 'Italian', but the overall proportions remain similar.

84 For instance, the poet and churchman Pietro Carmeliano, who arrived from Brescia in 1481: see chapter 9.

85 See chapter 10.

86 For further details, see Bradley, 'Italian Merchants in London'.

87 E 179/242/25, m. 7.

88 For Buonvisi, see Dizionario Biografico degli Italiani, www.treccani.it/ enciclopedia/antonio-buonvisi_(Dizionario-Biografico)/ (accessed 25 May 2017); E 303/8/10; C 66/685, m. 20. For Guercy, see *ODNB*, XXIV, pp. 167–8; C 1/1083/ 28; C 1/438/1. For other families in the area, see E 179/251/15b; LR 2/108; LMA, CLA/023/DW/01/247, nos 115–17.

89 Ruddock, 'Alien merchants in Southampton'; Ruddock, 'Alien hosting in Southampton'.

90 E 179/176/585; E 179/173/136; E 179/173/139; E 179/173/137, m. 1; E 179/17/133, m. 1; E 179/173/134, m. 1; E 179/173/132, m. 1; Ruddock, *Italian Merchants*, pp. 125–8.

91 E 179/173/132. The origins of one Italian were unspecified.

92 E 179/176/585, rot. 4.

93 Wallace, 'Overseas Trade of Sandwich', pp. 352–65.

94 E 179/242/9, rot. 2.

95 E 179/236/118, mm. 1–2.

96 E 179/73/109, m. 2.

97 E 179/180/111, rot. 4.

98 E 179/71/79, m. 7; E 179/235/18, m. 8; E 179/180/111, rot. 3.

99 E 179/113/192, m. 11.

100 E 179/124/188, fol. 4r; E 179/108/154, rot. 13d.

101 *CPR 1441–6*, p. 34; *CPR 1476–85*, p. 476; *LP*, I, pt 1, no. 1524 (33).

102 Bradley, 'Lucia Visconti'; Mackman, ' "Hidden gems" '.

103 *CPR 1405–8*, p. 22; *CPR 1408–13*, p. 392; *CPR 1429–36*, p. 294; *LP*, V, no. 232. See also entries in Talbot and Hammond, *Medical Practitioners*; Getz, 'Medical practitioners'. For Signorelli, see Colson and Ralley, 'Medical practice'; and for Agostini, see Hammond, 'Doctor Augustine'. For Nigarelli, see also chapter 8.

104 *CPR 1436–41*, p. 50; *LP*, XX, pt 1, no. 465 (50); www.oxforddnb.com/view/article/ 16813 (accessed 19 April 2017).

105 E 179/87/78, mm. 3–4.

106 E 179/95/100, rots. 4, 3d; E 179/180/92 Part 2, m. 12.

107 E 179/155/80, rot. 4; E 179/235/4, m. 4; E 179/103/83.

108 E 179/169/92, m. 1; E 179/155/80, rot. 3d.

109 E 179/155/80, rot. 2d (1440); E 179/387/4 (1443); E 179/157/469 (1444).

110 E 179/117/61, m. 2; E 179/236/135, m. 1; E 179/117/70, m. 1.

111 E 179/180/111, rot. 4.

112 E 179/241/327 Part 2, rot. 1; E 179/144/52, m. 7; E 179/242/25, m. 11.

113 Roth, 'Sir Edward Brampton'; *ODNB*, VII, 319.

114 E 179/242/25, m. 10d.

115 *CPR 1416–22*, p. 311; *CPR 1485–94*, p. 258; Ollard, *Fasti Wyndesoriensis*; Talbot and Hammond, *Medical Practitioners*, pp. 246–7.

116 *CPR 1494–1509*, p. 604; *CPR 1467-77*, p. 510; *LP*, IV, pt 3, no. 6418 (28); V, no. 364 (30).

117 WAM 12261, m. 31; *LP*, II, pt 2, no. 2747.

118 *LP*, II, pt 2, no. 2074 (5). For the influence of the royal household, see chapter 9.

119 PSO 2/6, May 1541, no. 37.

120 Chambers, *Imperial Age of Venice*.

121 Harris, *Greek Emigres*; Harris and Porfyriou, 'The Greek diaspora'.

122 E 179/144/52, m. 9; E 179/144/52, m. 10.

123 Harris, 'Two Byzantine craftsmen'.

124 For example, E 179/144/42, m. 25 (1441); E 179/242/25, m. 10 (1483, Alexius only). Andronicus (named as 'Andrew'), a native of 'Constantine', gifted all his goods to Alexius ('Alexander') in October 1471, suggesting that Andronicus died around that time: *CCR 1468-76*, no. 752.

125 E 179/144/42, m. 25; E 179/235/57, m. 2; E 179/242/25, m. 10.

126 E 179/236/107, m. 2; E 179/144/70; E 179/144/72; E 179/236/74.

127 E 179/236/96, m. 2. 'Coraunt Goldwyrdrawer', given no nationality, was also taxed in 1464: E 179/144/69.

128 Mueller, 'Greeks in Venice'.

129 *CPR 1429–36*, p. 604; E 28/57/112; Foffano, 'Tommaso Franco'; Harris, *Greek Emigres*, pp. 35–8, 59–61, 89–93. Thomas was sometimes given the surname 'Greek': see, for example, E 179/144/53, m. 15 (1443). He was also presumably the 'Thomas Fisicion' taxed in London's Broad Street ward in 1444: E 179/144/54, m. 6.

130 PSO 2/5, April 1541, no. 44.

131 *SR*, III, p. 865. Bent, 'Lords of Chios'.

132 *CPR 1467-77*, p. 65; Harris, *Greek Emigres*, p. 37.

133 C 82/344/2; C 1/1507/31; Cameron, *The Pardoner and his Pardons*, pp. 15–16.

134 C 244/160/20.

6

Supplying the market

Post-plague England and the consumer economy

During the century and a half that followed the arrival of the Black Death, England was particularly attractive to producers from abroad. The severe depopulation caused by successive outbreaks of the plague, other epidemics and famines made rents fall and agricultural prices plunge. Labour shortages led to an increase in real wages from the 1380s onwards.[1] As a result, the majority of the English population experienced an increase in purchasing power not paralleled, in relative terms, until the twentieth century. Numerous families were no longer forced to spend such a high proportion of their available money on mere subsistence and were left with a higher disposable income.[2] For the first time, they could exercise choice and taste, paving the way for the emergence of a consumer economy. Peasants and wage earners were able to diversify their diets, fashion became an important factor in the purchase of clothing, privacy and comfort in the construction and decoration of homes. The more elaborate consumption by the lower classes blurred social distinctions and stimulated the elites to spend more on luxuries, so as to set themselves apart from the rest of the population.[3]

Most of these consumer goods were produced within England, bringing about a boom in the manufacturing industries. This, in turn, attracted numerous foreign craftsmen, whose skills and capital sometimes allowed them to cater for the increasingly cosmopolitan and quickly changing tastes of English consumers more adequately than native producers. Many of these artisans employed fellow aliens as apprentices and journeymen, adding further to England's immigrant workforce. At the same time, the consumer revolution led to an intensification of international commerce, made possible by the significant numbers of traders who visited the country temporarily and the minority of alien merchants who stayed in the realm on a more permanent basis.

Developments independent of the consequences of the Black Death also encouraged people from abroad to find employment in England. The take-off of the native cloth industry from the early fourteenth century attracted thousands of textile workers from other parts of Europe. The numbers of people settling in later medieval England for professional reasons were high, and the contribution these groups made to the country's economy exceeded even their numerical strength. Immigrant workers brought skills and know-how that the English population lacked, introduced new products and technologies, and left a lasting imprint on England's economic history.

Dressing English consumers

One of the economic sectors that benefited most from the rising living standards and the increased consumer demand in post-plague England was that of the fashion industries. During the second quarter of the fourteenth century, dramatic changes took hold in aristocratic dress; tight-fitting clothes replaced the loose garments that had prevailed for centuries.[4] For the first time, and despite the criticisms of moralists and the imposition of sumptuary laws, the innovations were adopted by larger parts of the population, albeit often with a time lag.[5] Novelty started to dominate consumer taste and keeping up with the latest trends became crucial, to the extent that dress historians have identified the fourteenth century as the starting point of fashion.[6] The impact on the clothing industries was enormous. In London, the demand for tailors was high and the number of masters and apprentices in the business doubled between 1425 and 1465.[7] In York, the number of tailors who obtained the freedom of the city rose sharply from the 1330s onwards, outnumbering all other crafts over the later medieval period.[8]

These opportunities also attracted immigrants. Between 1440 and 1487, there are 308 instances of people recorded as tailors paying the alien subsidies. The majority of these were immigrants from the Low Countries and the German territories. They were concentrated in Southwark, the borough south of London, and various places in Suffolk and Essex. Ipswich, for example, had ten alien tailors in 1483, a mixture of Germans, Flemings and Zeelanders.[9] Fourteen alien tailors were assessed for the alien subsidy without having their places of origin recorded in Southwark in 1440.[10]

As their surnames are distinctively 'Dutch' and several of them swore the oath of fealty in 1436, it is safe to say that nearly all of them came from the Low Countries.[11] High numbers of Irish and Scottish tailors are also recorded in the alien subsidy returns. Irishmen were mainly concentrated in Wiltshire: Malmesbury had four Irish tailors in 1440, and Salisbury four in 1443.[12] Their actual numbers were probably even higher than those recorded in the subsidy returns. Fifteen alien tailors paid the tax in Bristol in 1440.[13] Their origins were not given, but considering the status of the city as a destination for Irish immigrants, it is likely that most were Irish as well.[14] In the licences that Irishmen were expected to take out in order to remain in England in 1394, tailor was also the second most frequent occupation, after chaplain.[15] The majority of the Scottish tailors recorded in the tax returns worked in Yorkshire and East Anglia.

Whereas most of the Irish and Scottish tailors who paid the alien subsidies had no recorded dependants, many of those from the Low Countries and the German dominions were noted as living with their alien wives and employing alien servants. John Conyng, from Utrecht, for example, swore the oath of fealty in 1436 and was assessed for the alien subsidy in 1440. He lived in Southwark with his wife Fia and three 'Dutch' servants, two male and one female.[16] Some of these tailors became quite prosperous. John Mountagu, a Norman resident in London, and Robert Loy, another Norman working in Canterbury, were able to afford letters of denization in 1447 and 1448.[17] The most prominent alien tailor active in fifteenth-century England, however, was George Lovekyn. Born in Paris, he had moved to London by 1470, where he employed four alien servants in 1483. Lovekyn was appointed sergeant-tailor by Edward IV in 1475 and was granted letters of denization a year later. He made the robes for the coronations of both Richard III and Henry VII, before falling on hard times during the later years of his career.[18] Some immigrants found work in a particular niche of the tailoring business, embellishing clothes with increasingly elaborate decorations. Thirteen embroiderers, the majority from the Low Countries but also including two 'Austrians', swore the oath of fealty of 1436 and paid the 1440 alien subsidy in Southwark and London.[19] One of these, William Outcamp from Holland, even took out letters of denization in 1444.[20] Richard Ducheman made a living off the new taste for snug-fitting jackets and worked as a doublet maker in Norwich in 1440.[21]

The market for smaller garments also expanded vastly. Fashions in headwear changed quickly and ever widening ranges of hats, caps and bonnets were produced by specialised artisans. The dominance of craftsmen from the Low Countries in this field was such that when the anonymous author of *London Lickpenny*, a poem of the 1420s, needed to portray a stereotypical Fleming, he had him sell felt hats.[22] In London in 1483, fifty-three alien cappers paid the alien subsidy.[23] Most of these were recorded as being 'Teutonic', but surnames such as 'de Anwarpe' ('of Antwerp') suggest that many came from Brabant, Flanders and Holland. In Ipswich, eight Flemings and one Zeelander worked as hat makers in 1483.[24] Some of these artisans supplied to highly influential customers. Philip Lecok, a capper who employed five servants in London's Langbourn ward in 1483, was even given royal permission in 1491 to ignore the price ceiling that usually applied to alien-produced fashion items.[25] Closely associated with the hat makers, and often trying to incorporate them, were the haberdashers, the dealers in small fashion objects such as buttons and needles.[26] Fourteen haberdashers from the Low Countries took the oath of fealty of 1436 in Southwark.[27] Even more specialised were the hosiers, producers of socks and stockings. Nine people identified with this trade appear in the alien subsidy returns between 1440 and 1487. Most were based in larger urban centres; but the small town of Harwich on the Essex coast was home to three immigrant hosiers, as well as a tailor and a glover, in 1484.[28]

Leatherworking was one of the most buoyant industries in the later Middle Ages. It involved many different trades. Tanners or barkers prepared cattle hides using oak bark, whereas tawyers and whit-tawyers treated the skins of other animals with oil or alum. Curriers made the leather strong, flexible and waterproof.[29] Forty-one immigrants employed in these trades were listed in the returns to the alien subsidies, most of them being tawyers and curriers from the Low Countries and the German territories. Yet most aliens did not work in the preparation of the raw material, but in the finishing of leather goods. Nowhere in the fashion industries was the impact of immigrant craftsmen stronger than in shoemaking. Growing consumer interest during the later Middle Ages resulted in a widening range of footwear, some more extravagant than others.[30] Cordwainers originally worked only with leather from Spain, but by the fifteenth century were understood to produce the highest-quality shoes. Corvisers also made new footwear, while cobblers and souters repaired or remade old shoes. Often these terms were used interchangeably, or workers were more generically called 'shoe makers'. Patten makers produced wooden clogs with leather straps or bands, a later medieval novelty.[31] There are a total of 434 instances of aliens engaged in these trades in the alien subsidy returns between 1440 and 1487. Fifty-four cordwainers from the Low Countries swore the oath of fealty in 1436, the single most recorded occupational group; twenty-four of them lived in Southwark.[32] Thirty 'Dutch' artisans worked in the shoemaking business in Cambridge in 1440, twenty-seven of them categorised as cordwainers.[33] Ipswich had twenty-four alien shoe makers in 1483, twenty of whom were Flemings.[34] In London, also in 1483, thirty-two cobblers and nineteen other shoe workers paid the subsidy.[35] They were designated as 'Teutonics' but, as with the hat makers, this must have included craftsmen from the Low Countries.

Immigrant shoe workers often ran very large workshops. Both William Jerusalem, a cordwainer from Zeeland working in Southwark during the 1430s and 1440s, and Herman Stone, a 'Teutonic' cordwainer who paid the subsidy in London's Dowgate ward in 1483, had no fewer than ten servants.[36] In Ipswich, the Fleming Ingoll Bolton brought several stages of the shoemaking process together under one roof. In 1483, he employed four Flemish servants, three of whom were shoe makers and one a tawyer.[37] Peter Gretloff, a German who lived in London and received letters of denization in 1473, could equally have combined interests in leather preparation and shoemaking.[38] Described as a cordwainer in the London letter books in 1480, he was identified as a tawyer with five immigrant servants in the alien subsidy three years later, in 1483.[39] No female aliens were recorded as working in the shoemaking business as servants or independent artisans, even among the curriers, for whom it was customary to employ women.[40] The majority of immigrant shoe workers did, however, have alien wives, who may have assisted their husbands on the shop floor. Smaller numbers of aliens, mostly from the Low Countries, Germany or Ireland and also exclusively male, worked in more specialised and highly fashionable leather crafts as glovers, pursers, girdlers and saddlers.[41]

Rivalling the shoe makers when it came to alien involvement in English manufacture, and possibly outnumbering them, were the goldsmiths. Increased purchasing power during the later Middle Ages made jewellery more affordable and created a demand for dress accessories. Eager to maintain the social distinction with the newly aspiring lower classes, the elites stepped up their spending on luxury.[42] As the market for goldsmiths' work in London grew, so did the attraction for immigrant artisans. After 1400, the sprinkle of alien goldsmiths in the capital became a flood.[43] Fifteen men from the Burgundian territories living in Southwark and involved in this trade swore the oath of fealty in 1436.[44] In London, twenty-eight people identified as goldsmiths paid the alien subsidy in 1483.[45] These figures come nowhere near the actual numbers active in and around the capital during the fifteenth century. 'Dutchmen' tried to escape the stringent controls of the London Goldsmiths' Company and may also have remained under the radar of the alien subsidy collectors. Even the numbers of those openly associating themselves with the company are markedly higher than the figures suggested by the oaths and the subsidies. In 1436, forty-two alien goldsmiths contributed to London's payment for the defence of Calais, more than half the total number of contributing goldsmiths. In 1469, the company compiled a list of an astonishing 113 foreigners, mainly Flemings, who were engaged in goldsmiths' work in the city, Southwark and Westminster. Between 1479 and 1510, 310 aliens swore to observe the company's rules.[46]

Openly or covertly, many of these alien goldsmiths worked for the most influential customers. Marcellus Maures, alias Selis, from Utrecht, repaired Edward IV's jewels and supplied the royal wardrobe during the 1480s. He made numerous silver-gilt objects for the coronations of both Richard III and Henry VII. Maures acquired letters of denization in 1482, but was still made to pay the alien subsidy in 1483, when he had seventeen alien servants.[47] A fellow supplier at Henry VII's coronation was John van Delff, who maintained connections with his homeland until the very end of his life, in 1504. He employed twenty-one 'Dutchmen' between 1499 and 1503 and still owned property overseas when drawing up his will.[48] Alexander Brusshel, from Baden in Germany, became Henry VII's chief engraver of new models for the coinage in 1494. At one time employing twenty-five alien servants, he probably left London for Antwerp in 1511.[49] There are no indications that immigrant women participated in the goldsmiths' business during these years.

Unlike the other livery companies, the London Goldsmiths' Company had control over the business of guilds elsewhere in England.[50] This, together with the concentration of elite demand in the capital, explains why the great majority of goldsmiths who paid the alien subsidies lived in London. Still, every major provincial town in fifteenth-century England had one or more alien goldsmiths working within its walls. In Salisbury, customers in the 1440s could choose between the Normans Stephen and Bartholomew Deschamps.[51] Bristol and Exeter offered promising career prospects: described as servants in 1440, the alien Richard Batyn and the Frenchman Tilman Cok were running their own workshops by the following year.[52] In York, the registers of the freemen document a steady stream of alien goldsmiths from the end of the fourteenth century.[53] They included Warimbald Harlam, likely from Haarlem, who, after twenty-four years of residence in England, obtained letters of denization in 1403.[54] The alien subsidy returns for York hardly ever specify occupations, but the freemen's registers allow us to identify at least seven taxpayers as goldsmiths. Among them was John Colan, a German. Possibly related to Nicholas Colayn, an alien goldsmith in York during the 1440s, John was active throughout the 1460s.[55] When he died, in 1490, he left his business to his son Herman, with his will providing one of the most detailed descriptions of a goldsmith's workshop in the whole medieval period.[56]

Aliens also worked in crafts connected to goldsmithing. Six jewellers from the Low Countries and the German territories swore the 1436 oath of fealty or were assessed for the alien subsidies, all of them based in London or Southwark. The art of goldwire drawing was highly specialised, involving the production of fine wires of precious metal that were then interwoven with silk thread.[57] The Greek brothers Alexius and Andronicus Effomatos, whom we met in chapter 5, are credited with introducing this craft in London.[58] Commonly working with less precious metals but equally bene-fiting from the growing demand for accessories were the pin makers: seven aliens involved in this trade are known to have set up shop in fifteenth-century England.[59] Surprisingly, given the constant context of warfare and the Germans' reputation in these industries, alien armourers were seem-ingly few, with fourteen armourers and one maker of plate swearing the oath of fealty or paying the alien subsidy.[60] However, they included highly prosperous artisans such as William Warter, who entered the freedom of York in 1419–20 and was still producing armour in 1443, and the 'Teutonic' Vincent Toteler, who could afford twelve immigrant servants in London in 1483.[61]

Brick, wood and glass: aliens in the building trades

Consumers in later medieval England not only spent more money on the latest fashion; they also invested a higher proportion of their income in housing. Higher-quality building materials were introduced, most not-ably brick. Although it was common in the Low Countries, Germany and Poland, brick was only used on a limited scale in England until the end of the fourteenth century, mainly for paving and vaulting.[62] Some of this work involved immigrant artisans such as Athelad of Brabant, who was responsible for the pavement of the canons' cloister at St George's Chapel, Windsor.[63] At the beginning of the fifteenth century, brick was adopted as a favoured building material by the royal court and various lords who had served in the Hundred Years War. Some of these patrons were aliens themselves, such as the Danish-born Andrew Ogard, commis-sioner of Rye House in Hertfordshire in 1440.[64] The interest of the elites, followed by many other English consumers, attracted craftsmen from the

Low Countries and the German territories, who introduced decorative innovations such as diapering and ornamental chimneys.[65]

Building accounts during this period, as well as the alien subsidy returns, distinguish between the work of brick makers, bricklayers and masons, although the terms could often be used interchangeably. The earliest surviving brick building in England known to have involved alien masons was the chapel tower at Stonor Park, in Oxfordshire, where Flemings worked in 1416–17. Henry V employed bricklayers from Holland for the construction of his Charterhouse at Sheen, funded in part out of the confiscated alien priories, and begun in 1414.[66] Some of these men may still have been active during the 1430s, as two masons from Guelders swore the 1436 oath of fealty in Isleworth, the site of the priory.[67] Several brick workers also paid the alien subsidies between 1440 and 1487. Among them were four 'Teutonic' masons at New Windsor in 1483.[68] It is likely they were working at Windsor Castle, possibly on the tomb of Edward IV, which was being built during these years. In Leicestershire, the chief brick maker Anthony Docheman and several fellow 'Dutchmen' built Kirby Muxloe Castle, until construction stopped on the execution of its patron, William, Lord Hastings, in 1483.[69]

Some alien masons were given much more far-reaching responsibilities. After providing brick for the king's manors at Sheen, William Veysey, who was probably 'Dutch', was instructed by the crown to run the newly built brick kiln at Slough in Berkshire in 1442. Over the next ten years, he supplied about 2.5 million bricks for the construction of the accommodation ranges of Eton College, the school for poor boys founded by Henry VI. His contribution to the king's building works proved the starting point of an illustrious career, as he went on to hold several offices and sat as MP for Lyme and Wareham.[70] The appearance of typically continental diapering, and the details of some surnames in the building accounts, suggest that alien masons were also involved in the construction of Eton College.[71] At Tattershall in Lincolnshire, Ralph, Lord Cromwell began building his new brick castle in the 1430s. The person responsible for the production of bricks, and probably also the master mason or architect of the building, was the 'Dutchman' Baldwin Brickmaker.[72] In 1443 and 1446 he paid the alien subsidy in Edlington, where the clay pits for the brickmaking were located. Listed in the same assessments were Arnekyn and John Brickmaker and others, such as the tiler Jacob Papelwyck, who must also have been involved in the construction of the castle.[73] After his death, Baldwin's widow continued to supply bricks to Tattershall in her own right.[74]

Aliens also settled in England to work on the decoration of houses and other buildings. In 1411, the wardens of London Bridge instructed a carver from the Low Countries to produce several pieces of decorative woodwork. In 1477, Dirick Vangrove and Giles Vancastell made wooden figures of St George and the dragon and St Edward, as well as a rood with the Virgin and St John, for St George's Chapel, Windsor.[75] In 1483, the Ipswich carver William Dew employed three carvers from the Low Countries. Two of them resided in Bury St Edmunds, probably carrying out work at the abbey there.[76] Also in Suffolk, Sir John Clopton, a wealthy landholder and former sheriff, tore down Holy Trinity Church in Long Melford and rebuilt it on a much larger scale in the 1480s.[77] Probably working for Clopton were a Flemish sculptor, Henry Phelip, and painter, Anthony Lammoson.[78] Among the recipients of denization in the 1540s were more than eighty men described variously as joiners and carvers, most of them from France and working in the South-West of England where stylistic evidence also points to a particularly strong tradition of northern French carving in both secular and ecclesiastical settings.[79]

Richard Marks has stated that, between the middle of the thirteenth and the late fifteenth centuries, 'there is little evidence in either documentary sources or in surviving windows to suggest that the presence of foreign glass-painters in England was any more than occasional'.[80] However, this claim needs some qualification in light of the evidence surveyed here. The early sixteenth century did indeed see a strong influx of alien glaziers, but this was actually an acceleration of a trend that went back to at least the 1430s. The alien subsidies reveal the presence of fifteen immigrant glaziers in the country between 1440 and 1487, most of them from the Low Countries. William Mundeford, a native of the bishopric of Utrecht, started his career as an apprentice in the workshop of the Englishman John Wighton in Norwich before 1432. He swore the oath of fealty in 1436 and was assessed for the alien subsidies from 1440 to 1468.[81] Written sources suggest that he worked on the dormitory windows in Norwich Cathedral; and a body of stained glass in Norfolk has been attributed to him on the basis of his style, which had a lot in common with that of the art of the Low Countries at the beginning of the fifteenth century.[82] Mundeford's son, Henry, worked in the same trade as an apprentice to the glazier Henry Piers, who entered the freedom of Norwich in 1426–7 and was assessed for the alien subsidies between 1440 and 1452, variously as a Fleming and a Frenchman. Piers may have mended windows in the church of St Giles in the city, but otherwise none of his work is known.[83] Another glazier who was probably from the Low Countries was John Pyle, who is known to have paid the alien subsidies in Canterbury between 1455 and 1463; the figures of Edward IV and his family in the cathedral's Royal Window, dated to the 1480s, which may have been Pyle's work, betray the hand of a 'Dutch' artist.[84] In Exeter, two glaziers from Frisia who were assessed for the 1440 subsidy were employed on work at the cathedral.[85]

Glaziers also came to England from other parts of Europe. At Leominster in Herefordshire, for example, the Irishman John Bygge paid the alien subsidy as a glazier between 1440 and 1443.[86] In the small town of Wickham Market in Suffolk, the Scot John Glacier ran a glaziers' workshop with two alien apprentices in 1483.[87] Apart from those who were explicitly recorded as working in the glazing business, there were also people recorded in the alien subsidy returns with the surname 'Glazier', or a variant thereof. Eleven of these lived in London; they may include some of the twenty-eight immigrant craftsmen mentioned in a complaint by the city's Glaziers' Company in 1474.[88]

Aliens resident in the country may also have been responsible for the production of the glass that was used by the glaziers' workshops. During the 1440s, two immigrants with the surname Glasswright and one called Glassmaker were assessed for the alien subsidies.[89] Craftsmen from the Low Countries may even have introduced the manufacture of coloured glass, which was more expensive than painted white glass, into England: in 1449, Henry VI granted John Utynam from Flanders a twenty-year monopoly to make glass of all colours for the windows of Eton College and King's College, Cambridge, and to instruct English natives 'because the said art has never been used in England'.[90] One of the possible glass makers assessed towards the alien subsidies, the 'Dutchman' Jacobus Glasswright, was also based at Cambridge and may have been one of Utynam's collaborators.[91] There is, however, much debate as to whether Henry's efforts met with any success, as there is no archaeological or documentary evidence that coloured glass was ever actually produced in England during this period.[92]

Providing food and drink

Higher standards of living allowed people in later medieval England to afford better food and drink. Wheat replaced less expensive grains such as barley and oats as the main ingredient for bread.[93] Only twenty-seven bakers are identified among those assessed for the alien subsidies between 1440 and 1487, which is a surprisingly low number for such an important trade. Most of these immigrant bakers were French. Agnes Hirde, an

Irishwoman at Kendal in Westmorland, was the only female among them.[94] In Southwark in the early 1440s, customers also had access to an immigrant pie baker.[95]

The consumption of meat also increased, particularly beef and mutton.[96] This was partly facilitated by a shift in agriculture: confronted with plummeting demand as a result of the population decline and the difficulty of finding enough manpower, landowners switched from grain farming to the grazing of cattle and sheep.[97] The numerous 'husbandmen' identified in the alien subsidy returns, discussed in detail in chapter 7, were probably mostly arable farmers, but may also have included some who responded to this new trend and supplied meat for the market. The connections to meat preparation of the fifteen butchers and two immigrant poulterers recorded in the alien subsidy returns are obviously straightforward. New techniques for the preservation of food were introduced, many of them requiring salt. Two Scottish salters were active in Northumberland in 1440.[98] As England had become heavily dependent on imported salt after the mid-fourteenth century, Henry VI's government tried to revive the native salt industry. In 1440, the crown invited the Hollander John of Schiedam and a team of sixty workers to prepare salt near Winchelsea.[99] This may have been the man of the same name who swore the oath of fealty four years later while living in Bury St Edmunds.[100] At the higher end of the social spectrum, the well-to-do employed foreign cooks to prepare ever more exquisite dishes. The University of Cambridge's Trinity Hall had a French chef in 1441, and an anonymous alien worked in the kitchen of the wealthy Italian merchant Benedetto Borromei in London in 1449.[101] The employers of the other fifteen immigrant cooks recorded in the alien subsidy returns remain unknown.

There is one notable exception to the limited involvement of alien residents in the supply of food and drink. From the 1370s onwards, beer brewed in the Low Countries was imported to cater for the tastes of 'Dutch' immigrants. After 1400, however, brewers from Flanders, Holland and Zeeland also began to produce beer within England itself. By the end of the fifteenth century, the new drink was not only supplying a growing English customer base but also being exported to the Low Countries. An important advantage was the use of hops, which allowed beer to be preserved longer and transported further than native ales. According to Bennett, the alien brewers in fifteenth-century England were 'few, but prosperous and powerful'.[102] The alien subsidy returns certainly suggest that fewer immigrants were involved in beer brewing than in the cordwainers' or goldsmiths' business, but at a local level the numbers could still be significant. In Ipswich in 1483, for example, no fewer than nineteen 'Dutch' and German beer brewers were assessed for the alien subsidy.[103] London also had twenty alien 'beermen' and four brewers assessed in 1483.[104] More importantly, there are also reasons to believe that the alien subsidy returns seriously under-represent the overall numbers of foreigners involved in beer brewing. In the Norfolk port of Great Yarmouth only one person was ever assessed for the alien subsidies with the occupational designation of brewer. Yet the borough court records show that dozens of residents from Holland and Zeeland were fined for brewing beer outside the civic franchise between 1430 and 1490.[105]

Bennett has characterised the alien beer business as very male-dominated, certainly in comparison with the brewing of ale.[106] The involvement of immigrant women in beer making as recorded in the alien subsidy returns was limited, but no more so than in other trades. In Lynn, Alice Hosedowyn from Brabant worked as an independent beer seller in 1483-4.[107] Also in 1483, Marion Duchewoman was a servant of an alien beer brewer in Dunwich in Suffolk, and Katherine Petirson similarly in Ipswich.[108] Here again, the Great Yarmouth borough court rolls provide a rather different and more nuanced picture. Most of the aliens fined for brewing in the town between 1430 and 1455 were engaged in multiple occupations and produced beer as a seasonal activity, supplying the traders from Holland and Zeeland who visited Great Yarmouth during the herring fair. These included several women. After the mid-1450s, however, brewing became the sole profession of a smaller group of aliens who now produced beer year-round for both 'Dutch' and native consumers. This involved few, if any, women.[109] The example of Great Yarmouth therefore suggests that female immigrants may have participated in the early stages of alien beer brewing in England, but that the increase in scale and costs resulting from a stronger demand in the following decades made the trade largely inaccessible to them. It is surprising that no immigrant widows were recorded as continuing their late husbands' brewing businesses, though it should be stressed that, as detailed in chapter 7, the alien subsidy returns hardly ever give information on widows' occupations.

Alien beer brewers certainly were, in Bennett's words, 'prosperous and powerful'. Of the twenty-four brewers in London in 1483, eight had five or more servants. Some beer makers concluded partnerships to finance their investments in equipment and raw materials. John Evynger and Peter Hounslowe, two 'Teutonic' partners in the brewing industry in London in 1483, employed no fewer than sixteen alien servants between them.[110] Four alien beer brewers took out letters of denization during the fifteenth century. One of them, Hillary Warner, did so on the condition that he could export thirty tons of beer each year.[111] At the same time, alien brewers and their beer houses were often subject to particular scrutiny. Capitalising on their prosperity, Parliament decided that alien owners of breweries had to be taxed separately from, and more heavily than, other immigrant householders in the alien subsidy of 1483.[112] Beer houses were seen as distinctive symbols of 'Dutch' presence and became the target of hostility whenever Anglo-Burgundian relations came under strain. In 1436, after the duke of Burgundy had abandoned his alliance with the English for the new pact with the French, rumours spread that Flemish beer was poisonous and alien brewers needed royal protection.[113] In 1470, supporters of the earl of Warwick, who strongly opposed a rapprochement between England and Burgundy, set beer houses in London and Southwark on fire.[114]

High skills from the Low Countries

That so many of the skilled artisans who plied their trade in England originated from the Low Countries should be no surprise. During the fourteenth century, the traditional Flemish and Brabantine cloth industries, which had been the bedrock of the regions' economies and provided work to very large parts of their population for centuries, were hit hard by falling demand and the competition from draperies elsewhere in Europe, causing massive unemployment. One of the responses to the decline was a shift in focus to the luxury industries, dependent on highly skilled labour, artisan creativity and fashionable refinements. The added value of human capital in this sector was high, difficult to replace and less subject to short-term economic changes. Fuelled by growing domestic demand as a result of rising standards of living, specialised artistic and luxury crafts blossomed in many of the larger towns of the Low Countries, organised in guilds which exerted control over workers' skills and the quality of the products.[115] The node in this system was the Flemish city of Bruges, where the Burgundian court and its administrators indulged in conspicuous consumption and an unequalled concentration of foreign merchants bought goods for export.[116] Artisans all over the Low Countries and further afield supplied the Bruges market and many migrated to the city, buying citizenship and setting up shop close to their customers.[117]

Nevertheless, if the Low Countries offered many assets that attracted skilled craftsmen, there were also factors that pushed them away. In the first quarter of the fifteenth century, a series of devastating floods struck the region, ravaging towns in Holland, Zeeland and Brabant. Some of these affected places were named as the places of origin of people who moved to England.[118] Adrian Arnoldson, for example, came from Aartswaarde, which disappeared in the St Elisabeth's Flood of 1421. He swore the oath of fealty in 1436 and paid the alien subsidy in 1441 while living in Rye in Sussex.[119] Gerard Jonson, who swore the 1436 oath as a resident of Strumpshaw in Norfolk, was from Nieuwenbosch, a village in Brabant that was lost in the same flood.[120] Unfortunately, these men's occupations were not recorded.

Probably more important was the constant political turmoil that troubled the Low Countries during the later Middle Ages. Duke Philip the Good's expansionist campaigns caused much damage in Holland in the years before so many from that county took the English oath of fealty in 1436–7.[121] Throughout the period, urban revolts, both by factions within the cities opposing each other and by urban groups against princely authority, were endemic.[122] The craft guilds, including those of the luxury industries, were often deeply involved in these clashes. Between 1436 and 1438, the city of Bruges, home to the strongest concentration of highly skilled artisans in all of the Low Countries, rebelled against the duke. Economic life came to a standstill, the numbers of craftsmen buying citizenship plunged, and many of those already established departed.[123] Sources on both sides of the Channel allow us to reconstruct the trajectories of some who left for England as a result of these disturbances. In 1427, Joris Peperlooc was one of the searchers of the guild of grey fur workers (the artisans who worked mainly with squirrel skins imported by merchants of the Hanse) in Bruges, and in 1429, 1432 and 1435 he acted as its dean.[124] After 1436, he disappears from the Bruges records, only to reappear in London's Aldgate ward in 1441, paying the alien subsidy together with his wife.[125] Two years later, Peperlooc, who worked in the capital as a skinner and whose name was now anglicised to 'George Peperlok', took out letters of denization.[126] In 1427 and 1431, Jan Danckaerd was a searcher in the guild of the goldsmiths in Bruges.[127] Five years later, one John Dankaerd, very likely the same person, swore the oath of fealty in Southwark.[128] He paid the alien subsidy between 1440 and 1443, running a goldsmith's workshop together with two alien servants.[129]

A revolt against Maximilian of Austria, then ruler of the Low Countries, broke out in 1483. This involved most of the Flemish cities and raged on, with intervals, for nine years.[130] The alien subsidy assessments carried out in 1483, the year the revolt started, also provide us with one of the most extensive censuses of alien, and particularly 'Dutch', artisan activity both in

London and in certain other English cities and towns. This raises the possibility that the migration of skilled craftsmen overseas, recorded in these
1483 assessments, was just a temporary response to political problems at
home, and that numbers would have tailed off once the political position
was again stable. After the Bruges Revolt, in 1440, the Burgundian duke
radically lowered the fees to acquire citizenship in order to attract more
artisans to the city again, a measure that met with considerable success.[131]
Yet there are no known examples of return migration by skilled artisans
from the Low Countries who had moved to England. Rather, the English
evidence suggests that a substantial number of them stayed in the country
for longer periods, often for the rest of their lives.[132]

Native and alien craftsmen

In some English cities and towns, tensions emerged between the economic activities of immigrants and the privileges that English workers had
enjoyed for centuries. Even though most foreigners originated from places
where participation in production and retail depended just as much, if not
more, on membership of privileged associations of workers, many aliens
practised their trades in England without joining the local craft guilds
or the civic franchise of their adopted places of residence. As such, they
escaped regulation and did not share in the obligations that were expected
of enfranchised artisans. From the 1380s onwards, for example, the
London goldsmiths used their right to check the standard of all gold and
silver produced in the city to search the 'chambers' of those working outside their company, mainly 'Dutchmen'.[133] Members of the company were
also forbidden to employ unlicensed immigrants or to sell precious metals
to them.[134] However, while attempts to persuade aliens to buy temporary
licences or the freedom of the company and the city brought some under
fuller surveillance, such measures proved ineffective with most. In 1404 the
Cordwainers' Guild of London petitioned the king to take action against
the aliens who were working in the city without regard for its franchises.
Interestingly, it took all malicious immigrants to be 'cobblers', usually the
name given to those who repaired old shoes.[135] In fifteenth-century Great
Yarmouth, aliens from Holland and Zeeland engaged in a wide range of
occupations without joining the civic franchise. Dozens were fined year
after year, but meanwhile continued to ply their crafts and businesses.[136]

The desire to avoid native control also had an impact on the spatial
distribution of immigrants in towns and cities. The majority of those
who swore the oath of fealty in 1436–7 were craftspeople from the Low

Countries. That about 10 per cent of them had settled in Southwark was certainly not a coincidence. Southwark was outside the jurisdiction of London's craft guilds, though wardens of some livery companies, such as the goldsmiths, also had the power to search shops there.[137] Similarly, in Great Yarmouth, alien beer brewers established themselves in Southtown, on the other side of the river Yare, where the bailiffs of Great Yarmouth had no authority.[138] English attitudes towards illicit alien labour, however, were not always as consistent as they may seem. London's Company of Merchant Tailors denounced the activities of aliens as a threat to the interests of its members, but native tailors simultaneously employed large numbers of immigrants in their own workshops.[139] In chapter 2, we saw that governors in some cities and towns tried to eliminate alien competition by denying immigrants entry to the franchise; yet this often resulted in aliens moving their economic activities outside the physical bounds of urban jurisdictions – and thus, ironically, in a loss of control for the civic authorities.

The relationship between native and alien craftsmen became more problematic after 1450. The mid-century economic slump reduced many people's purchasing power and, consequently, the demand for consumer goods. Yet evidence suggests that this recession affected the opportunities for native artisans more than those for alien craftspeople. In 1450, the London cordwainers petitioned the king that young English-born men in the city could no longer live by their occupation.[140] One year later, both the cordwainers and the London tailors expressed concern to the mayor and aldermen that native apprentices could not practise their craft anymore.[141] And in 1451 or 1452, the Goldsmiths' Company complained about the unemployment of London-born goldsmiths.[142]

London's native craft guilds argued that their members' problems were caused by the unfair competition from alien artisans and the latter's habit of employing only fellow immigrants, instead of English apprentices. They made these views clear in a further stream of petitions and, exceptionally, through violent action. In chapter 10, we shall see that several physical attacks on aliens in London were instigated by English craftsmen who believed that immigrants took away their livelihoods. The lobbying of the native craft guilds also resulted in the protectionist legislation discussed in chapter 2. In 1484, for example, a statute was passed that only aliens with letters of denization could exercise a craft or occupation and employ servants other than their sons or daughters.[143]

Unsurprisingly, these measures brought little relief, since the supposed evil of immigrant masters hiring exclusively alien servants was not, in reality, the reason why young English artisans were unable to attract custom and went out of business. What the native artisans' petitions actually reveal is that, in times of decreasing purchasing power, English consumers wanted the goods and services provided by immigrant craftsmen over those supplied by natives. Some evidence from this period even refers to a preference for alien skills. In the Essex village of Havering atte Bower, an English resident asked a friend to recommend him 'a mason that is a Dutchman or a Fleming' in 1469. The man wanted a brick chimney, and aliens, he believed, were better at making those. Only if no 'Dutchmen' or Flemings were available would he consider a young Englishman.[144] Complaints about the unemployment of English manufacturers and the immigrant population's responsibility for these problems continued well into the Elizabethan period.[145] By failing to address native producers' own shortages of skills, however, they were both unrealistic and, therefore, ineffective.

'Merchant strangers'

Many of the consumer goods that were in demand in later medieval England, as well as the raw materials needed by the manufacturing industries, were not available locally and had to be imported from abroad. In addition to bringing in more mundane goods, Italian ships supplied high-value commodities such as spices, satin, velvet and other silks, glass, jewellery and precious stones. Merchants of the Hanseatic League provided products from the Baltic, Scandinavia and Russia, including wood, furs, wax and amber. Traders from the Low Countries sold textiles, foodstuffs and haberdashery, while those from France and the Iberian Peninsula brought in wine and iron.[146] The Italian and Hanseatic merchants had their operational headquarters in London, but their agents also organised shipping in and out of Southampton and Sandwich (for the Italians) and Ipswich, Lynn, Boston and Hull (for the Hansards). Most of these merchants stayed in England only very briefly. The views of hosts, the records of the transactions of foreign merchants overseen by English hosts between 1440 and 1444, make clear that nearly all traders from the Low Countries made their sales and purchases within one day.[147] Italian merchants and shipping staff stayed for longer periods – the Venetian galleys sometimes up to several months – but many of them still returned home at the end of the trading season. A number of these transient Italians still got caught in the net of the alien subsidies. We have already encountered many of the more prominent merchants in question in chapter 5. There were also at least a few of menial status: in 1441 and 1456, six members of Italian shipping crews, all provided with the apt surname 'Galleyman', were assessed towards the alien taxes in London.[148]

A minority of foreign merchants resided in England on a more or less permanent basis. Between 1440 and 1487, Italian merchants and merchant staff were assessed for the alien subsidies on 873 occasions.[149] Several of these represent repeat appearances by the same individuals over several years; indeed, there are thirty-two Italians – all but one Genoese – whose presence in England is attested for at least ten years.[150] Those who considered broadening their activities in England became freemen of the city of London, joined one of its livery companies, and/or took out denizenship. Before 1550, nineteen of the fifty-six Italians in receipt of denization were specifically described as merchants in their letters patent, reflecting their wealth and conspicuous presence. In 1452–3, the Venetian Jacopo Falleron became a member of the London Drapers' Company and received denization.[151] The Lucchese Carlo Gigli brought his wife Camilla Cagnoli with him from Bruges and took out letters of denization for both of them in 1460.[152] A number of Italian merchants also married English women. The Genoese Percivalle Marchesani, who paid the subsidy in 1443, was married to the Londoner Alice Hill, member of an important mercer family; and the Florentine merchant banker and long-term taxpayer Belisardo de Bardi also had an English wife.[153] Some Italian merchants died in England and chose to be buried there.[154]

Some of the Italian merchants in London employed impressive alien households. Benedetto Borromei not only had a foreign cook but also an anonymous alien butler working for him in London.[155] Pancrazio Giustiniani, from Genoa and living in London's Langbourn ward in 1483, employed no fewer than eight foreigners in his service, while in Bishopsgate ward Gherardo Canigiani, the Florentine manager of the Medici Bank, had two.[156] Also living in with the Italian taxpayers were their so-called *garzoni*, youngsters who stayed with established merchants to learn the trade. The alien subsidies caught some of these in the early stages of a long and successful career. In 1444, Agnolo Tani worked as a servant in the household of the Florentine Gerozzo de' Pigli in Langbourn ward.[157] Ten years later, Tani would be appointed manager of the Bruges branch of the Medici bank and be immortalised as the subject of some of Hans Memling's paintings.[158]

The presence of the Hansards, the most important foreign merchant group in England alongside the Italians, is somewhat obscured by the exemptions from all forms of national taxation that the Hanseatic League had been claiming for centuries. The question of whether the leading merchants of the Hanse evident in the customs accounts and other English documentation were permanently located in England remains unanswered, but a glimpse of their activities within the alien subsidy returns provides some sense of which of their number were considered to be long-term residents.

No Hanseatic traders are known to have paid the alien subsidies during the 1440s. In London in 1456, however, three of them were assessed, either by accident or by design, in the newly introduced and more costly category for merchants.[159] In April and August 1457, fourteen Easterlings (the name commonly given to Hansards) were again assessed in London to pay the tax.[160] The year 1468 witnessed significant activity. English ships had been seized by the Danish king as a reprisal for depredations by English merchants. Confronted with the Danes' refusal to offer compensation for the damage and knowing that seamen from the Hanseatic city of Danzig had been involved in the action, the English crown ordered the arrest of all Hansards in England in July 1468.[161] It is impossible to determine whether the alien subsidy assessment for this year was made before or after the arrest, but the number of Hanseatic traders listed in the London tax return (twenty-eight) comes remarkably close to the known number of those arrested (thirty).[162] The taxpayers included the young Cologne merchant Gerhard von Wesel, mistakenly classified as a Clevelander, who at the time of the problems was the alderman of the Steelyard, the Hanseatic office in London. Von Wesel led the negotiations with the English crown with Peter Bodenclop, who was also assessed for the alien subsidy. Capitalising on the divisions within the Hanseatic League, Edward IV released from custody all the Hansards of Cologne, who were eager not to get entangled in the difficulties of Danzig and the other northern and eastern Hanseatic cities. Under pressure from his hometown, Von Wesel then established a separate Cologne Steelyard in London in May 1469, which was provided with its own privileges by the English crown.[163] This explains why, in the alien subsidy for June 1469, only eleven Easterlings from Cologne, including von Wesel and Bodenclop, were recorded as liable to the alien subsidy in London.[164] The other Hanseatic members were furious, and Cologne was expelled from the league in 1471. Even though all arrested Hansards were eventually released and the Hanse cities were reconciled in 1476, Gerhard von Wesel remained *persona non grata* for several more years. In 1483, fourteen 'Teutonic' merchants were made liable to the alien subsidy in London, together with four of their servants, but it is unclear whether any were actually Hansards.[165]

The records of the confiscation of alien property by the crown during the late thirteenth and early fourteenth centuries reveal that large numbers of Flemish and French merchants were then permanently based in England.[166] The alien subsidies paint a very different picture for the fifteenth century. During the time that the taxes were collected, only five people from the Low Countries were listed with the occupational designation of merchant. Two came from Brabant, one from Flanders and one from Liège; the other was described as 'Dutch'.[167] Two other Flemish men worked as mercers.[168] Letters of denization supply some additional names of traders from the Low Countries who established themselves in England. Godfrey and Peter van Upstall, both from Brabant, settled in York in the late fourteenth and early fifteenth centuries.[169] Laurence Swarfeld, who came from Bruges and Antwerp and took out letters of denization in 1468, exported cloth from London.[170] Hundreds of Burgundian subjects swore the oath of fealty to the English king in 1436, but none did so as a merchant. However, these figures do not reflect the total number of resident immigrants from the Low Countries involved in trade. Many of the men classified solely as artisans in the subsidies or the oaths combined manufacture with commercial activities. In Great Yarmouth, dozens of immigrants from Holland and Zeeland were fined for pursuing a craft and working as common merchants outside the civic franchise. Yet the alien subsidy returns and the records of the oath of fealty only mention people in Great Yarmouth, and elsewhere, by their occupations as craftsmen.[171]

Only one person from any other part of Europe, the Catalan Michael Desmas, was listed explicitly as a merchant in the alien subsidy rolls.[172] Five immigrants were referred to as mercers: Thomas Breknok (likely of Welsh extraction) and William Warde (whose origins are unknown), both working in Bristol in 1440; John White, an Irishman living at Westbury in Wiltshire in 1441–3; the Frenchman William Brown in Northampton between 1449 and 1458; and Henry Johnson, 'Teutonic', in London in 1483.[173] Moses Contarini, a Venetian-born merchant from Bordeaux who was very active in the import of wine and woad and the export of cloth in Bristol, acquired letters of denization in 1461: he was apparently the only person leaving Gascony at the end of the Hundred Years War to take out this privilege.[174] Here, too, however, the occupational categories used by jurors and tax assessors certainly obscured the overall number of resident aliens engaged in trade. Maryanne Kowaleski's research in Exeter's civic records has shown that a Gascon and two Guernseymen recorded in the alien subsidy without occupational designations worked as merchants in the city.[175]

The cloth industry

The large-scale involvement of immigrant workers in the English cloth industry predates the Black Death. In the 1330s, the crown launched a series of measures with the intention of transforming England from a wool- into a cloth-exporting country. All inhabitants of the realm were henceforth allowed to make woollen cloth. The import of foreign textiles was discouraged, except for the higher orders of society. The need for additional revenues to finance the start of the Hundred Years War was met by large increases in the duties levied on the export of wool, which acted as a disincentive to trading in this raw material. Skilled alien cloth workers were encouraged to settle and were promised all the necessary rights. This promotion of the native English cloth industry coincided with, and contributed to, a crisis in the Low Countries. After having dominated high-quality cloth production in Europe for centuries, the Flemish cities could no longer compete. These economic problems added to the social unrest that had characterised Flanders since the twelfth century. The politics of the Flemish towns were fraught with in-fighting and the autonomous cities opposed their overlord, the count of Flanders. Confrontations were customarily concluded with the banishment of the losing parties from Flemish soil.[176]

Cloth workers played a prominent role in each of these conflicts and, consequently, were sometimes exiled abroad. Their destination of choice was England. The most significant exodus of this kind took place in 1352. Having rebelled against the count and set up an alternative government, over 1,300 people were banished from Flanders, most of them involved in the production of cloth. After Edward III had granted letters of protection to all exiles who wished to settle in England, at least fifty-six of them established themselves with their families in London. Fifty-five took up residence in the Norfolk port of Great Yarmouth and twenty-seven in the Essex town of Colchester. Smaller numbers went to Lynn, Norwich and York. In each of these places, they engaged in the local cloth industry. Following the invasion of the duchy of Brabant and the imposition of an economic stranglehold by the Flemish count in 1356, Brabantine textile workers increasingly made their way to England as well.[177]

The contribution of these exiles and other immigrant cloth workers from the Low Countries to the development of the English textile industry remains a matter of debate. Considering Edward III's initiatives as a forerunner of later, mercantilist policies, nineteenth- and early twentieth-century historians believed the crown's efforts to attract skilled Flemish weavers were highly effective and jump-started the late medieval boom in the country's cloth industry. Later observers were far more sceptical and either nuanced or dismissed the effects of the immigration of cloth workers from the continent.[178] Yet, while there is no evidence that the influx of Flemish or Brabantine weavers had a nationwide impact, several of the places mentioned above experienced a growth of their cloth industry during the years when textile workers from the Low Countries settled there. Colchester, for example, did not have a sizable cloth production of its own before the start of the 1350s. In the years that followed the arrival of the Flemings, the manufacture of russets (grey and brown shaded cloth) took off. Business expanded dramatically so that, by the 1390s, Colchester had become the single most important cloth market in Essex and Suffolk, exporting to many parts of Europe. The strength of its textile industry allowed the town to ward off the economic and social problems that so many other English urban centres experienced during the late medieval period.[179] Similarly, although Great Yarmouth is often regarded as a prominent example of urban decay, its cloth manufacturers actually flourished throughout the second half of the fourteenth century, when Flemish textile workers arrived in the town.[180]

Even though the influx of cloth makers from the Low Countries started before the outbreak of the plague, the economic consequences of the Black Death undoubtedly influenced their work in England. The increase in purchasing power that occurred during the second half of the fourteenth century resulted in a stronger domestic demand for high-quality fabrics. Cloth workers from the Low Countries had the skills, capital and organisation to produce these types of textiles. The aulnage accounts, which record the payment of a fee for the measurement and sealing of cloth when it was sold on the domestic market, make clear that, in London, a small number of exiles and other immigrant workers from Flanders and Brabant dominated the manufacture of coloureds (the most expensive, heavily finished kind of cloth) and rays (medium-quality fabrics with striped bands or checks dyed in the yarn) during the 1370s. Employing their fellow Flemings in the different stages of the cloth making process, these men serviced the royal household and the nobility, substituting for the import of foreign cloth, and also exported small amounts abroad. The success of London's alien cloth makers created envy among the city's native weavers, who struggled with the falling demand for their lower-quality cloth and the competition of provincial textile workers. Determined to maintain control over the capital's cloth industry, they challenged the Flemings not only in Parliament but also, as we shall see in chapter 10, in the street.[181]

By the second quarter of the fifteenth century, the immigration of Flemish cloth makers had already passed its peak. Twenty-four weavers from the Low Countries swore the oath of fealty to the crown in 1436, making it only the fourth most common occupation among those receiving the resulting licences to remain. Most of these twenty-four came from Brabant and lived in the southern counties of Kent, Essex and Suffolk. Between 1440 and 1487, people were recorded as weavers on 224 occasions in the alien subsidies. Twenty of these taxpayers were recorded as 'Dutch', nineteen as 'Teutonic', another nineteen as Flemish, six as Brabanters and one as a Clevelander. Nine were Scottish, seven were French (including Normans), two came from Milan and one from Genoa. Five aliens were assessed as fullers, two of them from France and Normandy, and three as drapers. Seven alien women were recorded as spinsters (that is, spinners of wool).[182]

These alien cloth makers were spread over England, though with some notable concentrations. Most of the recorded French and Norman textile workers lived in Wiltshire, the Scottish ones in Yorkshire and Cambridgeshire. Three Italian weavers worked in the cloth town of Abingdon in Berkshire in 1483.[183] Throughout the 1440s, Boston in Lincolnshire was home to fifteen alien weavers, whose origins, unfortunately, were not specified.[184] Twelve alien cloth workers, all of them 'Dutch' or Flemish, lived in Northampton during the 1440s and 1450s.[185] Eighteen 'Teutonic' weavers worked in London in 1483.[186] Great Yarmouth and Colchester, the two other places that attracted so many Flemish weavers in the fourteenth century, only had one alien cloth worker each assessed towards the alien subsidies between 1440 and 1487.[187]

Between the middle of the fourteenth and the middle of the fifteenth century, the push factors that had driven numerous cloth makers from the Low Countries across the Channel had changed significantly. Provoked by the problems of the fourteenth century, many Flemish cities had reoriented their economies away from large-scale cloth production and towards the manufacture of high-value finished goods.[188] Unsurprisingly, then, highly skilled artisans, rather than weavers and fullers, made up the bulk of the immigrants from the Low Countries recorded in the alien subsidies. Following the arrival of the Burgundian dynasty in Flanders and the expansion of the apparatus of government from the end of the fourteenth century onwards, collective exile had also been progressively abandoned as a punishment for urban rebellions.[189] As a result, England no longer attracted the wealthy clothiers who had been banished for political subversion in the fourteenth century, and who had employed many of their fellow Flemish cloth workers. Only four alien cloth makers recorded in the English alien subsidy returns had more than two alien servants: the 'Dutchman' Lander Creto had three in Northampton in 1440; John Truner had five at Staines in Middlesex in 1455; and in London in 1483, Richard Hawke and Marchus Kyng, both 'Teutonic', had four and five respectively.[190] No alien cloth maker is known to have purchased letters of denization in the fifteenth century.

Tellingly, the biggest employer of alien textile workers during the second half of the fifteenth century was not an immigrant, but an Englishman. In 1483, the Londoner John Stanesby had no fewer than eleven alien cloth makers, including one woman, on the payroll in the Suffolk town of Bildeston. All were designated by the alien subsidy assessors as Italians, possibly because of Stanesby's Italian business connections. The names of the taxpayers, however, strongly suggest they originated from the Low Countries: Artisan [sic] Desmer, Barbett Fandermer, Peter Fanhobard, James Kacelotes and so on.[191] Drawing on his alien workforce, Stanesby was able to produce on a larger scale than his competitors and delivered 10 per cent of Suffolk's total cloth output.[192]

It is only in the second half of the sixteenth century that clear evidence survives to show cloth workers from the Low Countries once again migrating to England in numbers comparable to, and, indeed, higher than, those of the fourteenth century. Weavers and other related occupations are notably absent, again, from the letters of denization in the first half of the sixteenth century. In the 1560s, however, Protestant cloth workers from the Low Countries seeking to escape religious persecution settled in Canterbury, Sandwich, Colchester and London.[193] Most of this new wave of 'Dutch' immigrants went to Norwich, where, in the 1580s, they represented about a third of the city's population.[194] They would contribute significantly to the further development of the English cloth industry, just as their predecessors from the Low Countries had done in the fourteenth century.

Skilled immigrants from other parts of Europe thus made a vital contribution to the development of the English economy during the fourteenth, fifteenth and sixteenth centuries. Alien artisans filled labour shortages and introduced new technologies in the country's fashion industries, the building trades and the provision of food and drink. Together with Italian, German and other merchants, they catered for the quickly changing tastes of English consumers. Yet while their presence has received most attention, both from contemporaries and from historians, the relatively prosperous, high-status and predominantly male groups of immigrant craftspeople and merchants were only a minority of the aliens resident in England between the early fourteenth and late sixteenth centuries. The country was also home to thousands of unskilled workers, people of lower standing and women from abroad. Their lives and experiences will be explored in chapter 7.

Notes

1 Bolton, ' "The world upside down" ', pp. 22–45; Hatcher, 'Plague, population and the English economy'; Penn and C. Dyer, 'Wages and earnings'.
2 Dyer, *Standards of Living*, p. 276.
3 Kowaleski, 'A consumer economy'.
4 Sutton, 'Dress and fashions'.
5 Kowaleski, 'A consumer economy', pp. 247–9.
6 Newton, *Fashion in the Age of the Black Prince*, pp. 8–13.
7 Davies, 'The Tailors of London', pp. 250–1.
8 Swanson, *Medieval Artisans*, pp. 45–8.
9 E 179/180/111, rot. 6. See also Amor, *Late Medieval Ipswich*, p. 211.
10 E 179/184/212.
11 *CPR 1429–36*, pp. 542–62.
12 E 179/387/8, Part 1, mm. 3–5; E 179/196/100.
13 E 179/113/104.
14 Fleming, 'Identity and belonging', pp. 175–93; Childs, 'Irish merchants and seamen', pp. 34–42.
15 Bolton, 'Irish migration', 14.
16 *CPR 1429–36*, p. 544; E 179/184/212, rot. 9d.
17 *CPR 1446–52*, pp. 116, 123.
18 Sutton, 'George Lovekyn'.
19 *CPR 1429–36*, pp. 544, 555; E 179/144/42, m. 25; E 179/184/212; E 179/242/25.
20 *CPR 1441–6*, p. 316.
21 E 179/149/130, m. 2.
22 'London Lickpenny', p. 223, ll. 53–4.
23 E 179/242/25.
24 E 179/180/111, rot. 6. See also Amor, *Late Medieval Ipswich*, pp. 210–11.
25 *CPR 1485–94*, p. 371.
26 Archer, *History of the Haberdashers' Company*, pp. 8–9.
27 *CPR 1429–36*, pp. 537–52.
28 E 179/108/130, mm. 2–3.
29 Cherry, 'Leather'.
30 Swann, 'English and European shoes', pp. 17–20.
31 Cherry, 'Leather', pp. 308–10.
32 *CPR 1429–36*, pp. 539–87.
33 E 179/235/4, m. 4. See also Lee, *Cambridge and its Economic Region*, pp. 76–81.
34 E 179/180/111, rot. 6. See also Amor, *Late Medieval Ipswich*, p. 218.

35 E 179/242/25.

36 *CPR 1429–36*, p. 545; E 179/184/212, rot. 9d; E 179/43/5, m. 2; E 179/242/25.

37 E 179/180/111, rot. 6. Amor, *Late Medieval Ipswich*, pp. 239–40 identifies him as Jurgoll Bolton.

38 *CPR 1467–77*, p. 402.

39 *CLBL L*, p. 172; E 179/242/25, m. 16d. See also *Alien Communities*, p. 102.

40 Swanson, *Medieval Artisans*, p. 58.

41 William Feeld, for example, was an Irish glover in 1440 in Northampton: E 179/155/80, rot. 3.

42 Egan and Forsyth, 'Wound wire and silver gilt'.

43 Reddaway and Walker, *Goldsmiths' Company*, pp. 47–8, 79, 120.

44 *CPR 1429–36*, pp. 538–62.

45 E 179/242/25.

46 Reddaway and Walker, *Goldsmiths' Company*, pp. 120, 125–6, 171.

47 Sutton, 'Marcellus Maures'. For his alien subsidy assessment in 1483, see E 179/242/25, m. 9d.

48 *Alien Communities*, p. 108; Reddaway and Walker, *Goldsmiths' Company*, p. 172. For his alien subsidy assessment in 1483, see E 179/242/25, m. 10d.

49 Reddaway and Walker, *Goldsmiths' Company*, p. 172.

50 Reddaway and Walker, *Goldsmiths' Company*, p. 4.

51 E 179/196/100; E 179/196/105, m. 2; E 179/387/8, mm. 1, 3–5.

52 For Batyn, see E 179/113/104, m. 7; E 179/113/103 Part 2, m. 5. For Cok, see Kowaleski, 'Assimilation of foreigners', pp. 175–7.

53 Dobson, 'Aliens in the city of York', p. 262.

54 *CPR 1401–5*, p. 204.

55 For Nicholas Colayn, see E 179/217/45, m. 4; E 179/217/51, mm. 2, 5; E 179/217/50, m. 2. For his entry in the freemen's registers, see *Registers of the Freemen, I*, p. 157. For John Colan, see E 179/217/68; E 179/217/74, m. 2; E 179/21/76, m. 2; E 179/217/74, m. 2.

56 *Testamenta Eboracensia IV*, pp. 58–60.

57 Campbell, 'Gold, silver and precious stones', pp. 132–4.

58 Harris, 'Two Byzantine craftsmen', pp. 387–403.

59 For the trade in general, see Caple, 'The detection and definition of an industry'.

60 Blair, *European Armour*, pp. 77, 92–107.

61 For Warter, see *Registers of the Freemen, I*, p. 130; E 179/217/51, mm. 2, 4. For Toteler, see chapter 9.

62 Moore, 'Brick', pp. 211–12; Smith, *Medieval Brickmaking Industry*, pp. 2–3.

63 Salzman, *Building in England*, p. 147.

64 Moore, 'Brick', p. 214; Lambert, 'Scandinavian immigrants', pp. 118–19.

65 Moore, 'Brick', pp. 212–14; Smith, *Medieval Brickmaking Industry*, pp. 4–22.

66 Moore, 'Brick', pp. 214, 232–4.

67 *CPR 1429–36*, p. 560.

68 E 179/73/109, m. 2.

69 'Building accounts of Kirby Muxloe Castle', pp. 205–6, 208.

70 Harvey and Oswald, *English Medieval Architects*, p. 310.

71 Moore, 'Brick', p. 214. Surnames include 'German', 'Vryze' and 'Bruyn': Knoop and Jones, 'The building of Eton College', pp. 93, 103.
72 Smith, *Medieval Brickmaking Industry*, pp. 7, 69. See the many references to Baldwin in *The Building Accounts of Tattershall Castle*.
73 E 179/242/24, m. 1; E 179/136/215, Part 2, m. 2.
74 Smith, *Medieval Brickmaking Industry*, p. 69.
75 Salzman, *Building in England*, p. 259.
76 E 179/180/111, rots 5–6.
77 Dymond and Paine (eds), *Five Centuries of an English Parish Church*, pp. 14–20.
78 E 179/180/111, rot. 4.
79 Allan, 'Breton woodworkers'.
80 Marks, *Stained Glass*, p. 205.
81 *CPR 1429–36*, p. 578; E 179/235/6; E 179/149/31; E 179/149/138; E 179/269/42, m. 2; E 179/149/161.
82 King, 'A glazier from the bishopric of Utrecht'.
83 E 179/149/130, m. 4; E 179/149/145, m. 1; E 179/149/148, m. 2; E 179/149/150, m. 2; E 179/269/42, m. 2; King, *Medieval Stained Glass of St Peter Mancroft*, p. 139.
84 E 179/124/120, m. 2; E 179/253/63; E 179/124/129, m. 2; Caviness, *Windows of Christ Church Cathedral Canterbury*, pp. 251–73.
85 Kowaleski, 'Assimilation of foreigners', p. 177.
86 E 179/117/52; E 179/117/154, m. 2; E 179/117/49, m. 3.
87 E 179/180/111, rot. 2.
88 Marks, *Stained Glass*, p. 206.
89 E 179/149/126, m. 5; E 179/149/138, m. 2; E 179/253/3, m. 1.
90 *CPR 1446–52*, p. 255.
91 E 179/253/3, m. 1.
92 Marks, 'Window glass', pp. 265–7.
93 Dyer, 'Changes in diet', p. 28.
94 E 179/195/33, m. 2.
95 E 179/184212, rot. 10; E 199/43/5, m. 2.
96 Dyer, 'Changes in diet', p. 28.
97 Campbell, 'A fair field once full of folk'.
98 E 179/158/41.
99 Thielemans, *Bourgogne et Angleterre*, pp. 299–300.
100 *CPR 1429–36*, p. 581.
101 E 179/235/3, m. 1; E 179/235/23, m. 10.
102 Bennett, *Ale, Beer, and Brewsters*, pp. 79–82.
103 E 179/180/111, rot. 6.
104 E 179/242/25.
105 Liddy and Lambert, 'Civic franchise', pp. 130–3. The only immigrant assessed as a beer brewer was Clays Boone in 1450: E 179/235/37, m. 6.
106 Bennett, *Ale, Beer, and Brewsters*, pp. 83–90.
107 E179/149/177, m. 2.
108 E 179/180/111, rot. 3; rot. 6, m. 1.
109 Liddy and Lambert, 'Civic franchise', pp. 130–2.

110 E 179/242/25, mm. 7d, 12.

111 *CPR 1485–94*, pp. 205, 301.

112 See chapter 3.

113 *CLBL K*, pp. 205, 301. See also chapter 10.

114 Carlin, *Medieval Southwark*, pp. 160–1.

115 Van Der Wee, 'Structural changes', pp. 212–15.

116 Blockmans, 'The creative environment', pp. 11–20.

117 Thoen, 'Immigration to Bruges'.

118 Gottschalk, *Stormvloeden en rivieroverstromingen in Nederland, II*, p. 74.

119 *CPR 1429–36*, p. 583; E 179/242/9, m. 1d.

120 *CPR 1429–36*, p. 580.

121 Vaughan, *Philip the Good*, pp. 31–50.

122 Dumolyn and Haemers, 'Patterns of urban rebellion'.

123 Dumolyn, *De Brugse Opstand*.

124 Bruges City Archives, Registers Wetsvernieuwingen, 1422–43, fols 54v, 81v, 107r–v.

125 E 179/144/42, m. 24. For further assessments in 1443, see E 179/144/52, m. 15; E 179/144/53, m. 10; E 179/144/50, m. 25.

126 *CPR 1441–6*, p. 207.

127 Bruges City Archives, Registers Wetsvernieuwingen, 1422–43, fols 43v, 71r.

128 *CPR 1429–36*, p. 538.

129 E 179/184/212, rot. 9d; E 179/43/5, m. 2.

130 Haemers, *De strijd om het regentschap*.

131 Blockmans and Prevenier, *The Promised Lands*, pp. 168–9.

132 *Alien Communities*, pp. 26–7.

133 Forbes, 'Search, immigration and the goldsmiths' company'.

134 Reddaway and Walker, *Goldsmiths' Company*, pp. 47–8, 122–6.

135 SC 8/182/9055.

136 Liddy and Lambert, 'Civic franchise', pp. 128–41.

137 Carlin, *Medieval Southwark*, pp. 119–28.

138 Liddy and Lambert, 'Civic franchise', pp. 132–3.

139 Davies, 'The Tailors of London', p. 168.

140 SC 8/345/E1323.

141 *CLBL K*, pp. 335–8.

142 Reddaway and Walker, *Goldsmiths' Company*, p. 127.

143 *SR*, II, 489–93.

144 Thrupp, 'Aliens in and around London', p. 121.

145 Luu, *Immigrants and the Industries of London*, pp. 154–7.

146 Bolton, 'Alien Merchants', pp. 135–55; *Views of Hosts*, pp. xl–xliii.

147 *Views of Hosts*, pp. 140–1, 144–5, 149–50, 151–4.

148 E 179/144/42, mm. 9, 24; E 179/235/58, m. 1.

149 See further discussion in chapter 5.

150 Guidi-Bruscoli and Lutkin, 'Perception, identity and culture', pp. 98.

151 *CPR 1446–52*, p. 552; Bradley, 'Italian Merchants in London', pp. 314–15. For his continuing liability to the alien subsidies, see chapter 3; and for other aspects of his career, see chapter 10.

152 Lambert, '"Nostri fratelli da Londra"', pp. 97–8.
153 *Views of Hosts*, p. 293; C 1/31/321.
154 Guidi-Bruscoli and Lutkin, 'Perception, identity and culture', pp. 98–9.
155 E 179/235/23, m. 10.
156 *Alien Communities*, pp. 68, 72.
157 E 179/144/54, m. 23.
158 De Roover, *Rise and Decline of the Medici Bank*, pp. 87–9.
159 E 179/235/58, m. 1.
160 E 179/144/72; E 179/236/74.
161 Fudge, *Cargoes, Embargoes, and Emissaries*, pp. 50–6.
162 E 179/236/111.
163 For what follows, see *ODNB*, LVIII, 172–3; Fudge, *Cargoes, Embargoes, and Emissaries*, pp. 63–6.
164 E 179/144/67.
165 E 179/242/25, m. 8.
166 Lambert and Ormrod, 'A matter of trust', 208–26.
167 E 179/235/58/1; E 179/95/126 Part 1, m. 3; E 179/180/111, rot. 6.
168 E 179/180/111, rot. 5.
169 Twycross, 'Some aliens in York', pp. 367–8. For their denizations, see *CPR 1391-6*, p. 285; *CPR 1413-16*, p. 295.
170 *CPR 1467-77*, p. 87; *Overseas Trade of London*, pp. 450–1, 456, 505, 573, 577.
171 Liddy and Lambert, 'Civic franchise', pp. 136–7.
172 E 179/144/64, m. 3.
173 E 179/113/104, mm. 7, 11; E 179/196/105, m. 3; E 179/387/8 Part 1, m. 5; E 179/155/88, m. 4; E 179/155/104, m. 2; E 179/242/25, m. 10d.
174 *Overseas Trade of Bristol*, pp. 101–2, 111, 147–8, 151–3, 207, 213; *CPR 1461-7*, p. 41.
175 Kowaleski, 'Assimilation of foreigners', p. 176.
176 Dumolyn and Haemers, 'Patterns of urban rebellion'; Dumolyn and Pajic, 'Enemies of the count and of the city'.
177 Lambert and Pajic, 'Drapery in exile'; Lambert and Pajic, 'Immigration and the common profit'.
178 See the overview of the historiography in Lambert and Pajic, 'Drapery in exile', pp. 734–6.
179 Lambert and Pajic, 'Drapery in exile', pp. 749–53.
180 Saul, 'English towns', p. 8.
181 Lambert and Pajic, 'Immigration and the common profit', pp. 642–52.
182 See chapter 7.
183 E 179/73/109, m. 2.
184 E 179/136/206; E 179/136/243, m. 5; E 179/242/24.
185 E 179/155/80; E 179/155/95; E 179/155/100-1; E 179/155/104, m. 2.
186 E 179/242/25.
187 E 179/149/126, m. 5; E 179/108/113, m. 6.
188 Van Der Wee, 'Structural changes', pp. 212–15.
189 Dumolyn and Pajic, 'Enemies of the count and of the city', pp. 499–500.

190 E 179/155/80, rot. 3; E 179/235/57, m. 4; E 179/242/25, mm. 9, 10d.
191 E 179/180/111, rot. 4.
192 Amor, 'Merchant adventurer or jack of all trades', pp. 426–7.
193 Goose, 'The "Dutch" in Colchester'.
194 Wilson, 'The textile industry', p. 221.

7

Wealth, status and gender

'And great treasure is brought out of this your realm by the same aliens'[1]

One of the main driving forces behind the introduction of the alien subsidy and the hosting regulations in the Parliament of 1439–40 was the belief that aliens living in the realm possessed far greater wealth than native-born people. Foreign traders, it was assumed, sold their imports dear, yet spent hardly any of their profits on English goods. As a consequence, the Commons told the king, 'the same alien merchants are greatly enriched, and your subject denizen merchants of your same realm are grievously impoverished'.[2] The view that alien merchants deprived the country of its wealth went back at least to the late fourteenth century and had been brought up time and again ever since, particularly at times of economic recession.[3]

England certainly attracted affluent, high-status immigrants during the later Middle Ages. We have already met a number of them in chapters 5 and 6. During the 1490s, for example, London was home to the staff of the Florentine merchant company of the heirs of Giovanni de Bardi, who were the bank of choice for the city's mercers and grocers, supplied precious cloth to the royal wardrobe and financed John Cabot's voyages to the Americas.[4] Living in an eighteen-room house off Lombard Street, they spent £840 on their household in five years, and paid out £107 on silverware alone between January 1493 and March 1494.[5] Another very successful immigrant was Giovanni Gigli, son of the Lucchese silk merchant Carlo Gigli. Born in Bruges, Giovanni obtained a degree in canon and civil law and, following his move to England and denization in 1477, became a papal collector and nuncio. Both Edward IV and Henry VII employed him in a range of diplomatic missions, and in 1490 he was made the English ambassador to Rome. In 1483, when his main domestic base was in London's Coleman Street ward, Giovanni was assessed for the alien subsidy with an entourage of eight foreign employees. At the end of his life he was made bishop of Worcester, though he held the office *in absentia*. He was succeeded at Worcester by his cousin Silvestro Gigli, an appointment that seemed to confirm the Commons' general resentment of the nepotism and financial opportunism allegedly practised by the alien clergy.[6]

What is most striking from the documentary evidence, however, is the presence in England of very high numbers of aliens who lived in much more modest, and sometimes even rather miserable, circumstances. In 1441 in London, fifty-eight non-householders, both men and women, were found too poor to pay the alien subsidy.[7] In 1464, another fifteen immigrants in the capital did not have the means to contribute the relatively low non-householder rate.[8] It is, of course, possible that these people feigned poverty in order to evade the tax, confirming the prejudices about alien residents that existed among parts of the English population: the returns for the 1441 and 1464 collections in London also contain suspiciously high numbers of aliens recorded as 'moved' or 'deceased'.[9] But other annotations in the subsidy documents are more difficult to mistake. Eleven aliens, all of them men and living in different parts of England throughout the 1440s, were described as beggars. Robert Stratford, for example, was found begging in Newington in Surrey in 1440, but still paid the non-householder rate towards the alien subsidy.[10] On the Westminster Abbey denization roll of the 1540s, twelve immigrants were branded as poor, two as beggars. The latter included the aptly named John Beca, a man who had begged during sixteen of the forty years he had been in England.[11]

The alien subsidy returns and, to a lesser extent, the denization rolls of the 1540s also reveal the existence of countless immigrants working in low-status jobs, who are hardly ever considered in other documents of the period and, consequently, are ignored in the existing historiography. This chapter will examine a number of groups that operated at a relatively modest – and, in some cases, veritably abject – social level, and will address both the towns and the rural landscapes of later medieval England. After analysing the presence of aliens among the lower reaches of the clergy, we will focus on the relatively small number of foreigners who managed to eke out an existence as tenant farmers before considering the thousands of alien people, from all over Europe, who worked in domestic service or helped out as skilled or unskilled labourers in the agricultural and the artisanal sectors. Finally, attention will be given to one of the most understudied groups among England's immigrants. Though they never particularly figured in the complaints of Parliament, immigrant women appear in significant numbers in the alien subsidy returns. We will assess their presence and investigate to what extent they benefited from developments that affected other parts of English society during the period after the Black Death.

Alien lower clergy

High-grossing dignitaries such as Giovanni Gigli were the most visible alien clergy in England. Others moved in exalted circles at court: Michael Dyaconi, a Norman professor of theology, for example, served as confessor to Henry VII and was granted letters of denization in 1495.[12] But these men were hardly representative of the majority of foreign clerics in the country. Plague took a heavy toll among parish priests, who often had direct contact with sick parishioners.[13] Estimates of mortality among beneficed parish clergy in several English dioceses between 1348 and 1353 range from 40 per cent to as high as 60 per cent.[14] Having to replace many priests, bishops struggled to fill parish vacancies. Unsurprisingly, stipendiary priests now demanded higher fees, leading to the imposition of salary caps and complaints about clerical greed.[15] These conditions proved very attractive to churchmen from abroad.

Taxes on the clergy in late medieval England normally had to be imposed by the Convocations of the provinces of Canterbury and York, and collected under a separate system administered directly by the Church. The imposition of the alien subsidies is, in fact, the only instance before the Reformation where either beneficed or unbeneficed clergy were made routinely liable to a 'lay' poll tax granted in Parliament, and the fact that there was no recorded protest about this by the English clerical hierarchy may suggest that lower alien clergy were open to discrimination even from within their own order.[16] Aliens were assessed as parish clergy in the alien subsidy returns on 321 occasions between 1440 and 1487. In twenty-eight of these cases the immigrants were rectors, beneficed priests who lived off the endowment of their churches. In forty-eight cases the aliens had to content themselves with vicarages, caring for the souls of the parishioners where the rectories had been appropriated by religious houses or other patrons, who took most of the income for themselves. Most of the alien clergy assessed, however, did not hold benefices at all. In 188 instances they worked as chaplains, and in eleven cases as parish chaplains. On twenty-nine occasions, the immigrants were described more generically as priests, parish priests, pastors or parsons. Two alien 'celebrants' were assessed in Kent in 1440 and 1441.[17] Two Irish-born chantry priests, both working at Chippenham in Wiltshire in 1440, capitalised on the practice of saying daily masses for the spiritual benefit of wealthy benefactors.[18]

The wide range of clerical roles recorded in the alien subsidy documents provides a glimpse both of the importance of Catholic practice in England on the eve of the Reformation and of the English Church's significant reliance on people from abroad. Those who were in minor clerical orders, lower than that of priest or deacon, often had only very modest roles to fulfil. Nineteen aliens were annotated by the subsidy assessors as clerks or parish clerks, who attended on priests and were partly responsible for the upkeep of parish churches.[19] In the city of Lincoln, the Hollander Nicholas Jonson was described simply as 'servant' to the vicar of St Martin's in 1440, but as a 'former parish clerk' in 1441 and 1444.[20] One man, Gilam Frensshman at Feltham in Middlesex, paid the alien subsidy in 1440 as a holy water clerk; he was presumably charged with keeping the holy water safe and distributing it to households in the parish.[21] In London's Farringdon Within ward in 1483, the Scotsman John Porter worked as a summoner, calling people before the ecclesiastical courts.[22] Victims of Porter and his colleagues could resort to the likes of the Scotsman William Foster, who, as a pardoner, sold papal pardons and indulgences in Lincoln in 1451.[23] At the very bottom of the hierarchy, and usually outside all formal clerical orders, were the beadsmen, pensioners who said prayers for the benefactors of their almshouses. Elias Bourdeux, who had moved all the way from Gascony to end his days at Wylye in Wiltshire, was described as a beadsman in 1440.[24] The non-beneficed alien clergy and those in minor orders were part of what the historian William Pantin famously called the 'clerical proletariat' of late medieval England.[25]

Some of these alien churchmen had more than enough to get by. Fourteen, most commonly vicars, could afford one or, occasionally, two immigrant servants.[26] Six alien chaplains, coming from Scotland, Normandy and Germany, were prosperous enough to purchase letters of denization during the 1440s.[27] However, this did not automatically mean that people of such rank were free from financial worry. John Nesbit, a Scottish chaplain who purchased letters of denization in 1492, stated in his petition that he had lived in poverty for most of the fourteen years he had been in England and had to earn his keep by schoolteaching.[28] And in the 1540s, when the denization process was made more accessible for less well-off immigrants, three alien priests and a beadsman described as 'poor' took out denization papers.[29] Such instances reflect the wider possibility that members of the alien clergy looked to their patrons and parishioners to help subsidise the expense involved in the process of denization.

The alien clergy of England came predominantly from within the British Isles. In forty-eight of the 321 instances of clergy in the alien subsidy returns, the taxpayer was Irish. These figures reflect this presence imperfectly, since immigrants from Ireland were exempt from liability to the tax after 1442. Most of the people assessed were chaplains operating in Wiltshire and, to a lesser extent, in Kent. Their migration was clearly part of a longer and broader trend. The English ordination lists, the records of men wishing to be ordained to the priesthood, reveal a constant influx of Irish clergy, most of all to London, starting after the Black Death and continuing throughout the later Middle Ages.[30] When, in the 1390s, Irishmen living in England had to buy licences to remain, 141 of the 255 recipients who had their occupations recorded (55 per cent) were clergymen.[31] People from Ireland resident in the country were made to purchase licences again in 1413 and in 1430. In the first case twelve of the fifty-seven people recorded worked for the Church, and in the second case twenty-one out of sixty-seven.[32]

Men from Scotland account for thirty-seven of the instances of clergy assessed in the alien subsidy records. Most of these worked in Northumberland, but some also lived in the southern counties. The migration of Scottish clerics to England is very imperfectly recorded before the 1440s, but is corroborated in other sources of the later fifteenth century, most notably in the letters of protection granted by the Chancery. Of the 115 protections issued to Scotsmen in the 1480s, twenty-three were to churchmen. All but one of these people resided in England's southern counties.[33] As people from Wales were exempt from payment of the alien subsidies, it is hard to grasp the full scale of the migration of lower Welsh clergy to England. Nine Welsh clerics were granted licences to remain in England in 1413, but the sample here is very small and not indicative of the likely full extent of clerical migration.[34]

The alien subsidy returns record twenty-four churchmen from France, the Low Countries and Germany, but this is clearly an under-representation: the data are drawn predominantly from one county, Wiltshire, where an unusually high proportion of aliens were listed with both their nationality and their occupation. A better sense is derived from the Westminster denization roll of the 1540s, where 129 Norman, fifty-three French and twenty-seven Breton priests and other lower clergy are identifiable.[35] Whatever the precise scale of the phenomenon, it is clear that French clergymen were active in England long before the establishment of the Walloon churches and the immigration of Huguenots from the 1550s onwards.[36]

Husbandmen, yeomen and gentlemen

One of the largest social and occupational categories specified in the alien subsidy returns comprised the group known as husbandmen. Husbandmen were tenant farmers who rented land under a variety of forms of lease; crucially, the term was used to describe those who had sufficiently large holdings to support their families.[37] They were higher in status than people who in the high Middle Ages were often called cottars: those who held a tenancy of a few acres but made their living mostly by selling their own and their families' labour. Equally, though, husbandmen were very definitely inferior to the social group who, in the fifteenth century, became known as yeomen. These were substantial farmers who normally held by free tenure, had an income from their land of around £5–£10 a year and in some cases aspired to become members of the gentry.[38]

The label 'husbandman' was used in 368 instances in the surviving returns to the alien subsidies, almost all in the 1440s, and most frequently in three counties: Somerset (136), Dorset (106) and Buckinghamshire (seventy-eight). The remaining people identified with this occupation were scattered, in small numbers, in the regions to the south of the Severn–Wash line, from Somerset in the West to Norfolk in the East. Apart from seven cases in Lincolnshire, the term was not used to describe aliens anywhere else in the Midlands or the North, other than three isolated examples in Westmorland. This reflects the fact that husbandmen appeared mainly in the heavily manorialised regions of England that focused on grain production – though some may well have kept livestock, too. All these aliens, not surprisingly, were householders. Only a small number of husbandmen were ascribed a nationality, but these and the others that can be surmised from surname evidence indicates that the most numerous groups were the French (thirty-three, including four Normans and a Gascon), the Scots (fourteen) and the Irish (ten). A few also had other occupations: in Somerset in 1443, John White was described as a mill keeper and husbandman, and Gyllam Gylman (perhaps a Frenchman) as a cordwainer and husbandman.[39] It is especially striking that some alien husbandmen employed alien servants. Of the ten husbandmen recorded as doing so, the outstanding case is John Delf (presumably from Delft in Holland) who had no fewer than four aliens working for him on his farm in Somerset in 1443. (The exact location, unfortunately, is lacking.)[40] Alien husbandmen could therefore have acted as magnets for other foreigners looking for employment as labourers and servants in the agricultural economy. This may have been especially the case for the French, who were conspicuous both as husbandmen and as labourers.

With the possible exception of John Delf, however, it seems unlikely that many, if any, of the aliens described as husbandmen in mid-fifteenth-century England enjoyed much beyond a very basic level of self-sufficiency. It is striking that there are very few instances of first-generation immigrants in fifteenth-century England aspiring to the social labels used for the ranks of society immediately above husbandman: those of yeoman and gentleman. The term yeoman does occur very occasionally in the returns to the alien subsidies, but as often as not it is used in its older meaning, which continued to prevail in the fifteenth century, of a servant: clearly, a 'yeoman' non-householder was not the same thing as a substantial tenant farmer.[41] The nearest we come to an alien yeoman farmer may be James Skotte, presumably a Scotsman, who was enumerated for the alien subsidy at Chipping Camden in Gloucestershire in 1468.[42] Similarly, only one foreigner was ever described in the alien subsidy returns as a gentleman: that is, of the rank immediately above yeoman, and one that definitely considered itself to be part of gentle society. Revealingly, this case was not from the countryside, but from the city of London, in the person of John Griffyn, assessed in 1441.[43] He seems to have aspired to be part of a recognisable 'urban gentry' in England that sought to disguise its origins and trades by claiming equivalence with petty landed society in the shires.[44]

It is more than likely, of course, that the English-born descendants of at least a few of the first-generation immigrant husbandmen recorded in the alien subsidy returns subsequently rose up the social scale to establish themselves as yeomen farmers and even as minor gentry. Nevertheless, the impediments to such social mobility were real. In the towns, as we have seen in chapters 2 and 6, aliens could establish themselves in high-status crafts, be granted the franchise, and become core members of the civic elite. The absence of yeomen and gentlemen aliens in the countryside suggests that foreign husbandmen generally lived modest lives, and is an important indicator of the very limited opportunities for economic, social and political advancement generally available to immigrants in English rural society.

In search of better conditions: alien servants and labourers

Husbandmen were not the only people, of course, who employed alien servants. The economic conditions of post-plague England were particularly favourable to immigrant wage labourers. Many English servants died as a result of the successive outbreaks of plague – proportionately more, perhaps, than among the upper classes – and needed to be replaced.[45] Others took advantage of the labour shortage and moved into more rewarding occupations, leaving further gaps at the bottom of the occupational ladder that needed to be filled. Economic evidence also suggests that, certainly after 1380, real wages in England were higher than elsewhere in north-western Europe, making a service career in England an appealing prospect for potential migrants.[46]

It should be no surprise, then, that 'servant' was the single most frequent occupational label used in the alien subsidy rolls, attributed in 11,394 instances, or more than 71 per cent of those cases where status or work was identified. Another 162 had other, more specific jobs in the service sector. It should be stressed, however, that the definition of 'servant' during the later Middle Ages was a particularly fuzzy one, and could relate to a very wide range of professional activities. The term referred both to lifetime servants, who worked in service for their entire careers, and lifecycle servants, who only did so during a specific stage of their lives. The category comprised both live-in servants, who resided with their employers, and day labourers. Medieval servants could equally well be domestic personnel employed by wealthy households, junior commercial staff of merchant houses or agricultural workers helping out on manorial estates and tenant farms.[47]

Alien servants: nationalities

Alien servants' nationalities differed according to their places of residence in England. Even though their origins were often recorded only haphazardly, it seems clear that English cities and towns attracted waged labour from other parts of the British Isles and the nearest regions of continental Europe (apart from Scandinavia, which was remarkably absent).[48] The Italian merchants in London and Southampton hired mainly, though not exclusively, from their own lands. Of the eight members of staff working for the Genoese Pancrazio Giustiniani in London in 1483, for example, four were recorded as being Lombard and four as 'Teutonic' – although the names of at least two of the 'Teutonics', Pancrazio and Jacobus Piemonte, suggest that they, too, were Italians.[49] In exceptional cases, the Italians' personnel came from more distant locations. Filippo Cini, a Genoese merchant paying the alien subsidies in Southampton between 1466 and 1468, had a Moorish servant, Maria Moriana.[50]

Artisans from the Low Countries and Germany also preferred to employ people from their own regions of origin, sometimes including relatives. Gerard Johnson, from Flanders, had six fellow Flemings as servants in

Kent in 1488, one of whom, Harman Johnson, may have been related to his master.[51] Elias Cordwainer, a 'Dutch' shoe worker in Cambridge, also had six alien servants in 1440, five of them called 'Dutchman'.[52] In 1483, sixty-four alien women were working as servants in London, with English or alien craftspeople.[53] All of them were recorded as 'Teutonic'. Mariona Cornelys, for example, worked for the capper Gerard Codde, also 'Teutonic', together with two alien men in the city's Dowgate ward.[54] Unfortunately, the records do not allow us to establish whether these women were apprentices or household staff.

The proportion of servants among Scottish immigrants in fifteenth-century England was particularly high. On 763 instances (72 per cent) of the 1,050 occasions in which an occupation was given for Scottish men or women in the alien subsidy returns, the individuals in question were recorded as working in service. The overwhelming majority of these lived in England's northern counties: there are 223 recorded cases in Cumberland, 187 in York and Yorkshire, 132 in Northumberland and sixty-nine in Westmorland. Only 152 instances of Scottish servants were recorded south of the Humber.[55] The number of women in this group was unusually high. Whereas only 18 per cent of all instances of aliens in the subsidy returns were female, 38 per cent of those described as Scottish servants were female, rising to 43 and 46 per cent respectively in the northern counties of Cumberland and Westmorland.

Everything suggests that these Scots were unskilled immigrants of humble social backgrounds. They included far fewer fathers and husbands and more female heads of families than other alien taxpayers. Most of the Scottish servants lived alone and isolated, often being the only Scots in their places of residence. They flocked to towns and baronial seats, hoping to make some money helping craftsmen and artisans or in seasonal agricultural activities.[56] In Yorkshire, Scotsmen were found working as swineherds and cattle-herders.[57] Sixteen others in this county earned their living as labourers. Many of these Scottish immigrants were very mobile, having left their recorded English place of residence by the time the alien subsidy had to be paid. In Yorkshire again, eighteen Scottish women and thirteen Scottish men were explicitly labelled as 'vagabonds' during the 1440s and 1450s.[58] This term denoted people who travelled the country in search of employment, something that caused particular concern in a period when English authorities were desperately trying to establish control over the labour force. So lowly were these itinerant Scots that some were not recorded by name in the alien subsidy records, and in some cases it is not even possible to determine their gender.[59] They were probably people who migrated out of desperation, rather than aspiration. The fact that so many came to northern England, a region which, at this time, was struck by an agrarian crisis of its own and where attitudes towards Scots could be hostile, says a lot about the economic circumstances in their homelands beyond the Scottish border.[60]

Alien servants working in the South and West of England came, in most cases, from other parts of Europe. Unfortunately, the numbers of those hailing from Ireland are obscured by the fact that the Irish were only liable to pay the alien subsidy until 1442; and even before that date, Irish occupations were given in only 30 per cent of cases.[61] Despite this, Irishmen and women were described as servants in 227 instances between 1440 and 1442, by far the most frequent occupational designation for Irish immigrants in this period. Most of these servants lived in the West Country.

More remarkable is the significant presence of French servants in England's southern counties. Between 1440 and 1487, people from France (including Normandy and Brittany) working in English service were listed in the alien subsidy records on 1,382 occasions. The highest incidences were in Wiltshire (339), Devon (157) and Kent (108). Only sixty-one of these cases (4 per cent) are clearly recognisable as female. Some French servants may have been brought back by English landowners from their campaigns in the Hundred Years War and employed on their estates. Walter Hungerford, first Baron Hungerford, veteran of the Battle of Agincourt, former treasurer of England and speaker of the Commons, had a Norman serjeant at arms, Peter Herispin, who, in 1439, took out letters of denization.[62] In addition, Hungerford employed five alien servants on his estates in Heytesbury in Wiltshire, four of whom were French.[63] Sir John Pelham, who had also earned his spurs in the French wars and had served as chamberlain in the household of Henry V's consort, Queen Katherine, had four French servants in Shiplake hundred in Sussex in 1440.[64] Sir William Beauchamp, later Lord St Amand and Chamberlain of North Wales and son of a distinguished military commander in France, employed three alien servants, at least one of them French, at Bromham in Wiltshire in 1440.[65] Members of the county gentry may have followed the nobility's example. The Turberville family of Bere Regis in Dorset had two French grooms in 1440.[66] Eight other grooms from France or Normandy worked in Dorset, Wiltshire and Cornwall in the 1440s, while John Baynton, sheriff of Wiltshire in 1429 and 1443, had two French servants on his manor of Faulston.[67]

The particular tastes of the English upper class for overseas household staff account for only some of the French servants in southern England.

Ecclesiastical estates employed equally high numbers of Frenchmen. In Devon, four men recorded as Norman and one as French worked for Cowick Priory in 1440.[68] The fact that the institution was one of the alien priories that survived Henry V's cull, and that the prior at the time, William Dounebaunt, was himself of Norman birth (duly paying the alien subsidy in 1440), could have facilitated the employment of these people.[69] Yet Bradenstoke Priory in Wiltshire had no such links, but also had two French servants between 1440 and 1442.[70] In 1440, the prior of Christchurch in Hampshire had two Frenchmen working for him, and the prior of Leeds in Kent had one.[71]

In some of the towns and cities of the South, French immigrants found jobs in artisans' workshops. In Salisbury, sixty-seven men from France (including Normandy and Brittany) were assessed to pay the alien subsidy in 1440. Of the fifty-one whose occupations were given, forty-one were employed as servants.[72] They worked either for native craftspeople or, more exceptionally, for one of the alien artisans who originated from other parts of Europe. For example, John Bote, an English baker in Salisbury, had three immigrant servants – one French, one Breton and one Norman – assisting him between 1440 and 1443.[73]

It therefore seems that all employers in the South of England, and particularly in the South-West, whether noble, ecclesiastical or artisanal, benefited from the availability of high numbers of cheap, unskilled French workers. As we saw in chapter 5, economic conditions in northern France and the English withdrawal from the occupation of Normandy in 1450 may have encouraged people from a wide social and economic range to seek refuge in England. In fact, the surnames Frenchman and Frenchwoman occur so frequently in relation to low-status occupations in the alien subsidy returns – some 683 instances of servants and labourers, in the Midlands and Yorkshire, as well as in the South – as to suggest that the French presence, especially in the countryside, was proverbial. 'John the Frenchman' was not just a name; he was also a recognisable type among the servant class of later medieval England.

Working conditions of alien servants in England

As a result of the labour shortages following the Black Death, the working conditions of wage labourers in England improved. In an attempt to safeguard employers' interests, authorities tried to limit their increases in wages and to prohibit their movement from their home areas in search of better conditions, often to no avail.[74] In this context of increasing regulation, alien workers, who were not bound to a specific location or to previous employers in England, may have sought more flexible working arrangements than their English-born counterparts. In the alien subsidy rolls, sixty-one immigrants of different nationalities living all over England, most of them male, were recorded as 'former' or 'late' servants, which suggests that they had moved on to other, perhaps better, occupations. Some of the records contain examples of social mobility by alien servants in an urban context. William Feber was the immigrant son of a servant, Lucia, who paid the alien subsidy herself in 1440. Yet in the same year William was running a tailor's workshop in Southwark and employing three alien assistants of his own.[75]

Other evidence provides us with glimpses of people with less secure circumstances. From 1349 onwards, day rates for work in a range of agricultural, manufacturing and retailing activities were pegged, at first to a national maximum and later as local conditions allowed. There is no particular indication that the Statute of Labourers (the catch-all term for what was actually an evolving body of legislation) was used with any more vehemence against aliens than against denizen workers, and the occasional prosecutions of aliens can of course be taken two ways: on some occasions, as indicating their vulnerability to malicious employers; but on others, as evidence of their confidence in demanding what they regarded as an appropriate payment for their work. Sometimes, indeed, the records of the resulting legal cases reveal that recalcitrant alien servants were in the employ of fellow aliens.[76] Journeymen in the guild of alien weavers in London, drawing on the culture of civic action in their native land, effectively went on strike for better pay from the alien master weavers in 1355.[77] There may also have been some collusion between the three Brabanter weavers who were fined in Coventry in 1358 for taking high wages in breach of the national code.[78] In more remote areas, alien labourers who were isolated from kinship and friendship networks may have been forced to accept the lower rates of pay sometimes given to women, children, the elderly and the infirm.[79]

There are also some signs of forced labour. At Glassonby in Cumberland, the Englishman Robert Bate employed two anonymous Scottish women in 1440. Each was described not by the usual Latin term used for a servant in the lay subsidy returns – *serviens* – but as an *ancilla*, a word that, in a lay context, has strong connotations of subjection and bondage.[80] In 1472, Filippo Cini tried to sell his Moorish servant Maria Moriana to a Genoese acquaintance in Southampton. When she objected, he had her thrown into gaol.[81] Virtual slavery may even have been a reality for a whole group of immigrants working in later medieval England. As we saw in chapter 5, the alien subsidy returns reveal concentrations of Icelanders in the ports of Hull and Bristol and the landlocked communities of Nottingham and Coventry. Most of them were servants, and one in three were women – a higher proportion than among most other nationalities. Both English and Icelandic sources of the period document the trafficking of people by Englishmen. In 1429, for example, Icelandic youths were being offered for sale in Lynn, where they were spotted by a visiting bishop from Iceland and rescued. At Bristol the enumerators for the alien subsidies often left out the names of Icelandic servants or referred to them simply as 'boys'. In Fleming's view, at least some of these are likely to have been abducted by English seafarers or been sold on by their desperate parents in Iceland, and thus lived a life of forced labour in England.[82]

A golden age for immigrant women?

In an article published in 1989, Caroline Barron provocatively posited that women living in late medieval England experienced a 'golden age'. Following the Black Death, the argument goes, the depletion of the workforce resulted in a strongly increased demand for labour. This allowed women to engage in economic activities that had previously been inaccessible to them, in the same way as it did for unskilled workers. The newly acquired economic power afforded them more autonomy and an improved position in relation to men. Many of these achievements were undone again in the sixteenth century, as an increase in the population brought more men back into the labour market.[83] Jeremy Goldberg also argued that women in post-plague England enjoyed economic opportunities that had been unavailable to their predecessors.[84] However, Bennett subsequently contended that, even if opportunities increased after the Black Death, women's status remained confined by patriarchal structures, and women continued to work in the lowest-status and lowest-paid occupations.[85] Sandy Bardsley has also argued that there was no discernible reduction in the gap between male and female wages in the fifteenth century.[86] More recently, Marjorie McIntosh placed herself between Barron's emphasis on change and Bennett's insistence on continuity, by concluding that, while nothing much changed for most women in post-plague England, some could claim more independent control over their lives and livelihoods.[87]

In the context of late medieval immigration, the question arises as to whether women living in England but coming from elsewhere enjoyed anything of a 'golden age' after the Black Death. Did they benefit from greater economic opportunities and a rise in status in the same way that English-born women are supposed to have done? Could they, like their male alien counterparts discussed in chapter 6, capitalise on the increased demand for wage labour and the general growth of demand for manufactured and luxury goods?

Before investigating the fortunes of female immigrants, their presence in the country needs to be considered. Between 1440 and 1487, women were listed in the alien subsidy returns on 5,998 occasions. This represents 11 per cent of all instances in which people were recorded towards the subsidy in nominal returns. However, this gender ratio was not constant throughout the period in which the tax was collected. In 1440, when the alien subsidy was first collected, 2,372 of the 15,901 people listed, or 15 per cent, were female. During the 1440s as a whole, women account for 14 per cent of all entries. In the 1450s, the ratio drops to 7 per cent, and in the 1460s to 4 per cent. In the 1470s, when the amount of data is especially sparse, women were responsible for only 9 per cent of all entries. In the 1480s, however, the proportion rose again to 14 per cent.

Rather than accurately reflecting the ups and downs of female migration to England, these trends should remind us of the quirks of the evidence. During the 1450s and 1460s, the alien subsidies were administered less rigorously than in the 1440s and 1480s, and details of the immigrants listed, such as their nationalities, were recorded less often.[88] In this context, the subsidy collectors were also more inclined to leave out the names of taxpayers' alien wives, who were not liable for the subsidy but were occasionally recorded in the assessment rolls. So, whereas immigrant wives account for 6 per cent of all entries in the alien subsidy returns during the 1440s and 7 per cent in the 1480s, they represented only 2 per cent in the 1450s and 0.01 per cent in the 1460s. While no returns provide an exhaustive enumeration of all alien women living in the realm, it thus seems likely that the figures of the 1440s and 1480s, and those of the first collection in 1440 in particular, provide the best approximation to the gender ratio among immigrants in England.

Gender ratios also varied according to the different national groups of immigrants coming to England. Only one female Italian was recorded by the alien subsidy assessors, and women were responsible for only 4 per cent of all instances in which French people were recorded.[89] By contrast, female immigrants accounted for 19 per cent of all occasions on which Icelanders were listed and no fewer than 25 per cent of instances of Scots. To some extent, these figures reflect the different migration patterns characteristic for each group. As explained in chapters 5 and 6, the majority of Italian immigrants to England were merchants who arrived as young, single men and stayed in the country only for a phase of their lives; in most cases, it appears that they did not marry while resident in England. The very high proportion of males among French incomers could also reflect the emergency in northern France at the end of the Hundred Years War, discussed in chapter 5, and the possibility that young, single men had more choice and freedom than women or married men about leaving the region and seeking refuge abroad. Yet, here again, we should be careful not to take the sources at face value. Women account for 11 per cent of the instances in which immigrants were recorded as 'Dutch', the designation used for people coming from the Low Countries and Germany. Among the 'Teutonics', the alternative label applied to aliens from the Low Countries and Germany in London and Berkshire during the 1480s, however, female immigrants were responsible for 24 per cent of all entries. The difference is accounted for, at least in part, by the fact that more alien wives were recorded in the 1480s and in London than in earlier decades and in other places in the country. Other groups of immigrant women were never covered by the alien subsidy returns, regardless of their nationalities. Most noteworthy in this respect are the alien wives of English and Welsh men, who were exempt from payment of the alien subsidies, and whose experiences will be explored in chapter 10.

Female occupations

Occupations are given in 1,464 (24 per cent) of the 5,998 occasions on which women were assessed for the alien subsidies. This is slightly less than for the male entries, where occupations were specified in 31 per cent of cases. In no fewer than 1,382 (94 per cent) of the 1,465 instances in which female occupations were recorded, women were identified as servants, 'common' servants or 'former' servants. As has been explained, servant was a catch-all term that covered a range of activities. Some alien women, for example, were clearly employees of immigrant and English-born artisans. Katherine Cornelis and Elena Nele worked for the cobbler and fellow-'Teutonic' Reginald Egbson in London's Cordwainer Street ward in 1483.[90] But although women like Katherine and Elena could theoretically have trained with their employers as apprentices, the very low numbers of female immigrants recorded in the alien subsidy rolls as independent craftspeople during later stages of their lives suggest otherwise. In fact, the overwhelming majority of the women assessed as servants in the subsidy returns probably earned their living as domestic workers or as unskilled helpers in the agricultural and artisanal sectors. 289 of such instances represented single women from Scotland found in England's northern counties. Most of them were given the blanket surname 'Scot', and some were recorded without a name.[91] The general vulnerability of this group is shown by the fact that they had to travel further south than their male counterparts in search of work, and were arguably even more mobile than Scottish men. The second most common occupational designation among females in the alien subsidies, recorded on thirty-two occasions, was 'vagabond', a term that explicitly denotes the absence of a fixed residence and employment. In thirty-one instances, women were assessed generically as labourers. Taken together, this means that in 99 per cent of the cases in which female occupations were given, women were employed in low-status and, one can assume, low-paid jobs – or no jobs at all. Men were described as servants, labourers or vagabonds in only 73 per cent of the male entries in the alien subsidy rolls in which occupations were specified. Moreover, as we noted in chapter 6, male servants included apprentices, who would go on to work as master artisans in their own right.

The other sectors where female immigrants were employed were exactly those which, according to Barron, became more accessible for English women during the period after the Black Death. However, it should be stressed that the numbers of alien women engaged in these more highly skilled jobs were very low.[92] Fourteen female foreigners were employed in the clothing trade. Eight of these, four of them from Ireland, worked as spinsters.[93] Two 'Teutonic' flaxwives (women involved in the production of linen) lived in London in 1483, and a female Scottish weaver, the widow Marion Scot, was maintaining her own household (and presumably her own business) at Cawood in Yorkshire in 1440.[94] In the same year, at Southwark, Joan Yonge worked together with her father as a capper.[95] In Suffolk in 1483, Alice Josip from Flanders worked independently as a hat maker in Ipswich, and the wife of Nicholas Blok, who was also Flemish but whose first name is unknown, teamed up with her husband in the tailoring business in Stoke by Nayland.[96] One alien woman managed to get a foothold in a skilled trade in which English women were very strongly represented. Protected by the mercers, the London silkwomen had obtained a monopoly on the retail of small silk items in the city.[97] Among them was the 'Teutonic' Mariona Jerbray who, in 1483, had her own alien servant, Margaret Symond.[98]

Similar patterns – and small numbers – are evident in the victualling trades. Two female immigrants made a living in the beer industry. An alien tapster called Rosa worked in Bristol's Broad Street in 1440; and in Lynn, Alice Hosedowyn from Brabant sold beer in 1483–4.[99] Three women from the Low Countries were also assessed as servants to male beer sellers and brewers in Suffolk in 1483, but it is not clear whether they were involved in the trade themselves.[100] Three female immigrants provided food in 1440. The Irishwoman Agnes Hirde was an independent baker in Kendal; Emma Benton was a huckster in Newcastle upon Tyne; and Isabella Hukster did the same, together with her alien servant, in Southwark.[101]

We should bear in mind that the occupations listed in the alien subsidy returns do not necessarily tell the whole story. A study of the borough court rolls of Great Yarmouth has made clear that several alien women who were assessed for the subsidies without an occupation actually participated in a range of economic activities in the town, including retail and hostelling. They were also active in the beer trade, at least until it became a larger-scale, year-round business from the mid-1450s onwards.[102] Most of such work was done on an informal basis in the context of the household, and this may be the reason why it was only acknowledged intermittently in the alien subsidy returns.

One economic activity in which foreign women were more heavily involved was hardly recorded in the alien subsidy rolls at all. According to Ruth Karras, it was very common for female immigrants, who lacked their usual support networks abroad and were often barred from more morally accepted occupations, to engage in prostitution in English towns, either as prostitutes or as brothel keepers. She argues that women from the Low Countries were particularly prominent in this line of work.[103] Many late medieval sources support Karras's claims. A London proclamation of 1393 concerning prostitution specifically targeted 'Flemish women, who profess and follow such a shameful and dolorous life'.[104] In fourteenth-century Colchester, women from the Low Countries were fined for receiving men.[105] Southwark had several Flemish 'stews', and one of them was attacked by the rebels at the time of the Peasants' Revolt in 1381. In the hostile climate of the 1430s, petitions denounced the Southwark stews as meeting places for enemy aliens.[106] In Great Yarmouth, at least five brothels operated by 'Dutch' immigrants were active between 1430 and 1490. Three of these were run by men, two by women.[107] English literary sources, such as Langland's *Piers Plowman* and Chaucer's *Pardoner's Tale*, also represented Flemings and others from the Low Countries as being commonly associated with paid sex.[108] Yet the alien subsidy returns provide only a few traces of immigrant prostitution. In Southwark in 1440, an alien called Arnold Lovell was assessed as a hosteller 'of the stews', and two immigrant women, Katherine Mason and Katherine Wytte, were described as servants 'of the stews'. Probably Arnold was a brothel keeper and the two Katherines were either his aides or prostitutes working for him.[109] In Essex, also in 1440, two alien women, one living in Chelmsford and the other in Maldon, were designated with the term 'frowe', a word that usually denoted sex workers.[110] Similarly, as we shall see in chapter 8, 'Blaak Margaret', recorded as an alien householder in Boston in 1440, may have run a brothel there.

Fiscal, marital and legal status

Occupations are not the only indicator of female status provided by the subsidy records. Women were listed as householders in 571 of the 5,598 instances in which they were recorded, or just over 10 per cent. This is significantly lower than the 43 per cent of entries in which males were considered householders. Women employed servants on twenty-one occasions, or 0.4 per cent of all female entries, whereas men were classified as masters in 2 per cent of all male entries. Eight of these female employers also had male servants. Elena Pytte, for example, had two alien women and one alien man working for her in Bristol's St Nicholas parish in 1440, all of who shared her surname.[111] One woman, the 'Teutonic' widow Barbara Frean, was recorded as lodging other aliens: she had six 'Teutonics', three male and three female, staying in her house in London's Dowgate ward in 1483.[112] Immigrant men provided accommodation to other aliens on twenty-eight occasions, lodging both men and women, between 1440 and 1487.

A factor that greatly influenced medieval women's social and economic position was marital status. As we have seen in chapter 2, alien women married to alien men were effectively exempted from liability to the alien subsidies on the basis (which applied in so many legal and fiscal contexts) that they were 'covered' by their husbands. Nevertheless, the assessors of the tax sometimes chose to include information about alien wives, and there are 2,403 instances of this in the alien subsidy returns between 1440 and 1487. The evidence is not evenly spread; and as we noted above, almost all of it falls within the 1440s and the 1480s. Nor is it clear how much credence can be given to information that may have been added on only a very ad hoc basis. This is why, in chapter 3, we chose not to rely on very erratic and perhaps unrepresentative samples but to take a theoretical approach to calculating the overall proportions, and global numbers, of male aliens married to female aliens (and to English women) in the era of the alien subsidies.

Despite these caveats, the data still represent a sufficiently large sample to make some further analysis worthwhile. The most striking point is that marital status, like the gender ratio itself, seems to have differed greatly according to nationality. The ethnic origins of alien wives were not stated, so we have to assume that they were generally married to men of their own nationality, and thus rely on the labels attached to their husbands. (This also tends to suppose, of course, that the marriage had taken place before the migration, which may not always be strictly the case.) Taking all this ambiguity into account, we may note that between 1440 and 1487, 40 per cent of all instances of women recorded as coming from the Low Countries and the German territories, and 28 per cent of those from Ireland, were described as married to men of those nationalities residing in England. This seems to reflect other social realities encountered elsewhere in this study. As we have seen (male) immigrants from the Low Countries and the German territories and, to a lesser extent, from Ireland included many people who were householders and had established occupations. They are more likely to have migrated to England with their wives and families, and often drew on the skills of their spouses in running the family business. By contrast, 98 per cent of instances of Icelandic women, 88 per cent of French women and 87 per cent of Scottish women in the alien subsidy returns were single. Female immigrants of these nationalities came to England mostly on their own (or with their parents) – though a proportion of them, if they remained in the country, presumably later married English husbands.

According to Barron, one of the major improvements for women during the post-plague period in England was that wives could claim *femme sole* status, which provided them with legal and economic independence from their husbands.[113] Thirteen women, six of them living at Boston in Lincolnshire, were labelled as 'singlewomen' in the alien subsidy records, but it is unclear whether this refers to *femme sole* status or simply means that they had not married. The fact that seventy-four men were equally described as 'singlemen' in the subsidies probably makes a *femme sole* qualification rather unlikely in these cases. Similarly, we need to be cautious not to impose the modern ambiguity of the word 'spinster', which originally simply meant a (female) spinner of wool but which, by the seventeenth century, was used to denote the status of single woman. We have already encountered seven spinsters assumed, in this analysis, to be wool workers. While such women are likely to have been single, their occupational label did not definitively announce them as such. There is also very slight evidence for the presence of alien mothers residing or having other acknowledged connections with their alien-born children over the taxable age of twelve. Fifty-three alien women were described as mothers to other aliens, both male and female, between 1440 and 1487. Only twenty-three of these were married; the rest of these women were presumably widowed, or had had children born from extramarital affairs.

Among medieval women, widows traditionally enjoyed most economic freedom. They had inherited part of the property of their late husbands and, unlike married women, had the right to use these resources autonomously.[114] It is unclear, however, how the legal position of alien widows in England compared to that of native-born ones. Like all other immigrants, foreign-born widows of alien men were not entitled to own and inherit real property, unless they had purchased letters of denization. In 1420, anticipating a higher frequency of international marriages following the recent Treaty of Troyes and the union of Henry V and Katherine of Valois, Parliament confirmed the rights of foreign wives of English men to their dowries on the deaths of their husbands.[115] Yet alien widows of English men also continued to take out denization in order to claim their share in their late husbands' estates, possibly as a means of obtaining additional security. Katharine Carpenter, from Zeeland, acquired denization papers in 1446 following the death of her spouse, the prominent London official John Carpenter.[116] Jaquelina May, from Normandy, did the same after her English-born husband John had died in 1443.[117] The letters granted to Gertrude, the alien wife of London citizen and merchant William de Limes, in 1440 expressly made her capable of claiming dower on the death of her husband.[118]

The alien subsidy returns certainly make clear that widows were among the economically most prominent of immigrant women in England. Nine of the twenty-one women who employed alien servants and the only woman who lodged other immigrants in the subsidies were widows, as were two of the nineteen female immigrants involved in skilled occupations, the silkwoman Mariona Jerbray and the weaver Marion Scot. Unfortunately, the occupations of most of the other widows assessed were not recorded. Given the relatively high marriage rate among immigrants from the Low Countries and the German territories, it should be no surprise that most of the alien widows in the returns hailed from the same regions. Seventy-seven widows were assessed between 1440 and 1487, fifty-one of them being attributed a nationality. Twenty-eight of these, or more than half, were 'Teutonic'. No information is given on any of their late husbands, though it seems likely that many would have been involved in the artisan businesses so common among 'Dutch' and German immigrants.

The experiences of female immigrants in England did not necessarily compare well with the opportunities they would have enjoyed in their homelands. In the Low Countries, customary law allowed women relatively high levels of legal freedom. Whereas in England, the wife's goods and chattels belonged to the husband, wives in Flanders maintained a right to any property brought into the marriage. Any increase of the property after the marriage belonged equally to both spouses. Debts left after the death of the husband could only be recovered from his or the community assets, not the woman's personal belongings.[119] A study of legal practice in Ghent, the largest city in Flanders, shows that until the emergence of a more patriarchal legal culture later in the fifteenth century, women also had far-reaching control over their assets and could use them relatively freely, regardless of their marital status. Married women could prosecute in cases relating to a wide variety of economic activities. Unlike in England, they did not need *femme sole* status, or their husbands' consent, to do so.[120] In Bruges, one of the most commercialised cities of late medieval Europe, both widows and married women were involved in a range of economic undertakings, though the latter usually acted together with their husbands.[121] For women from the Low Countries, or at least from their biggest cities, migrating to England could thus have resulted in a loss of status.

The experiences of immigrant women in England were not only influenced by where they came from, but also by where in the country they settled. In an article from 1994, Barron nuanced her earlier claims about a 'golden age' by stating that the phenomenon was primarily confined to the major urban centres in England, and to London and York in particular.[122] The alien subsidy returns confirm that female aliens living in the capital may have had better opportunities than female aliens living elsewhere. 40 per cent of all alien female householders were assessed in London, as were eleven of the twenty-one alien mistresses. Yet even there, immigrant women worked in service in more than 97 per cent of the entries in the alien subsidy rolls for which an occupation was given. The alien subsidy records only cover the period 1440–87 and do not allow us to document much of an evolution over time, but they do make clear that female aliens in England benefited far less than alien men from the increase in real wages and the emergence of a consumer economy after the Black Death. They also suggest that immigrant women were worse off than their English counterparts who, even if they remained confined by a patriarchal system, gained access to a widening range of more skilled occupations. Even the happy few of London-based, mainly 'Dutch' immigrant women who could afford to run a shop or employ a servant might have enjoyed better legal conditions in their place of origin. If there was a golden age for women in late medieval England, it seems safe to say that it did not apply to immigrants.

Notes

1 *PROME*, XI, 291.
2 *PROME*, XI, 291.
3 Bolton, 'London and the anti-alien legislation', pp. 34–41; *Views of Hosts*, pp. xv–xvii.
4 Guidi-Bruscoli, 'John Cabot'.
5 Guidi-Bruscoli and Lutkin, 'Perception, identity and culture', p. 100.
6 *ODNB*, XXII, 152–3; Lambert, ' "Nostri fratelli da Londra" ', p. 99. For Carlo Gigli, see chapter 6.
7 E 179/236/85.
8 E 179/144/69.
9 See chapter 3.
10 E 179/184/212, rot. 13d.
11 WAM 12261, m. 35.
12 *CPR 1494–1509*, p. 25.
13 Davies, 'Effect of the Black Death'.
14 Benedictow, *Black Death*, pp. 342–57.
15 *Black Death*, p. 241.
16 McHardy, 'Clerical taxation'.
17 E 179/124/107, rot. 6; E 179/124/138, rot. 3d.
18 E 179/196/100, rot. 2.
19 McKay, 'Duties of the medieval parish clerk'.
20 E 179/270/32 Part 1, m. 3; E 179/269/28, m. 2; E 179/136/210, m. 2.
21 E 179/141/69, m. 4v; Duffy, *Stripping of the Altars*, p. 124.
22 E 179/242/25, m. 16d.
23 E 179/136/228, m. 2.
24 E 179/196/100, rot. 3.
25 Pantin, *English Church*, p. 28.
26 John Obses, rector of Stepney in Middlesex, had two alien employees in 1444: E 179/269/38, m. 3.
27 *CPR 1441–6*, p. 285; *CPR 1446–52*, pp. 5, 37, 123, 232.
28 *CPR 1485–94*, p. 381; Thomson, 'Scots in England', p. 9.
29 WAM 12261, mm. 11, 12, 20.
30 Davis, 'Irish clergy'; Davis, 'Material relating to Irish clergy'.
31 *CPR 1391–6*, pp. 452–86; Bolton, 'Irish migration', pp. 13–16.
32 *CPR 1413–16*, pp. 122–5, 296; *CPR 1416–22*, p. 112.
33 *CPR 1476–85*, pp. 189–218; Thomson, 'Scots in England', 6–9.
34 *CPR 1413–16*, pp. 124–5.
35 WAM 12261.

36 See chapter 8.
37 Goldberg, *Medieval England*, pp. 72–3.
38 Rigby, *English Society*, pp. 190–1.
39 E 179/235/14, m. 3.
40 E 179/235/14, m. 6.
41 See, for example, E 179/108/125, m. 2; E 179/177/70, m. 2; E 179/196/100, rot. 2d.
42 E 179/113/128, m. 2. Other examples come from Northumberland, but the meaning of the term as used there is unclear: E 179/158/55, mm. 1, 3, 4; E 179/158/57, mm. 1, 4.
43 E 179/144/73, rot. 1, m. 1.
44 Horrox, 'Urban gentry'.
45 Benedictow, *Black Death*, p. 377.
46 Munro, 'Urban wage structures'; Thielemans, *Bourgogne et Angleterre*, p. 211.
47 Goldberg, 'What was a servant?'; Hettinger, 'Defining the servant'.
48 Lambert, 'Scandinavian immigrants', pp. 114–17.
49 *Alien Communities*, p. 68.
50 E 179/173/131, m. 1; E 179/173/132, m. 2; E 179/173/134, m. 1; Ruddock, *Italian Merchants*, pp. 126–7.
51 E 179/124/154, m. 2.
52 E 179/235/4, m. 4.
53 E 179/242/25.
54 E 179/242/25, m. 8d.
55 For the general distribution of Scottish immigrants in England during the later Middle Ages, see chapter 4.
56 Rees Jones, 'Scots in the North of England', pp. 60–9, 72–4.
57 E 179/270/31, mm. 14, 20, 23–4.
58 E 179/217/67, mm. 1–3; E 179/270/31, mm. 23, 26.
59 See, for example, E 179/136/244, m. 2.
60 Pollard, 'North-eastern economy'; Neville, 'Local sentiment and the "national" enemy'.
61 Bolton, 'Irish migration', p. 8.
62 *ODNB*, XXVIII, 825–6; *CPR 1436–41*, p. 360.
63 E 179/196/100, rot. 3d.
64 Salzman, 'Early heraldry of Pelham', p. 67; E 179/184/212, rot. 5.
65 *Complete Peerage*, XI, 301–2; E 179/196/100, rot. 1d.
66 E 179/103/83.
67 E 179/196/10, m. 2.
68 E 179/95/100, rot. 7.
69 E 179/95/100, rot. 5; Smith (ed.), *Heads of Religious Houses*, III, 171. In spite of the exemption of regular clergy from the alien subsidies, Dounebaunt paid the tax in 1440: E 179/95/100, rot. 5.
70 E 179/176/585; E 179/196/100; E 179/387/8, Part 1, mm. 6–7.
71 E 179/176/585; E 179/124/107.
72 E 179/196/100.
73 E 179/196/100, rot. 4; E 179/196/150, m. 2; E 179/387/8, Part 1, mm. 3–5.
74 Given-Wilson, 'Problem of labour'.

75 E 179/184/212, rot. 10.
76 Amor, *Late Medieval Ipswich*, pp. 239–40; Pajic, 'Migration of Flemish Weavers', p. 135.
77 Lambert and Pajic, 'Immigration and the common profit', p. 645.
78 Pajic, 'Migration of Flemish Weavers', p. 140.
79 For (English) women and vulnerable men, see Bardsley, 'Women's work reconsidered'.
80 Bennett, 'Women (and men) on the move', p. 24.
81 Ruddock, *Italian Merchants*, pp. 126–7.
82 Fleming, 'Icelanders in England', pp. 79–81.
83 Barron, ' "Golden age" of women'.
84 Goldberg, 'Female labour'; Goldberg, *Women, Work and Life-Cycle*, pp. 336–40.
85 Bennett, 'Medieval women, modern women'; Bennett, *History Matters*, pp. 83–6.
86 Bardsley, 'Women's work reconsidered', pp. 3–29.
87 McIntosh, *Working Women*, pp. 250–3.
88 See chapter 3.
89 Bete Currour was assessed as a 'Lombard' non-householder in London in 1483: E 179/242/25, m. 10d.
90 E 179/242/25, m. 14d.
91 Bennett, 'Women (and men) on the move', pp. 5, 6, 7, 27–8.
92 Barron, ' "Golden age" of women', p. 47.
93 E 179/95/100, rot. 5d; E 179/113/107, m. 2; E 179/217/59, m. 7; E 179/235/8, m. 2; E 179/270/31, m. 8.
94 E 179/242/25, m. 7d; E 179/270/31, m. 8.
95 E 179/184/212, rot. 12.
96 E 179/180/111, rot. 6, m. 1d; E 179/180/111, rot. 4.
97 Dale, 'London silkwomen', pp. 324–35.
98 E 179/242/25, m. 10.
99 E 179/113/104, m. 4; E 179/149/177, m. 2.
100 E 179/180/111, rot. 3d. rot. 6, m. 1.
101 E 179/195/33, m. 2; E 179/158/115, m. 2; E 179/184/212, rot. 10.
102 Liddy and Lambert, 'Civic franchise', p. 131.
103 Karras, *Common Women*, pp. 56–7.
104 *Memorials of London and London Life*, p. 535.
105 Rodziewicz, 'Order and Society', p. 98.
106 Carlin, *Medieval Southwark*, pp. 158–60. See also chapter 10.
107 Liddy and Lambert, 'Civic franchise', p. 131 n. 38.
108 Chaucer, *Canterbury Tales*, p. 195, ll. 1–3; Langland, *Piers Plowman*, p. 89, ll. 152–4.
109 E 179/184/212, rot. 13.
110 E 179/108/113, m. 5; Carlin, *Medieval Southwark*, p. 212.
111 E 179/113/104, m. 11.
112 E 179/242/25, m. 9.
113 Barron, ' "Golden age" of women', pp. 39–40.
114 Loengard, ' "Which may be said to be her own" '.

115 *PROME*, IX, 260.
116 *CPR 1441–6*, p. 408.
117 *CPR 1441–6*, p. 205.
118 *CPR 1436–41*, p. 430.
119 Howell, *Women, Production and Patriarchy*, pp. 14–21.
120 Hutton, '"On herself and all her property"'.
121 Murray, *Bruges*, pp. 300–43.
122 Barron, 'Introduction: the widow's world', pp. xiii–xxxiv.

8

Old worlds, new immigrants

Much of this book is taken up with studying the European immigrants who are readily visible in the official records as having a presence in England between 1300 and 1550. As we have seen, English jurors, administrators and politicians used a well-established range of labels to describe these incomers, ranging from the readily recognisable labels of 'French', 'Scottish', 'Irish' and 'Icelander' to the more generic forms of 'Dutch' and 'Teutonic' and the various descriptors used for Iberians, Italians and 'Greeks'. In that they were markers of national and/or linguistic difference, such labels may be said, to some degree, to have carried ethnic connotations.

It was very rare in late medieval England, however, for persons coming into and residing in the country to be identified by explicitly racial or ethno-religious markers that readily reveal the presence of groups from the Middle or Far East, North Africa or other areas of the known wider world.[1] In the sixteenth century we begin to find clearer references to the presence in England of various racial and religious minorities, and many historians of the early modern period assume that this new documentation denotes the arrival of new categories of immigrants not previously present in the realm. One of the most widespread of these historiographical traditions relates to the well-known black trumpeter of Henry VII and Henry VIII, known as John Blanke (his surname, seemingly, a racist joke derived from the French *blanc*, for white). John is often said to have been part of the very first group of African immigrants coming into England, arriving supposedly as part of a Moorish contingent in the entourage of the Spanish princess, Katherine of Aragon, in 1501.[2] The real reason for singling out Blanke, however, is that he happens not only to be documented in the royal household accounts, but also offers us the first known 'portrait' of a black person in England, in the visual record compiled to commemorate a royal tournament at Westminster in 1511.[3] In fact it is this, rather than his colour alone, that makes Blanke 'a first' in England.

Rather than perpetuating the notion that Europeans' travels of discovery in the fifteenth and sixteenth century turned England from a monoracial to a multiracial country, we need to recognise that there was a weak but discernible presence of minority groups right across the Middle Ages and early modern periods. The purpose of this chapter is to explore that continuum in relation particularly to a number of recognisable groups, including those defined by religion (Jews and Muslims) and those singled out by race (people from North Africa and the Middle East). We will investigate the nature and extent of the evidence for the presence of such minorities during the fourteenth and fifteenth centuries before going on to discuss the ways in which the early Tudor state sought more assertively to manage the more general process of immigration to England in the first half of the sixteenth century.

The Jews before and after 1290

Prior to the royal order for their expulsion in 1290, the Jews were the most visible of all ethnic or racial minorities in England.[4] The Jews did not conform to the normal rules that emerged in the thirteenth century about place of birth as the defining marker of legal status, for they were defined by their religious faith and therefore included both first-generation immigrants and significantly larger numbers of descendants of immigrants. In Norman and Angevin England, Jews were regarded as a royal possession and an exploitable asset. In return for promises of general protection and freedom of religious expression, the Jewish community was expected to pay heavy taxes and make available its liquid capital in the form of large loans to the crown. As early as 1233 the crown was adamant that only those Jews who provided practical service to the king should remain in the kingdom: all others should leave. In 1253 this was followed up with draconian legislation limiting the Jews to the towns where they already had recognised communities. A year later, faced with crippling fiscal demands, the leaders of the Jews in England actually requested that they be released from their obligations and be allowed to leave the country. Henry III's government refused, and in the 1270s the crown again attempted a programme of enforced conversion and integration. Eventually, in 1287, Edward I set the vital precedent by deciding to expel the Jews from his duchy of Gascony. On his return to England two years later, the king also set about eradicating the Jewish community from the realm.

There has been a good deal of debate about Edward I's motivations in ordering the forced expulsion of all Jews from England in July 1290. We can attempt to equate this process with the threats and actions undertaken against specific alien groups, such as French and Italian moneylenders under Henry III or the entire French-born resident population in 1294. The expulsion of the Jews, however, was different in a number of respects. First, it was an irrevocable policy: the persons of the Jews, previously considered a royal asset, could never thereafter be effectively reunited with the property confiscated from them. Secondly, it was a process strikingly lacking in exceptions: whereas it became regular practice to protect certain aliens during general orders for Flemish or French expulsions, there is abundant evidence of a general exodus of Jews in 1290, and the most that the crown was prepared to do for prominent members of the Jewish community was to allow the sale of their assets so that they left the country with the wherewithal to start up their businesses elsewhere. Finally, there was little by way of fiscal motivation behind the expulsion. The crown benefited in theory from the confiscated property and assets of the Jews, including the unpaid debts owed to them by English borrowers; but no concerted attempt was made by the state to exploit these already depleted resources, which instead were shared out with the elites of those towns that had previously had a visible Jewish presence.

The comparative ease with which the English crown seems to have effected the expulsion of 1290 is most obviously explicable in terms of the ways that Jews were marked out from their host society. Jewish physiognomy was widely caricatured in late medieval representational art. However, the English did not rely on facial features alone: instead, from the early thirteenth century at least, all Jews resident in the realm were required to wear the *tabula*, the badge of the Ten Commandments, and other forms of distinctive dress that made for ready and formal identification. As an existing asset of the crown, the Jews were one of the most highly documented groups in the whole of English society, and are now readily traceable via the extant bureaucratic records of taxation and money lending. The focused nature of the expulsion process may also explain why it was so notably low-key: while there are examples of lay and clerical attacks on Jews in 1290, there is no sign of a general outpouring of anti-Semitic violence, and the crown itself was at pains to stress that the departures should take place under its protection. Although relatively little is known of the practicalities of the forced exodus, it would seem that the majority of those who left England in 1290 fled to France. It is one of the ironies of national and racial labelling that significant numbers of people who ended up there were subsequently ascribed the surname 'English'.[5]

It is a commonplace of historical scholarship that the expulsion of 1290 and the effective outlawry of Judaism that resulted from it meant that, for at least two and a half centuries, there were no Jews in England. As Patricia Skinner put it, 'If Jews remained in Britain after 1290, it was purely in the literary imagination.'[6] The extraordinary outpouring of imaginative writing on the theme of the Jew, most often distinctly hostile and sometimes viciously violent, seems to have found licence in the very absence of living Jews from late medieval English society.[7] One trope that developed in the twelfth century and remained an abiding preoccupation of English culture in the later Middle Ages was that of the Jews who stole Christian children from their families and subjected them to ritualistic murders. Nor was this simply a literary device. Actual accusations of child abduction and murder by Jews before 1290 had resulted in the establishment in England of no fewer than seven shrines to child martyrs, three of which – at Norwich, Bury St Edmunds and Lincoln – survived until the Reformation.[8] Other general themes in the literature of the later Middle Ages include the idea of the Jewish desecration of the consecrated bread, or host, of the Christian Eucharist. There is a good deal of debate as to whether these and other stories are simply to be read as anti-Semitic sentiment or as devices to promote Christian devotion. Even taking into account the fact that there were no Jews available to persecute in a direct sense after 1290, however, it is difficult to resist seeing the objectification and demonisation of the imaginary Jew in late medieval England as a form of deep-seated, communal racism.[9]

In strict terms, the idea that Jewish people were completely absent from England after 1290 cannot altogether be true. The key evidence comes from those Jews who accepted Christianity and resided in the so-called House of Converts, or Domus Conversorum, in London. This was a royal foundation set up by Henry III in 1232; tellingly, it continued on beyond the expulsion of 1290 and was still admitting converts in the early sixteenth century.[10] Before 1290, there were perhaps up to a hundred inmates. The numbers inevitably declined after the expulsion, but there were still fifty-one persons living there in 1308 and twenty-two in the early 1330s.[11] The last survivor of the pre-expulsion converts was Claricia of Exeter (d. 1356), who divided her long life between residence at the Domus and marrying and having children in the city of Exeter; her (Christian) husband and a number of their (Christian) children also ended up living at the Domus under a grace and favour arrangement provided by the government of Edward III.[12] As the case of this family shows, not all those who were given rights of residence in the House of Converts during the fourteenth and fifteenth centuries were born as Jews. Nevertheless, their acquisition of such rights through Jewish-born parents who had converted to Christianity represents a residual understanding of the ancestral identities of such second-generation converts.

The Jews who accepted conversion and entered the House of Converts in the generations after 1290 originated mainly from Iberia, France, Germany and the Low Countries. Some attracted the attention of the crown because of their high status. Elizabeth, the daughter of one Rabbi Moses, called 'bishop [*sic*] of the Jews of France and Germany', entered the Domus in 1400 and subsequently married David Pole, a London tailor.[13] In other cases it seems that the individuals had resided for some time in English provincial towns before accepting conversion and seeking royal protection. This explains the fact that, long after the expulsion, persons admitted to the House of Converts were referred to by surnames that denoted their previous presence in English provincial towns. Henry 'of Stratford', for example, who was baptised under the patronage of Henry IV, actually seems to have originated from France.[14] The records of the alien subsidies also yield a suggestive example. Oswald 'the Convert', who was assessed for the tax on aliens in Bridge Street ward in London in 1444, was evidently one of those immigrant converts who chose not to live within the protected confines of the Domus Conversorum but to make his home within an urban and commercial environment where he could go readily about his own business transactions.[15] As we saw in chapter 5, the case of Duarte Brandão/Edward Brampton, the Portuguese Jew converted to Christianity before his arrival in England, proves that Jewish birth was no impediment in itself to a mainstream career even in the highest social circles in England.

Brandão's Jewish heritage is well attested. However, historians have sometimes been too quick to assert Jewish origins for other prominent medieval immigrants to later medieval England. For instance, Davino Nigarelli, doctor to Henry IV, who came originally from Lucca in Italy, was claimed as Jewish in a much-cited publication from 1905; but the evidence adduced was entirely circumstantial and further research indicates that the attribution is almost certainly erroneous.[16] We must also be very careful about assuming that names which might be regarded as Jewish carried any particular ethnic significance and force in medieval Christian society.[17] For example, forenames such as 'Isaac' and 'Moses', and the surname 'Jew', are all found reasonably regularly in the English public records of the fourteenth, fifteenth and early sixteenth centuries. The contexts in which they occur, however, provide no suggestion that the individuals were under some form of scrutiny or special dispensation: in most cases, they were straightforwardly parties to litigation taking place in the king's courts.[18] It is also evident that 'Jew' could be an alternate spelling for the relatively common English surname Yeo, which is a topographical name denoting a river.[19] In the alien subsidy returns of the later fifteenth century we encounter a handful of instances of persons with the forenames 'Abraham' and 'Isaac' living variously in London, Canterbury, Lynn and Penzance, as well as the case of Peter 'Jewe', a householder in Broad Street or Bishopsgate within the city of London in 1449.[20] None of these examples, however, can be said to point unambiguously to the presence of individuals or communities of Jews, converted or otherwise, either in the English capital or in provincial towns.

It therefore seems likely that Jewish immigrants to England in the fourteenth and fifteenth centuries could be counted in mere tens of instances. It is perhaps as well, though, to recognise that the more obvious presence of Jews in England from the early sixteenth century was also a very small-scale affair. After the 1490s we know that a certain number of Portuguese Jews fled persecution in their natal land and took up residence in London, ostensibly again as Christian converts but in this case maintaining a stronger sense of their Jewish inheritance.[21] By the middle of the sixteenth century it was apparently possible to be quite open about the presence at least of visiting Jews: around 1540, for example, William Beryff of Brightlingsea was in dispute with Anthony Delorenya, 'a Spanish Jew', over the seaworthiness of the vessel that the latter had used to transport goods from Boston to Lisbon.[22] It would take another hundred years, and the onset of the English Commonwealth, before the ban imposed in 1290 was informally raised and, in 1656, for Jews to be once again allowed to enter England. Even then, the motives were not straightforwardly about freedom of religious expression. The Jews were to be resettled in England, it was argued, in order that they could be persuaded to convert to Christianity; in the interim, they were assumed to be a good source of taxation.[23]

'Saracens', 'Moors' and people of 'Inde'

Whereas persons of Jewish extraction were formally forbidden to live in England after 1290, there was never any such ban on the presence of the people who the contemporary sources usually call 'Saracens': that is, Muslims from the Middle East, North Africa and Iberia. Much of the scholarship on Saracens focuses on the literary and art-historical representation of Islam and its followers in later medieval England, and generally tends to treat the group in the same way as the Jews: that is, as an absent 'other', and thereby all the more susceptible to imaginative flights of fancy. The relationship between the Christian and the Saracen as exemplified in romance literature of the later Middle Ages certainly remained rooted in ideas of religious conflict and brutal violence, not least because so much writing was set in the context of the Crusades. However, scholars have also noted a difference between the way that such texts viewed Jews and Saracens. Saracens were considered to be capable of a certain nobility of thought and purpose, and were represented as embodying some of the values of Christian chivalric society. Partly for this reason, the literary conceits about the conversion of Saracens to Christianity incorporated, in a way that is not apparent for the Jews, a sense of the moral worth of the convert.[24]

The scholarly emphasis on the literary representation of the Saracen has meant, as for the Jews, that little attention has been given to the possibility of an actual Muslim presence in later medieval England. The evidence is admittedly very scarce, but is certainly enough to give the lie to the claim that 'the very first Muslim about whom some information has survived arrived in England in the mid-1580s'.[25] One reason for pursuing such evidence is that, in contrast to the Jews, whose diaspora meant that they did not have a *territorial* presence in the known world, the Saracens were firmly associated with the southern Mediterranean and the Middle East, where the English (and others) acknowledged them as a discernible political and commercial presence. Writing to his brother-in-law, Alphonso the Wise of Castile, in 1276, King Edward I stressed the collective duty of Christian monarchs to maintain the crusading tradition against 'the Saracens'; over the following century, English nobles and knights participated extensively in the continuing Crusades against the Moors in Spain and against the Ottoman Turks in the eastern Mediterranean.[26] In 1377, in a very different kind of context, the cloth workers of Norfolk complained of restrictions placed on their ability to export the low-quality woollen cloth known as worsted; their main market, they declared, was not at home or on the continent, but among 'the Saracens', and had now been disastrously cut off.[27] These examples indicate ready contact, both hostile and friendly, between English and Islamic culture. They still, however, fall short of proving that Muslims were actually present in England.

The strongest evidence in support of that presence comes not from historical documents but from archaeology, where the study of facial characteristics has permitted the distinguishing of race in human remains.

Skeletons found both in the city of York and at Fairford in Gloucestershire have, by this methodology, been classified respectively as a North African male and a sub-Saharan female who lived in England in the tenth or eleventh century.[28] The most significant evidence for the later Middle Ages came to light in 2010 when it was revealed that a human skeleton previously exhumed from a medieval cemetery in the East Anglian town of Ipswich comprised the remains of a North African male buried there at some point in the thirteenth century. The most likely channel by which the latter had reached his final home was the crusading movement, and specifically the Ninth Crusade, the campaign to the eastern Mediterranean led by Edward I of England (as prince) in 1271. The scientific analysis, combined with the context of the burial, suggests that the individual was a Muslim prisoner brought back to England by one of the leaders of the campaign and baptised somewhere along the way as a Christian. A further eight of the 150 bodies found in this cemetery were also identified as having African origins.[29]

Nor are these tantalising pieces of archaeology the only evidence of such long-distance travel. As with Jews, so with Saracens, the best documentary evidence from the later Middle Ages concerns people who were converted to Christianity under royal sponsorship. Numbered among those maintained in the household of the Black Prince in 1351 were 'Sigo and Nakok, the Saracen children'; the names suggest that these had not (yet) accepted Christian baptism.[30] In 1363–4, during a visit to the English court by King Peter I of Cyprus to drum up support for a new crusading enterprise, Edward III was presented with a candidate for baptism who called himself the 'lord of Jerusalem'. The English king stood as godfather to the assumed potentate and, as was customary in such cases, bestowed on him his own forename, Edward.[31] There is also a strong possibility that some of those who found their way into the London House of Converts in the later Middle Ages had been born not as Jews but as Muslims.[32] Henry IV, who took quite seriously his role as sponsor to converts, acted as godfather variously to Jews, Muslims and pagans from Lithuania (a place where he himself had been on Crusade), and seems to have treated all categories as worthy of consideration for inclusion in the House of Converts.[33] In special cases, the crown was also prepared to employ the assistance of Muslims without the requirement of conversion: Francis Panizonus was an Arab doctor, originally from Alexandria, who served as personal physician to Henry VI and his queen, Margaret of Anjou, in the 1440s.[34]

A further term used occasionally to denote a racial minority in later medieval England was the description 'of Inde'. The records of the fifteenth-century alien subsidies refer to three people with this designation: the husband and wife Benedict and Antonia Calaman, non-householders resident in London in 1483; and James Black, a servant living in Dartmouth in Devon in 1484.[35] The forenames of these individuals indicate that they were all Christians, either by birth or more probably by conversion in England. 'Inde' was a catch-all term used in medieval geography and imaginative literature to denote the great land mass that stretched out eastwards beyond the Holy Land: it was not restricted to, and did not necessarily carry connotations of, modern India. The haziness with which this remote area was understood is well exemplified in the case of John Balbat, who appeared at the court of Edward III in 1366 claiming to be no less than the son of the 'king of Inde'. In the end, it was decided that John was an imposter, and he was unceremoniously deported from the realm later that same year.[36] The general vagueness of the designation also makes it very difficult to construe what distinctive ethnicity the assessors of the alien subsidy thought they were ascribing to the three individuals whom they labelled as 'of Inde'. In the case of James Black, however, it could be argued that a double designation was intended, with the surname conceivably referring to the perceived colour of the man's skin and the 'nationality' expressed in terms of a land situated beyond the territory of the 'Saracens' in the Middle East.

Medieval English culture was emphatic that 'Saracens' and people 'of Inde' were black (or, as often stated in texts and represented in art, blue-black). One of the ways in which the literature of the time represented the supposed superiority of the Caucasian – and of Western Christianity – over other world religions was in the notion that, at conversion, a former Saracen was transformed from a black skin tone to a white one.[37] Medieval notions of race did not readily distinguish between types of blackness, or between what we would call North African and Middle Eastern. One reason perhaps why it is still commonly believed that there were no black people in England before the early sixteenth century is the fact that medieval records rarely deploy the terminology of the 'Moor' or the 'black-amoor' that became prevalent in Tudor times. One rare exception is that of Maria Moriana, the servant in Southampton in the 1460s whom we met in chapter 7; she was specifically described as 'Moorish' to denote a North African ancestry. As with Jews and 'Saracens', so with black Africans, identifying key cases is hampered by the fact that Christian converts were given forenames that are usually indistinguishable from those of the white host community. We are therefore left to speculate as to the use of 'black' as a surname or nickname, and what this may or may not signal about an African presence in late medieval and early Tudor England.

'Black' (usually spelled as 'Blak' or 'Blake') was a fairly regular surname in the alien subsidy returns of the fifteenth century, but – except conceivably in the case of James Black – it cannot be assumed to have any direct racial connotations. Where nationality was declared alongside this surname, it appears that the immigrants were Caucasian, coming variously from Ireland, Scotland, the Low Countries and northern France.[38] In the past there has been a tendency to assume rather too readily that other versions of the surname 'black' denote race. It was long argued, for example, that Sir Pedro Negro, a Spanish mercenary who found service with Henry VIII, was black; but the latest research suggests that this is a fallacy.[39] Where the surname Negro (or Negre) occurs in the alien subsidies – as it does in seventeen instances – it is always in relation to Italians in London, Southampton and Sandwich, most of whom seem to have been members of the di Negro trading family of Genoa; no one has ever suggested that this clan had African roots.[40] The only instance where 'black' was used as a nickname in the alien subsidies is that of 'Blaak Margaret', a householder in Boston (Lincolnshire) in 1440.[41] Here, the label may most likely refer to Margaret's involvement in the sex industry. 'Black Meg', a Manxwoman living in late medieval Chester, was specifically recorded as a brothel keeper.[42] In spite of efforts by literary scholars to assert that the famous sixteenth-century prostitute 'Black Luce' was indeed African (and therefore the 'Dark Lady' of Shakespeare's *Sonnets*), her name too seems to fit more likely with this social practice of identifying prostitutes as implicitly 'dirty'.[43]

It should be no particular surprise, however, that the taxation records fail to yield unambiguous evidence of the presence of black people in fifteenth-century England. Even though the assessments of 1440 reached a long way down, they still left out the most abject members of society. Maria Moriana is known to us not because she was named by the tax collectors but because her master, Filippo Cini, got into trouble over his promise to sell her, as a slave, to a Genoese merchant.[44] At Southampton in 1491–2, one of the officials of the town was said to have become involved in an affray with a 'blackman' employed on the Genoese ships in the port; the context strongly suggests that the man in question was one of the African slaves used as oarsmen by the Italians in this period.[45] The black presence that historians have been able to document in the sixteenth century was almost entirely the result of a single, new phenomenon: England's participation in the emerging slave trade out of West Africa. The black people who entered England during the Tudor period therefore did so against their will, and were treated as the chattels of their masters.[46] Even those who progressed to *de facto* freedom and to successful careers tended to do so only in quite prescribed ways. It is no accident, for example, that John Blanke was a trumpeter: African musicians and dancers were already a relatively common and visible presence in many southern European courts during the fifteenth century.[47] Searching for – and failing to find – black people in the records of English government during the later Middle Ages is therefore to miss the point: namely, that such individuals were given no independent legal status, had no possessions of their own and usually fell entirely outside the normal systems of administration and justice.

There is little doubt that the age of European discovery and trade with new worlds had the effect of increasing the range and size of discernible racial minorities within England during the sixteenth century, and of diversifying the economic activities and social standing of emergent minority groups. Among these were Jewish converts to Christianity arriving from Portugal and Spain; North and West Africans, now increasingly referred to as blackamoors; and Muslims, often from the Ottoman and Persian empires, and known variously as Moors or Turks. The documentary and archaeological evidence discussed above indicates, however, that this early modern racial diversity cannot have been an entirely new phenomenon. We make no false claims about the presence of minorities in late medieval England, which was clearly of a much lower order of magnitude than the overall alien presence. Nor, most emphatically, can we suppose that the general absence of racial markers in the documents signals that the later Middle Ages was some kind of progressive regime in which government agents pursued a policy of 'colour blindness'. In certain other parts of Europe there are indications that ethnic and racial discrimination became a more frequent and forceful phenomenon during the later Middle Ages.[48] England too would exhibit some signs of intolerance as soon as ethnic and religious minorities became more visible in the Tudor period.

Aliens, minorities and the early Tudor state

During the first half of the sixteenth century a number of trends converged to create a more cohesive and sustained approach in English government and society to the whole question of immigration. One very important development that underpinned and facilitated this new outlook was the change in the constitutional relationship between the kingdom of England and its dependencies.[49] Henry VII made attempts to resolve the status of the Channel Islands by negotiating a transfer of episcopal authority from the diocese of Coutances in Normandy to that of Salisbury or Winchester in England. Much more ambitiously, Henry VIII finally made an explicit statement in 1536 that resolved a century of ambiguity over the status of Calais by formally declaring the town a parcel of the English crown. Between 1535 and 1542, the English government incorporated both the Marches and the principality of Wales into its direct jurisdiction, and declared Henry VIII as king, rather than merely lord, of Ireland. The legislation for Wales put an end to the discrimination that had applied since the Glyn Dŵr revolt. The new dispensation was clearly not driven simply by compunction over the civil rights of the king's subjects outside England. Rather, it was a reassertion of control after significant challenges to English authority in Ireland and Wales during the late fifteenth century, and a necessary and timely articulation of 'imperial' authority such as to reinforce the parallel process by which Henry VIII claimed his independence from the jurisdiction of the pope and established himself as Supreme Head of the Church in England.

This last development also helps to explain the increasing visibility of some European immigrant groups in English society during this time. From the 1520s, the fissures in European Christianity resulted in the arrivals of Protestant refugees, partly from northern France but principally at first from Walloon areas in the Low Countries. With the adoption of Protestant practice in the English Church after 1547, the flow of such refugees very visibly increased, most especially in London. Already in 1551 it was alleged that the rush of refugees had increased the 'stranger' community in the capital to over 40,000 people. Although the real number is likely to have been only around 5,000, it still represented a major new presence in the city.[50] While we tend to refer to them as Huguenots (the term used for French protestants), the capacious term 'Dutch' also now took on distinctly religious connotations.[51] Around the middle of the sixteenth century, too, the number of black Africans trafficked to England increased significantly, creating a new rhetoric of racial difference around the categories of 'moor' and 'blackamoor'.[52]

The arrival of immigrants who were recognisably different from their English neighbours in ethnic, racial and/or religious terms, and who tended to form more tight-knit communities with their own kind than had been the case in the fifteenth century, was inevitably treated with some suspicion. 'Turks' (that is, Muslim subjects of the Sultan) were formally expelled from England in 1503, but seemingly as a result of a diplomatic rapprochement with Emperor Maximilian rather than on explicitly ideological grounds.[53] A much more ethnically driven initiative came in 1531, when Parliament passed the first so-called 'Egyptian' Act. This was focused directly on the Romany people whose presence had recently begun to be noted in England. The statute forbade any gypsies from coming to England in the future, and those who were already there were given only sixteen days to quit the realm on pain of forfeiture.[54]

It is difficult to resist seeing this legislation as the prelude to further discriminatory policies adopted towards Africans and other ethnic and racial minorities in England during the later sixteenth century.[55] However, it is possible that the notorious Elizabethan decree of 1596 ordering the expulsion of black people from the realm has been taken out of context and greatly exaggerated. In spite of its abhorrent rhetoric on the expendability of the black workforce to the economy of England, it seems that the ordinance was never intended to be applied generally, and only related to the specific endeavours of one slave merchant.[56] The common idea that the 1596 measure is equivalent to the Egyptian Act, let alone to the 1290 ordinance against the Jews, is therefore wrong.

Discriminatory measures against minorities were mainly the result of concerns about the economy. The population of England began to grow again in the early sixteenth century, reaching around 3 million people by 1550.[57] The longer-term impact of economic recession and the increasing desire to protect English jobs for English men led to concerns about under-employment among both the native-born and immigrants. Tellingly, the 1531 Egyptian Act complained that Romany people did not make their living by the practice of crafts or the buying and selling of goods, but went from place to place telling fortunes and committing robberies and other felonies. At the same time, the more generalised neurosis about those who wandered about without a fixed place of abode or useful occupation resulted in a new vagrancy act requiring the flogging of offenders and their forced return to the places where they had been born or had previously resided for at least three years.[58] Tudor political culture regarded the idle poor as anathema, whatever their ethnic or racial background. It is interesting in this respect that, when the Egyptian Act was amended in 1554, it was specified that those who would abandon the nomadic lifestyle and adopt a stable home and useful employment would be allowed to remain in the realm.[59]

In terms of the treatment of immigrants who were of European ethnicity and of the Christian faith, the official line actually remained quite differentiated and nuanced. On the one hand, early Tudor governments were keen to take up opportunities to sponsor foreigners with special skills who could help to drive new economic activity and set up state-owned industries. The northern French workers introduced into the nascent iron works of the Sussex Weald made a significant contribution to the expansion of the arms industry in the reign of Henry VIII.[60] In 1528 Henry appointed Joachim Hechstetter, a German engineer, as surveyor and master of the king's mines; although Joachim did not stay long in England, his son Daniel later took up the same office.[61]

On the other hand, wider trends in the economy and economic thinking tended simply to reinforce pre-existing protectionism. Although Henry VII abandoned the separate alien subsidy after the grant of 1487, he and his son began to experiment with new forms of general direct taxation, now known as the Tudor subsidies. From 1512, the fiscal alien therefore became, once more, an active reality in direct taxation. Those holding land and/or goods were assessed in the same ways as denizens, but paid double the rates; and those reliant on wages were charged a poll tax reminiscent of the non-householder rate of 1440, and again set at a higher rate than for native people.[62] Meanwhile, continuing concerns about the under-employment of English-born men, coupled with the dominance of the Londoners in the making of national policy in Parliament, kept up the pressure to identify and marginalise aliens in the crafts. A statute of 1523 prohibited alien masters from employing alien apprentices and any more than two alien journeymen, in order to encourage them to take on the native-born.[63] This was reiterated in 1529, when parliamentary legislation also required that all aliens involved in trades should swear oaths of allegiance to the king through the masters of the relevant urban guilds.[64]

Mass denizations, 1540–4

As had often been the case in the fourteenth and fifteenth centuries, national policy towards aliens during the early Tudor period was frequently driven by the exigencies of diplomacy and war. In 1538–40, in the face of deteriorating relations with Francis I and a major threat of invasion from France, Henry VIII prepared for hostilities on a grand scale.[65] The Parliament of 1540 granted a series of heavy taxes on the expectation of a major commitment against England's old enemy.[66] Amongst the legislation granted in return for these fiscal concessions was a major new initiative with regard to resident aliens. 'Calling to his … remembrance the infinite number of strangers and aliens of foreign countries and nations which daily increase and multiply within his … realm and dominions', the king announced that previous legislation to limit the rights of immigrants had been confounded by the too liberal interpretation of denization. Those in receipt of letters of denization thought themselves to be 'as free as

Englishmen naturally born', so that the existing laws regulating strangers did not apply to them. From 1 September 1540, however, all current legislation would apply to anyone born abroad, unless they held letters of denization specifically exempting them from the associated liabilities. This was followed by further limitations on aliens' rights to keep servants or to take leases on houses, shops and land, with fines to be levied on those who broke the law.[67]

Not since Edward I's confiscation of French assets in 1294 had there been such a direct attack on the commercial interests of the alien community resident in the realm. Since the 1430s, moreover, the only real public challenge to the rights of aliens holding letters of denization had been around the issue of tax liability. Now, by contrast, it seemed that all aliens were to be victimised for the deteriorating relationship with France, and that even the holding of existing letters of denization would be no protection against the forfeiture of property and assets. Over the summer of 1540, ambassadors in London and Paris frantically sought clarifications over the manner in which the legislation would be enforced, and the possibility of compensation for those suffering any resulting loss of livelihood.[68]

In certain respects, the episode proved something of a damp squib. Diplomatic efforts successfully avoided the immediate opening of war, and no attempt was made to put the general confiscation into commission. There was still, however, the prospect that Anglo-French animosities would be played out in the looming conflict between Francis I and Emperor Charles V. As a result, there remained strong interest among the resident alien population of England in securing denizations that could provide guarantees against future application of the 1540 statute. In the first four decades of the sixteenth century, letters of denization had generally been granted at the rate of about ten per year, spiking in 1535, when 164 were issued.[69] Now, quite suddenly, there was an explosion of applications, such as to necessitate the creation of new Chancery rolls recording the resulting royal grants. The first of these rolls, which seems to have been compiled between 1539 and 1541, contains 446 grants made to people mainly from France but also from Scotland, the Low Countries, Iberia, Italy and Scandinavia.[70]

The outbreak of the so-called Italian War of 1542–6 (one actually fought out over a much wider European theatre) created fresh anxieties and expectations. In July 1544, as Henry VIII was crossing to Boulogne to lead his forces there, further measures were put in place to require all immigrants to England – but this time, much more explicitly, those who were *French*-born – to take out the appropriate letters of denization.[71] We have already noted in chapter 2 that a minimum of 2,500 denizations were issued from the Chancery in response to this measure – by far the largest peak in the annual number of denizations issued at any time between the fifteenth and the seventeenth century. The resulting documentation bears striking testimony to the extraordinary rush of activity among those – predominantly of French extraction, but also from the Low Countries and Scotland, and living mainly in the South and South-West of England – who sought the protection of the English state in 1544.[72]

The threats to alien security in 1540–1 and the anti-French initiative of 1544 were, like most of the equivalent measures taken since the thirteenth century, reactions to emergencies rather than long-term solutions. Once the threat of confiscation and expulsion was called off in September 1544, the impetus for mass denization also rapidly fell away.[73] In the interim, however, all manner of people had been caught up in the process. In 1540, the Privy Council sent instructions to the mayor and sheriffs of the capital 'for the punishment of [those who] do injuries to the strangers' during the planned campaign of enforced removal.[74] Anne of Cleves, divorced from Henry VIII in 1540, was one of those who thought it best to sue out denization in the febrile atmosphere of 1541.[75] Particularly significant was the expansion of the process into the lower orders of society. In 1544, the recipients of denization included not just merchants, master craftsmen, clergy and professionals, but those in a wide range of urban and rural occupations including apprentices and servants, husbandmen and labourers, and the occasional beggar. To adjust to the expectations of these social levels, the Chancery extended the scale of fees and fines downwards below the usual bottom limit of £2, with most of the humbler sort (or their employers, on their behalf) now paying 6s. 8d. for their letters of denization.[76]

It was perhaps in response to this perceived devaluation of denization that more prominent aliens now began to press for an alternative and possibly enhanced route to denizen status. Aristocrats and merchants alike had been making requests for denization in the form of petitions to the Commons in Parliament since at least the 1420s.[77] From 1539, however, the legislative output of Parliament began to include a discreet category of 'private acts' passed in favour of named individuals and corporate bodies.[78] In 1542 and 1543 this section of the statutes included statements on behalf of English-born men (various London merchants, a former member of the king's household, a royal herald and a lawyer working for the Company of the Merchant Adventurers) who were married to foreign-born women and had children born abroad: one of the recipients of the new status was Edward Castelyn, whose mixed parentage was detailed in chapter 5.

Although these children's rights ought to have been covered adequately by the statute of 1351, it was now decided that private legislation could be issued confirming the full denizen status of individual, named persons.[79] Many of the private acts that followed in the sixteenth and seventeenth centuries were similarly in favour of the children of English-born parents. Partly for this reason, the process of securing a private act of Parliament according denizen status came gradually to be referred to as 'naturalisation', denoting a full and unconditional grant of adopted nationality beyond the conventional limits of denization by letters patent.[80] In particular, acts of naturalisation categorically freed the recipients from paying the alien rates of customs duties, and allowed them (if they were male) to participate in the parliamentary franchise.[81] Like denizations, naturalisations were the preserve of the well-to-do, and were issued in only small numbers: only eighty-three such acts were passed in the Parliaments of Elizabeth I.[82] In this way, however, the mass processes conducted in 1540 and 1544 may be said to have prompted new and higher expectations about the legal position of aliens in England and to have paved the way for the development of a more coherent law of naturalisation in the eighteenth and nineteenth centuries.

The greater degree of interest taken by central government and civic authorities in the regulation of aliens during the later fifteenth and early sixteenth centuries may have contributed, either deliberately or inadvertently, to the development of a sharper sense of institutionalised discrimination against foreigners and racial and religious minorities. While the royal council was generally quick to distance itself from the popular victimisation of immigrant groups, its own policies may have unintentionally given licence to manifestations of suspicion and hatred. In the two chapters that follow, we will look in more detail at the ways in which aliens contributed to the life of the realm and at the reactions, both positive and negative, to their presence. This will provide a more rounded understanding of the ways in which immigrants were variously encouraged, supported and protected, as well as more occasionally objectified, vilified and victimised, by the English state and society.

Notes

1 For English engagement with and understandings of the world within and beyond Europe in the later Middle Ages, see Phillips, *Medieval Expansion of Europe*; Frame, 'The wider world'.

2 Habib, *Black Lives*, p. 274. For more judicious use of this material, see Kaufmann, 'Tudor Britain', pp. 486-7; Kaufmann, *Black Tudors*, pp. 7-31.

3 *Great Tournament Roll of Westminster*, II, plates III and XVIII.

4 For this and the next two paragraphs, see Rigby, *English Society*, pp. 284–302; Mundill, *England's Jewish Solution*; Mundill, *The King's Jews*, pp. 145–66; Cohn, *Popular Protest*, pp. 273–83.

5 Mundill, *The King's Jews*, p. 164.

6 Skinner, 'Introduction', p. 3.

7 For indicative studies, see Delaney (ed.), *Chaucer and the Jews*; Krummel (ed.), *Crafting Jewishness*.

8 Stacey, 'Anti-semitism', p. 170.

9 Heng, 'Jews, Saracens'; Bale, *Feeling Persecuted*, pp. 168–89.

10 Adler, *Jews of Medieval England*, pp. 279–379.

11 Stacey, 'Conversion of Jews'; Fogle, 'Jewish Converts', pp. 214–26.

12 Adler, *Jews of Medieval England*, pp. 313–14, 316–20.

13 Fogle, 'Jewish Converts', pp. 210–11.

14 Kelly, 'Jews and Saracens', p. 139; Fogle, 'Jewish Converts', p. 211.

15 E 179/144/54, m. 10.

16 Weiner, 'Note on Jewish doctors'; Lazzareschi, 'Le ricchezze di due medici lucchesi della Rinascenza'. We are grateful to Christine Meek for information drawn from her unpublished research in the archives of Lucca, which shows that neither Nigarelli's paternal nor his maternal ancestry included any reported Jewish heritage. Nigarelli was betrothed to Caterina, the sister of Paulo Guinigi, lord of Lucca, in 1401, in what was planned as a Christian union: Archivio di Stato di Lucca, Diplomatico, Archivio di Stato, 1401 4 Giugno. It is highly unlikely that Guinigi would have allowed a match with either a Jew or a convert. For Henry IV's request to Guinigi that Nigarelli be allowed to remain in England, see Archivio di Stato di Lucca, Diplomatico, Archivio di Stato – Tarpea, 1412 Ottobre 14.

17 Hirschman and Yates, *Early Jews and Muslims of England and Wales*, argues for a Jewish presence in England across the Middle Ages, based mainly on very ambiguous surname evidence. For problems surrounding Jewish forenames, see Clark, *Words, Names and History*, p. 254 and n. 65.

18 For 'Isaac' see C 1/278/22 (1504–15); C 241/69/206 (1307); E 150/21/11 (1526); etc. For 'Moses' see SP 46/183, fol. 29 (1440); WARD 2/5/20A/3 (1479); etc. For 'Jew', see C 44/25/13 (1422–3); C 241/139/118 (1359); C 241/158/63 (1376); C 241/212/40 (1418); SC 8/221/11030 (1390–1); SC 8/267/13313 (1390).

19 See, for example, C 1/15/201 (1443–56); C 1/23/5 (1353–4).

20 For 'Isaac', see: E 179/87/133, rot. 5d; E 179/124/107, rots 1, 7. For 'Abraham', see: E 179/150/219, rot. 4; E 179/150/279, rot. 1d; E 179/241/327 Part 2, rot. 3d. For Peter Jewe, see E 179/235/23, m. 2.

21 Samuel, 'London's Portuguese Jewish community'.

22 C 1/946/28.

23 Katz, *Philo-Semitism and the Readmission of the Jews*; Walsham, *Charitable Hatred*, pp. 245, 259.

24 Calkin, *Saracens and the Making of English Identity*; Akbari, *Idols in the East*; Bartlett, 'Looking at t'Other'.

25 Matar, 'First Turks and Moors in England', p. 261.

26 SC 1/12/105; SC 1/62/30; Housley, *Later Crusades*, pp. 278–81.

27 SC 8/85/4243.

28 Gover, 'The first black Briton?'; Keefe and Holst, *Osteological Analysis*, pp. 7–8.

29 Passmore, 'Medieval black Briton found'; 'Historical Ipswich skeleton finally identified'.

30 *Register of Edward the Black Prince*, IV, 10.

31 Ormrod, 'John Mandeville', pp. 335–6.

32 Fogle, 'Jewish Converts', p. 212.

33 Fogle, 'Jewish Converts', pp. 152–4, 157.

34 Griffiths, *Reign of King Henry VI*, p. 554.

35 E 179/242/25, m. 10; E 179/95/126 Part 1, m. 3. *Alien Communities*, p. 29 n. 72 erroneously extends 'Black' to 'Blackman'.

36 Ormrod, 'John Mandeville', pp. 336–8.

37 Heng, 'Jews, Saracens', pp. 260–1.

38 See, for example: Richard Blake, Irish, at Salisbury in 1440 (E 179196/100, rot. 4); Christina Blak, Scot, at Newbiggin (Northumberland) in 1440 (E 179/158/41, m. 5); the husband and wife Herman and Gunna Blake, 'Dutch', at Huntingdon in 1440 (E 179/235/4, m. 5); and the Norman John Blake at Eastbury (Dorset) in 1524 (E 179/103/119, rot. 14d).

39 Ungerer, 'Recovering a black African's voice', p. 267 n. 4; Kaufmann, 'Sir Pedro Negro'.

40 London: E 179/144/42, m. 15; E 179/144/72; E 179/235/23, m. 2 (five instances), m. 8; E 179/236/74. Southampton: E 179/173/32, m. 1; E 179/173/134, m. 1; E 179/173/136; E 179/173/137, m. 1 (two instances); E 179/173/139. Sandwich: E 179/235/55, m. 1 (three instances). See also 'de Nigrone' in London in 1443: E 179/144/52, m. 3.

41 E 179/136/206, m. 3.

42 Laughton, 'Mapping the migrants', p. 176.

43 Ungerer, 'Prostitution', p. 199.

44 C 1/148/67.

45 Ruddock, 'Alien merchants in Southampton', pp. 11–12; *Alien Communities*, p. 29.

46 Habib, *Black Lives*, pp. 63–4.

47 Lowe, 'Stereotyping of black Africans', pp. 35–41.

48 Bartlett, *Making of Europe*, pp. 236–42; Wickham, *Medieval Europe*, pp. 207–8, 240.

49 For the remainder of this paragraph, see Griffiths, *King and Country*, pp. 52–3.

50 Pettegree, 'Foreign population of London', pp. 141–6.

51 Pettegree, *Foreign Protestant Communities*, pp. 9–76. See also, in general, Terpstra, *Religious Refugees*.

52 Habib, *Black Lives*, pp. 63–119.

53 *Tudor Royal Proclamations I*, no. 52.

54 *SR*, III, 327; Cressy, 'Trouble with gypsies'.

55 Kaufmann, 'Tudor Britain'.

56 Kaufmann, 'Caspar van Senden'. See also Fraser, 'Slaves or free people?'.

57 Guy, *Tudor England*, pp. 30–52.

58 *SR*, III, 328–32; McIntosh, *Poor Relief*, pp. 121–3.

59 *SR*, IV, 242–3.

60 Awty, 'Continental origins of Wealden ironworkers'.
61 Ash, *Power, Knowledge, and Expertise*, pp. 45–6.
62 Jurkowski, Smith and Crook, *Lay Taxes*, pp. 130–2, 137–9, 140–1, 143–4.
63 *SR*, III, 208–9.
64 *SR*, III, 297–8.
65 For the full details of the diplomatic and military context for the ensuing dispute, see Potter, *Henry VIII and Francis I*.
66 *SR*, III, 744, 812–24; Jurkowski, Smith and Crook, *Lay Taxes*, pp. 141–2. In principle, all exemptions from subsidies were cancelled for the running of the new tax: R. Schofield, *Taxation under the Early Tudors*, pp. 91–2.
67 *SR*, III, 765–6. For exemptions granted to members of the royal household, see *POPC*, VII, 21, 23, 28.
68 *POPC*, VII, 63; *LP*, XV, no. 995.
69 *LP*, I–XIII, passim.
70 C 67/72.
71 *LP*, XIX, pt 1, nos 936, 969.
72 C 67/73; WAM 12261.
73 *LP*, XIX, pt 2, no. 332.
74 *POPC*, VII, 7.
75 *LP*, XVI, no. 503. For other considerations behind this grant, see Warnicke, *Marrying of Anne of Cleves*, p. 246.
76 For the beggars, see chapter 7.
77 These were recorded on the patent rolls: see summaries of cases in *PROME*, X, 316, 433, 481; XI, 63, 64, 156, 191. There is one instance of a resulting denization being recorded on the parliament roll in 1433 (*PROME*, XI, 114–15), but denizations were not treated as statutes in the fifteenth century.
78 Clifford, *History of Private Bill Legislation*, I, 270.
79 *SR*, III, 865; *LP*, XVIII, pt 1, no. 66 (31, 33).
80 *Letters of Denization, 1509–1603*, pp. 43, 86, 90, 167, labels the parliamentary acts of denization of 1542 and 543 as naturalisations. However, see Parry, *British Nationality Law*, pp. 43–6, 50–2, 60–3, 74–8, for the continuing ambiguity between denization and naturalisation.
81 *Letters of Denization, 1603–1800*, I, vi–vii.
82 Selwood, *Diversity and Difference*, pp. 49–50.

9

Cultural contact

The previous chapters have given a lot of consideration to the legal and fiscal definitions of the alien, and to the means by which aliens could acquire formal rights equivalent to those of the native-born. It is now time to address the processes by which immigrants may have aspired, and/or were deemed, to 'become English' in a social and cultural sense. It may not be altogether useful to refer to this as a process of 'assimilation', a term which can imply the effective loss of natal heritage and the voluntary or enforced acceptance of the totality of the adopted culture. Rather, the social phenomena that we will observe in this and the next chapter were about different degrees of acculturation, in which both immigrants and host communities had to negotiate the process of inclusion or exclusion, and in which both therefore experienced elements of adjustment and change.

The idea of England

To propose that foreign immigrants to England during the later Middle Ages thought consciously about 'becoming English', we first have to be clear as to whether there was a tangible sense of Englishness by which they could navigate such a tricky path. Nationality had different connotations in the Middle Ages from today, and was not by any means always the primary marker of social identity. Nevertheless, national attributes were clearly understood as a very important element of a shared culture.

In recent generations, medieval historians have been increasingly pre-occupied with the 'idea of England': that is, with the political-cultural concept that framed both the development of the English state and the attitudes and identities of those who lived under its rule.[1] A sense of

Englishness was certainly not new in the later Middle Ages, and had a recognisable lineage stretching back to the times of Bede and of Alfred the Great. There was, however, a clear quickening of such sentiment from the thirteenth century onwards. An older generation of historians argued that the loss of the Norman and Angevin possessions in northern France during the first half of the thirteenth century was, in effect, a moment of liberation that allowed the laws and customs of the realm, after three centuries of Scandinavian and French rule, to become fully 'English'.[2] Today, the step change is more usually associated with the ambitions of Edward I. This king's firm intention of stamping his dominance in the British Isles and retaining his dynasty's remaining possessions in France is seen to have played a key role in the development of a more adamant expression of English nationhood.[3] Paradoxically, then, the encouragement and harnessing of national sentiment in the era of the Hundred Years War was not the consequence of English isolationism, but part of the Plantagenets' continued commitment to their wider dominions and of their close engagement with their European neighbours, enemies and friends alike.[4] This is precisely the vision presented by Thomas Polton, a clerical lawyer and member of the English delegation at the great church council at Constance in 1417. Responding to French suggestions that the English did not deserve their status as a 'principal nation' alongside the Italians, the French, the Germans and the Spanish, Polton argued strongly that England's voice in Europe relied on her cultural and political dominance across the British Isles – and in parts of France, too.[5]

Over the period covered by this book, the ruling elite actively promoted the idea of England for explicit purposes of internal and external propaganda. Whatever their own cultural instincts, kings from the later thirteenth century gradually came to display a characteristically nationalistic public persona. This was first exemplified in the patronage of the cults of English-born or English-adopted saints, especially Edward the Confessor and St George. Later, under Henry IV and Henry V, it was also manifested in the self-conscious rejection of French and the adoption of Middle English as a language of authentic communication between the king and his subjects.[6] Another very important element of the new Englishness was an emphasis on independence and self-determination, captured in the concept of sovereignty, which entered English political rhetoric from the time of Edward I. The idea was used across the period to argue both for the territorial integrity of English dependencies (especially Gascony) and for English immunity from the universalist claims of the Holy Roman Empire and the papacy. Sovereignty also became the device by which Henry VIII's regime argued its right to set up the independent Church of England, free of all other temporal authorities.[7] Finally, there was an observable change of tone towards the end of our period when, with the close of the Hundred Years War, the domestic preoccupations attendant upon the Wars of the Roses, and the onset of the Reformation, there developed an increasingly insular and exceptionalist view of Englishness that defined the country's attributes in reference to a discreet and stable territorial state.[8]

In spite of this emergent isolationism, English notions of ethnicity did not, as so often in medieval and modern societies, result in some assertion of a ring-fenced racial purity. The cultural and political constructions of ethnic identity in the Anglo-Saxon kingdoms of the early Middle Ages may have subscribed quite forcefully to a notion of exclusive ethnogenesis, in which self-identification with continental Germanic ancestors became the means of differentiating the dominant culture from those of subaltern 'natives'.[9] However, historical writing of the high and later Middle Ages was much more nuanced, consistently representing England as a place of ethnic diversity where the descendants of the country's first inhabitants, the Britons, mingled with those of Roman, Scots, Pictish, Germanic, Viking and Norman descent. The 'people of the English' (*gens Anglorum*) was therefore regarded not as a single whole but, emphatically, as a hybrid: a 'people of diverse birth' (*pople de diverse nacioun*), as the English writer Peter Langtoft put it (in French) at the beginning of the fourteenth century.[10] This was also acknowledged to be potentially problematic: according to the chroniclers, the social homogeneity and political unity that had been achieved in England was the product not of innate racial superiority but of God's providence. The supremacist myths that later developed around the Germanic invasions of the Roman Empire and led nineteenth-century British historians to see English identity as exclusively bound up in a stable and exclusive Anglo-Saxon 'race' was therefore no part of later medieval thinking, even amongst the most jingoistic of commentators.[11]

National stereotypes

To understand the impact that these ideas had on their intended audiences within the realm, we can turn to the chronicles, imaginative literature and art of the period. Perhaps not surprisingly, these sources tended to couch Englishness mainly in opposition to other – and always seemingly baser – cultures. Because the Welsh and the Irish were seen to be so often resistant to their English overlords, for example, and because the Scots actively resisted the attempts of Edward I and Edward III to bring the kingdom into the Plantagenet orbit, the inhabitants of all the Celtic parts of the British Isles were customarily cast as unworthy, treacherous, irrational, fickle and degenerate. 'A barbarous, brutal and foolish people' is how the Scots were described in a Latin poem commemorating the English victory at the battle of Falkirk in 1298. English commentators were also stinging in their assessments of the 'wild' Welsh and Irish: 'May Wales be sunk deep to the Devil!' exclaimed Peter Langtoft.[12]

Many of these stock images were also applied to people living on the continent of Europe, particularly those with whom England was regularly at war.[13] The French elite was usually acknowledged to share in the same international code of chivalry to which the English aristocracy subscribed, and was therefore given credit, where it was due, for its part in upholding the values of honour, prowess, courage and mercy. This, however, did not stop the English from branding the generality of the French as infected with the sin of pride and fatally weakened by a supposed tendency to lasciviousness.[14] The anonymous Latin poem *The Dispute between an Englishman and a Frenchman*, written in England during the triumphalism following Edward III's victories at Crécy and Calais in 1346–7, defamed French men as eunuchs: 'Because French womanhood has emasculated the effeminate French, take on the name and style of "capon", Frenchman!'[15] The Flemish – the term used by the English from the end of the fourteenth century to describe all the subjects of the duke of Burgundy – were cast as especially treacherous. Among the Middle English political texts written in the aftermath of the defection of Burgundy to the French in 1435 and the Franco-Burgundian siege of English Calais in 1436 was one now known as *The Scorn of the Duke of Burgundy*, in which Duke Philip of Burgundy was cast as the epitome of duplicity, the 'founder of new falsehood'.[16] Repeated English comments about the drunken, riotous and promiscuous tendencies of people from Flanders represented a second order of characterisation, perhaps derived from more direct observation of beer-brewing and -drinking immigrants from the Low Countries.[17] The Middle English poem the *Libelle of Englyshe Polycye*, written to advocate the safekeeping of Calais after the threat of 1436, claimed that two Flemings would attempt to drink a barrel of beer in one sitting, urinating in their clothes as they did so.[18] Not, of course, that the English had a monopoly on such slurs. A very common trope in medieval Europe, one to which the French and Scots enthusiastically subscribed, stated that the English, like dogs and demons, had tails.[19]

When it came to those peoples with whom England retained formal or friendly association, however, the stereotypes were rather less loaded and not usually overtly satirical or critical. At various points from the late thirteenth century, for example, the royal Exchequer used visual representations of 'nations' as a means of cataloguing and cross-referencing its rapidly expanding archive. Here, the weapons, hairstyles and dress (or undress) of the Welsh, Irish and Scots clearly referenced barbarianism.[20] In contrast, the king's subjects in Aquitaine were simply depicted in the act of tending vines and treading grapes, a reference to the heavy English dependency on the Gascon wine trade. Aragon was represented by horsemen riding à la jineta, a distinctively Spanish style associated with the small, light breed of horses known as jennets. The inhabitants of northern Italy were identified by what was apparently seen as a characteristic male headgear of the region, a capacious and luxurious hat with a broad headband.[21] In a rather different context, the Libelle of Englyshe Polycye had much to say about the characteristic commodities being brought into England from the various countries with which the kingdom traded. Although he resorted to the stock stereotypes of the 'wild' Irish and the drunken Flemish, however, the anonymous author of the Libelle was relatively restrained in his deployment of hostile ethnic comment: here, questions of nationalism focus on economic questions rather than simply resolving into straightforward ridicule or hatred of foreigners.[22]

Allegiant nationality and its limitations

One of the key challenges in studying the history of immigration is to understand how, and whether, ethnic stereotyping affected the actual functioning of individual relationships between members of the immigrant and host communities. One way to examine this topic is via what Andrea Ruddick has called 'allegiant identity', in which those not born in England acquired – or were excluded from – full participation in 'Englishness'. As Ruddick has remarked, the main evidence for people 'becoming English' by simple transfer of their affective allegiance (rather than, for example, by the process of denization) comes in relation to foreign aristocrats and soldiers who, for a range of reasons, decided to throw in their lot with the English cause during the Scottish and French wars.[23] In some cases the decision to go over to the English had long-term consequences that made for a real sense either of exclusion or of integration. Guichard d'Angle, the Poitevin nobleman who became a prominent member of the English court under Edward III and Richard II, remembered in his will 'my people who have served me and who have lost their country for me'.[24] By contrast, the chronicler Jean Froissart commented that the family of Thierry (or 'Canon') Robessart, a nobleman of Hainaut who re-established his family's long connections with the Plantagenet court by doing homage to Edward III in 1365, soon became 'English at heart'.[25]

In other cases, especially those where the laws of chivalry did not prevail, the choices made and identities espoused seem a good deal more pragmatic. An outstanding case is Gervase le Vulre, a native of Bruges in Flanders whose natal surname was de Vulre ('the fuller'). Gervase spent his early career in the 1420s and early 1430s in the service of the English regime in northern France.[26] The defection of the overlord of Flanders, the duke of Burgundy, to the Valois cause in 1435 proved decisive for Gervase's sense of identity. By this stage he was expressing his name in a French form, as le Vulre, in order to minimise his Flemish birth and identify himself professionally with the Plantagenets' 'French' regime. In 1436 Gervase moved to England and became secretary for French affairs to Henry VI.[27] When he applied for letters of denization in 1441, le Vulre actually stated that he had been born in the kingdom of France.[28] He defended this position again in the 1450s, claiming as a result to be 'perfectly versed in French' and therefore fully equipped for his specialist role in Henry VI's service.[29] It was only in his will of 1467 that Gervase once more openly acknowledged his Flemish birth.[30] For le Vulre and others like him, nationality was a matter of practicality, and was defined by personal and professional experience rather than simply by birth and name.

The reaction of English society to cases of 'allegiant identity', even when these were followed up with acts of denization, could be one of suspicion and resistance. As we saw in chapter 2, the crown undertook a series of measures across the course of the fourteenth century to ensure that the foreign-born inmates of the alien priories were placed under proper surveillance, culminating in the development of the idea that the priories themselves could enjoy denizen status. This, however, did not stop local people, or the political community at large, from believing that the alien priories were filled with infiltrators and spies. In 1295, a man named Warin of Northampton took advantage of the recent proclamations announcing the confiscation of the alien priories and possessions of other French people resident in England to claim that the head of the alien priory of St Neots (Huntingdonshire) had raised the standard of the king of France over his house.[31] Shortly before the general expulsion ordinance of 1378, the parliamentary Commons alleged that, in spite of the wartime seizure of their estates, many alien priories were still under the effective control of foreigners, who were acting as informants for the French enemy, to the general ruin of the realm.[32]

Even royal protection could not ultimately do much to prevent the bubbling up of local and personal animosities. Reginald Newport, who came originally from Nieuwpoort in Flanders, made a career over thirty years in the household service of Edward III and as keeper of the fisheries of the Thames Valley. The easy anglicisation of his surname, together with the fact that he was also often known as 'Reginald of the Chamber', served to disguise his origins very effectively. When he came into conflict with the authorities of London over the city's rights to regulate its own waterways, however, the civic elite submitted a petition to Richard II's first Parliament, which tellingly labelled Reginald as a 'Fleming' and immediately thereby associated him with the Flemish community of weavers who were so unpopular in the capital around this time.[33]

There are a number of similar examples of the way in which host communities could sustain memory and prompt suspicion about 'enemies' of lesser social status, too. The Scottish woman Alicia Emson was said to have lit beacons to warn the inhabitants of Galloway of an imminent English raid upon them in 1384. The record of her case revealed that Alicia had lived in England for around forty years and had married, had children and been widowed there. Ironically, the finding that she had never sworn a formal oath of fealty to the king of England or to the wardens of the March saved her from further inquiry, since she was felt not to be entirely subject to the English court that heard the allegation.[34] At Maldon in Essex in 1459 a more complicated case arose when Giles Morvyle, a tailor who had earlier been admitted as a burgess of the town on the basis that he came from Jersey, and was therefore born in the allegiance of the king, was suspected of being 'a Spaniard or a Breton'. Upon further investigation it was revealed that Giles, in fact, was none of these things, but was rather a native of Flanders. Interestingly, again, the truth set the suspect free: upon admitting his deception and paying a fine in 1460, Morvyle was allowed to resume his place as a member of the town's franchise.[35] These two examples reveal much not only about the simmering distrust that must often have prevailed towards those of foreign extraction over long periods of time, but also to the inability or reluctance of formal legal systems to deal too harshly with mildly seditious activity or false claims of nationality.

Such reactions to the presence of long-term alien residents in the realm serve to suggest the sense of conditionality under which many such immigrants must have lived. Similar uncertainty is also evident in the assessment and payment of the alien subsidies. In chapter 3 we noted a number of cases from London where recipients of letters of denization were nonetheless made liable to the alien subsidies. Gervase le Vulre again provides a particularly interesting example of this phenomenon. His letters of denization were granted in January 1441; given the timing, it seems quite likely that he intended these specifically as a guarantee against the tax imposed in the Parliament of 1439–40. Yet Gervase was assessed repeatedly for the subsidy throughout the decade 1441–51, and in 1456 he even went to the length of securing a royal intervention to persuade the tax officials in London not to press him for further payments.[36] The pressure brought upon le Vulre was not typical, and may have been the consequence of some other antipathy between him and the authorities of the city. Nevertheless, this and the other cases discussed earlier serve to exemplify the limits of denization. Being legally granted the equivalence of denizen status was not the same as 'becoming English', and in some cases at least the motivations and actions of persons who had received letters of denization were evidently sufficient to raise real questions in English officialdom about their integrity as sworn subjects of the crown.

The royal court

While it was never a primary driver of policy towards aliens, the royal court continued throughout the later Middle Ages to be a focus for wider cultural and political attitudes to foreigners. It also provides us with a useful index of the success of the formal measures put in place to protect foreigners and their rights in England, and of the take-up of letters of denization.

Throughout the thirteenth, fourteenth and first half of the fifteenth centuries, English kings tended to marry foreign wives of high birth: it was only under the Yorkists and early Tudors that monarchs more generally made matches with English-born women. Social commentators (most of whom were members of the clergy) were fond of suggesting that the entourages of foreign queens threatened the morals and mores of English fashionable society. Under normal circumstances, this discourse was relatively harmless fun: witness, for example, the contemporary comments on the decadent and indecent styles of clothing supposedly introduced by the Hainauters and Bohemians who arrived in England in the trains respectively of Edward III's queen, Philippa, and Richard II's first wife, Anne.[37] At moments of high tension, however, the political community looked to the king to set a proper example by limiting the influence of the queen and, if necessary, expelling foreigners from his and her households. The public announcement of emergency measures on the outbreak of war with France in 1324 included the statement that all persons 'of the lordship and dominion of the king of France', including those in the household of the queen, would be sent out of the realm; and since Queen Isabella was herself the sister of the king of France, Edward II's government actually seized all her landed property in England – albeit compensating her immediately with a cash income.[38]

Later, under Henry IV and Henry V, a cluster of factors – rebellion in Wales, the presence of the king of Scotland in England as a prisoner of war, the reopening of hostilities with France and the Breton connections of Henry IV's second wife, Joan of Navarre – led to demands for the expulsion of various alien groups from the king's and queen's households in 1404, 1406, 1413 and 1416.[39] The political pursuit of Joan of Navarre's Breton entourage went a good deal further than most previous attempts at purges of the court. In 1406, the parliamentary Commons actually presented the steward of the king's household with a list of forty-four named individuals in the queen's service, including her cook and laundresses, who they insisted should not be allowed to wriggle out of the new expulsion ordinance.[40]

We can see the consequences of such a position working out in terms of applications for denizenship. In 1410, in response to a further request for a general removal of aliens from the realm, the king insisted that 'those who are now resident in England' should be allowed to remain so long as they were 'sworn to be loyal to the king and to the realm'.[41] Soon afterwards the Breton John Peryan, a long-standing courtier of Richard II and Henry IV who had escaped inclusion on the Commons' 1406 hit list, took out letters patent of denization for himself and for his wife, Joan, the principal lady-in-waiting of the queen.[42] By Henry VI's reign, denization was a relatively routine resort for 'above-stairs' members of the king's and queen's households.[43] It was also now considered appropriate to grant denizations to foreign women marrying into the royal family and titled nobility. Following the precedent set by Lucia Visconti, countess of Kent, in 1408, two Portuguese ladies, both named Beatrice, who were the widows of Lord Talbot and the earl of Arundel, sought the benefits of denization in order to have incontrovertible right to their dowers in 1419 and 1421.[44] Anne of Burgundy and Jacqueline of Hainaut, the wives of Henry VI's uncles the dukes of Bedford and Gloucester, received such grants in the Parliament of 1423, and Bedford's second wife, Jacquetta of Luxembourg, was similarly licensed in 1433.[45]

Royal and princely courts were obvious magnets for aliens as a result of their cosmopolitan outlook, their international dynastic links and their desire to attract the brightest and best artists and scholars of the day. In the thirteenth and fourteenth centuries, the prevailing influences on the English court were from France and the Low Countries. The military households of Edward I and Edward III included significant numbers of knights and esquires from Gascony (in the first instance) and from Flanders, Brabant and Hainaut (in the second).[46] James of St George, who hailed from Savoy, was the architect of many of the great castles erected in North Wales in the 1280s and 1290s to solidify and symbolise Edward I's recent conquest of the region.[47] In the 1360s, Queen Philippa acted as patron and protector to Jean Froissart, the Hainaut-born writer and chronicler, who spent the years before the queen's death in 1369 writing what he called 'pretty ditties and treatises of love' for her entertainment.[48]

It was by no means only the francophone areas of Europe, however, that contributed to the cosmopolitanism of the English court in the fourteenth century. The royal family, for example, retained physicians from Mediterranean lands. The medical expert (and financier) Pancio da Controne, who came from Lombardy, was in the service of Edward II, Queen Isabella and Edward III, while both Edward III and Richard II employed the services of a Spanish doctor, Paul Gabrielis.[49] We encountered a number of Henry IV's Italian physicians in chapter 5; and the French surgeon Thomas Belwel, who received denization in 1443, was one of a group of experts who sought remedies for Henry VI's 'madness' in the mid-1450s.[50] In cultural terms, too, the range of influences was diverse. Peter of Spain was retained as one of the court painters to Edward I, who himself adopted the Spanish gown and biretta as his costume of relaxation.[51] Later, under Edward III and Richard II, close connections with Emperor Charles IV, king of Bohemia, encouraged a steady to and fro of musicians and artists between Prague and Westminster.[52] The late fourteenth-century poet Geoffrey Chaucer, so often hailed as the father of English literature, was deeply influenced by contemporary writing in France and Italy. A century later, after William Caxton set up the first printing press in England, a number of continental experts moved to England to exploit the new demand for books, including William Machlinia, from Mechlin in the Low Countries, Wynkyn de Worde, from the Rhineland, and John Letowe, who seems to have been born in Lithuania.[53]

In the fifteenth century there was a significant shift in the alien presence at court as the rise of humanism encouraged English royals to patronise Italian scholars and artists. Humphrey, duke of Gloucester, uncle of Henry

VI, brought the Ferrara-born Tito Livio Frulovisi to England for several years in the late 1430s, during which time Livio wrote a Latin *Life* of Henry V, later translated into English, and a number of anti-Burgundian political tracts. His successor, Antonio Beccaria, originally from Verona and working in England in the early 1440s, deployed his humanistic training as a speechwriter for the duke.[54] It would be a mistake to see such figures as permanent residents, since the duration of their stay depended entirely on the nature of their employment and the opportunities arising in other courts and metropolitan centres. By the late fifteenth century, however, the English crown set sufficient store by the presence of highly educated Italians to offer special inducements to them to remain in the king's service. Pietro Carmeliano, who arrived in England from Brescia in 1481, secured a pension from Henry VII in 1486 and letters patent of denization in 1488. In 1490, he became the king's Latin secretary, and remained in England for the rest of his life, residing in Westminster and dying eventually in 1527.[55] One of Carmeliano's successors as Latin secretary to Henry VIII, Andreas Ammonius, established himself as a major figure in the intellectual world of London before entering the king's service in 1511, and died in England in 1517.[56] The best known such case is that of Polydore Vergil, born near Urbino in c. 1470, who arrived in England in 1502. Under encouragement from Henry VII, Polydore began his Latin *English History* in 1506–7, completing the first version in 1513 and continuing the project in further editions down to his death. Vergil spent most of his time in England, though he retained close contact with Italy, where he died in 1555.[57]

As the intellectual force of the Renaissance began to express itself in literature, art and architecture, the English court also opened up to the influence of a wider range of scholars and artists from both Italy and elsewhere. The Italian sculptor Pietro Torrigiano, who was commissioned to prepare tombs for Lady Margaret Beaufort and for Henry VII and Elizabeth of York, was in England from about 1507 to the early 1520s.[58] The painter Antonio Toto, also Italian, arrived in Torrigiano's wake and stayed in England for the rest of his career, dying in 1528.[59] The great humanist scholar Desiderius Erasmus, a native of Rotterdam, resided intermittently in England for about ten years between 1499 and 1514, and for the rest of his career made occasional visits from his various bases on the continent.[60] Those involved in making and performing on musical instruments also arrived in England. Four organ makers, three of them specified as coming from the Low Countries and Germany, appear in the oaths of fealty and the alien subsidy returns of the fifteenth century, two of them based in Westminster and one in London (with the other residing in Norwich).[61]

No fewer than ten members of the great Venetian family of instrument makers and performers, the Bassanos, received denization in 1545 as 'the king's musicians'.[62]

The outstanding example of a Renaissance figure in long-term residence in England is that of Hans Holbein the younger, born in Augsburg, who lived more or less permanently in England under the patronage of Henry VIII from 1526 to 1528 and again from 1531/2 to his death in 1543.[63] Holbein's membership of the resident alien population in early Tudor England is nicely typified by his reaction to the 1540 statute, discussed in chapter 8, which threatened to place significant restrictions on the rights of aliens to keep servants or to take leases on houses, shops and land. In June 1541, Holbein took the same step as hundreds of other aliens in the capital and elsewhere and sued out letters patent of denization by way of an insurance policy against the application of the 1540 legislation.[64] The denization represented a distinctly pragmatic move, driven particularly by the restrictions that would otherwise have been placed on Holbein's ability to staff his London workshop. If, in a legal sense, denization made Holbein 'English', then in his work as an artist he exemplified the continued and reinforced theme of internationalism in the world of the courts and the arts.

The status of the English language

The most powerful marker of aliens' identity in the later Middle Ages was undoubtedly language. First-generation immigrants not easily distinguishable from members of the English host community in terms of their dress and lifestyle were nonetheless instantly identifiable as foreigners once they spoke. England in the fourteenth and fifteenth centuries was still very far off the assumptions made in modern states that immigrants seeking citizenship have to demonstrate the ability to communicate in the appropriate language. It is clear, however, that language was in many respects both the primary barrier to, and the primary vector of, social integration. There is a huge body of written evidence from which we can deduce much about the nature of the spoken languages of England in this period. Ironically, however, that evidence yields remarkably little by way of insight into the challenges that confronted those who sought to acquire the English vernacular as a second (or third, or fourth) language of oral communication.

What is clear is that English was virtually unknown, and certainly not taught in any systematic way, outside the British Isles. This was partly a matter of politics. In 1377 it was declared in Parliament that no one having

English as a first language was tolerated 'in the lands of our enemies'.[65] But it was also a fact that English – unlike French, the default language of the courts and of diplomacy – had virtually no international currency. None of the continental-born clerics who gathered at the Council of Constance in the early fifteenth century, for example, claimed any proficiency in English.[66] European intellectuals were indeed much more inclined to deprecate English and to see it as inferior to those other vernacular languages – notably French and Italian – that were making headway as mediums of literary expression in the fourteenth and fifteenth centuries. The French poet Eustace Deschamps may have congratulated his contemporary, Geoffrey Chaucer, on his English translation of the French *Roman de la Rose*, but he did so in the context of a general condemnation of the English vernacular as an inelegant hybrid (as he saw it) of Latin, German and French.[67]

English-born commentators shared the sense of uncertainty about the validity of their vernacular. Chaucer's writings have often been upheld as marking the final 'triumph of English' over the other written languages of medieval England, Latin and Anglo-Norman French.[68] At the time, however, people were much less confident. Chaucer's contemporary, John Trevisa, highlighted the problem of regional dialects in pointing out that southern-born English people could barely comprehend what they regarded as the harsh and unruly language of their compatriots in the North.[69] Ironically, the increasing tendency to borrow words from French (and other continental languages) caused something of a crisis among the purists: the fourteenth-century chronicler Ranulf Higden felt that the 'native tongue' of England was becoming bastardised or contaminated.[70] All of this clearly had an impact on the perceptions of non-English speakers: the author Thomas Usk, writing in the 1380s, posed the pertinent question as to how anyone could possibly expect a Frenchman (or, by extension, any foreigner) to cope with such a wayward language.[71]

The fact that English people themselves were much less disposed than their modern counterparts simply to assume that foreigners could or should speak English made for much more pragmatic linguistic encounters. English people at many different levels in society were themselves capable of speaking or understanding more than their own native vernacular. Recent work has done much to emphasise that Anglo-Norman French remained a living language in England throughout the fourteenth century – certainly written and read, and also spoken at least in elite contexts – and that it only really began to falter with the more widespread adoption of Middle English as a language of record from the 1420s and 1430s.[72] Visitors from France, or from other European regions where versions of French were also used, might have found it possible to communicate in their own language in a variety of contexts: not just in the royal court and in aristocratic households, but among gentry and merchant society, and even on rural manors.[73] Peter Scolemaister, servant to Sir John Montgomery at Faulkbourne in Essex in 1440, was likely a French-born member of the knight's retinue who followed him home from the wars in Normandy, and presumably taught his children (and maybe some of his other servants) at least a smattering of French.[74] Similarly, a number of the French-born parish clergy whom we met in chapter 6 may have provided rudimentary educations in French for the children of parishioners, especially those intended to move on to Latin and, thus, to jobs in the Church or in legal services.

Similar claims are made, to a lesser extent, about those who came from the Low Countries and spoke various forms of Middle Dutch and Middle Low German. The number of loan words from these latter languages found in Middle English, especially in relation to the process of trade and to specific activities such as fishing and beer brewing, suggests that the English may have found it comparatively easy to comprehend the native vernaculars of their near neighbours from across the North Sea.[75] The early fifteenth-century satirical poem *London Lickpenny* deploys the Dutch word 'koepen' as a synonym of the English word 'buy' in an apparent evocation of the mixed speech of the quayside and market place.[76] At Playden near the port town of Rye in Sussex, the tomb slab of the brewer Cornelis Roetmans, made in the fifteenth or early sixteenth century, has an inscription in Middle Dutch: *Hier is begraven Cornelis Roetmans bidt voer de ziele* (Cornelis Roetmans is buried here: pray for [his] soul'). The context may be sufficient to suggest that literate English parishioners knew intuitively what the inscription meant – though there was also sufficient of a 'Dutch' presence in the locality to make it possible that Roetmans' (or his family's) choice also represented the self-conscious assertion of a small linguistic community.[77]

An argument might be made that immigrants who spoke languages that were not part of the West Germanic or Romance linguistic groups might have been particularly disposed to use their native tongues in a private setting as part of a self-conscious expression of their sense of exile from the homeland. One instance is provided, albeit at a high social level, by the use of the West Slavic language, Czech, by Richard II's queen, Anne of Bohemia and the followers whom she brought with her from her father's court in Prague. Anne and her ladies did not just know Czech, of course: they were also educated to read and/or speak Latin, French and German; and Anne herself seems to have acquired a good comprehension of English after her marriage.[78] Like the characteristically Bohemian forms that can be seen to have influenced the art of Richard II's court, however, Czech served as an emotional bond within the group of Czech exiles and to their relatives back home. One of Anne's cousins and attendants, Margaret of Teschen, who married the Norfolk knight, Simon Felbrigg, had a Czech translation of a Latin prayer written into her English family's book of hours as though by way of a personal commemoration of her own origins and connections – and perhaps as a means of giving her offspring a smattering of the language of their maternal forebears.[79] The Latin inscription on the memorial brass that Sir Simon commissioned after Margaret's death in 1413 and which still survives in the parish church of Felbrigg described his wife as 'of the nation and noble blood of Bohemia' (*nacione et generoso sanguine Boema*).[80]

Acquiring English

It would be highly disingenuous, however, to assume that all those who moved to England in the later Middle Ages were able to get by effectively on the basis of speaking their own languages more slowly, or deploying a few common or borrowed words in English. Profession and occupation sometimes demanded a degree of linguistic proficiency. The Church had an explicit requirement that parochial clergy should be able to communicate in the vernacular, and this seems to have been quite vigilantly enforced. In 1283, for example, the archbishop of Canterbury stressed that Queen Eleanor's physician (and presumably Castilian compatriot) Nicholas de Montimer was unsuitable for appointment to an English benefice because he had no knowledge of English.[81] Equally, by the fifteenth century, fostering arrangements and indentures of apprenticeship not uncommonly included the requirement that boys put into service with artisan masters would be educated to a basic level of literacy; in cases where those youths came from overseas, it was occasionally specified that they were expected to become fluent in English.[82]

Higher forces may also have played a part in driving immigrants to become functionally anglophone. From the time of Edward I, royal propaganda played on the emotive idea that the enemy French were intent on eradicating the English language from the face of the earth.[83] The concomitant was that those foreigners living in the realm who could not communicate effectively in the vernacular were not only selfish but potentially seditious. This proposition became part of the wider rhetoric against aliens that developed in London and in Parliament from the second half of the fifteenth century. There were certainly cases of clustering that fed the belief that aliens communicated with, and helped, only their own. The London-based 'Teutonic', Vincent Toteler, taxed for the alien subsidy in 1483, had a wife, Antonia, and daughter, Margaret, both ascribed the same nationality, and twelve servants (nine 'Teutonic' and three French, with one having a 'Teutonic' wife), as well as a live-in associate, Matthew, 'Teutonic', who had his own servant, also 'Teutonic'.[84] There can surely be no doubt either that the default language of the household was the Middle Dutch or Middle Low German of the master and mistress. Yet this is an extreme example, and can hardly be taken as typical even of the capital. The cultural pressures applied on foreign-born residents to acquire some knowledge of English are likely to have increased as our period went on, and to have resulted in levels of proficiency at least appropriate to the social status of most immigrants.

The specific evidence to support such a proposition comes from a handful of cases where English-born people made comments and judgements about the level of trustworthiness of an alien based on his or her use of language, or where particular communities of aliens explicitly recognised the utility of their being represented by people fluent in English. In 1347, during a security emergency on the south coast, the mayor of Salisbury made representations against the expulsion of a French-born resident, Jean Gournay, on the grounds that he was only there 'to improve his English'.[85] Lacking the status of a freeman of the city or letters of protection from the crown, Jean had rather cleverly persuaded the civic authorities that his interest in acquiring linguistic proficiency eliminated any sense that he was a threat to national security. Not so in the case of Thomas Scott, a Scotsman who had been living in England for nearly twenty years when he was called before the ecclesiastical court in York to provide evidence in a divorce case in 1364. The examiner found that it was impossible to believe Scott's testimony because he kept changing his style of speech, sometimes pretending to be an English southerner, sometimes a northerner, and sometimes betraying his origins by pronouncing English words in a Scottish accent.[86]

Much more dramatically, there is the episode during the Peasants' Revolt of 1381 in which the rebels were said to have identified their targets among the members of the Flemish community in London by requiring people to pronounce 'cheese and bread' in the English idiom: those who made the mistake of saying 'case and brode' in the 'Dutch' style were instantly put to death. This is a striking example of the popular belief that a privileged group such as the Flemish weavers of London tended only to look after their own people and interests, and reinforced their sense of exclusiveness through the use of their own native language.[87] A very different perspective is encountered in 1446, when the Medici bank decided not to appoint its own man, Agnolo Tani, as head of the London branch because he was not competent in English, and instead took on Tani's former London employer, the Florentine Gerozzo de' Pigli, who had no previous formal links with the company but had good linguistic skills.[88]

The idea that aliens worked, and lived, by and for themselves became a good deal stronger after the arrival of Protestant dissenters in the middle of the sixteenth century and the setting up of separate churches in which they could practise their religion in their own native tongue.[89] Prior to the Reformation, by contrast, there is comparatively little to suggest that aliens residing in England brought very obviously different forms of religious observance to their adopted country. There is no evidence, for example, that the small number of 'Greeks' in the capital, discussed in chapter 5, had access to the services of Eastern Orthodox priests, even supposing that they would have been allowed to perform the sacraments in their own tradition. Significantly, George Vranas, an Athenian who rose to become bishop successively of Dromore and Elphin in Ireland, and also spent a limited amount of time in England at the very end of the fifteenth century, received all the stages of his ordination and consecration in the Roman tradition after he had fled from Greece as a refugee to the West.[90]

The outstanding – but highly unusual – example of a conscious English emulation of continental religious practice comes from Norwich, where at least two houses of women living under a vow of chastity were recorded in the fifteenth century. These are very likely to have drawn direct inspiration from the Beguine movement in the Low Countries, in which groups of women who did not take formal religious orders lived together under a general regime of poverty and piety. The link is all the more likely given the fact that one of the Norwich houses was patronised by the merchant John Asger, whose wife Catherine originated from Flanders.[91] Otherwise the only institutional manifestations of alien influence on religious practice come again from London, where by the end of the fifteenth century (as we shall see in chapter 10) there were a number of fraternities set up by and/ or patronised by alien residents of the city. In contrast to the suspicion that later attached to alien Protestant churches, however, there is no sense from the records that the pre-Reformation alien fraternities in London were regarded as closed or covert associations intent on pursuing the economic and political interests of their members.[92]

Names

One of the most important markers of the influence of English on the lives of immigrants is that provided by the names ascribed to incomers in their host communities.[93] The alien subsidy rolls of 1440–87 are a uniquely rich source in this respect, though inevitably not an unproblematic one. Traditions of record keeping meant that most standard forenames were written up in their Latin form. This means that we cannot immediately detect the valences, for example, around the name rendered in the returns as 'Jacobus': would the man in question have been known by the still comparatively rare English form James, or did he retain a clearer sense of his origins by calling himself, and being called, Jacques (for Frenchmen), Jacob (for the 'Dutch'), Giacomo (for Italians) or Jaime (for Iberians)? In other cases, however, vernacular variety was preserved: people with the equivalent of the English name 'William' were referred to not, in general, by the Latin 'Gulielmus' but by a whole variety of mainly French-derived forms, including 'Guillaume', 'Guillam' and 'Gylmyn'. Where forenames without particularly ready English equivalents were encountered, the clerks to the assessors strived to create comprehensible versions. The names Ingelram and Ingelbert appear in both vernacular and Latin versions, with many variant spellings. Gonzales is a recognisable forename for a Portuguese immigrant in Plymouth in 1440.[94] The name Balthazar, not in currency in England, is also identifiable in a number of cases, including the Italian Balthazar Lirica who paid the alien subsidy in London in 1441.[95]

It is fortunate that surnames in Latin records were usually given in their vernacular forms, making it much easier to know how the individuals and their hosts described them in their spoken language. As a general trend, we can say that the immigrants to later medieval England who were most likely to retain their original surnames were people of higher status: aristocrats, merchants, clergy and at least a proportion of artisans. There are, inevitably, some significant exceptions: it is important to notice that Duarte Brandão, the Portuguese adventurer whom we encountered in chapter 5, became Sir Edward Brampton not by an approximate transliteration of his name, but because he took his forename from his godfather, Edward IV, and his surname from the Northamptonshire manor that he was granted by the king.[96] Lower down the social scale, there was also considerable flexibility of identity: it was only in the fourteenth century that English peasant society began regularly to use hereditary surnames at all, and many people who moved to England in the later Middle Ages would not necessarily have had a stable family name that would readily survive the process of migration.[97] The conventions of bureaucratic registration were such, however, as to require the use of surnames, and the ways in which English jurors and assessors went about declaring these for the purpose of the alien subsidies tell us a lot about how foreigners were marked out in their host society.

In cases where surnames relate to occupations, the evidence can sometimes be rather ambiguous. For example, over two hundred people, most from the Low Countries, appear in the alien subsidy returns with the anglicised surname 'Beerbrewer'. Since the modern German form is *Bierbrauer*, and the modern Dutch equivalent is *bierbrouwer*, it is quite possible that these people had already acquired their business-based identities before leaving their places of birth. Similarly, the oaths of fealty of 1436 and the alien subsidy returns yield a number of examples of people variously described as Flemings, Zeelanders and a 'Spaniard', all with the recognisable surname 'Scrivener', denoting one who wrote business documents and provided paralegal services.[98] Again, the modern Dutch and German forms (*schrijver* and *Schreiber*) are not so distant as to make it impossible that these individuals (though perhaps not the Spaniard) arrived with their own professional identities enshrined in existing surnames. A similar sense of self-determination is much more doubtful, however, in the case of the many English-language surnames found in the alien subsidy rolls for people working in low-status jobs in the agricultural and service sectors: 'Husband' (husbandman), 'Ploughman', 'Carter', 'Shepherd', 'Sherman' (shearer of sheep) and so on. These are much more likely to have been allocated pragmatically on the basis of the occupation understood to be undertaken by the relevant individual at the moment of enumeration.

If these kinds of occupational labels were straightforward, factual descriptions, the national and linguistic surnames deployed by the English jurors and assessors were sometimes freighted with rather more cultural meaning. The use of words such as 'French', 'Dutch', 'Scot' or 'Irish' as designators of surnames often seems quite arbitrary. In the city of Cambridge in 1440, for example, twenty-three of the twenty-seven reported 'Dutch' cordwainers, masters and servants were identified simply by forenames followed by 'Dutchman'.[99] This habit of applying '-man' or '-woman' to the national labels was very common: whereas there are only 161 instances of people named 'French' in the alien subsidy rolls (along with 177 called 'Norman', eighty called 'Picard', fifty-nine called 'Breton' and twenty-six called 'Gascon'), there are an extraordinary 1,861 instances of 'Frenchman', as well as fifty-two of 'Frenchwoman'. Similar proportions apply for 'Dutch' and 'Irish', though not for 'Scot': in the latter case the simple form prevailed (1,021 instances), and it was quite rare to refine the vocabulary to 'Scotsman' or 'Scottishman' (twenty-nine cases) and the female equivalents (just ten cases). Many (though not all) of the people who appear in the alien subsidy rolls with such names were non-householders and servants; where other occupations are given, they again tend to be relatively low-status ones, such as husbandman and labourer, weaver and tanner, mariner, seaman and fisherman. All of this suggests that national and linguistic labels were applied in the main to people who arrived without established skills that would give them a craft-based surname, and without the social cachet to insist on the use of an existing familial name – even supposing they had ever had one. Very occasionally we know of instances where local society provided qualifiers or nicknames to distinguish between people with such generic names: at Harwich in 1484, the enumerators listed one John Ducheman 'with the red face'.[100] In the most abject cases, as we have seen, the alien subsidy assessors simply ignored names altogether and recorded people just by status, nationality and/or occupation, like the labouring women from Scotland and the trafficked youths from Iceland discussed in chapter 7. It is hard to resist the notion that national or linguistic tags used as surnames, or surrogates for names, were at least sometimes a means of objectifying – and even, at times, of commodifying – the alien.

Finally, we may note the cases where the clerks responsible for writing up official documents were clearly nonplussed or even made the butt of foreigners' jokes. There are eighteen instances in the alien subsidy rolls, scattered across the South and the Midlands, where immigrants were listed with the surname 'English'. The dynamics of such an identifier are hard to unravel. In one of these instances, at Sutton in Cambridgeshire, the man in question was stated as having two names: 'Robert Iryssh' and the alias 'Robert English'.[101] Were such people known by their denizen and alien neighbours to have 'turned English' in some way? More comical were the stumbles over forenames. In 1436, a Swede from Stockholm who lived in Southwark swore the oath of fealty. Either the man had a very evocative name or, more likely, the Chancery official responsible for preparing his licence struggled with interpretation: he was entered on the patent roll with the name 'All Good'. At Warminster in Wiltshire in 1440, one of the non-householders declared liable to the alien subsidies was a Flemish man identified as 'Ymond Dyer'. Ymond is not a medieval (or modern) Dutch or Flemish name, but instead seems to be a variant of *iemand*, which in modern Dutch means 'someone'. Other Middle Dutch-speakers – perhaps the man named next on the roll, the Fleming James Coppin – must have informed the assessors that 'so-and-so Dyer, a groom', was also an alien, and that this was then mistaken as representing the man's forename.

This chapter has examined a number of ways in which the English expressed their views of their own nationhood through engagement with other peoples of the British Isles and Europe, and particularly with the aliens they encountered in their midst. The 'idea of England' included important and enduring concepts of kingship, sovereignty and language, and it behoved even the rarefied international culture of the royal court to pay lip service to some of the precepts of this powerful political and cultural phenomenon. Englishness was also the set of values and practices to which immigrants wishing to be fully accepted in the host society could aspire and adhere. As we shall see in the next chapter, however, immigrants made their own contribution to a culture that was open to influence and change. Acculturation and acceptance were therefore both gradual and incomplete: 'becoming English' was about degrees of adjustment on both sides, rather than a straightforward process of assimilation.

Notes

1 See the review of this debate by Ruddick, *English Identity*, pp. 2–22.
2 Powicke, *Loss of Normandy*, pp. 297–307.
3 See, as an exemplar, Davies, *First English Empire*, pp. 41–3, 142–71.
4 Ruddick, *English Identity*, pp. 17–20, 136–55.
5 Genet, 'English nationalism'; Ruddick, 'The English "nation" and the Plantagenet "empire"'.
6 Richardson, 'Henry V'; Nilson, *Cathedral Shrines*, pp. 117–21; Good, *Cult of St George*.
7 Armitage, *Ideological Origins*, pp. 33–6; Genet, 'Empire and English identity'.
8 Watts, 'Plantagenet Empire and the continent', pp. 412–20.
9 Among a huge literature on the subject, see the critical appraisals of Geary, *Myth of Nations*, pp. 1–14, 93–119; and Gillett, 'Ethnogenesis'.
10 Ruddick, *English Identity*, p. 170.
11 Ruddick, *English Identity*, pp. 123, 170, 181–2.
12 Davies, 'Peoples of Britain and Ireland, 1100–1400: I'; Ruddick, *English Identity*, pp. 136–55, with quotes at p. 144.
13 Menache, *The Vox Dei*, pp. 191–209.
14 For this paragraph in general, see Linsley, 'Nation, England and the French', pp. 98–129, 144–57.
15 Green, 'Further evidence', p. 308.
16 Doig, 'Propaganda, public opinion and the siege of Calais', p. 100; Bellis, *Hundred Years War in Literature*, p. 125.
17 Ruddick, *English Identity*, pp. 139–40.

18 Linsley, 'Nation, England and the French', p. 150 n. 95.

19 Ditchburn, 'Anglo-Scottish relations', p. 311; Butterfield, *Familiar Enemy*, pp. 125–6.

20 Crooks, 'Before Humpty Dumpty', p. 272.

21 Luxford, 'Drawing ethnicity'.

22 *Libelle of Englyshe Polycye*; Scattergood, 'The *Libelle of Englyshe Polycye*'. For the most recent assessment of this text and the likely Irish connections of its anonymous author, see Bennett, 'The *Libelle of English Policy*'.

23 Ruddick, *English Identity*, pp. 239–56.

24 *ODNB*, II, 162.

25 Ormrod, *Edward III*, p. 458.

26 Harriss, *Cardinal Beaufort*, p. 196; Curry, 'Coronation expedition', p. 45.

27 Otway-Ruthven, *King's Secretary*, p. 53.

28 C 66/450, m. 12, calendared in *CPR 1436–41*, p. 555.

29 SC 8/145/7237.

30 LMA, DL/C/B/004/MS09171/006.

31 *Select Cases in the Court of King's Bench under Edward I*, pp. 50–2.

32 *Early Common Petitions*, no. 27. See also, more generally, Alban and Allmand, 'Spies and spying'.

33 Ormrod, 'Reynauld de Nieuport'; and see chapter 10.

34 JUST 3/176, m. 28; Summerson, 'Responses to war', pp. 158, 170–1; Ruddick, *English Identity*, p. 244.

35 Johnson, '"Some said he was a Spaniard"'.

36 E 179/144/42, m. 15; E 179/144/64, m. 4; E 179/144/73, rot 1d, m. 2; E 179/144/52, m. 3; E 179/144/57; E 179/235/23, m. 2; *CLBL K*, p. 380.

37 Newton, *Fashion in the Age of the Black Prince*, p. 9; Saul, *Richard II*, p. 348.

38 Benz St John, *Three Medieval Queens*, p. 88.

39 *PROME*, VIII, 239–40, 335–6; IX, 10, 155; Given-Wilson, *Henry IV*, pp. 333–4. The campaign against the aliens in Queen Joan's service was revived in 1426: *PROME*, X, 308; Griffiths, *Reign of King Henry VI*, p. 170.

40 *PROME*, VIII, 331, 333–7, 351–2.

41 *PROME*, VIII, 465–6.

42 *CPR 1408–13*, pp. 368, 460; Given-Wilson, *Royal Household*, p. 202.

43 See, for example, *PROME*, X, 316–17; *CPR 1446–52*, p. 240.

44 *CCR 1419–22* pp. 24–5; *PROME*, IX, 268. For the countess of Kent, see chapter 5.

45 *PROME*, X, 162–4; XI, 133–4.

46 Vale, *Angevin Legacy*, p. 31; Ormrod, *Edward III*, p. 458.

47 Brown, Colvin, and Taylor, *History of the King's Works*, I, 293–408.

48 Butterfield, 'French culture', pp. 89–93; Ormrod, *Edward III*, p. 457.

49 Getz, *Medicine in the English Middle Ages*, pp. 28, 30.

50 Rawcliffe, 'Master surgeons', p. 199.

51 Vale, *Princely Court*, pp. 95, 263.

52 Ormrod, *Edward III*, p. 458; Saul, *Richard II*, p. 348.

53 Sutton, 'Merchants', p. 129. For Letowe, see also chapter 10.

54 Saygin, *Humphrey, Duke of Gloucester*, pp. 72–80, 118, 254–62.

55 Clough, 'Late fifteenth-century English monarchs', pp. 314–15; *ODNB*, X, 165–7. For his accommodation in the hospital of St James, Westminster (1511–27), see Eton College Archives, ECR 60/03/01, fols 152r, 199r.

56 *ODNB*, I, 963–4.

57 Hay, *Polydore Vergil*.

58 *ODNB*, LV, 61–3.

59 *ODNB*, LV, 72–3.

60 Schoeck, *Erasmus of Europe*.

61 *CPR 1429–36*, p. 549; E 179/141/89; E 179/149/145, m. 1; E 179/235/57, m. 1; E 179/242/25, m. 10d.

62 *LP*, XX, pt 1, no. 465 (50); Lasocki and Prior, *The Bassanos*.

63 Foister, *Holbein and England*.

64 Holbein did not have his letters patent enrolled on the patent roll, so the record of the issue is derived from the fee he paid into the hanaper for the writing and sealing of the original letters: E 101/223/10.

65 *PROME*, VI, 49.

66 Wallace, 'Constance'.

67 Butterfield, *Familiar Enemy*, pp. 139–51.

68 Cottle, *Triumph of English*.

69 Davies, 'Peoples of Britain and Ireland, 1100–1400: IV', p. 3.

70 Bellis, *Hundred Years War in Literature*, pp. 43, 68–9.

71 Usk, 'The Testament of Love', p. 30, ll. 22–4.

72 Curry, Bell, Chapman, King and Simpkin, 'Languages in the military profession', pp. 82–5.

73 Ingham, 'Mixing languages'; Kowaleski, 'French immigrants', pp. 206–24.

74 E 179/108/113, m. 5; Bognor, ' "Military" knighthood'.

75 Kerling, *Commercial Relations*, pp. 167–9; Wright, 'Trade between England and the Low Countries'.

76 Hsy, 'City', p. 319.

77 Bertram, 'Incised slabs', pp. 389, 391. Two aliens were recorded at Playden in 1440 (E 179/184/212, rot. 3d); thirty-three were assessed at Rye in 1441 (E 179/242/9, mm. 1–1d), and ten in 1483 (E 179/236/134, m. 10). Nationalities are given in only a handful of these cases, but the surnames suggest a preponderance of 'Dutch'.

78 Hudson, *Lollards and their Books*, p. 155.

79 Thomas, 'Margaret of Teschen's Czech prayer'; Thomas, *Reading Women*, p. 4.

80 Milner, 'Sir Simon Felbrigg'.

81 Richardson, 'A Bishop and his Diocese', p. 60. For the background, see Gunn, *Ancrene Wisse*, pp. 91–138.

82 Kowaleski, 'The French of England', p. 115; Kowaleski, 'French immigrants', p. 213.

83 Curry, Bell, Chapman, King and Simpkin, 'Languages in the military profession', p. 75.

84 *Alien Communities*, pp. 50, 52.

85 Ormrod, 'French residents in England'.

86 Owen, 'White Annays and others', p. 332. We owe this reference to Joshua Ravenhill.

87 Justice, *Writing and Rebellion*, pp. 71–3.

88 Guidi Bruscoli, 'I mercanti italiani', p. 116. We owe this reference to Megan Tidderman. For the connection between Tani and de' Pigli, see chapters 6 and 10.

89 Pettegree, 'Foreign population of London', pp. 141–6; Luu, 'Assimilation or segregation'.

90 Harris, 'Greeks at the papal curia', pp. 429–31.

91 Tanner, 'Religious practice', pp. 140–1. For the national identities of the couple, see chapter 10.

92 *Alien Communities*, p. 36.

93 For an exemplary study, see Clark, *Words, Names and History*, pp. 241–79, esp. pp. 271–9.

94 E 179/95/100, rot. 4.

95 E 179/144/42, m. 23.

96 Roth, 'Sir Edward Brampton'.

97 McClure, 'Patterns of migration'.

98 See, for example, *CPR 1429–36*, pp. 556, 564; E 179/124/188, fol. 5r; E 179/180/111, rot. 5.

99 E 179/235/4, m. 4.

100 E 179/108/130, m. 2d.

101 E 179/235/4, m. 2.

10

Integration and confrontation

Working and living together

Having understood the nature of the 'Englishness' that aliens
encountered on their entry and settlement in the kingdom, and the
various contributions that immigrants in turn made to the evolving culture of their adopted country, we now turn to consider some of the social
interactions that resident aliens had, both with people of their own ethnicity and with their English neighbours. This includes the generally peaceful
contacts revealed in the workplace and in the practice of religion, as well as
issues such as intermarriage and the settlement patterns of aliens in some
of the major towns. Finally, we shall address the evidence for organised,
violent conflict between English people and the groups of foreigners who,
from time to time, they identified as a focus of suspicion or hatred. Taking a
balanced view of this broad range of evidence will allow us to gain a firmer
impression of the true extent, and limits, of English toleration of foreigners.

The contacts between England's immigrant and native populations
were manifold and diverse. Numerous aliens in the country entertained
long-standing relationships with English men and women for professional
and personal reasons. Even though the alien subsidy assessors were not
expected to record the names of English masters or mistresses, the returns
still provide us with countless examples of immigrant residents employed
by native people as domestic staff or apprentices. In Toltingtrough hundred in Kent, William Doget had one female and two male 'Dutch' servants
in 1440.[1] Also in 1440, the aliens Cornelius Ducheman, Simon Diryke and
Cornelius Garlof worked for Henry Breuer in Newbury in Berkshire.[2]
In the hamlet of Landulph in Cornwall, Thomas Roberd employed two
Breton members of staff.[3] In Scarborough in Yorkshire, thirty-six native

employers had alien servants in 1440, and in Reading in Berkshire nine-teen.[4] In London, local citizens and artisans often worked with immigrants from the Low Countries and the German territories, who probably trained with them as apprentices. In 1483, five 'Teutonic' men were assessed towards the alien subsidy as servants of the English draper John Saunder in Portsoken ward, and four as employees of the English fruiterer and beer brewer Martin Blondell in Queenhithe ward.[5]

Unfortunately, the alien subsidy returns do not tell us anything about English servants, making it impossible to determine to what extent they had contact with immigrant masters or to investigate whether there was much truth to the accusation that their alien counterparts only employed their own countrymen as apprentices. The Tudor subsidies, however, did record English servants, and reveal that they also worked in immigrant households. Of the ten aliens assessed with servants in the 1523 return for Canterbury, for example, four employed only other aliens, three both aliens and Englishmen, and three only Englishmen.[6] Immigrant apprentices and domestic staff certainly worked with and for fellow aliens of different nationalities. Thomas Fuller, an Englishman living in Hatfield Peverel in Essex, had an employee from France and one from the Low Countries in 1440.[7] John Grene, a goldsmith from Prussia active in Exeter during the 1430s and 1440s, made use of the services of the Frenchman Tilman Cok.[8] Gerozzo de' Pigli, manager of the London branch of the Florentine Medici bank, had five alien servants in 1444. One of them, Agnolo Tani, was Italian, while the names of three of the four others, Philip de Bulle, Severius Mastrik and Dederik Esterlyng, suggest they came from the Low Countries, Germany or northern Europe.[9]

Native businessmen sometimes stood surety for foreign merchants in commercial transactions, and Italians such as the Venetians Giovanni and Lorenzo Marcanova or the Lucchese Giovanni Micheli represented their English colleagues as agents.[10] Londoners also acted as sureties when alien merchants or artisans obtained the freedom of the city and became members of one of its livery companies. In 1356, the London cloth workers John Payn, Richard atte Boure and John Bennet helped the Fleming John Kempe join the guild of native weavers and acquire citizenship, allowing him to trade retail in the city.[11] In 1453, the London drapers John Walshawe, William Russell, Henry Waver and Henry Kent stood surety for the Venetian Jacopo Falleron, so that he could buy the freedom and enter their livery company.[12] Occasionally, alien and English entrepreneurs set up business ventures that went far beyond day-to-day buying and selling. John Evynger, the 'Teutonic' brewer who paid the alien subsidy in London in 1483 and whose activities were explored in chapter 6, joined forces with an English maltster from Hertfordshire.[13] After he had become a London citizen, Jacopo Falleron engaged in mining enterprises in Devon and the West Country together with another Venetian and Londoners Richard Acreman and Robert Glover.[14] William Wilcokkys, a London draper and merchant adventurer and an acquaintance of William Caxton, invited John Letowe, the Lithuanian book printer, to England, sponsored his freedom of the city and helped him establish a printing press. Drawing on Wilcokkys' support, Letowe ran a shop in London's Dowgate ward in 1483, together with his alien wife, Elizabeth, a Brabantine associate and four alien servants.[15]

Many English men and women also provided accommodation to immigrant newcomers. The alien subsidy records provide evidence of immigrants renting property all over the country. Nine aliens were described as 'tenants', five of them living in Lynn in 1440.[16] Numerous others were recorded as 'staying with' English people. In the village of Wellington in Herefordshire in 1440, Robert Frencheman lodged with the Englishman John Harper.[17] In the same year, a Scot named Patrick was staying with Thomas Bakworth at Black Hedley in Northumberland.[18] In various places in Cambridgeshire, Englishmen accommodated fifteen immigrants in 1440 and 1441, most of whom came from France.[19] In Southwark in 1440 and London in 1483, a total of sixty-five aliens, mainly 'Teutonics' and Scots, were said to be 'holding' (*tenens*) a room or chamber. Unfortunately, the documents do not specify the householders from whom they were renting.[20] In Derbyshire and Herefordshire in 1483, aliens were described as having a room.[21] Members of the English clergy appear to have been particularly keen to provide immigrants with a place to stay. In Suffolk in 1440, Jacobus Ducheman lodged with the rector of Coney Weston.[22] Guyllaum Francheman resided with the vicar of Gedney in Lincolnshire in 1443.[23] John Hallowe, from France, was staying with the prior of Brooke in Rutland in 1457.[24] Bearing in mind, as we emphasised in chapter 2, that alien residents in England were not entitled to own real property without urban citizenship or denization, it is very likely that their impact on the English rental market was far greater than has previously been understood.

Mixed marriages

The relationships between immigrants and English people were not limited to the world of business and property contracts: it also included mixed marriages.[25] As alien wives of English men and English wives of immigrant men were exempt from payment of the alien subsidies, intermarriage usually went unrecorded in the subsidy returns. Occasionally, however, subsidy assessors exceeded their brief and included details about them. In Rutland, twenty-six immigrants were assessed in 1440, most of them Frenchmen or 'Dutchmen', fifteen of whom were recorded as having married English women (whose names were not given).[26] In Herefordshire, fifty-seven aliens were enumerated in 1443, mostly from France, Ireland and the Low Countries, of whom seven (or about 12 per cent) were recorded as married to women from England or nearby Wales.[27]

Neither in Rutland nor in Herefordshire were alien wives of native English men recorded. The alien subsidy returns do contain thirty scattered entries in other places, mainly London and the East Riding of Yorkshire, of immigrant women married to men whose names do not appear in the records. This means one of several things: that these women's husbands had died; that the husbands were from one of the groups exempt from payment; or that the husbands were English, and that the women had therefore been unjustly assessed. In Aldeburgh in Suffolk in 1483, for example, the Scottish labourer Isabella Hopkyn was described as the wife of Thomas Hopkyn, whose name does not figure elsewhere in the document.[28] In the inquest for London's Tower ward in 1483, the 'Teutonic' Mariona Pope was even said to be married to an Englishman, but was still taxed.[29] Other sources, such as letters of denization, also give isolated references to alien wives of Englishmen, including some of London's political heavyweights, such as Robert Warner, MP for Middlesex in 1425, who was married to Margaret Roos, a woman from the Flemish town of Sluys.[30] Even John Carpenter, MP for London in 1437 and 1439, long-term common clerk of the city and one of the assumed architects of the anti-alien legislation of 1439–40, had an immigrant wife, Katharine, who came from Zeeland.[31]

On the denization rolls of the early 1540s, 278 aliens are specified as married to English women or men. In the great majority of entries on these rolls, no marital status is specified. The first of the rolls, however, compiled in 1539–41 and containing a total of 446 entries, has marital information in 90 per cent of cases.[32] Ruddick has calculated that no fewer than 197 (44 per cent) of this sample of aliens were married to an English spouse, whereas 140 (31 per cent) had fellow aliens as wives or husbands. Fifty-nine (13 per cent) were described as single, and the remaining immigrants were widows or widowers. Alien wives of Englishmen were recorded, though their numbers are very low: only 6 per cent of all immigrant women in the sample were specified as married to native-born husbands. Out of the 371 alien men in this group, 53 per cent had English wives, while 19 per cent had immigrant spouses. The sample is inevitably skewed, since the recipients of denization were predominantly settled people who were more likely to marry local women or men. Ruddick's findings for the early sixteenth century suggest, however, that endogamy may also have been less the norm among immigrants than has previously been assumed for the fifteenth century, and support the cautious multipliers that we deployed in chapter 3 to calculate the number of alien–alien marriages among those assessed for the subsidy of 1440.[33]

Ruddick has also observed a link between intermarriage and aliens' length of residence in the records of the 1440s for Rutland and Herefordshire. However, it is not clear whether immigrants stayed in the country for longer periods as a consequence of being married to English women, or whether they were already long-term residents of the realm when they married and were therefore simply more likely to choose a local spouse. The connection between length of stay and mixed marriage is less obvious in the denization rolls of the 1540s, but aliens who had migrated to England during their childhood were certainly more likely to marry native women. Some immigrant residents found English partners even before they moved to England. The Fleming Oliver Bowthin, for example, married Alianore, an Englishwoman, in the city of Bruges. He then settled with her in Southwark, where he started working as a vintner.[34] John Asger, an English merchant and mayor of Norwich in 1426, had a Flemish wife, Catherine, whom he had probably met in Bruges, where he sold tombstones during the 1420s. They had a son, called John, while in Zeeland and then moved to England, where the older John purchased letters of denization for his wife and child.[35]

Marriages to women of well-established local families often provided alien residents with an entrée into the social and political elites of their new places of residence. Having married Agnes de Barden, daughter of a former mayor of York, the Hanseatic merchant Henry Wyman obtained the freedom of the city and took out letters of denization in 1388–9, and was subsequently elected mayor for three annual terms in 1407, 1408 and 1409.[36] In Dartmouth, Edmund Arnold, a Gascon heavily involved in overseas trade, took a local widow as his wife and served as an MP and as mayor at the end of the fourteenth and the beginning of the fifteenth centuries.[37]

The relationships that aliens built up with others of their kind, as well as with their denizen neighbours and adopted families, proved useful when it came to drawing up their wills. Thus, Italian merchants in London preferred to use fellow Italians as their executors – although when looking for witnesses to testify to the authenticity of the will, they usually called on the aid of native Londoners, whose word was expected to carry more weight in English courts.[38] Hanseatic merchants did sometimes use Englishmen as executors, and acted as executors for them.[39] Other alien testators also depended on native acquaintances, either as witnesses or executors. In Ipswich, Henry Foslowe, a beer brewer from Zeeland who paid the alien subsidy in 1483, named his wife as his executrix but asked an English clerk, John Squyer, and a merchant, Robert Wentworth, to supervise her in his will in 1487.[40] In Southampton, the French resident Philippe le Leyvre chose an Englishman, Sampson Thomas, as his only executor in 1537.[41]

Alien collectives in politics and religion

As we saw in chapter 2, the emerging body of legislation that defined the legal and fiscal rights and obligations of first-generation immigrants had the effect both of forging a social status group of 'aliens' and of representing a perceived 'alien problem'. The question therefore arises as to whether aliens were inclined to form meaningful collectives, networks or 'communities' dedicated to the pursuit of some common goal. At a national level, aliens as a whole seem to have lacked a political voice. Petitions to parliament very occasionally asserted the existence of more particular alien collectives, such as the 'alien religious' (presumably largely meaning the residents of the alien priories) who complained of their lot around the time of the expulsion ordinance in 1377–8.[42] Not surprisingly, though, merchants were by far the most vocal in this respect. In the first half of the fourteenth century, the crown often negotiated with the 'Estate of Merchants', an ad hoc group called together to represent the mercantile interest of the realm, and which on some occasions could include aliens.[43] This explains the occasional petitions made in Parliament during this period by groups claiming to speak on behalf of alien merchants at large, lobbying either on their own or in concert with the 'merchants of England'.[44] This rhetoric did not, however, mean that there was a coherent national network of alien merchants, but rather that smaller interest groups operating outside as well as inside the realm – the Hansards, for example, or the Gascon merchants of Bordeaux and Bayonne – sought to claim wider legitimacy for their cause by declaring themselves the spokespersons of aliens at large. It is much rarer to find a parliamentary petition that came explicitly from the alien mercantile interest *inside* England, such as one from 1389 made by 'the merchants of Genoa resident in London'.[45]

The particular ability of the Italians to organise in this way is hardly surprising. In addition to their well-established business links, merchants originating from the same city-states in Italy established formal communities in London during the later Middle Ages, known as 'nations', albeit that these were organised less strictly than in other places in Europe such as Bruges. The 'nations' defended Italians' economic interests, promoted social cohesion and provided spiritual care. In this respect they replicated the mixed political, social and religious roles of English craft guilds. Many of their more explicit practices were pious in purpose. The Lucchese nation, for example, had a chapel dedicated to the Volto Santo or the Holy Face, a much-venerated crucifix in Lucca, in London's church of St Thomas of Acon, where its members met for mass.[46] There is some limited evidence that the Italian merchants resident in London employed confessors from Italy.[47] These may have provided the nations with religious services in their native tongue.

Other alien residents in the English capital also set up fraternities. Like English parish guilds, these provided social activities for their members, supported the sick and incapacitated, and acted as communal chantries that performed masses for the souls of deceased members and their families. Unlike the English lay fraternities in London, however, the immigrant ones did not gather in the city's parish churches but in mendicant houses, where friars coming from other countries might supposedly cater for aliens' needs in their own language. Even though the evidence left by alien fraternities is scant, the options available to immigrants in London appear to have been diverse. There was a Fraternity of the Holy Blood of Wilsnack that met at the Austin Friars in the 1490s and was a focus of activity for immigrants from Saxony.[48] One of its members was Oliver Wyst, a 'Teutonic' capper who was assessed for the alien subsidy in Castle Baynard ward in 1483.[49] In the 1490s, the Fraternity of St Katherine, based at the Crutched Friars, welcomed 'Dutch' immigrants such as the 'Teutonic' Matthew Godfrey who, together with his wife Elena, was recorded in the alien subsidy inquest for Langbourn ward in 1483.[50] Both of these associations may have been offshoots of a group that had convened at the Crutched Friars since the 1450s and had members of different social standings. By contrast, the Fraternity of the Holy Trinity at the Friars Preachers may have attracted 'Teutonics' with a higher status. Godfrey Sperying, the keeper of a beer house who was assessed for the alien subsidy in Portsoken ward together with his wife and five servants in 1483, left a bequest to this fraternity in his will of 1489.[51]

Some of these fellowships targeted immigrants with specific occupations. The Fraternity of the Blessed Lady and the Holy Trinity aimed at alien shoe makers, the Fraternity of St Eligius or St Eloi at 'Dutch' goldsmiths. One of the latter was John van Delff, the enterprising supplier of the royal court whose activities were discussed in chapter 6 and who made a bequest to the brotherhood of St Eligius in his will in 1502.[52] French residents in London, such as the Gascon Anthony Odet, the recipient of letters of denization in 1512, patronised the Fraternity of the Immaculate Conception at the Blackfriars.[53] Other than the reference to a local German relic in the name of the Saxon brotherhood, however, we know nothing as to whether the liturgical practices of these guilds followed any recognisably continental traditions or fashions. The decision to set up separate alien fraternities could be interpreted as reflecting a refusal to join English worshippers or a reaction to immigrants' exclusion from other bodies. Yet, as Justin Colson has argued, the alien fraternities could also simply be considered as part of the wide range of possibilities for religious expression on offer in a large city such as London, both for immigrants and for English people.[54] No alien fraternities are known to have existed in England outside the capital. In Boston, merchants of the German Hanse did flock together at the local Franciscan friary: the sixteenth-century anti-quarian John Leland reported that they were benefactors of the Greyfriars' church and that many of them were buried there. The incised slab of one of them, Wissel Smalenburg of Münster, who died in Boston in 1340, was found on the site of the Franciscans' church in the late nineteenth cen-tury and is now in St Botolph's church.[55] However, the few studies of popular religion that explicitly acknowledge the presence of aliens before the Reformation suggest that most immigrants did not set themselves apart in the practice of religion and engaged fully with mainstream parish life. In Southwark and in Sandwich during the fifteenth and early sixteenth centuries, for example, immigrants attended parish services, joined parish guilds and held parish offices.[56]

It appears, then, that immigrants to England did sometimes form communities that were organised along national lines. Yet none of these precluded wider engagement with other aliens and denizens in England – or indeed, with other foreigners abroad. Many immigrants to England continued to pursue interests in their places of origin, in spite of appearing to be fully integrated into their English host society. In his will of 1494, John Gyse, a merchant who had migrated from Antwerp in the Low Countries to London, instructed his executors to give a significant part of his prop-erty to people in his native Brabant. Equally, though, he socialised with native-born Londoners in the Fraternity of Our Lady in his local parish of St Botolph Billingsgate, and made considerable bequests to the city's Austin and Crutched Friars.[57] John Tubbac came from Heist op den Berg, also in Brabant, and settled in York at the end of the fourteenth century. In his will, drawn up in 1438, he made legacies to his sisters' children 'in the parts overseas' and to other acquaintances in Antwerp. Yet, during his life, he had also been a freeman of the city of York, had joined the local Mercers' Guild, had been involved in numerous charitable activities as one of the brethren of the Hospital of the Trinity, the Blessed Virgin Mary and All Saints in Fossgate, and had rubbed shoulders with the city's elites as a member of the Corpus Christi Guild.[58] For the residents of smaller towns and rural areas, connections forged by religion and good works could spread out some way: the prosperous mariner Downe Bek, taxed as an alien in the Tudor subsidy in 1524, made provision in his will for the sale of one of his boats to pay for a silver and gilt cross in his local church at Easton Bavents in Suffolk; but he also left money for the upkeep of the bridge at nearby Kessingland, for repairs to Southwold church and for the saying of masses by the friars of Dunwich.[59]

Aliens in the townscape

Did aliens' sense of community also have a spatial dimension and, in particular, did they cluster together physically in their new places of residence? As described in chapter 3, one of the most striking features of the geographical distribution of taxpayers in the alien subsidy records is the occurrence of small groups of immigrants, and frequently even of single individuals, in some of the remotest places in the country. Where they were found in larger numbers, however, there are key questions to be asked about their distribution across the townscape, and how this may have affected their own and others' views. Laughton's study of late medieval Chester has revealed that newcomers tended to congregate in certain parts of the city: the Welsh in the south and the Manx in the west. Her work has also revealed, however, that immigrants 'did not live in ethnic enclaves', and that participation in the economic, governmental, religious and ceremonial aspects of city life meant that there was a high level of integration.[60] How much does the alien subsidy data help us to identify similar or contrasting patterns in other English towns and cities?

In larger towns and cities, the spatial distribution of immigrants did not follow any general pattern. Figures 3, 4 and 5 show the distribution of aliens by parish or ward in York and Bristol in 1440 and in London in 1441.

In York, eighty-three aliens were assessed towards the alien subsidy and had their parish of residence recorded in 1440.[61] We explained in chapter 3 that this return may have under-recorded the city's alien population, women and servants in particular. That the 1440 data for York are suspiciously low can also be deduced from Figure 3: aliens were assessed in only twenty-three of the city's fifteenth-century parishes, while no immigrants were recorded in the other twenty-two. Many of those enumerated in the city in 1440 crop up again, but in different parishes, in subsequent assessments of the alien subsidies. This may indicate either that there was much internal mobility or that the parish information is less reliable than it seems. If we take the 1440 data at face value, however, it seems that aliens were most numerous in the central parishes north of the River Ouse. The highest number, twelve, were recorded in St Michael Spurriergate, while eight were assessed in Holy Trinity, King's Court. These parishes were part of the Ousegate and Petergate areas: wealthy, commercially bustling neighbourhoods where, during this period, most of the city's leading office holders lived.[62] Information on the occupations of York's resident aliens in 1440 is scanty, but we do know that the immigrants living in these parishes included skilled artisans, such as a capmaker and a goldsmith.[63] An exception to the pattern of central concentration is the more peripheral parish of All Saints and St Helen, Fishergate, where six aliens were enumerated. A prosperous neighbourhood during the twelfth and thirteenth centuries, Fishergate had lost much of its allure during the subsequent period and by the mid-fifteenth century was one of the less affluent parts of the city.[64] This also seems to be reflected in the occupations of the immigrants living in the area: three of the six aliens assessed in All Saints and St Helen were servants.[65]

In spite of the fact that parts of the document are illegible and information for some parishes may be missing or incomplete, the return for Bristol in 1440, which contains details on 648 alien taxpayers and a further fifty-three foreign-born residents who did not pay, is one of the richest sources of information on the distribution of immigrants within an English city. As can be seen in Figure 4, aliens were spread relatively evenly across Bristol's jurisdictional areas. However, and in contrast to York, the highest recorded concentrations were to be found in the large outer parishes, which included or bordered some of the city's ecclesiastical estates and comprised the area across the River Avon where Bristol's cloth industry was situated. Nearly all of the immigrants living in these peripheral parishes – St Michael (eighty-five), Temple (sixty-four), St Stephen (sixty), St Nicholas (fifty-five) and St James (fifty-two) – were servants, labourers or mariners. Of the

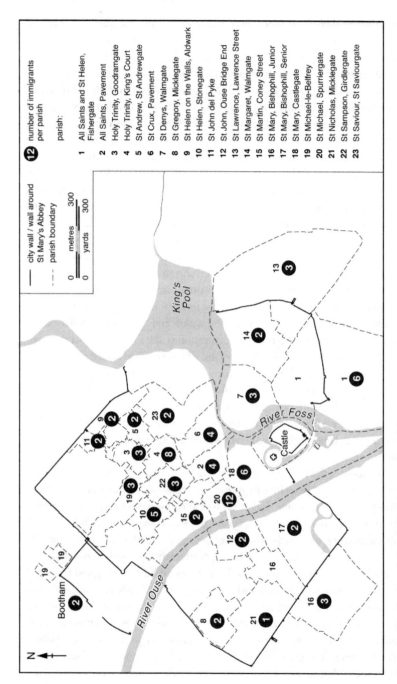

Figure 3 Distribution of aliens in York in 1440, by parish

Legend:

⑫ number of immigrants per parish

parish:

1 All Saints and St Helen, Fishergate
2 All Saints, Pavement
3 Holy Trinity, Goodramgate
4 Holy Trinity, King's Court
5 St Andrew, St Andrewgate
6 St Crux, Pavement
7 St Denys, Walmgate
8 St Gregory, Micklegate
9 St Helen on the Walls, Aldwark
10 St Helen, Stonegate
11 St John del Pyke
12 St John, Ouse Bridge End
13 St Lawrence, Lawrence Street
14 St Margaret, Walmgate
15 St Martin, Coney Street
16 St Mary, Bishophill, Junior
17 St Mary, Bishophill, Senior
18 St Mary, Castlegate
19 St Michael-le-Belfrey
20 St Michael, Spurriergate
21 St Nicholas, Micklegate
22 St Sampson, Girdlergate
23 St Saviour, St Saviourgate

city wall / wall around St Mary's Abbey
parish boundary

0   metres   300
0   yards   300

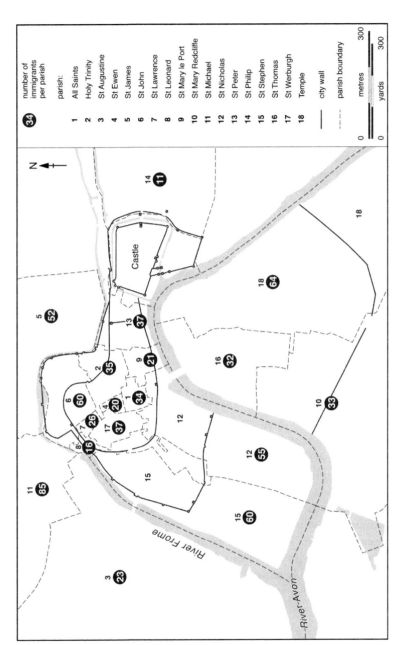

Figure 4 Distribution of aliens in Bristol in 1440, by parish

number of immigrants per parish

parish:

1 All Saints
2 Holy Trinity
3 St Augustine
4 St Ewen
5 St James
6 St John
7 St Lawrence
8 St Leonard
9 St Mary le Port
10 St Mary Redcliffe
11 St Michael
12 St Nicholas
13 St Peter
14 St Philip
15 St Stephen
16 St Thomas
17 St Werburgh
18 Temple

——— city wall
- - - parish boundary

0 metres 300
0 yards 300

parishes in the old walled city, only St John had more than fifty recorded aliens (sixty). The immigrants enumerated in these central parishes, where many of Bristol's merchants and craftspeople lived, included more skilled artisans than those in the outer parishes: eleven of Bristol's fifteen alien tailors, six of its seven foreign corvisers and all of its immigrant butchers were assessed in the old walled city. The exceptions to this pattern were the alien carpenters and skinners, who were concentrated in the outer parishes of St Michael and St Nicholas.[66]

It is obvious from Figure 5 that London did not have a particular alien quarter either. In 1441 – as also in 1483, the other year for which the London data are high in quantity and quality – the highest concentrations of immigrants were located in the outer ring of the city's wards, most of all those on the waterfront such as Tower and Dowgate wards, and in the separate borough of Southwark, south of the Thames. Then came the wards around the city walls and the eastern, northern and western suburbs.[67] Some nationalities flocked to specific areas. The Italians, for example, lived mainly around Lombard Street in Langbourn ward.[68] In the 1550s, and possibly also earlier, St Olave's parish in Southwark was a hotspot for the 'Dutch'.[69] Yet no neighbourhood in the city was monopolised by a particular group, and throughout the capital aliens would have encountered native Englishmen and immigrants of other nationalities. The high mobility of a large part of London's immigrant population, attested in chapter 3, would also have made any tendencies towards spatial segregation difficult to achieve.

The reasons behind the distribution of aliens in the English capital during the later Middle Ages are mainly of an economic and logistical nature. There were no official instructions to avoid certain areas in the city or obligations to settle in specific wards, let alone to confine immigrants to separate ghettos, as happened with the Jewish populations in sixteenth-century Venice and Florence.[70] Aliens settled in areas of London because they were close to points of entry into the city, because of the availability of commercial and industrial space and housing, and because of the presence of other producers and the proximity of customers.[71] A particular attraction in Southwark, both to aliens and Englishmen who had not obtained the civic freedom, was that it was situated outside the jurisdiction of the city and that residents could therefore escape the control of London's guilds.[72]

The only place in London that could potentially be considered as an alien enclave was the Steelyard, the walled community in Dowgate ward where merchants of the Hanseatic League resided. The marking off of

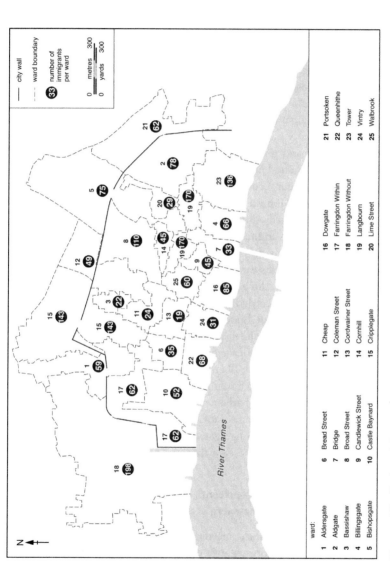

ward:

1	Aldersgate	6	Bread Street
2	Aldgate	7	Bridge
3	Bassishaw	8	Broad Street
4	Billingsgate	9	Candlewick Street
5	Bishopsgate	10	Castle Baynard

11	Cheap
12	Coleman Street
13	Cordwainer Street
14	Cornhill
15	Cripplegate

16	Dowgate
17	Farringdon Within
18	Farringdon Without
19	Langbourn
20	Lime Street

21	Portsoken
22	Queenhithe
23	Tower
24	Vintry
25	Walbrook

Figure 5 Distribution of aliens in London in 1441, by ward

this physical space was done not so much out of a desire to segregate from the rest of the city's inhabitants, but because of the specific ways in which Hanse colonies abroad were organised, based on a high degree of self-governance and separate jurisdiction. Similar Hanseatic enclaves existed at Bergen in Norway and at Novgorod in Russia.[73] However, the Hansards in London were still very much the exception amongst England's immigrants, and the overwhelming majority of aliens in the country lived closely together with English men and women and with other newcomers.

The jurisdictional boundaries in Figures 3, 4 and 5 are based on the situation in the early 1540s, when information about the layout of parishes in English cities and towns becomes more abundant. As such, though, they do not show any liberties or areas of peculiar jurisdiction held by monasteries or other ecclesiastical institutions abolished during the Dissolution of the Monasteries, on which mapping information is only very patchy. It is equally difficult to find firm data about the aliens who lived in such liberties in the fifteenth century. None of the alien subsidy grants or inquests provides any clarity in this respect, and it was probably left to the local assessors, on an informal basis, to decide whether or not to intervene within the boundaries of peculiar jurisdictions. In York, two immigrants were recorded as living in Bootham in 1440 (see Figure 3). This was a suburb outside Bootham Bar, where jurisdictional rights were heavily disputed between the urban authorities and St Mary's Abbey.[74] In 1446, the mayor and the aldermen of London complained to the king's council that strangers in the liberty of St Martin le Grand, a refuge for aliens throughout the later Middle Ages and the Tudor period, refused to pay 'the impositions laid by parliament'.[75] Later in this chapter we shall see that one of the most important complaints voiced by the rebels on Evil May Day in 1517 was that aliens congregated in London's liberties, including St Martin le Grand, in order to escape the city's regulation and taxation.

Confrontation in the fourteenth century: Janus Imperial and the massacre of the Flemings

Peaceful cohabitation, mixed marriages and bequests to local parishes may have been most representative of the daily reality of aliens' lives in England, but they were not the whole story. At times, English natives and immigrants confronted each other, sometimes with violence. Most of these disturbances remained limited to verbal abuse and, at worst, damage to alien property. Yet some were more difficult to contain and resulted in the loss of lives. Not much evidence has been preserved to tell us about anti-alien hostility in England during the first three quarters of the fourteenth century, and what does survive is restricted to London – though, as we shall see, the concentration of such activity in the capital is a feature of the whole of our period. In 1357, several London mercers carried out a premeditated attack on Francesco Bochel and Reymund Flamy, two Italian merchants in Old Jewry. The fight was broken up, and nobody was killed. Some of the mercers were taken to the Tower but were soon released again. Only after persistent Italian pressure were the main culprits convicted and punished in 1359. Nicolao Sarducci was a Lucchese merchant who fell out with the mercers because of his attempts to force up the price of silk in the capital. In 1369, his enemies managed to have him convicted for evasion of customs duties, but he regained his freedom after buying a pardon. Eighteen months later, Sarducci was killed in a brawl with three mercers; all the perpetrators were pardoned.[76]

Members of the Mercery were also involved in the case of Janus Imperial. On the night of 26 August 1379, two English apprentices, the mercer John Kirkby and the grocer John Algor, had an altercation with a Genoese resident, Janus Imperial, in front of the latter's house in London's Langbourn ward. In the skirmish that followed, Kirkby stabbed Imperial to death. In September 1379, the two Londoners were indicted for felony, but in June 1380 they secured acquittal on the grounds that the confrontation had been unpremeditated and that Kirkby had acted in self-defence. This, however, was not the end of the case. Imperial had arrived in England as the official ambassador of the Genoese state. His intention was to discuss a plan to make Southampton the main port of call for the Genoese in north-western Europe, whence English wool could be exported directly to Italy. Imperial had been granted royal protection for the duration of his visit, which turned his killing into a major diplomatic embarrassment.

Under pressure from the royal council and the chief justices, Algor now changed his statement. He admitted that he and Kirkby had gone to Langbourn ward with the deliberate intention of provoking and murdering Imperial. The indictment was changed to treason; and in December 1380, at a Parliament in Northampton, Kirkby was sentenced to death. Algor's life was saved, albeit that he was committed to prison. The grocer's confession strongly suggests, however, that the two apprentices were not lone wolves and had acted at the instigation – possibly even on the instruction – of some of London's leading capitalists. Algor named the grocers Nicholas Brembre and John Philipot and the fishmonger William Walworth. These three men, who served numerous times as mayors and aldermen in the city, virtually controlled the trade in English wool via the staple in Calais. Imperial's plans for large-scale wool exports through Southampton would have seriously damaged their interests, and thus gave them the perfect motive to eliminate the ambassador. Yet the involvement of Brembre, Philipot and Walworth in the murder was never investigated.[77]

Six months after Kirkby's conviction, the English capital was the scene of an attack on resident immigrants of significantly larger dimensions. On 14 June 1381, as the Peasants' Revolt raged in the capital, thirty-five to forty Flemings were dragged out of churches and houses in Vintry ward and were beheaded. 'Mounds of corpses were to be seen in the streets and various spots were littered with the headless bodies of the slain,' commented the *Westminster Chronicle*.[78] Italians and other aliens had their houses looted, though their lives seem to have been spared. The carnage among the Flemings was not confined to London. Artisans from Lynn killed some residents from Flanders in the town and in nearby Snettisham later in June. Flemings were also murdered in Great Yarmouth, and in Colchester, Manningtree and Maldon in Essex.[79] On 13 June, the day before the massacre in Vintry ward, rebels from Kent had also sacked a brothel in Southwark where Flemish women worked.[80]

The sources fail to say who was behind the London attack, but there are strong reasons to believe that English weavers were involved. As explained in chapter 6, London's native cloth workers struggled with the slackening demand for cheaper textiles in the wake of the Black Death and the competition from producers in the provinces, while immigrant weavers from the Low Countries were highly successful in manufacturing high-quality cloth in the capital. The native cloth workers believed that the incorporation of the Flemings into their guild would solve their problems and, from the 1350s onwards, petitioned the king to support them. The crown, however, rejected their requests, arguing that the independence of the alien weavers was to the common profit of the whole realm. Each time the London weavers were confounded in this campaign, they resorted to physical violence against their Flemish colleagues. In March 1380, a year before the slaughter in Vintry ward, their final attempt at reaching a political settlement was crushed. It is reasonable to suppose, then, that the attack on the Flemings during the Peasants' Revolt was a piece of direct action orchestrated by guild members entirely frustrated at the repeated rebuffs they had received from the crown. In the aftermath of the Peasants' Revolt, several London cloth workers were pardoned for their involvement in the rising; but the crown was less than inclined to pursue the details of the massacre, and the perpetrators were never explicitly named.[81]

Assaults on the 'Dutch' and the Italians in the 1430s and 1450s

The first quarter of the fifteenth century was relatively uneventful in terms of anti-alien hostility. In 1425, at the time of a bitter power struggle between Cardinal Beaufort, the pro-Burgundian bishop of Winchester, and the duke of Gloucester, who opposed any rapprochement with the duke of Burgundy, bills against the Flemings were nailed on the door of the former's palace in Southwark. Beaufort used the event as an excuse to take control of the Tower of London and to garrison it with his men.[82] Ten years later, the Flemings in the capital faced much more considerable hostility and danger. In 1435, at the Congress of Arras, Duke Philip the Good of Burgundy renounced his alliance with the English and made a pact with the French. When the news of his *volte-face* broke in London, people turned against the duke's subjects. According to the chronicler Enguerrand de Monstrelet, 'no one who was well bred was sparing of the grossest abuse against the duke of Burgundy and his country. Many of the common people collected together to search for Flemings, Hollanders, Brabanters, Picards, Hainauters and others of the lands of the duke ... Several were seized in the heat of their rage and murdered.'[83] Jean Lefèvre de Saint-Remy, who was one of the diplomats who delivered the news of the duke's decision to Henry VI and the royal council, stated that people in England had 'killed and drowned a certain number of Flemings'.[84]

The council intervened and brought those responsible for the riots to justice.[85] Meanwhile, the subjects of the Burgundian duke living in England were invited to the Chancery to confirm their trustworthiness, offering the oaths of fealty of 1436–7 that are an important source for the 'Dutch' presence in late medieval England. Philip the Good's decision to besiege the English garrison in Calais complicated matters further. In June, when the Burgundian militia were being mustered, rumours were spread that the beer produced by 'Dutchmen' in England had been poisoned. Sheriffs were instructed to tell the latter 'to continue their art', as 'such attacks have caused many brewers to cease brewing'.[86] In January 1437, a petition was presented to the Commons in Parliament alleging that the Flemings held secret meetings in brothels, hostelries and taverns in Southwark where they betrayed vital matters of national security to the French and others of England's enemies. The petitioners suggested that, to prevent such sedition, no alien should be allowed to operate such premises.[87]

The available sources do not provide any clear evidence as to who was responsible for the disturbances in London in 1435 and 1436. Whipped up by a particularly vitriolic spate of anti-Burgundian propaganda and polemic, the rioters may have acted spontaneously to developments that were well understood to be ruinous both in political and, even more so, in economic terms.[88] The wool trade through the staple at Calais, which was the main source of both bullion and customs revenues for England, was brought to a complete standstill by the break with Burgundy. At the same time, the export of English cloth was devastated by the war and by Philip the Good's ban on its sale throughout his territories.[89] The actions of some members of the English royal council clearly did not help to calm things: according to Monstrelet, they denounced Philip's treachery, but conveniently forgot that their own Bullion and Partition Ordinances had both devastated the English economy and soured relations with the duke since 1429.[90]

There is every sign, however, that some of those who stirred up or took part in the anti-Burgundian demonstrations did so for personal gain. Both the slander against beer from the Low Countries and the petition against the Southwark brothels and hostelries could be read as deliberate attempts to disrupt the burgeoning 'Dutch' brewing and prostitution industries. In Southwark, the Flemish resident and vintner, Oliver Bowthin, was abused by the skinner William Hough and the hackneyman William atte Ende, both Englishmen. According to Bowthin's petition to the Chancery, they called him 'bawd, traitor, Fleming, thief and other horrible names, without any matter between them than to seek strife, debate and rancour'. The assailants drew their daggers and would have murdered him, 'had there not been succour of the neighbours there'. Possibly inspired by the petition against the Flemish brothels, Hough, who was also the bailiff of the part of Southwark known as the Guildable Manor, then indicted Bowthin for 'bawdry and receipt of thieves' and locked him up. The Fleming was released, but only after he had given 20 marks' worth of his goods and jewels to Hough.[91]

During the 1440s, the decade in which the alien subsidies were introduced, there were no known attacks on aliens recorded in London or elsewhere. In 1450, at the time of Jack Cade's Rebellion, men from nearby Romsey entered the town of Southampton and threatened the Italians there. The latter imported cloth from the Low Countries and had it finished in Hampshire villages; the Romsey men's grievance was that they offered unacceptable working conditions. In London, Cade demanded money and supplies from the Italians and warned that he would kill them if they did not comply. Even though looting took place during the rebellion, the Italians and their property were eventually left untouched.[92]

This was not the case in 1456. On 28 April of that year, in Cheapside, servants of the London mercers attacked Alessandro Palastrelli, a merchant from Lucca.[93] The following day, the houses of other Italians in the capital city were ransacked. The mayor and sheriffs dispersed the assailants, but turmoil continued. Only on 5 May could order be restored and two or three men were hanged for their role in the riots. A more thorough investigation into the event followed, which eventually concluded in July 1456. The responsibility for the attacks was clearly laid on the mercers and on their master, William Cantelowe, who was imprisoned. What had particularly infuriated the attackers was the government's habit of raising money by granting licences to the Italians. These enabled them to export wool directly to Italy without going through the wool staple in Calais. This practice seriously undermined the position of the powerful Londoners (including Cantelowe) who controlled the staple – precisely the same group that had earlier had a hand in the murder of Janus Imperial.

Tensions continued into the next year. On 16 June 1457, Thomas Graunt, a servant of the Mercers' Company who had been involved in the riots in 1456, and several other servants of the London guilds conspired to murder Italian merchants. Their main target was Galeotto Centurione or Galiot Scot, a Genoese who was heavily engaged in the shipping of wool by royal licence.[94] Their plot was discovered and prevented by the mayor and the sheriff. On 27 June, however, Graunt again attempted to persuade others to kill Lombards in the city. This time, he was immediately detained.[95]

York, Lancaster and the Flemings in 1468–71

The attacks on the Italians in 1455 and 1456 had unfolded against the background of the beginning of the Wars of the Roses, which saw two rival factions fighting for the English crown. The conflict between the houses of York and Lancaster had a more direct impact upon the immigrant communities of London at the end of the 1460s and the start of the 1470s. On 24 July 1468, a skinner named William Shawe tried to gather men from the city's goldsmiths, tailors, cordwainers and skinners to molest the immigrants from the Low Countries in Southwark. His plans were clearly triggered by the crisis of native producers in the city. 'For that the Flemyngs there take away the living of English people', he said, he 'purposed to have cut off their thumbs or hands, so that they should never have helped themselves again by the means of crafts.'[96] In chapter 6 we explained how London's craft guilds failed to keep up with the competition of aliens in the capital during the later fifteenth century, and thus faced the spectre of unemployment. The craft associations where Shawe hoped to find his allies were exactly those which, since the early fifteenth century, had been petitioning the crown for more restrictions on immigrant labour. Before Shawe could carry out his plans, however, the plotters were informed upon and imprisoned.

The London narrative account known as *Gregory's Chronicle* tells us that, in the summer of 1468, Englishmen who had attended the wedding of Edward IV's sister, Margaret, to the Burgundian duke, Charles the Bold, in Flanders returned home with the intention of landing at night at Horsleydown, just east of Southwark, and slaying the Flemings in their beds. The motive, according to the chronicle, was that these men had been treated badly during their stay in the Low Countries.[97] They may have been supporters of the earl of Warwick, who was strongly opposed to the marriage and to Edward's alliance with Burgundy, and favoured a pact with the French. It is not clear whether the conspirators were intending to carry out a second, separate attack on the Flemings or were involved in Shawe's plans, possibly capitalising on the discontent among English craftsmen in order to realise their more politically inspired goals.

Whatever the relationship of this episode to Shawe's plot, the scheme was foiled. Two years later, however, the opponents of Edward's Burgundian alliance did manage to attack London's 'Dutch' population. In the summer of 1469, the earl of Warwick, who had now openly turned against Edward IV, captured the king. Charles the Bold realised that this endangered his subjects in London and sent a letter to the city's mayor and aldermen urging them to keep the peace.[98] The king was released again, and Warwick left the country. In September 1470, however, the latter invaded England, making Edward flee the realm into the protection of the duke of Burgundy.[99] Some days after the king's flight, Warwick's Kentish supporters entered the capital and proceeded to the precinct of St Katharine by the Tower and to Southwark, where, according to the *Great Chronicle of London*, 'Dutchmen dwelled and held beer houses, and there robbed and spoiled without mercy'. The earl's retainer, Geoffrey Gate, opened the Marshalsea gaol and released the prisoners, who burned down more 'Dutch' beer houses and attacked any Flemings they could find.[100]

A petition to the Chancery brings home how this politically inspired hostility could impact upon the lives of immigrants in the capital. Bartholomew Deux was a 'Dutch' merchant who rented a room from the Englishman Roger Dawson in London. When Deux was absent, however,

Dawson stole all of his goods and chattels. The case was brought before the sheriffs of London, where the landlord 'rebuked your said suppliant, he being a subject of the duke of Burgundy, calling him Fleming, saying it was allowed to cut his throat or else to throw a dagger at his heart'.[101] By a bitter irony, Deux came from Guelders, which fought off its incorporation into the Burgundian dominions until 1473. Perhaps it was his experiences with Dawson that inspired him to take out letters of denization in October 1473, eight months after Guelders had finally become part of the Burgundian territories.[102]

Anti-alien hostility during the Tudor period: the attack on the Steelyard and Evil May Day

There are not many cases of violence against aliens known from the early Tudor period. In the early hours of 15 October 1493, a mob assembled at the gates of the Steelyard, the Hanseatic base in London. One month earlier, Henry VII had imposed an embargo on all direct trade with the Low Countries. The Hansards in the country were asked to refrain from trading with Flanders, but the official announcement of their agreement was made very late. As a result, some may have continued their business with the Low Countries, creating the impression that they were trying to gain an advantage at the expense of London's mercantile companies. Incited to action by one of the servants of the mercers, the crowd at the Steelyard damaged warehouses and started a fire, which was put out with the help of Flemish residents. The mayor dispersed the unruly mob, arrested the main perpetrators and installed a nightly guard at the Steelyard for the following seven days in order to guarantee the Hansards' safety.[103] This is one of very few documented cases of organised violence against members of the Hanseatic League operating in England. Some years before the London riots, at an unspecified time during Edward IV's reign, a Hanseatic merchant was also killed in the port of Boston. According to John Leland, the perpetrator was Humphrey Littlebury, a local merchant and customs collector. Unfortunately, nothing is known about Littlebury's motives or about the wider context of the murder.[104]

The competition from alien craftsmen and merchants again triggered disturbances in the capital in the spring of 1517, in an event that later became known as Evil May Day. In April 1516, bills had been spread complaining that the king's wool policy greatly enriched foreigners. Early in 1517, the Mercers' Company had asked Thomas Howard, earl of Surrey, for his help in subduing those aliens who broke regulations in London. Tensions rose when, around mid-April, a native pedlar called John Lincoln convinced a preacher to exhort all Englishmen to stand up against aliens. Isolated attacks against immigrants in London took place over the following two weeks and, because of rumours that more aliens would be slain, the aldermen imposed a curfew on 1 May. When a young man was arrested for ignoring the order, a riot broke out. Around a thousand people, mainly apprentices and servants, gathered in Cheapside and went to Newgate prison, where a number of those involved in the earlier attacks on aliens were released. The houses of Genoese and Florentine traders were damaged, as well as the property of John Meautys, a merchant from Picardy and secretary to the king who was suspected of sheltering unlicensed French wool workers. The insurgents also headed to the liberty of St Martin le Grand, a royal sanctuary where 'Dutch' and French artisans were assumed to escape trade regulations, and to Blancheappleton, a private manor near Aldgate, where the shops of alien shoe makers were ransacked. The rioting stopped early in the morning of the following day. Three hundred people were arrested for their involvement in Evil May Day and several instigators, including John Lincoln, were executed.[105] Although aliens in England continued to be threatened after 1517, there is no evidence of similar large-scale attacks at any other time in the sixteenth century.

Causes of violence against aliens in England during the later Middle Ages

Some historians have seen instances of popular anti-alien hostility in England in the later Middle Ages as being a result of the development of national sentiment. The emergence of the more assertive sense of Englishness charted in chapter 9 not only promoted cohesion among those born in the realm but also supposedly excluded those who originated from elsewhere. In his analysis of the massacre of the Flemings during the Peasants' Revolt, for example, Erik Spindler has claimed that the rebels' eagerness to create an English community made them intuitively and violently opposed to outsiders.[106] According to Ralph Griffiths, fifteenth-century English society was characterised by patriotism and an 'instinctive anti-alien feeling'. Intensified by the Burgundian defection and related propaganda, it was this sentiment that made English people persecute the nation's enemies in the 1430s.[107] For Laura Yungblut, the attacks on the Flemings in 1381 and Evil May Day in 1517 were the result of a permanent anti-alien sentiment that continued to exist in England into the more recent past.[108]

Yet these explanations fail to answer many of the questions that are raised by the surviving evidence. First of all, they do not make clear why violence against aliens was limited to particular moments and why amicable relations between English and immigrant residents prevailed for most of the time. Admittedly, developments such as Philip the Good's defection of 1435 and his attack on Calais in 1436 seem to have stirred up national feeling and provoked hostility against those associated with England's foreign enemies. It is unclear, however, why the much more sustained hostilities with the French during the Hundred Years War would not have had a similar effect. As demonstrated in chapter 5, England had large numbers of French people living within its borders during the later Middle Ages. Yet the only recorded instances of aggression against Frenchmen in this period are the murder of a Breton spy in 1429 after he had battered to death a London widow, and the assault on John Meautys and the cloth workers he was hiding in 1517 – when England and France were not actually at war.[109] Similarly, the recurring context of war with the Scots resulted in additional scrutiny of Scottish residents by the English authorities and a degree of mistrust among Englishmen, certainly in the North. As far as is known, however, this resulted in no large-scale physical attacks on the many Scots living in the country.

Nor do accounts based on the emergence of national identity or ethnic hostility explain why the violence against aliens happened almost exclusively in London. Apart from the isolated murders of Flemings in Norfolk and Essex at the time of the Peasants' Revolt in 1381 and of the Hanseatic merchant in Boston in Edward IV's reign, all the confrontations under consideration here took place in the capital. In many cities and towns outside London, violent encounters between immigrants actually seem to have outnumbered conflicts between aliens and Englishmen.[110] The 1440 alien subsidy returns make clear that London was home to far higher numbers of immigrants than any other place in the country. However, the analysis presented in chapter 3 suggests that aliens represented an equally large part of the total population of Bristol and Southampton, if not larger. Why, then, did English national or ethnic sentiment only make casualties of aliens in the capital?

Many of the existing interpretations do not take into account the interests of those who can be identified behind the attacks. Apart from Monstrelet's claim that it was 'the common people' who chased the subjects of the Burgundian duke in 1435, there is no evidence to conclude that all of the English population, or even a majority, ever turned against alien residents. The case of Oliver Bowthin, who was rescued by his neighbours, even suggests that some Englishmen were disposed to protect immigrants from those who would harass them. The above analyses have revealed that two specific groups were involved in the majority of the incidents throughout the period. The mercers and, to a lesser extent, the other mercantile mysteries of London played a crucial part in the confrontations in the 1350s, 1360s and 1370s, in 1456, 1457, 1493 and 1517 – or at least, their servants and apprentices did. The capital's artisans and craftsmen participated in the disturbances of 1381, 1435–6, 1468 and 1517. Demagogues and political magnates alike – Jack Cade in 1450, the supporters of the earl of Warwick in 1468 and 1470 and possibly even Cardinal Beaufort in 1425 – can be said to have taken advantage of existing antagonisms to further their own interests at times when central authority was weak.

It is equally important to consider the backgrounds of the victims of the attacks. On nearly all occasions, violence was directed towards specific national groups. The mercers and the other mercantile companies of London mainly confronted the Italians and, in 1493, the Hansards. The capital's artisans had a particular issue with immigrants from the Low Countries. These groups were not targeted because they were alien, Italian, German or 'Dutch'. They were challenged because the Italians and, to a lesser extent, the Hansards organised international trade in the city, the wool trade in particular, and because the 'Dutch' dominated many of its crafts and industries, while London's own merchants and producers were losing out. These specific alien groups were often granted privileges by the crown, while the city's native traders and artisans felt the authorities did not adequately address their issues. In this respect, as Ian Archer suggested, attacks on aliens functioned as a device to prod the central government into action.[111] Such an interpretation also helps explain why those who actually performed the acts of violence were so susceptible to political exploitation by opportunists such as Cade. While their animosity may have fed off, and contributed to, an emerging sense of Englishness and the developments of national stereotypes, there is no indication that national feelings ever acted as a primary driver for organised attacks on aliens. London during the later Middle Ages, then, was not a city characterised by anti-alien sentiment. Rather, it was a place where English merchants and producers struggled with international competition and fought fierce battles for political control. The main group to bear the brunt of these tensions was its alien population: or, more accurately, certain groups of aliens labelled as public enemies of the city and the realm.

Notes

1 E 179/124/107, rot. 5.
2 E 179/73/91, m. 5.
3 E 179/87/78, m. 3.
4 E 179/270/31, m. 42; E 179/236/84.
5 E 179/242/25, mm. 12, 15. See also *Alien Communities*, pp. 82, 98.
6 E 179/124/188.
7 E 179/108/113, m. 5. John Cook was assessed as a Fleming in 1440 but swore the oath of fealty in 1436 as an immigrant from Herck in Liège: *CPR 1429-36*, p. 570.
8 *CPR 1429-36*, p. 542; E 179/270/31, m. 5; E 179/95/100, rot. 7; Kowaleski, 'Assimilation of foreigners', p. 175.
9 E 179/144/54, m. 23. For de' Pigli and Tani, see also chapters 6 and 9.
10 *Views of Hosts*, pp. 291-2, 294-5.
11 Lambert and Pajic, 'Immigration and the common profit', p. 644.
12 Bradley, 'Italian Merchants in London', p. 315.
13 *Alien Communities*, p. 51.
14 Bradley, 'Italian Merchants in London', p. 318.
15 E 179/242/25, m. 8d; *Alien Communities*, pp. 57-8.
16 E 179/149/126, m. 3.
17 E 179/117/71, m. 2.
18 E 179/158/41, m. 6.
19 E 179/235/3, m. 2; E 179/235/4, mm. 3-4.
20 E 179/184/212; E 179/242/25.
21 E 179/236/130, m. 15; E 179/117/77.
22 E 179/180/92, Part 2, m. 4.
23 E 179/136/215, Part 2, m. 5.
24 E 179/165/83, m. 1.
25 For references to Ruddick's work throughout this section, see Ruddick, 'Immigrants and intermarriage'.
26 E 179/165/68, m. 2.
27 E 179/117/49, m. 3.
28 E 179/180/111, rot. 2.
29 E 179/242/25, m. 7d.
30 *CPR 1436-41*, p. 352.
31 *CPR 1441-6*, p. 408; Bolton, 'London and the anti-alien legislation', p. 47.
32 C 67/72. For context, see chapter 8.
33 For previous judgements on the fifteenth century, see *Alien Communities*, pp. 8, 35; Thrupp, 'Aliens in and around London', pp. 264-5, 269-72.
34 C 1/45/55.
35 *CPR 1429-36*, p. 116; *PROME*, IV, p. 387; Bruges City Archives, City Accounts, 1422-3, fol. 81r; 1423-4, fol. 34v. Most of the English historiography considers John Asger to be a Bruges native: see, among others, Tanner, 'Religious practice', pp. 140-1. However, the Bruges sources categorically classify him as an Englishman.
36 Kermode, *Medieval Merchants*, p. 346.

37 Roskell, Clark and Rawcliffe, *History of Parliament*, II, 53–4.
38 Bradley, 'Italian Merchants in London', pp. 291–4.
39 Jenks, 'Hansische Vermächtnisse in London', pp. 51–2.
40 E 179/180/111, rot. 6, m. 1; Amor, *Late Medieval Ipswich*, pp. 249–50.
41 Ruddock, 'Alien merchants in Southampton', p. 17.
42 SC 8/88/4384.
43 Ormrod, 'Origins of tunnage and poundage'.
44 For example, SC 8/127/6303; SC 8/329/E939.
45 SC 8/216/10773, with resulting action in *CPR 1388–92*, p. 27.
46 Lambert, ' "Nostri fratelli da Londra"', pp. 91–3.
47 Bradley, 'Italian Merchants', p. 294.
48 Colson, 'Alien communities and alien fraternities'.
49 E 179/242/25, m. 16. He was called 'Oliverus Weste' in the ordinances of the fraternity.
50 E 179/242/25, m. 10.
51 E 179/242/25, m. 12; Colson, 'Alien communities and alien fraternities', p. 112.
52 *Alien Communities*, p. 36; Reddaway and Walker, *Goldsmiths' Company*, p. 129.
53 *LP*, I, pt 1, no. 1365 (15).
54 Colson, 'Alien communities and alien fraternities', pp. 111–43.
55 Badham, 'Introduction', p. 11.
56 Carlin, *Medieval Southwark*, p. 156; Ford, 'Marginality and the assimilation of foreigners'.
57 Thrupp, 'Aliens in and around London', p. 114; Colson, 'Alien communities and alien fraternities', pp. 118, 125–6.
58 Twycross, 'Some aliens in York', 265–6.
59 J. Hanley, 'Aliens and religion in Suffolk, c. 1330–1550', www.englandsimmigrants.com/page/individual-studies/aliens-and-religion-in-suffolk-c-1330-1550 (accessed 4 October 2017).
60 Laughton, 'Mapping the migrants', pp. 169–83 (quotation at p. 178).
61 E 179/217/45, mm. 2–4. This is a much larger number than the ten stated to have had their parish of residence recorded by Dobson, 'Aliens in the city of York', p. 256.
62 Rees Jones, *York*, pp. 193–201, 264–6, 302–6.
63 E 179/217/45, m. 2.
64 Rees Jones, *York*, pp. 193–201, 302–6.
65 E 179/217/45, m. 2.
66 E 179/113/104; Carus-Wilson, *Medieval Merchant Venturers*, pp. 2–4, 75–6.
67 Bolton, 'La répartition spatiale'.
68 Bradley, 'Italian Merchants in London', pp. 12–22.
69 Carlin, *Medieval Southwark*, pp. 154–5. The fifteenth-century alien subsidy returns for Southwark do not specify taxpayers' nationalities and parishes of residence.
70 Calimani, *Ghetto of Venice*; Siegmund, *Medici State and the Ghetto of Florence*.
71 Bolton, 'La répartition spatiale', pp. 425–35.
72 See chapter 6.
73 Keene, 'Du seuil de la cité à la formation d'une économie morale'.
74 Tillott (ed.), *Victoria History of the County of York: City of York*, pp. 68–9.
75 *POPC*, VI, viii–ix; McSheffrey, 'Stranger artisans'.

76 Sutton, *Mercery of London*, pp. 115–17.
77 Strohm, 'Trade, treason and the murder of Janus Imperial'.
78 *Westminster Chronicle*, pp. 6–8.
79 Prescott, 'Judicial Records', pp. 99, 117; Pajic, 'Migration of Flemish Weavers', pp. 199–208.
80 Carlin, *Medieval Southwark*, p. 158.
81 Lambert and Pajic, 'Immigration and the common profit'.
82 Harriss, *Cardinal Beaufort*, p. 140.
83 De Monstrelet, *Chronique, V*, pp. 192–3.
84 Lefèvre de Saint-Remy, *Chronique, II*, p. 378.
85 *POPC*, IV, 331.
86 *CLBL K*, p. 205.
87 SC 8/27/1309.
88 Doig, 'Propaganda, public opinion and the siege of Calais'; Bellis, *Hundred Years War in Literature*, pp. 114–26.
89 Thielemans, *Bourgogne et Angleterre*, pp. 165–212.
90 De Monstrelet, *Chronique, 1400–1444*, p. 192.
91 C 1/45/55. The petition is undated, but Bowthin asked the chancellor to consider the truce with Flanders. Burgundy and England concluded a series of these truces from February 1439 onwards: Thielemans, *Bourgogne et Angleterre*, p. 121.
92 Harvey, *Jack Cade's Rebellion*, pp. 127–8.
93 For Palastrelli's assessments towards the alien subsidies between 1449 and 1457, see E 179/235/23, m. 2; E 179/144/64, m. 11; E 179/144/72; E 179/236/74.
94 Centurione was assessed towards the alien subsidies continuously between 1456 and 1469: E 179/235/58, m. 1; E 179/236/74; E 179/236/107, m. 2; E 179/144/67.
95 Bolton, 'The city and the crown'.
96 LMA, COL/CC/01/01/007, fols 178–178v.
97 *Historical Collections of a Citizen of London*, pp. 237–8.
98 *Alien Communities*, p. 39.
99 Hicks, *Warwick the Kingmaker*, pp. 271–85.
100 *Great Chronicle of London*, pp. 211–12.
101 C 1/46/452.
102 *CPR 1467–77*, p. 374. In 1476, an Edward Deux, also from Guelders, acquired denization as well: *CPR 1467–77*, p. 604.
103 Fudge, *Cargoes, Embargoes and Emissaries*, pp. 135–6.
104 Badham, 'Introduction', pp. 25–6.
105 Holmes, 'Evil May Day'; Rappaport, *Worlds within Worlds*, pp. 15–17; Wilson, 'Evil May Day'.
106 Spindler, 'Flemings in the Peasants' Revolt'.
107 Griffiths, *Reign of King Henry VI*, pp. 169, 171.
108 Yungblut, *Strangers Settled Here Amongst Us*, pp. 37–40.
109 For the Breton spy, see Griffiths, *Reign of King Henry VI*, p. 134.
110 Kissane and Mackman, 'Aliens and the law', p. 120; Lambert and Pajic, 'Drapery in exile', pp. 741–2; Ruddock, 'Alien merchants in Southampton', p. 12.
111 Archer, *Pursuit of Stability*, pp. 131–3.

11

Conclusion: nationalism, racism and xenophobia

The later medieval state created the alien as a social category in England. As we detailed in chapters 2 and 3, it was the application of new laws concerning the rights of aliens and the development of special taxes on people born outside the realm that established, for the first time, a formal framework for the regulation of foreigners at a national level. In the process, as we saw in chapters 4 and 5, the agents of local government applied labels to foreigners living in their midst in such a way as to define nationality more precisely (though not necessarily more accurately) than ever before. Moreover, as we discussed in chapters 6, 7 and 8, it was the willingness of late medieval and early Tudor governments to respond to the lobbying of interest groups within the realm that created a legislative programme that variously promoted and restricted the working lives especially of the skilled immigrant labour force.

The institutionalisation of the alien also went hand in hand with a more confident expression of nationalism by the English monarchy and a growing sense of exclusiveness and superiority over other kingdoms and nations. One important manifestation of this development, as we noted in chapter 9, was the increasingly strident isolationism that seems to have crept in during the late fifteenth and early sixteenth centuries. A number of the foreign visitors (mainly Italians) who began to write reports of their experiences within the kingdom during this period commented on the English population's view that there was 'no other world but England'.[1]

The major question that arises, in light of the evidence discussed in chapters 8, 9 and 10, is whether this increasingly self-confident and inward-looking nationalism also bred forms of racial and ethnic hatred. Historians of the high and later Middle Ages in Europe have remarked the development of what R. I. Moore famously called a 'persecuting society': one in which a previous toleration of difference – whether race, ethnicity, class, gender, sexuality or disability – gave way to growing prejudice, discrimination and hostility.[2] It would be a gross mistake, of course, to suppose that people in England only started to have hostile intent towards minorities from the twelfth century onwards. Len Scales has collected examples of attacks on ethnic groups during the early and high Middle Ages, including what was probably by far the worst case in England over the whole of the medieval millennium, the state-sponsored massacre of the Danes on St Brice's Day 1002.[3] Equally, it has often been remarked that England actually avoided the bloodshed that accompanied continental programmes of racial and ethnic victimisation in the later Middle Ages: the crown was very insistent that the expulsion of the Jews in 1290 be carried out without violence, and after the Black Death there was virtually nothing in England akin to the pogroms of minorities (mainly Jews) that were a frequent manifestation of social and psychological turmoil in other parts of Europe.[4] There remains, though, an unanswered question as to whether people in later medieval England may still be described as racist and/or xenophobic in their attitudes, and particularly in their behaviour, towards those foreigners who were settled among them.

The terminology of racism and xenophobia is both fraught and entangled, and there are no clear boundaries between the two. Our choice of words is inevitably influenced by contemporary experience. In 1966, for example, the medieval historian Rees Davies deployed a word from the institutionalised racism then obtaining in South Africa to describe the discrimination applied by the English against the native Welsh in the later Middle Ages as a form of 'apartheid'.[5] Equally, the new vocabulary that emerged in the early 1990s to describe atrocities in the former Yugoslavia led Davies in 1995 to use the term 'ethnic cleansing' for the violent recriminations that the English applied against the Welsh after the revolt of Owain Glyn Dŵr.[6] Scales has also argued for the use of the twentieth-century neologism 'genocide' to describe pogroms of ethnic groups in medieval Europe.[7] Given the political and cultural baggage associated with such emotive terminology, it is clear that there are no truly definitive or objective ways in which to describe or evaluate the treatment of minorities in a given historical period. For the purposes of this study, however, it may be helpful to draw a clear distinction between racism and xenophobia. Racism is here understood as a form of prejudice expressed specifically against a minority group identified by colour and/or the practice of a non-Christian religion (specifically, in the instances discussed in this book, Judaism and Islam). Xenophobia, on the other hand – which literally means the fear of the foreign – may be defined as the suspicion or hatred of people of the same race and creed as the host community (for present purposes, 'European' Christians) but having a recognisably different ethnicity manifested in language, customs and sometimes (more especially after the Reformation) Christian denomination.

The accusation of systematic racism can and must be directed against the English state for its decision to expel the Jews in 1290, and thereafter to prevent the practice of Judaism in England for three and a half centuries. As we saw in chapter 8, the expulsion did not serve to weaken anti-Semitism in England: rather, it allowed popular and polite culture to vent its continued prejudices against the 'imagined' Jew. It could be conjectured that this anti-Semitic culture deflected attention from the other minority groups that were still present in the realm: we noted in chapter 8 that policy towards Muslims and black people was not as straightforwardly intolerant, even in the sixteenth century, as was once thought. However, the continued assumption that such people could obtain an identity in England only by converting to Christianity (Catholic before the Reformation, Protestant after it) shows the severe limits of diversity in the fourteenth to sixteenth centuries. In this sense the expulsion of the Jews in 1290, and its legal and cultural legacy, simply serve to highlight the existence of more widespread, institutionalised racism in late medieval England.

A more considerable challenge remains around the issue of xenophobia. In recent years, there has been a lively discussion among early modern historians as to whether sixteenth- and seventeenth-century England can properly be described as xenophobic. Given both the uncertainty of the criteria used to define the phenomenon and the necessarily subjective nature of the evidence, it is perhaps unsurprising that little consensus has emerged.[8] Those historians who have consciously used the term at all in relation to the fourteenth and fifteenth centuries have tended to treat xenophobia simply in relation to top-down nationalism, seeking evidence for its existence in those same rhetorical texts – parliamentary orations, official proclamations, sermons, chronicles and political poems – that promoted nationalistic spirit in support of the public enterprise of war. In other words, xenophobia in the later Middle Ages is generally seen as a facet of the wider process of state building.[9] Until this point, however, there has been virtually no consideration of whether a generalised distrust of enemy nations also drove the attitudes and responses of English people to the foreigners whom they encountered at home. This book has provided insights into the personal histories of many thousands of men and women who moved from other parts of the British Isles and continental Europe to spend some or all of the rest of their lives in England. It is the attitude to *them* that we need to make the focus of our final judgements about xenophobia.

The implication of the discussion in previous chapters is that a significant proportion – and probably a majority – of the indigenous population of later medieval England must have had some direct contact, even if only fleeting, with first-generation immigrants. The labels that the jurors and assessors for the alien subsidies applied to the people enumerated for these taxes demonstrate that the English did not regard such foreigners simply as an undifferentiated and anonymous bloc, but knew them individually by name, thought at least that they knew their nationalities, had some reliable details about their families and households and could identify many of them according to their status and jobs. This explains why, on the whole, the debates that took place over the legal rights and economic freedoms of foreigners were not accompanied by regurgitations of the demonising stereotypes deployed in war propaganda. The people under discussion were, after all, the fellow freemen, suppliers, household staff, employees, neighbours – and even, in some cases, the in-laws – of the English-born people who helped determine their fates. Nor should we forget that a certain proportion of these 'English-born' knew themselves to be the descendants of recent immigrants. It is our contention that, in those cases where anti-alien attitudes can indeed be said to have become more virulent, they almost never arose simply from some latent and generalised animosity to foreigners. Rather, they were prompted by specific pressures – political, social and, in particular, economic – and tended to be applied not against foreigners at large but against smaller groups defined by nationality and/or occupation.

The outstanding example of this model, which we have pursued in chapters 2, 6, 8 and 10, is that of urban society. We have seen that the welcome provided to immigrant merchants and artisans in the thirteenth century could give way, during the fifteenth, to a more discriminatory approach, in which some people born outside the realm were restricted in their ability to practise their crafts and were denied the right to participate in the public life of the town through joining the franchise or holding office. We have also argued, however, that these measures were directed not against aliens as a whole but against very specific categories: usually the skilled manufacturers and traders who could be made subject to the relevant civic guilds. In spite of the vehemence with which some of the national legislation against alien artisans was expressed, we would contend that the official discrimination applied against alien craftspeople was not driven by simple xenophobia, but was determined by the ups and downs of the economy at the local level. This explains why the restrictions on the rights of artisans can be shown to have been applied only in London and in certain larger towns, and seem not to have been taken up more generally in provincial urban contexts.

There are also, of course, instances covered in this book where particular national groupings were singled out for special surveillance, discrimination or persecution. In a formal sense, the Welsh were the minority with the fewest rights in the fifteenth century, since the disabilities applied within Wales in the aftermath of revolt also officially applied, as we saw in chapter 2, to Welsh-born people living in England. In reality, however, large numbers of Welsh émigrés to England were of too low a social standing to be worried about rules governing urban franchises and property-holding, while Welsh people of higher status were seemingly accommodated quite successfully in the civic hierarchies of those towns, such as Bristol and Chester, where they had a significant presence. The Irish in England stood in rather a different relationship to the rules that governed their homeland, not least because many of them, as we saw in chapter 3, seem to have come from the 'English' and legally privileged parts of Irish society. While they may have been marginalised from participation in civic life, however, there is every indication, as we demonstrated in chapters 4 and 6, that Irish men and women were more generally integrated into English society, in urban as well as in rural locations and in a wide range of occupations from labourers to clergy. In short, the formal disabilities that the Plantagenet regime applied to the 'native' peoples living in its dependencies did not operate on a consistent basis within England, and allowed for significantly more discretion in terms of the way that local elites chose to treat immigrants from the dominions.

A stronger test as to whether later medieval England can be described as a xenophobic society lies in the attitude to the longest-standing enemies of the period, the Scots and the French. The arrest of French-born people and their assets in 1294 was conducted with some thoroughness, but in later general seizures and expulsion ordinances, both against French and against Scots, numerous loopholes and exceptions were allowed. As we saw in chapter 2, careful strategies were also worked out by the government at Westminster and the officers of the English March towards Scotland to guarantee the rights of those who would otherwise be suspected as enemy strangers. The legal process of denization was itself a specific response to the needs of French people marooned in England after the reopening of the Hundred Years War in the 1370s. If the population at large remained vigilant towards those born in hostile nations, it was, as we remarked in chapter 10, remarkably restrained in its treatment of them. This level of acceptance is something that would be quite impossible in the modern era of total war, when enemy aliens were often interned for reasons of national security, as well as for their own safety. The explanation for the difference must be that English people in the later Middle Ages distinguished, rather more readily than their descendants, between the enemy as an abstract collective existing outside the realm and the individuals from that nation who happened to live within it.

A final test of xenophobia comes in the relative frequency of observable abuse and violence committed by denizens against foreigners. The Gascons' complaint in 1411 about the name-calling to which they were subject in England is evidence of a low-level latent hostility that no doubt manifested itself, at times, in physical attacks: at the turn of the sixteenth century, for example the Italian visitor Andreas Franciscus claimed that the Londoners despised his compatriots and beat them up on the streets at night.[10] Much more important as a measure of the instrumental nature of popular xenophobia, however, are discernible examples of scaled-up, premeditated attacks on targeted groups of immigrants. As chapter 10 made clear, the Peasants' Revolt is virtually the only occasion on which we find evidence of such organised violence taking place outside London over the entire period covered by this book – and even then, the instances beyond the capital were confined to a small number of places in East Anglia. In particular, our analysis has highlighted the way that generalised contempt of foreigners was channelled by specific elite groups to further their political programmes: the model of London guildsmen deploying mobs to intimidate foreign merchants and/or craftspeople holds for most of the periodic attacks on aliens in the capital from the Peasants' Revolt of 1381 to the Evil May Day of 1517.

The later Middle Ages is the first time when the archives allow us to go beyond the level of generalisation and to humanise the immigrant experience in England. Above all, the records of the alien subsidies of 1440–87 demonstrate vividly that thousands of people of alien birth continued, in each generation, to move into England, some as permanent and some as temporary residents, many responding to the economic opportunities understood to be on offer, and all presumably aware of the challenges that such a move would present. Contrary to widespread scholarly assumptions about the 'closed' nature of English society in this period, the alien subsidy returns reveal a larger and more varied immigrant presence than ever before appreciated, spread out across the rural landscape as well as clustered in towns and including people of low, middle and elite status. This body of evidence also allows us to offer a serious corrective to notions of English prejudice against foreigners by demonstrating just how many immigrants got on with their lives in reasonably peaceful coexistence with their native-born neighbours, going about their business and their work, in some instances intermarrying with local men and women, and in the vast majority of cases being integrated into the social and cultural networks of their adopted land.

In contemplating such a predominant model of integration, it is worth considering how the various treatments of and attitudes towards foreigners surveyed in this book fed off, and contributed to, notions of Englishness. As we saw in chapter 9, English writers of the later Middle Ages did not generally subscribe to a notion of racial supremacism: they were acutely aware of the mixed genetic heritage of people born within the kingdom, a position made all the more striking by their understanding that this reality potentially threatened the otherwise carefully constructed notion of an inclusive *gens Anglorum*. The acculturation of immigrants within each generation was therefore understood as a complex and subtle process that required adjustment not just by aliens but also by denizens. For most permanent arrivals, cut off as they were from all but rare contact with their families back home and from conscious minority communities in England, migration meant a significant loss of ethnic heritage. For those born inside the realm, ironically, the process of intermixing with foreigners had palpable results on mainstream culture, bringing in high-prestige foreign imports of goods, fuelling further demand for expert services and skills from abroad, and leaving permanent markers on spoken and written language. We therefore need to reflect not only on how immigrants to England in the later Middle Ages were able, so comparatively easily, to become 'English', but also on how Englishness itself adapted and changed to reflect a continuous and creative process of acculturation.

Notes

1 *A Relation ... of the Island of England*, pp. 20–1. See the similar reflections in *Calendar of State Papers Relating to English Affairs in the Archives of Venice, VI*, pt 3, App. no. 171.
2 Moore, *Formation of a Persecuting Society*.
3 Scales, 'Bread, cheese and genocide'.
4 Cohn, 'Black Death'.
5 Davies, 'Twilight of Welsh law'.

6 Davies, *Revolt of Owain Glyn Dŵr*, p. 284. More generally on the complexities of European ethnicity, see most recently Geary, 'European ethnicities'.

7 Scales, 'Bread, cheese and genocide'.

8 Luu, ' "Taking the bread out of our mouths"'; Goose, ' "Xenophobia"'; Birchwood and Dimmock, 'Popular xenophobia'.

9 Barnie, *War in Medieval English Society*; Menache, *The Vox Dei*, pp. 190–209; Griffiths, 'The island of England', pp. 198–200. See also the nuanced comments of Ruddick, *English Identity*, pp. 130–1; Green, 'National identities'; Green, *Hundred Years War*, pp. 230–47.

10 *Two Italian Accounts of Tudor England*, p. 37.

BIBLIOGRAPHY

Manuscripts

Bruges, City Archives
  City Accounts
  Registers Wetsvernieuwingen
Eton, Eton College Archives
  ECR 60/03/01
London, London Metropolitan Archives
  CLA/023/DW (Court of Husting, City of London, Deeds and Wills)
  COL/CC/01/01/001–10 (Corporation of London, Journals of the Common Council)
  DL/C/B/004/MS09171 (Diocese of London, Court Records, Commissary Court of London)
London, The National Archives
  C 1 (Chancery: Proceedings)
  C 44 (Court of Chancery: Common Law Pleadings: Tower Series)
  C 66 (Chancery and Supreme Court of Judicature: Patent Rolls)
  C 67 (Chancery: Patent Rolls Supplementary)
  C 76 (Chancery: Treaty Rolls)
  C 82 (Chancery: Warrants for the Great Seal, Series II)
  C 241 (Chancery: Certificates of Statutes Merchant and Statutes Staple)
  C 244 (Chancery: Petty Bag Office: Files, Tower and Rolls Chapel Series, Corpus Cum Causa)
  CP 40 (Court of Common Pleas: Plea Rolls)
  E 101 (King's Remembrancer: Accounts Various)
  E 150 (Exchequer: King's Remembrancer, Escheators' Files, Inquisitions Post Mortem, Series II)
  E 159 (Exchequer: King's Remembrancer: Memoranda Rolls and Enrolment Books)
  E 179 (Exchequer: King's Remembrancer: Subsidy Rolls)
  E 359 (Exchequer: Pipe Office: Accounts Rolls of Subsidies and Aids)
  JUST 2 (Coroners' Rolls and Files, with Cognate Documents)
  JUST 3 (Justices of Gaol Delivery: Gaol Delivery Rolls and Fines)
  PSO 2 (Privy Seal Office: Signet and Other Warrants for the Privy Seal, Series II)
  SC 1 (Special Collections: Ancient Correspondence of the Chancery and the Exchequer)

SC 8 (Special Collections: Ancient Petitions)
SP 46 (State Papers Domestic: Supplementary)
WARD 2 (Court of Wards and Liveries: Deeds and Evidences)
London, Westminster Abbey Muniments, WAM 12261
Lucca, Archivio di Stato
   Diplomatico, Archivio di Stato
   Diplomatico, Archivio di Stato-Tarpea.

Primary sources

The Alien Communities of London in the Fifteenth Century: The Subsidy Rolls of 1440 and 1483-4, ed. J. L. Bolton (Stamford, 1998).

The Black Death, ed. R. Horrox (Manchester, 1994).

Bronnen tot de Geschiedenis van den Handel met Engeland, Schotland en Ierland, 1150–1585, ed. H. J. Smit, 2 vols ('s Gravenhage, 1928–50).

'The building accounts of Kirby Muxloe Castle, 1480–84', ed. A. H. Thompson, *Transactions of the Leicestershire Archaeological Society*, 11 (1913–20), 193–345.

The Building Accounts of Tattershall Castle 1434-1472, ed. W. P. Simpson, Lincoln Record Society, 55 (1960).

Calendar of the Close Rolls Preserved in the Public Record Office, Henry III–Henry VII, 61 vols (London, 1892–1963).

Calendar of Documents relating to Scotland preserved in Her Majesty's Public Record Office, London, ed. J. Bain, 4 vols (Edinburgh, 1888).

Calendar of the Fine Rolls Preserved in the Public Record Office, Edward I–Henry VII, 22 vols (London, 1911–62).

Calendar of Inquisitions Miscellaneous, 1219-1485, 8 vols (London and Woodbridge, 1916–2003).

Calendar of the Letter Books of the City of London, A–L, ed. R. R. Sharpe, 11 vols (London, 1899–1912).

Calendar of the Patent Rolls Preserved in the Public Record Office, Henry III–Henry VII, 54 vols (London, 1891–1916).

Calendar of State Papers Relating to English Affairs in the Archives of Venice, VI: 1555–1558, ed. R. Brown (London, 1877).

Chaucer, Geoffrey, *The Canterbury Tales: Fifteen Tales and the General Prologue*, ed. V. A. Kolve (New York, 1989).

de Monstrelet, Enguerrand, *Chronique, 1400-1444, V*, ed. L. Doüet d'Arcq (Paris, 1861).

Early Common Petitions in the English Parliament, c. 1290–c. 1420, ed. W. M. Ormrod, H. Killick and P. Bradford, Camden Society, 5th series, 52 (2017).

The Great Chronicle of London, ed. A. H. Thomas and I. D. Thornley (London, 1938).

The Great Tournament Roll of Westminster, ed. S. Anglo, 2 vols (Oxford: Clarendon Press, 1968).

The Historical Collections of a Citizen of London in the Fifteenth Century, ed. J. Gairdner, Camden Society, n.s., 17 (1876).

Langland, William, *Piers Plowman*, ed. E. Salter and D. A. Pearsall (London, 1967).

The Lay Subsidy for Shropshire, 1524-7, ed. M. A. Faraday (Keele, 1999).

Lefèvre de Saint-Remy, Jean, *Chronique, 1400-1444, II*, ed. F. Morand (Paris, 1881).

The Libelle of Englyshe Polycye: A Poem on the Use of Sea-Power, 1436, ed. G. F. Warner (Oxford, 1926).

Letters and Papers, Foreign and Domestic, of the Reign of Henry VIII, ed. J. S. Brewer, J. Gairdner and R. H. Brodie, 37 vols (London, 1862-1932).

Letters of Denization and Acts of Naturalization for Aliens in England, 1509-1603, ed. W. Page, Publications of the Huguenot Society of London, 8 (1893).

Letters of Denization and Acts of Naturalization for Aliens in England and Ireland, 1603-1800, ed. W. A. Shaw, 2 vols, Huguenot Society of London Publications, 18, 27 (1911, 1923).

'London Lickpenny', in *Medieval English Political Writings*, ed. J. M. Dean (Kalamazoo, 1996), pp. 222-5.

Memorials of London and London Life in the XIIIth, XIVth and XVth Centuries, ed. T. H. Riley (London, 1868).

The Overseas Trade of Bristol in the Later Middle Ages, ed. E. M. Carus-Wilson, Bristol Record Society, 7 (1937).

The Overseas Trade of London: Exchequer Customs Accounts, 1480-1, ed. H. S. Cobb, London Record Society, 27 (1990).

The Parliament Rolls of Medieval England, ed. P. Brand, S. Phillips, W. M. Ormrod, G. Martin, C. Given-Wilson, A. Curry and R. Horrox, 16 vols (Woodbridge, 2005).

The Poll Taxes of 1377, 1379 and 1381, ed. C. C. Fenwick, Records of Economic and Social History, new series, 27, 29, 37 (1998-2005).

The Pre-Reformation Records of All Saints' Church, Bristol, II, ed. C. Burgess, Bristol Record Society, 53 (2000).

Proceedings and Ordinances of the Privy Council of England, ed. N. H. Nicolas, 7 vols (London, 1834-7).

Records of the Borough of Leicester, II: 1327-1509, ed. M. Bateson (London, 1901).

The Register of Edward the Black Prince, 4 vols (London, 1930-33).

Registers of the Freemen of the City of York, I: 1272-1558, ed. F. Collins, Surtees Society, 96 (1897).

A Relation, or Rather a True Account, of the Island of England ... about the Year 1500, ed. C. A. Sneyd, Camden Society, 37 (1847).

Responsiones Vadstenenses: Perspectives on the Birgittine Rule in Two Texts from Vadstena and Syon Abbey, ed. E. Andersson, Studia Latina Stockholmiensia, 55 (2011).

Returns of Strangers in the Metropolis, 1593, 1627, 1635, 1639, ed. I. Scouloudi, Publications of the Huguenot Society of London, 57 (1985).

Select Cases in the Court of King's Bench under Edward I, ed. G. O. Sayles, Selden Society, 58 (1939).

Statutes of the Realm, 11 vols (London, 1810-28).

Testamenta Eboracensia IV, ed. J. Raine, Surtees Society, 53 (1868).

Tudor Royal Proclamations, I: The Early Tudors (1485-1553), ed. P. L. Hughes and J. F. Larkin (New Haven, 1964).

Two Italian Accounts of Tudor England, trans. C. V. Malfatti (Barcelona, 1953).

Usk, Thomas, 'The Testament of Love', in *The Idea of the Vernacular: An Anthology of Middle English Literary Theory, 1280–1520*, ed. J. Wogan-Browne, N. Watson, A. Taylor and R. Evans (Exeter, 1999), pp. 28–33.

The Views of the Hosts of Alien Merchants, 1440–1444, ed. H. Bradley, London Record Society, 46 (2012).

The Wealth of Shrewsbury in the Early Fourteenth Century: Six Local Subsidy Rolls, 1297 to 1322, ed. D. Cromarty and R. Cromarty (Shrewsbury, 1993).

Unpublished dissertations

Bartlett, J., 'Looking at t'Other: Robert Thornton's Yorkshire Oryent, c. 1400–1473' (PhD dissertation, University of York, 2015).

Bolton, J. L., 'Alien Merchants in England in the Reign of Henry VI, 1422–61' (B.Litt dissertation, Oxford, 1971).

Bradley, H. L., 'Italian Merchants in London, c.1350–c.1450' (PhD dissertation, University of London, 1992).

Davies, M. P., 'The Tailors of London and their Guild, c. 1300–1500' (D.Phil dissertation, University of Oxford, 1994).

Fogle, L., 'Jewish Converts to Christianity in Medieval London' (PhD dissertation, University of London, 2005).

Linsley, C. D., 'Nation, England and the French in Thomas Walsingham's *Chronica Maiora*, 1376–1420' (PhD dissertation, University of York, 2015).

Pajic, M., 'The Migration of Flemish Weavers to England in the Fourteenth Century: The Economic Influence and Transfer of Skills 1331–1381' (PhD dissertation, Université de Strasbourg/Ghent University, 2016).

Prescott, A., 'Judicial Records of the Rising of 1381' (PhD dissertation, Bedford College, University of London, 1984).

Richardson, J., 'A Bishop and his Diocese: Politics, Government, and Careers in Hereford and Winchester Dioceses, 1282–1317' (PhD dissertation, University of York, 2016).

Rodziewicz, J., 'Order and Society: Great Yarmouth, 1366–1381' (PhD dissertation, University of East Anglia, 2008).

Wallace, J., 'The Overseas Trade of Sandwich, 1400–1520' (M.Phil dissertation, University of London, 1974).

Secondary studies

Adler, M., *The Jews of Medieval England* (London, 1939).

Akbari, S. C., *Idols in the East: European Representations of Islam and the Orient, 1100–1540* (Ithaca, 2009).

Alban, J. R. and C. T. Allmand, 'Spies and spying in the fourteenth century', in C. T. Allmand (ed.), *War, Literature, and Politics in the Late Middle Ages* (New York, 1976), pp. 73–101.

Allan, J. P., 'Breton woodworkers in the immigrant communities of south-west England, 1500–1550', *Post-Medieval Archaeology*, 48 (2014), 320–56.

Allen, M., *Mints and Money in Medieval England* (Cambridge, 2012).

Allmand, C. T., *Lancastrian Normandy: The History of a Medieval Occupation, 1415–1450* (Oxford, 1983).

Allmand, C. T., 'A note on denization in fifteenth-century England', *Medievalia et Humanistica*, 17 (1966), 127–8.

Amor, N., *Late Medieval Ipswich: Trade and Industry* (Woodbridge, 2011).

Amor, N., 'Merchant adventurer or jack of all trades: the Suffolk clothier in the 1460s', *Proceedings of the Suffolk Institute for Archaeology and History*, 40 (2004), 414–36.

Archer, I. W., *The History of the Haberdashers' Company of London* (Chichester, 1991).

Archer, I. W., *The Pursuit of Stability: Social Relations in Elizabethan London* (Cambridge, 1991).

Armitage, D., *The Ideological Origins of the British Empire* (Cambridge, 2000).

Arnold, B., *Princes and Territories in Medieval Germany* (Cambridge, 1991).

Ash, E. H., *Power, Knowledge, and Expertise in Elizabethan England* (Baltimore, 2004).

Awty, B. G., 'The continental origins of Wealden ironworkers, 1451–1544', *Economic History Review*, 2nd series, 34 (1981), 524–39.

Badham, S., 'Introduction', in S. Badham and P. Cockerham (eds), *'The beste and fayrest of al Lincolnshire': The Church of St Botolph, Boston, Lincolnshire and its Medieval Monuments*, British Archaeological Reports, British Series, 554 (2012), pp. 1–28.

Baker, J., *The Oxford History of the Laws of England, VI: 1483–1558* (Oxford, 2003).

Baker, R. L., *The English Customs Service, 1307–1343: A Study of Medieval Administration* (Philadelphia, 1961).

Baldwin, F. E., *Sumptuary Legislation and Personal Regulation in England* (Baltimore, 1926).

Bale, A., *Feeling Persecuted: Christians, Jews and Images of Violence in the Middle Ages* (London, 2010).

Bardsley, S., 'Women's work reconsidered: gender and wage differentiation in late medieval England', *Past & Present*, 165 (1999), 3–29.

Barnie, J., *War in Medieval English Society: Social Values in the Hundred Years War, 1337–99* (London, 1974).

Barrell, A. D. M. 'The Ordinance of Provisors of 1343', *Historical Research*, 63 (1991), 264–77.

Barron, C. M., 'The "golden age" of women in medieval London', *Reading Medieval Studies*, 15 (1989), 35–58.

Barron, C. M., 'Introduction: England and the Low Countries, 1327–1477', in C. M. Barron and N. Saul (eds), *England and the Low Countries in the Late Middle Ages* (Stroud, 1995), pp. 1–28.

Barron, C. M., 'Introduction: the widow's world in later medieval London', in C. M. Barron and A.F. Sutton (eds), *Medieval London Widows, 1300–1500* (London, 1994), pp. xiii–xxxiv.

Bartlett, R., *The Making of Europe: Conquest, Colonization and Cultural Change, 950–1350* (London, 1993).

Beardwood, A., 'Mercantile antecedents of the English naturalization laws', *Medievalia et Humanistica*, 16 (1964), 64–76.

Bellis, J., *The Hundred Years War in Literature, 1337–1600* (Woodbridge, 2016).

Bendiner, K., *The Art of Ford Madox Brown* (University Park, 1998).

Benedictow, O. J., *The Black Death, 1346–1353: The Complete History* (Woodbridge, 2004).

Bennett, J. M., *Ale, Beer, and Brewsters in England: Women's Work in a Changing World, 1300–1600* (Oxford, 1996).

Bennett, J. M., *History Matters: Patriarchy and the Challenge of Feminism* (Philadelphia, 2006).

Bennett, J. M., 'Medieval women, modern women: across the great divide', in A. L. Shapiro (ed.), *Feminists Revision History* (New Brunswick, 1994), pp. 147–75.

Bennett, J. M., 'Women (and men) on the move: Scots in the English North c. 1440', *Journal of British Studies*, 57 (2018), 1–28.

Bennett, M., 'Late medieval Ireland in a wider world', in B. Smith (ed.), *The Cambridge History of Ireland, I: 600–1500* (Cambridge, 2017), pp. 371–97.

Bennett, M., 'The *Libelle of English Policy*: the matter of Ireland', in L. Clark (ed.), *The Fifteenth Century XV: Writing, Records and Rhetoric* (Woodbridge, 2017), pp. 1–22.

Bennett, M., 'The Plantagenet Empire as "enterprise zone": war and business networks, c. 1400–50', in P. Crooks, D. Green and W. M. Ormrod (eds), *The Plantagenet Empire, 1259–1453* (Donington, 2016), pp. 335–58.

Bent, J. T., 'The lords of Chios', *English Historical Review*, 4 (1889), 467–80.

Benz St John, L., *Three Medieval Queens: Queenship and the Crown in Fourteenth-Century England* (Basingstoke, 2012).

Bergs, A. and L. J. Brinton (eds), *English Historical Linguistics: An International Handbook, II*, Handbooks of Linguistics and Communication Science, 34.2 (2012).

Berresford Ellis, P., *The Cornish Language and its Literature* (London, 1974).

Bertram, J., 'Incised slabs in Sussex', *Transactions of the Monumental Brass Society*, 13 (1984), 387–96.

Birchwood, M. and M. Dimmock, 'Popular xenophobia', in A. Hadfield, M. Dimmock and A. Shinn (eds), *The Ashgate Research Companion to Popular Culture in Early Modern England* (Farnham, 2014), pp. 207–20.

Blair, C., *European Armour: Circa 1066 to Circa 1700* (London, 1958).

Blockmans, W., 'The creative environment: incentives to and functions of Bruges art production', in M. W. Ainsworth (ed.), *Petrus Christus in Renaissance Bruges* (Turnhout, 1995), pp. 11–20.

Blockmans, W. and W. Prevenier, *The Promised Lands: The Low Countries under Burgundian Rule, 1369–1530* (Philadelphia, 1999).

Bois, G., *The Crisis of Feudalism: Economy and Society in Eastern Normandy, c. 1300–1550* (Cambridge, 1984).

Bognor, G., '"Military" knighthood in the Lancastrian era: the case of Sir John Montgomery', *Journal of Medieval Military History*, 7 (2009), 104–26.

Bolton, J. L., 'The city and the crown, 1456–61', *London Journal* 12 (1986), 11–24.

Bolton, J. L., 'Irish migration to England in the late Middle Ages: the evidence of 1394 and 1440', *Irish Historical Studies*, 32 (2000), 1–21.

Bolton, J. L., 'London and the anti-alien legislation of 1439–40', in W. M. Ormrod, N. McDonald and C. Taylor (eds), *Resident Aliens in Later Medieval England* (Turnhout, 2017), pp. 33–47.

Bolton, J. L., *The Medieval English Economy, 1150–1500* (London, 1980).

Bolton, J. L., 'La répartition spatiale de la population étrangère à Londres au XVe siècle', in J. Bottin and D. Calabi (eds), *Les étrangers dans la ville: Minorités et espace urbain du bas Moyen Âge à l'époque moderne* (Paris, 1999), pp. 425–35.

Bolton, J. L., '"The world upside down": plague as an agent of economic and social change', in W. M. Ormrod and P. Lindley (eds), *The Black Death in England* (Stamford, 1996), pp. 17–78.

Bradley, H., 'Lucia Visconti, countess of Kent (d. 1424)', in C. M. Barron and A. F. Sutton (eds), *Medieval London Widows, 1300–1500* (London, 1994), pp. 77–84.

Brand, P., 'Irish law students and lawyers in late medieval England', *Irish Historical Studies*, 32 (2000–1), 161–73.

Brown, R. A., H. M. Colvin and A. J. Taylor, *The History of the King's Works: The Middle Ages*, 2 vols (London, 1963).

Burgtorf, J., '"With my life, his joyes began and ended": Piers Gaveston and King Edward II of England revisited', in N. Saul (ed.), *Fourteenth Century England, V* (Woodbridge, 2008), pp. 31–51.

Butterfield, A., *The Familiar Enemy: Chaucer, Language, and Nation in the Hundred Years War* (Oxford, 2009).

Butterfield, A., 'French culture and the Ricardian court', in A. J. Minnis, C. C. Morse and T. Turville-Petre (eds), *Essays on Ricardian Literature in Honour of J. A. Burrow* (Oxford, 1997), pp. 89–93.

Calimani, R., *The Ghetto of Venice* (New York, 1987).

Calkin, S. B., *Saracens and the Making of English Identity: The Auchinleck Manuscript* (London, 2005).

Cameron, K. W., *The Pardoner and his Pardons: Indulgences Circulating in England on the Eve of the Reformation* (Hartford, 1965).

Campbell, B. M. S., 'A fair field once full of folk: agrarian change in an era of population decline, 1348–1500', *Agricultural History Review*, 41 (1993), 60–70.

Campbell, M., 'Gold, silver and precious stones', in J. Blair and N. Ramsay (eds), *English Medieval Industries: Craftsmen, Techniques, Products* (London, 1991), pp. 107–66.

Caple, C., 'The detection and definition of an industry: the English medieval and post-medieval pin industry', *Archaeological Journal*, 148 (1991), 241–55.

Carlin, M., *Medieval Southwark* (London, 1996).

Carr, A. D., 'Wales: economy and society', in S. H. Rigby (ed.), *A Companion to Britain in the Later Middle Ages* (Oxford, 2003), pp. 125–41.

Carus-Wilson, E., *Medieval Merchant Venturers: Collected Studies* (London, 1954).

Carus-Wilson, E. and O. Coleman, *England's Export Trade, 1275–1547* (Oxford, 1963).

Cavill, P. R., *The English Parliaments of Henry VII* (Oxford, 2009).

Caviness, M. H., *The Windows of Christ Church Cathedral Canterbury* (Oxford, 1981).

Chambers, D., *The Imperial Age of Venice, 1380–1580* (London, 1970).

Chaplais, P., 'English arguments concerning the feudal status of Gascony in the fourteenth century', *Bulletin of the Institute of Historical Research*, 21 (1948), 203–13.

Chaplais, P., *English Diplomatic Practice in the Middle Ages* (London, 2003).

Cherry, J., 'Leather', in J. Blair and N. Ramsay (eds), *English Medieval Industries: Craftsmen, Techniques, Products* (London, 1991), pp. 295–307.

Cheyette, F., 'Kings, courts, cures and sinecures: the Statute of Provisors and the common law', *Traditio*, 19 (1963), 295–349.

Childs, W. R., 'The *George* of Beverley and Olav Olavesson: trading conditions in the North Sea in 1464', *Northern History*, 31 (1995), 108–22.

Childs, W. R., 'Irish merchants and seamen in late medieval England', *Irish Historical Studies*, 32 (2000), 22–43.

Clanchy, M. T., *England and its Rulers, 1066–1307*, 4th edn (Oxford, 2014).

Clark, C., *Words, Names and History*, ed. P. Jackson (Cambridge, 1995).

Clay, C. G. A., *Economic Expansion and Social Change: England, 1500–1700, I: People, Land and Towns* (Cambridge, 1984).

Clifford, F., *A History of Private Bill Legislation*, 2 vols (Abingdon, 1968).

Clough, C. H., 'Late fifteenth-century English monarchs subject to Italian Renaissance influence', in J. Mitchell (ed.), *England and the Continent in the Middle Ages: Studies in Honour of Andrew Martindale* (Stamford, 2000), pp. 298–317.

Cohn, S. K., *Popular Protest in Late Medieval English Towns* (Cambridge, 2013).

Cokayne, G. E. (ed.), *The Complete Peerage of England, Scotland, Ireland, Great Britain and the United Kingdom*, rev. V. Gibbs et al., 13 vols (London, 1910–59).

Colson, J., 'Alien communities and alien fraternities in later medieval London', *London Journal*, 35 (2010), 111–43.

Colson, J. and R. Ralley, 'Medical practice, urban politics and patronage: the London 'commonalty' of physicians and surgeons of the 1420s', *English Historical Review*, 130 (2015), 1102–31.

Contamine, P., 'The Norman "nation" and the French "nation" in the fourteenth and fifteenth centuries', in D. Bates and A. Curry (eds), *England and Normandy in the Middle Ages* (London, 1994), pp. 215–34.

Conway, D., *A Nation of Immigrants? A Brief Demographic History of Britain* (London, 2007).

Cosgrove, A., 'The emergence of the Pale, 1399–1447', in A. Cosgrove (ed.), *A New History of Ireland, II: Medieval Ireland, 1169–1534* (Oxford, 1987), pp. 533–56.

Cottle, B., *The Triumph of English, 1350–1400* (London, 1969).

Cressy, D., 'Trouble with gypsies in early modern England', *Historical Journal*, 59 (2016), 45–70.

Crooks, P., 'Before Humpty Dumpty: the first English empire and the brittleness of bureaucracy, 1259–1453', in P. Crooks and T. Parsons (eds), *Empires and Bureaucracy in World History: From Late Antiquity to the Twentieth Century* (Cambridge, 2016), pp. 250–88.

Crooks, P., 'State of the union: perspectives on English imperialism in the late Middle Ages', *Past & Present*, 212 (2011), 3–42.

Cunningham, W., *Alien Immigrants to England* (London, 1897).

Curry, A., 'The coronation expedition and Henry VI's court in France, 1430 to 1432', in J. Stratford (ed.), *The Lancastrian Court* (Donington, 2003), pp. 30–54.

Curry, A., *The Hundred Years War*, 2nd edn (Basingstoke, 2003).

Curry, A., A. Bell, A. Chapman, A. King and D. Simpkin, 'Languages in the military profession in later medieval England', in R. Ingham (ed.), *The Anglo-Norman Language and its Contexts* (York, 2010), pp. 82–5.

Dale, M. K., 'The London silkwomen of the fifteenth century', *Economic History Review*, 2nd series, 4 (1932–4), 324–35.

d'Alteroche, B., *De l'étranger à la seigneurie à l'étranger au royaume: XIe–XVe siècle* (Paris, 2002).

Davies, M., 'London lobbying: the London companies in the fifteenth century', *Parliamentary History*, 23 (2004), 136–48.

Davies, R. A., 'The effect of the Black Death on the parish priests of the medieval diocese of Coventry and Lichfield', *Historical Research*, 62 (1989), 85–90.

Davies, R. R., *The First English Empire: Power and Identities in the British Isles, 1093–1343* (Oxford, 2000).

Davies, R. R., 'The peoples of Britain and Ireland, 1100–1400: I. Identities', *Transactions of the Royal Historical Society*, 6th series, 4 (1994), 1–20.

Davies, R. R., 'The peoples of Britain and Ireland, 1100–1400: II. Names, boundaries and regnal solidarities', *Transactions of the Royal Historical Society*, 6th series, 5 (1995), 1–20.

Davies, R. R., 'The peoples of Britain and Ireland, 1100–1400: III. Laws and customs', *Transactions of the Royal Historical Society*, 6th series, 6 (1996), 1–23.

Davies, R. R., 'The peoples of Britain and Ireland, 1100–1400: IV. Language and historical mythology', *Transactions of the Royal Historical Society*, 6th series, 7 (1997), 1–24.

Davies, R. R., *The Revolt of Owain Glyn Dŵr* (Oxford, 1995).

Davies, R. R., 'The twilight of Welsh law, 1284–1536', *History*, 51 (1966), 143–64.

Davis, J., *Medieval Market Morality: Life, Law and Ethics in the English Marketplace, 1200–1500* (Cambridge, 2012).

Davis, V., 'Irish clergy in late medieval England', *Irish Historical Studies*, 32 (2000), 145–160.

Davis, V., 'Material relating to Irish clergy in England in the late Middle Ages', *Archivium Hibernicum*, 66 (2002), 7–50.

Dawson, J. E. A., 'The Gaidhealtachd and the emergence of the Scottish Highlands', in B. Bradshaw and P. Roberts (eds), *British Consciousness and Identity: The Making of Britain, 1533–1707* (Cambridge, 1998), pp. 259–300.

Delaney, S. (ed.), *Chaucer and the Jews: Sources, Contexts, Meanings* (New York, 2002).

De Roover, Raymond, *The Rise and Decline of the Medici Bank 1397–1494* (Cambridge, Mass., 1963).

Dickinson, J. R. and J. A. Sharpe, 'Courts, crime and litigation in the Isle of Man, 1580–1700', *Historical Research*, 72 (1999), 140–59.

Dimes, F. G. and M. Mitchell, *The Building Stone Heritage of Leeds* (Leeds, 1996).

Ditchburn, D., 'Anglo-Scottish relations in the later Middle Ages: the other side of the coin', in P. Crooks, D. Green and W. M. Ormrod (eds), *The Plantagenet Empire, 1259–1453* (Donington, 2016), pp. 310–34.

Dobson, R. B., 'Aliens in the city of York during the fifteenth century', in J. Mitchell (ed.), *England and the Continent in the Middle Ages: Studies in Honour of Andrew Martindale* (Stamford, 2000), pp. 249–66.

Doig, J. A., 'Propaganda, public opinion and the siege of Calais in 1436', in R. Archer (ed.), *Crown, Government and People in the Fifteenth Century* (Stroud, 1995), pp. 79–106.

Down, K., 'Colonial society and economy in the High Middle Ages', in A. Cosgrove (ed.), *A New History of Ireland, II: Medieval Ireland, 1169–1534* (Oxford, 1987), pp. 439–91.

Dresser, M. and P. Fleming, *Bristol: Ethnic Minorities and the City, 1000–2001* (Chichester, 2007).

Duffy, E., *The Stripping of the Altars: Traditional Religion in England 1400–1580* (London, 1992).

Dumolyn, J., *De Brugse Opstand van 1436–1438* (Heule, 1997).

Dumolyn, J. and J. Haemers, 'Patterns of urban rebellion in medieval Flanders', *Journal of Medieval History*, 31 (2005), 369–93.

Dumolyn, J. and M. Pajic, 'Enemies of the count and of the city: the collective exile of rebels in fourteenth-century Flanders', *Legal History Review*, 84 (2016), 461–501.

Dyer, C., 'Changes in diet in the late Middle Ages: the case of the harvest workers', *Agricultural History Review*, 36 (1988), 21–37.

Dyer, C., 'A golden age rediscovered: labourers' wages in the fifteenth century', in M. Allen and D. Coffman (eds), *Money, Prices and Wages: Essays in Honour of Professor Nicholas Mayhew* (Basingstoke, 2015), pp. 180–95.

Dyer, C., *Making a Living: The People of Britain, 850–1520* (London, 2002).

Dyer, C., *Standards of Living in the Later Middle Ages: Social Change in England c. 1200–1520* (Cambridge, 1989).

Dyer, C., 'Taxation and communities in late medieval England', in R. H. Britnell and J. Hatcher (eds), *Progress and Problems in Medieval England: Essays in Honour of Edward Miller* (Cambridge, 1996), pp. 168–90.

Dymond, D. and C. Paine (eds), *Five Centuries of an English Parish Church: The State of Melford Church, Suffolk* (Cambridge, 2012).

Egan, G., and H. Forsyth, 'Wound wire and silver gilt: changing fashions in dress accessories c. 1400–c. 1600', in D. Gaimster and P. Stamper (eds), *The Age of Transition: The Archaeology of English Culture 1400–1600* (Oxford, 1997), pp. 215–38.

Emlyn, R., 'Serving Church and state: the careers of medieval Welsh students', in L. Clark (ed.), *The Fifteenth Century, XI: Concerns and Preoccupations* (Woodbridge 2012), pp. 25–40.

Fleming, P., 'Bristol and the end of empire: the consequences of the fall of Gascony', in P. Crooks, D. Green and W. M. Ormrod (eds), *The Plantagenet Empire, 1259–1453* (Donington, 2016), pp. 371–83.

Fleming, P., 'Icelanders in England in the fifteenth century', in W. M. Ormrod, N. McDonald and C. Taylor (eds), *Resident Aliens in Later Medieval England* (Turnhout, 2017), pp. 77–88.

Fleming, P., 'Identity and belonging: Irish and Welsh in fifteenth-century Bristol', in L. Clark (ed.), *The Fifteenth Century, VII: Conflict, Consequences and the Crown in the Late Middle Ages* (Woodbridge, 2007), pp. 175–93.

Foffano, T., 'Tommaso Franco, medico Greco, alla corte del cardinale d'Inghilterra Henry di Beaufort e di Carlo VII di Francia', *Aevum*, 74 (2000), 657–67.

Foister, S., *Holbein and England* (London, 2004).

Forbes, J., 'Search, immigration and the goldsmiths' company: a study in the decline of its powers', in I. A. Gadd and P. Wallis (eds), *Guilds, Society and Economy in London, 1450–1800* (London, 2002), pp. 115–25.

Ford, J. A., 'Marginality and the assimilation of foreigners in the lay parish community: the case of Sandwich', in K. L. French, G. G. Gibbs and B. A. Kümin (eds), *The Parish in English Life 1400–1600* (Manchester, 1997), pp. 203–16.

Frame, R., 'The wider world', in R. Horrox and W. M. Ormrod (eds), *A Social History of England, 1200–1500* (Cambridge, 2006), pp. 435–53.

Fraser, P. D., 'Slaves or free people? The status of Africans in England, 1550–1750', in R. Vigne and C. Littleton (eds), *From Strangers to Citizens: Immigrant Communities in Britain, Ireland and Colonial America, 1550–1750* (London, 2001), pp. 254–60.

Freeman, J., '"And he abjured the realm of England, never to return"', in P. Horden (ed.), *Freedom of Movement in the Middle Ages* (Donington, 2007), pp. 287–304.

Fudge, J. D., *Cargoes, Embargoes, and Emissaries: The Commercial and Political Interaction of England and the German Hanse 1450–1510* (Toronto, 1995).

Galloway J. A. and I. Murray, 'Scottish migration to England, 1400–1560', *Scottish Geographical Journal*, 112 (1996), 29–38.

Geary, P. J., 'European ethnicities and European as an ethnicity: does Europe have too much history?' in G. A. Loud and M. Staub (eds), *The Making of Medieval History* (York, 2017), pp. 57–69.

Geary, P. J., *The Myth of Nations: The Medieval Origins of Europe* (Princeton, 2002).

Genet, J.-P., 'Empire and English identity: reflections on the king of England's *dominium*', in P. Crooks, D. Green and W. M. Ormrod (eds), *The Plantagenet Empire, 1259–1453* (Donington, 2016), pp. 35–48.

Genet, J.-P., 'English nationalism: Thomas Polton at the Council of Constance', *Nottingham Medieval Studies*, 28 (1984), 60–78.

Getz, F. M., 'Medical practitioners in medieval England', *Social History of Medicine*, 3 (1990), 245–83.

Getz, F. M., *Medicine in the English Middle Ages* (Princeton, 1998).

Gillett, A., 'Ethnogenesis: a contested model of early medieval Europe', *History Compass*, 4 (2006), 241–60.

Giuseppi, M. S., 'Alien merchants in the fifteenth century', *Transactions of the Royal Historical Society*, new series, 9 (1895), 75–91.

Given-Wilson, C., *Henry IV* (London, 2016).

Given-Wilson, C., 'The problem of labour in the context of English government, c. 1350–1450', in J. S. Bothwell, P. J. P. Goldberg and W. M. Ormrod (eds), *The Problem of Labour in Fourteenth-Century England* (York, 2000), pp. 85–100.

Given-Wilson, C., *The Royal Household and the King's Affinity: Service, Politics and Finance in England, 1360–1413* (London, 1986).

Goddard, R., *Credit and Trade in Later Medieval England, 1353–1532* (London, 2016).

Goldberg, P. J. P., 'Coventry's "Lollard" programme of 1492 and the making of utopia', in R. Horrox and S. Rees Jones (eds), *Pragmatic Utopias: Ideals and Communities, 1200–1630* (Cambridge, 2001), pp. 97–116.

Goldberg, P. J. P., 'Female labour, service and marriage in the late medieval urban North', *Northern History*, 22 (1986), 18–38.

Goldberg, P. J. P., *Medieval England: A Social History, 1250–1550* (London, 2004).

Goldberg, P. J. P., 'What was a servant?', in A. Curry and E. Matthew (eds), *Concepts and Patterns of Service in the Later Middle Ages* (Woodbridge, 2000), pp. 1–20.

Goldberg, P. J. P., *Women, Work and Life Cycle in a Medieval Economy: Women in York and Yorkshire, c. 1300–1520* (Oxford, 1992).

Good., J., *The Cult of St George in Medieval England* (Woodbridge, 2009).

Goose, N., 'The "Dutch" in Colchester: the economic influence of an immigrant community in the sixteenth and seventeenth centuries', *Immigrants and Minorities*, 1 (1982), 261–80.

Goose, N., '"Xenophobia" in Elizabethan and early Stuart England: an epithet too far?', in N. Goose and L. Luu (eds), *Immigrants in Tudor and Early Stuart England* (Brighton, 2005), pp. 110–35.

Gottschalk, E., *Stormvloeden en rivieroverstromingen in Nederland, II: 1400–1600* (Assen, 1975).

Gover, D., 'The first black Briton?', *International Business Times* (2 October 2013).

Grant, A., *Independence and Nationhood: Scotland, 1306–1469* (London, 1984).

Green, D., *The Hundred Years War: A People's History* (London, 2014).

Green, D., 'National identities and the Hundred Years War', in C. Given-Wilson (ed.), *Fourteenth Century England, VI* (Woodbridge, 2010), pp. 115–30.

Green, R. F., 'Further evidence for Chaucer's representation of the Pardoner as a womanizer', *Medium Ævum*, 71 (2002), 307–9.

Gribling, B., *The Image of Edward the Black Prince in Georgian and Victorian England: Negotiating the Late Medieval Past* (Woodbridge, 2017).

Griffiths, R. A., 'Crossing the frontiers of the English realm in the fifteenth century', in H. Pryce and J. L. Watts (eds), *Power and Identity in the Middle Ages: Essays in Memory of Rees Davies* (Oxford, 2007), pp. 221–5.

Griffiths, R. A., 'The island of England in the fifteenth century: perceptions of the peoples of the British Isles', *Journal of Medieval History*, 29 (2003), 198–200.

Griffiths, R. A., *King and Country: England and Wales in the Fifteenth Century* (London, 1991).

Griffiths, R. A., *The Reign of King Henry VI* (London, 1980).

Grummitt, D., *The Calais Garrison: War and Military Service in England, 1436–1558* (Woodbridge, 2008).

Guidi-Bruscoli, F., 'John Cabot and his Italian financiers', *Historical Research*, 85 (2012), 372–93.

Guidi-Bruscoli, F., 'I mercanti italiani e le lingue straniere', in I. L. Sanfilippo and G. Pinto (eds), *Comunicare nel Medioevo: La conoscenza e l'uso delle lingue nei secoli XII–XV* (Rome, 2015), pp. 103–32.

Guidi-Bruscoli, F. and J. Lutkin, 'Perception, identity and culture: the Italian communities in fifteenth-century London and Southampton revisited', in W. M. Ormrod, N. McDonald and C. Taylor (eds), *Resident Aliens in Later Medieval England* (Turnhout, 2017), pp. 89–104.

Gunn, C., *Ancrene Wisse: From Pastoral Literature to Vernacular Spirituality* (Cardiff, 2008).

Gunn, S., D. Grummitt and H. Cools, *War, State and Society in England and the Netherlands, 1477–1559* (Oxford, 2007).

Guy, J., *Tudor England* (Oxford, 1988).

Habib, I., *Black Lives in the English Archives, 1500–1677: Imprints of the Invisible* (Aldershot, 2008).

Haemers, J., *De strijd om het regentschap over Filips de Schone: Opstand, facties en geweld in Brugge, Gent en Ieper (1482–1488)* (Ghent, 2014).

Hamil, F. C., 'Presentment of Englishry and the murder fine', *Speculum*, 12 (1937), 285–98.

Hammond, E. A., 'Doctor Augustine, physician to Cardinal Wolsey and King Henry VIII', *Medical History*, 19 (1975), 215–49.

Hanawalt, B. A., *The Ties that Bound: Peasant Families in Medieval England* (Oxford, 1986).

Hanley, J., 'Aliens and religion in Suffolk, c. 1330–1550', www.englandsimmigrants. com/page/individual-studies/aliens-and-religion-in-suffolk-c-1330–1550.

Harding, V., 'Cross-Channel trade and cultural contacts: London and the Low Countries in the later fourteenth century', in C. M. Barron and N. Saul (eds), *England and the Low Countries in the Late Middle Ages* (Stroud, 1995), pp. 153–68.

Harris, J., *Greek Emigres in the West, 1400–1520* (Camberley, 1995).

Harris, J., "Greeks at the papal curia in the fifteenth century: the case of George Vranas, bishop of Dromore and Elphin', in M. Hinterberger and C. Schabel (eds), *Greeks, Latins, and Intellectual History, 1204–1500* (Leuven, 2011), pp. 423–38.

Harris, J., 'Two Byzantine craftsmen in fifteenth century London', *Journal of Medieval History*, 21 (1995), 387–403.

Harris, J. and H. Porfyriou, 'The Greek diaspora: Italian port cities and London, c.1400–1700', in D. Calabi and S. T. Christensen (eds), *Cultural Exchange in Early Modern Europe, II: Cities and Cultural Exchange in Europe, 1400–1700* (Cambridge, 2006), pp. 78–86.

Harriss, G. L., *Cardinal Beaufort: A Study of Lancastrian Ascendancy and Decline* (Oxford, 1988).

Harriss, G. L., *Shaping the Nation: England, 1360–1461* (Oxford, 2005).

Harvey, I. M. W., *Jack Cade's Rebellion of 1450* (Oxford, 1991).

Harvey, J. and A. Oswald, *English Medieval Architects: A Biographical Dictionary down to 1550* (Gloucester, 1984).

Hastings, A. *The Construction of Nationhood: Ethnicity, Religion and Nationalism* (Cambridge, 1997).

Hatcher, J., 'The great slump of the mid-fifteenth century', in R. Britnell and J. Hatcher (eds), *Progress and Problems in Medieval England: Essays in Honour of Edward Miller* (Cambridge, 1996), pp. 237–72.

Hatcher, J., 'Plague, population and the English economy, 1348–1530', in M. Anderson (ed.), *British Population History: From the Black Death to the Present Day* (Cambridge, 1996), pp. 9–94.

Hay, D., *Polydore Vergil: Renaissance Historian and Man of Letters* (Oxford, 1952).

Heath, P., *Church and Realm, 1272–1461* (London, 1988).

Heaton, H., *The Yorkshire Woollen and Worsted Industries, from the Earliest Times up to the Industrial Revolution* (Oxford, 1920).

Helmholz, R. H., *The Oxford History of the Laws of England, I: The Canon Law and Ecclesiastical Jurisdiction from 597 to the 1640s* (Oxford, 2004).

Heng, G., 'Jews, Saracens, "black men", Tartars: England in a world of racial difference', in P. Brown (ed.), *A Companion to Medieval English Literature and Culture, c. 1350–c. 1500* (Oxford, 2007), pp. 249–55.

Hettinger, M. J., 'Defining the servant: legal and extra-legal terms of employment in fifteenth-century England', in A. J. Frantzen and D. Moffat (eds), *The Work of Work: Servitude, Slavery, and Labor in Medieval England* (Glasgow, 1994), pp. 206–28.

Hicks, M., *Warwick the Kingmaker* (Oxford, 1998).

Higgs, E., *Making Sense of the Census Revisited: Census Records for England and Wales, 1801–1901* (London, 2005).

Hirschman, E. C. and D. N. Yates, *The Early Jews and Muslims of England and Wales: A Genetic and Genealogical History* (Jefferson, 2014).

'Historical Ipswich skeleton finally identified', *East Anglian Daily Times* (5 May 2010).

Holmes, M., 'Evil May Day, 1517: the story of a riot', *History Today* 15:9 (1965), 642–50.

Holt, J. C., *Magna Carta*, 2nd edn (Cambridge, 1992).

Horrox, R., 'The urban gentry in the fifteenth century', in J. A. F. Thomson (ed.), *Towns and Townspeople in the Fifteenth Century* (Gloucester, 1988), pp. 22–44.

Housley, N., *The Later Crusades, 1274–1580* (Oxford, 1992).

Howell, M. C., *Women, Production and Patriarchy* (Chicago, 1986).

Hunnisett, R. F., *The Medieval Coroner* (Cambridge, 1961).

Hutton, S., '"On herself and all her property": women's economic activities in late-medieval Ghent', *Continuity and Change*, 20 (2005), 325–49.

Hsy, J., 'City', in M. Turner (ed.), *A Handbook of Middle English Studies* (Oxford, 2013), pp. 315–29.

Ingham, R., 'Mixing languages on the manor', *Medium Aevum*, 78 (2009), 80–97.

Jenks, S[tuart], 'Hansische Vermächtnisse in London ca.1363–1483', *Hansische Geschichtsblätter*, 104 (1986), 35–111.

Jenks, S[usanne], 'Justice for strangers: the experience of alien merchants in medieval English common law courts', in C. M. Barron and A. F. Sutton (eds), *The Medieval Merchant* (Donington, 2014), pp. 166–82.

Johnson, T., '"Some said he was a Spaniard; some said he was a Breton": the case of Giles Morvyle', www.englandsimmigrants.com/page/individual-studies/some-said-he-was-a-spaniard-some-said-he-was-a-breton-the-case-of-giles-morvyle.

Jones, G. P., 'The building of Eton College, 1442–1460: a study in the history of operative masonry', *Transactions of the Quatuor Coronati Lodge*, 46 (1933), 70–114.

Jones, J. G., 'Government and the Welsh community: the north-east borderland in the fifteenth century', in H. Hearder and H. R. Loyn (eds), *British Government and Administration: Studies presented to S. B. Chrimes* (Cardiff, 1974), pp. 1–22.

Jones, M., *The Creation of Brittany: A Late Medieval State* (London, 1988).

Jordan, W. C., *From England to France: Felony and Exile in the High Middle Ages* (Princeton, 2015).

Jurkowski, M., C. L. Smith and D. Crook, *Lay Taxes in England and Wales, 1188–1688*, Public Record Office Handbook, 31 (1999).

Justice, S., *Writing and Rebellion: England in 1381* (Berkeley, Cal., 1994).

Karras, R. M., *Common Women: Prostitution and Sexuality in Medieval England* (Oxford, 1996).

Katz, D. S., *Philo-Semitism and the Readmission of the Jews to England, 1603–1655* (Oxford, 1982).

Kaufmann, M., *Black Tudors: The Untold Story* (London, 2017).

Kaufmann, M., 'Caspar van Senden, Sir Thomas Sherley and the "blackamoor" project', *Historical Research*, 81 (2008), 366–71.

Kaufmann, M., 'Sir Pedro Negro: what colour was his skin?', *Notes and Queries*, 253:2 (2008), 142–6.

Kaufmann, M., 'Tudor Britain', in D. Dabydeen, J. Gilmore and C. Jones (eds), *The Oxford Companion to Black British History* (Oxford, 2007), pp. 486–7.

Keefe, K. and M. Holst, *Osteological Analysis: 12–18 Swinegate, 14 Little Stonegate & 18 Back Swinegate, York, North Yorkshire*, York Archaeological Trust Reports 1,815 (2015).

Keene, D., 'Metropolitan values: migration, mobility and cultural norms: London, 1100–1700', in L. Wright (ed.), *The Development of Standard English, 1300–1800* (Cambridge, 2000), pp. 93–114.

Keene, D., 'Du seuil de la cité à la formation d'une économie morale: l'environnement hanséatique à Londres entre XIIe et XVIIe siècle', in J. Bottin and D. Calabi (eds), *Les étrangers dans la ville: Minorités et espace urbain du bas Moyen Âge à l'époque moderne* (Paris, 1999), pp. 413–20.

Kelly, H. A., 'Jews and Saracens in Chaucer's England: a review of the evidence', *Studies in the Age of Chaucer*, 27 (2005), 125–65.

Kerling, N. J. M., 'Aliens in the county of Norfolk, 1436–85', *Norfolk Archaeology*, 33 (1963), 200–15.

Kerling, N. J. M., *Commercial Relations of Holland and Zeeland with England from the Late 13th Century to the Close of the Middle Ages* (Leiden, 1954).

Kermode, J., *Medieval Merchants: York, Beverley and Hull in the Later Middle Ages* (Cambridge, 2002).

Kim, K., *Aliens in Medieval Law: The Origins of Modern Citizenship* (Cambridge, 2001).

King, D. J., 'A glazier from the bishopric of Utrecht in fifteenth-century Norwich', in E. de Bievre (ed.), *Utrecht, Britain and the Continent: Archaeology, Art and Architecture* (London, 1996), pp. 216–25.

King, D. J., *The Medieval Stained Glass of St Peter Mancroft Norwich* (Oxford, 2006).

Kissane, A. and J. Mackman, 'Aliens and the law in late medieval Lincolnshire', in W. M. Ormrod, N. McDonald and C. Taylor (eds), *Resident Aliens in Later Medieval England* (Turnhout, 2017), pp. 105–23.

Knowles, D. and R. N. Hadcock, *Medieval Religious Houses, England and Wales* (London, 1953).

Kowaleski, M., 'The assimilation of foreigners in late medieval Exeter: a prosopographical analysis', in W. M. Ormrod, N. McDonald and C. Taylor (eds), *Resident Aliens in Later Medieval England* (Turnhout, 2017), pp. 163–79.

Kowaleski, M., 'A consumer economy', in R. Horrox and W. M. Ormrod (eds), *A Social History of England, 1200–1500* (Cambridge, 2006), pp. 238–59.

Kowaleski, M., 'French immigrants and the French language in late-medieval England', in T. Fenster and C. P. Collette (eds), *The French of Medieval England: Essays in Honour of Jocelyn Wogan-Browne* (Woodbridge, 2017), pp. 206–24.

Kowaleski, M., 'The French of England: a maritime *lingua franca*?', in J. Wogan-Browne et al. (eds), *Language and Culture in Medieval Britain: The French of England, c. 1100–c. 1500* (York, 2009), pp. 90–102.

Krummel, M. A. (ed.), *Crafting Jewishness in Medieval England: Legally Absent, Virtually Present* (New York, 2011).

Lambert, B., '"Nostri fratelli da Londra": the Lucchese community in late medieval England', in H. Fulton and M. Campopiano (eds), *Anglo-Italian Cultural Relations in the Later Middle Ages* (York, 2018), pp. 87–102.

Lambert, B., 'Scandinavian immigrants in late medieval England: sources, problems and patterns', in S. Suppersberger Hamre (ed.), *Foreigners and Outside Influences in Medieval Norway* (Oxford, 2017), pp. 111–23.

Lambert, B. and W. M. Ormrod, 'Friendly foreigners: international warfare, resident aliens and the early history of denization in England, c. 1250–c. 1400', *English Historical Review*, 130 (2015), 1–24.

Lambert, B. and W. M. Ormrod, 'A matter of trust: the royal regulation of England's French residents during wartime, 1294–1377', *Historical Research*, 89 (2016), 208–26.

Lambert, B. and M. Pajic, 'Drapery in exile: Edward III, Colchester and the Flemings, 1355–1366', *History*, 99 (2014), 733–53.

Lambert, B. and M. Pajic, 'Immigration and the common profit: native cloth workers, Flemish exiles, and royal policy in fourteenth-century London', *Journal of British Studies*, 55 (2016), 633–57.

Lasocki, D. and R. Prior, *The Bassanos: Venetian Musicians and Instrument Makers in England, 1531–1665* (Aldershot, 1995).

Laughton, J., 'Mapping the migrants: Welsh, Manx and Irish settlers in fifteenth-century Chester', in C. A. M. Clarke (ed.), *Mapping the Medieval City: Space, Place and Identity in Chester, c. 1200–1600* (Cardiff, 2011), pp. 169–83.

Lavaud, S., *Bordeaux et le vin au Moyen Age: Essor d'une civilisation* (Bordeaux, 2003).

Lazzareschi, E., 'Le ricchezze di due medici lucchesi della Rinascenza', *Rivista di Storia delle Scienze Mediche e Naturali*, 16 (1925), 112–39.

Leader, D. R., *A History of the University of Cambridge, I: The University to 1546* (Cambridge, 1988).

Lee, J. S., *Cambridge and its Economic Region 1450–1560* (Hatfield, 2005).

Le Neve, J., *Fasti Ecclesiae Anglicanae 1300–1541, V: St Paul's, London*, comp. J. M. Horn (London, 1963).

Lewis, B. J., 'Late medieval Welsh praise poetry and nationality: the military career of Guto'r Glyn revisited', *Studia Celtica*, 45 (2011), 111–30.

Liddy, C., *Contesting the City: The Politics of Citizenship in English Towns, 1250–1530* (Oxford, 2017).

Liddy, C. and B. Lambert, 'The civic franchise and the regulation of aliens in Great Yarmouth, c. 1430–c. 1490', in W. M. Ormrod, N. McDonald and C. Taylor (eds), *Resident Aliens in Later Medieval England* (Turnhout, 2017), pp. 125–43.

Linsley, C., 'The French in fifteenth-century England: enmity, ubiquity and perception', in W. M. Ormrod, N. McDonald and C. Taylor (eds), *Resident Aliens in Later Medieval England* (Turnhout, 2017), pp. 147–62.

Lipson, E., *The Economic History of England, I: The Middle Ages*, 10th edn (London, 1949).

Lloyd, T. H., *England and the German Hanse, 1157–1611* (Cambridge, 1991).

Lloyd, T. H., *The English Wool Trade in the Middle Ages* (Cambridge, 1977).

Lloyd, T. H., 'Overseas trade and the English money supply in the fourteenth century', in N. J. Mayhew (ed.), *Edwardian Monetary Affairs (1279–1344)*, British Archaeological Reports, 36 (1977), pp. 96–124.

Loengard, J. S., '"Which may be said to be her own": widows and goods in late-medieval England', in M. Kowaleski and P. J. P. Goldberg (eds), *Medieval Domesticity: Home, Housing and Household in Medieval England* (Cambridge, 2008), pp. 162–76.

Lowe, K., 'The stereotyping of black Africans in Renaissance Europe', in T. F. Earle and K. J. P. Lowe (eds), *Black Africans in Renaissance Europe* (Cambridge, 2005), pp. 35–41.

Lutkin, J., 'Settled or fleeting? London's medieval immigrant community revisited', in M. Allen and M. Davies (eds), *Medieval Merchants and Money: Essays in Honour of J. L. Bolton* (London, 2016), pp. 137–55.

Luu, L. B., 'Assimilation or segregation: colonies of alien craftsmen in Elizabethan London', *Proceedings of the Huguenot Society of London*, 26 (1994–7), 160–72.

Luu, L. B., *Immigrants and the Industries of London 1500–1700* (Aldershot, 2005).

Luu, L. B., '"Taking the bread out of our mouths": xenophobia in early modern London', *Immigrants and Minorities*, 19 (2000), 1–22.

Luxford, J., 'Drawing ethnicity and authority in the Plantagenet Exchequer', in P. Crooks, D. Green and W. M. Ormrod (eds), *The Plantagenet Empire, 1259–1453* (Donington, 2016), pp. 72–88.

Mackay, A., *Spain in the Middle Ages: From Frontier to Empire, 1000–1500* (Basingstoke, 1977).

Mackman, J., '"Hidden gems" in the records of the common pleas: new evidence on the legacy of Lucy Visconti', in L. Clark (ed.) *The Fifteenth Century, VIII: Rule, Redemption and Representations in Late Medieval England and France* (Woodbridge, 2008), pp. 59–72.

Marks, R., *Stained Glass in England during the Middle Ages* (London, 1993).

Marks, R., 'Window glass', in J. Blair and N. Ramsay (eds), *English Medieval Industries: Craftsmen, Techniques, Products* (London, 1991), pp. 265–94.

Martin, D., 'Prosecution of the Statutes of Provisors and Premunire in the King's Bench, 1377–1394', in J. S. Hamilton (ed.), *Fourteenth Century England, IV* (Woodbridge, 2006), pp. 109–23.

Masschaele, J., *Peasants, Merchants, and Markets: Inland Trade in Medieval England, 1150–1350* (Basingstoke, 1997).

Matar, N., 'The first Turks and Moors in England', in R. Vigne and C. Littleton (eds), *From Strangers to Citizens: Immigrant Communities in Britain, Ireland and Colonial America, 1550–1750* (London, 2001), pp. 261–7.

Matthew, D., *The Norman Monasteries and their English Possessions* (Oxford, 1962).

Matthew, H. C. G. and B. H. Harrison (eds), *Oxford Dictionary of National Biography*, 61 vols (Oxford, 2004).

McClure, P., 'Patterns of migration in the late Middle Ages: the evidence of English place-name surnames', *Economic History Review*, 2nd series 32 (1979), 167–82.

McHardy, A. K., 'The alien priories and the expulsion of aliens from England in 1378', *Studies in Church History*, 12 (1975), 133–42.

McHardy, A. K. and N. Orme, 'The defence of an alien priory: Modbury (Devon) in the 1450s', *Journal of Ecclesiastical History*, 50 (1999), 303–12.

McIntosh, M., *Poor Relief in England, 1350–1600* (Cambridge, 2012).

McIntosh, M., *Working Women in English Society 1300–1620* (Cambridge, 2005).

McKay, D., 'The duties of the medieval parish clerk', *Innes Review*, 19 (2010), 32–9.

McSheffrey, S., 'Stranger artisans and the London sanctuary of St. Martin le Grand in the reign of Henry VIII', *Journal of Medieval and Early Modern Studies*, 43 (2013), 545–71.

Menache, S., *The Vox Dei: Communication in the Middle Ages* (Oxford, 1990).

Miles, D., *The Tribes of Britain* (London, 2005).

Miller, E. and J. Hatcher, *Medieval England: Towns, Commerce and Crafts, 1086–1348* (London, 1995).

Milner, J. D., 'Sir Simon Felbrigg, KG: the Lancastrian revolution and personal fortune', *Norfolk Archaeology*, 38 (1978), 84–91.

Moore, M. J., 'Brick', in J. Blair and N. Ramsay (eds), *English Medieval Industries: Craftsmen, Techniques, Products* (London, 1991), pp. 211–36.

Moore, R. I., *The Formation of a Persecuting Society: Power and Deviance in Western Europe, 950–1250* (Oxford, 1987).

Morgan, M., 'The suppression of the alien priories', *History*, 26 (1941), 204–12.

Mueller, R. C., 'Greeks in Venice and "Venetians" in Greece: notes on citizenship and immigration in the late Middle Ages', in C. A. Maltezou (ed.), *Ricchi e poveri nella società dell'Oriente Grecolatino* (Venice, 1998), pp. 167–80.

Mundill, R. R., *England's Jewish Solution: Experiment and Expulsion, 1262–1290* (Cambridge, 1998).

Mundill, R. R., *The King's Jews: Money, Massacre and Exodus in Medieval England* (London, 2010).

Munro, J. H. A., 'Urban wage structures in late-medieval England and the Low Countries: work-time and seasonal wages', in I. Blanchard (ed.), *Labour and Leisure in Historical Perspective, Thirteenth to Twentieth Centuries* (Stuttgart, 1994), pp. 65–78.

Munro, J. H. A., *Wool, Cloth, and Gold: The Struggle for Bullion in Anglo-Burgundian Trade, 1340–1478* (Toronto, 1972).

Murray, J. M., *Bruges, Cradle of Capitalism, 1280–1390* (Cambridge, 2005).

Murphy, N., 'War, government and commerce: the towns of Lancastrian France under Henry V's rule, 1417–22' in G. Dodd (ed.), *Henry V: New Interpretations* (York, 2013), pp. 249–72.

Neville, C. J., 'Local sentiment and the "national" enemy in northern England in the later Middle Ages', *Journal of British Studies*, 35 (1996), 419–37.

Neville, C. J., *Violence, Custom and Law: The Anglo-Scottish Border Lands in the Later Middle Ages* (Edinburgh, 1998).

Newton, S. M., *Fashion in the Age of the Black Prince: A Study of the Years 1340–1365* (Woodbridge, 1980).

Nightingale, P., *A Medieval Mercantile Community: The Grocers' Company and the Politics and Trade of London, 1000–1485* (London, 1995).

Nilson, B., *Cathedral Shrines of Medieval England* (Woodbridge, 1998).

Ollard, S. L., *Fasti Wyndesoriensis* (Windsor, 1950).

Ormrod, W. M., 'The DNA of Richard III: false paternity and the royal succession in later medieval England', *Nottingham Medieval Studies*, 60 (2016), 197–236.

Ormrod, W. M., *Edward III* (London, 2011).

Ormrod, W. M., 'French residents in England at the start of the Hundred Years War: learning English, speaking English and becoming English in 1346', in T. Fenster and C. P. Collette (eds), *The French of Medieval England: Essays in Honour of Jocelyn Wogan-Browne* (Woodbridge, 2017), pp. 190–205.

Ormrod, W. M., 'John Mandeville, Edward III, and the king of Inde', *Chaucer Review*, 46 (2012), 314–39.

Ormrod, W. M., 'The origins of tunnage and poundage: parliament and the Estate of Merchants in the fourteenth century', *Parliamentary History*, 28 (2009), 209–27.

Ormrod, W. M., 'Poverty and privilege: the fiscal burden in England (XIIIth–XVth centuries)', in S. Cavaciocchi (ed.), *La fiscalità nell'economia europea secc. XIII–XVIII* (Florence, 2008), pp. 637–56.

Ormrod, W. M., 'Reynauld de Nieuport or Reginald of the Chamber? The hazards of being Flemish in fourteenth-century London', www.englandsimmigrants.com/page/individual-studies/reynauld-de-nieuport-or-reginald-of-the-chamber.

Ormrod, W. M. and J. Mackman, 'Resident aliens in later medieval England: sources, contexts and debates', in W. M. Ormrod, N. McDonald and C. Taylor (eds), *Resident Aliens in Later Medieval England* (Turnhout, 2017), pp. 3–31.

Otway-Ruthven, A. J., *The King's Secretary and the Signet Office in the Fifteenth Century* (Cambridge, 1939).

Owen, D. M., 'White Annays and others', in D. Baker (ed.), *Medieval Women* (Oxford, 1978), pp. 331–46.

Page, W. and J. W. Willis-Bund (eds), *The Victoria History of the County of Worcester, IV* (London, 1924).

Pantin, W. A., *The English Church in the Fourteenth Century* (Cambridge, 1955).

Parry, C., *British Nationality Law and the History of Naturalization* (Milan, 1954).

Passmore, G., 'Medieval black Briton found', *Sunday Times* (2 May 2010).

Pearl, V., 'Social policy in early modern London', in H. Lloyd-Jones, V. Pearl and B. Worden (eds), *History and Imagination: Essays in Honour of H. R. Trevor-Roper* (London, 1981), pp. 115–31.

Pearsall, D. A. 'Strangers in fourteenth-century London', in F. R. P. Akehurst and S. C. Van Delden (eds), *The Stranger in Medieval Society* (Minneapolis, 1997), pp. 46–62.

Penn, S. A. C. and C. Dyer, 'Wages and earnings in late medieval England: evidence from the enforcement of the labour laws', *Economic History Review*, 2nd series, 43 (1990), 356–76.

Pettegree, A., 'The foreign population of London in 1549', *Proceedings of the Huguenot Society of London*, 24 (1983–4), 141–6.

Pettegree, A., *Foreign Protestant Communities in Sixteenth-Century London* (Oxford, 1986).

Pettegree, A., 'The stranger community in Marian London', *Proceedings of the Huguenot Society of Great Britain and Ireland*, 24 (1987), 390–402.

Phillips, J. R. S., *The Medieval Expansion of Europe* (Oxford, 1988).

Pollard, A. J., 'The north-eastern economy and the agrarian crisis of 1438–40', *Northern History*, 25 (1989), 88–105.

Pollock, F. and F. W. Maitland, *The History of English Law before the Time of Edward I*, 2nd edn, 2 vols (Cambridge, 1898).

Potter, D., *Henry VIII and Francis I: The Final Conflict, 1540–47* (Leiden, 2011).

Power, E., 'The wool trade in the fifteenth century', in E. Power and M. M. Postan (eds), *Studies in English Trade in the Fifteenth Century* (London, 1933), pp. 39–90.

Powicke, F. M., *The Loss of Normandy, 1189–1204*, 2nd edn (Manchester, 1961).

Prestwich, M., 'England and Scotland during the Wars of Independence', in M. Jones and M. Vale (eds), *England and her Neighbours, 1066–1453: Essays in Honour of Pierre Chaplais* (London, 1989), pp. 181–97.

Prestwich, M., *English Politics in the Thirteenth Century* (Basingstoke, 1990).

Rappaport, S., *Worlds within Worlds: Structures of Life in Sixteenth-Century London* (Cambridge, 2002).

Rawcliffe, C., 'Master surgeons at the Lancastrian court', in J. Stratford (ed.), *The Lancastrian Court* (Donington, 2003), pp. 192–210.

Reddaway, T. F. and L. E. M. Walker, *The Early History of the Goldsmiths' Company 1327–1509* (London, 1975).

Redstone, V. B., 'Alien settlers in Ipswich in 1485', in *East Anglian Miscellany 1937* (Ipswich, 1937), pp. 16–19.

Rees Jones, S., 'Scots in the North of England: the first alien subsidy, 1440–43', in W. M. Ormrod, N. McDonald and C. Taylor (eds), *Resident Aliens in Later Medieval England* (Turnhout, 2017), pp. 51–75.

Rees Jones, S., *York: The Making of a City 1068–1350* (Oxford, 2013).

Richardson, M., 'Henry V, the English Chancery and Chancery English', *Speculum*, 55 (1980), 726–50.

Ridgeway, H., 'King Henry III and the "aliens", 1236–1272', in P. R. Coss and S. D. Lloyd (eds), *Thirteenth Century England, II* (Woodbridge, 1988), pp. 81–92.

Rigby, S. H., *English Society in the Later Middle Ages: Class, Status and Gender* (Basingstoke, 1995).

Rigby, S. H., 'Introduction: social structure and economic change in late medieval England', in R. Horrox and W. M. Ormrod (eds), *A Social History of England, 1200–1500* (Cambridge, 2006), pp. 1–30.

Rigby, S. H., 'Urban population in late medieval England: the evidence of the lay susbidies', *Economic History Review*, 2nd series, 63 (2010), 393–417.

Roskell, J. S., L. Clark and C. Rawcliffe, *The History of Parliament: The House of Commons, 1386–1421*, 4 vols (Stroud, 1993).

Ross, C., *Richard III* (London, 1981).

Rosser, G., *Medieval Westminster, 1200–1540* (Oxford, 1989).

Roth, C., 'Sir Edward Brampton: an Anglo-Jewish adventurer during the Wars of the Roses', *Transactions of the Jewish Historical Society of England*, 16 (1952), 121–7.

Ruddick, A., *English Identity and Political Culture in the Fourteenth Century* (Cambridge, 2013).

Ruddick, A., 'The English "nation" and the Plantagenet "empire" at the Council of Constance', in P. Crooks, D. Green and W. M. Ormrod (eds), *The Plantagenet Empire, 1259–1453* (Donington, 2016), pp. 109–27.

Ruddick, A., 'Immigrants and intermarriage in late medieval England', in W. M. Ormrod, N. McDonald and C. Taylor (eds), *Resident Aliens in Later Medieval England* (Turnhout, 2017), pp. 181–200.

Ruddock, A. A., 'Alien hosting in Southampton in the fifteenth century', *Economic History Review*, 1st series, 16 (1946), 30–7.

Ruddock, A. A., 'Alien merchants in Southampton in the later Middle Ages', *English Historical Review*, 61 (1946), 1–17.

Ruddock, A. A., *Italian Merchants and Shipping in Southampton 1270–1600* (Southampton, 1951).

Salzman, L. F., *Building in England down to 1540: A Documentary History* (Oxford, 1967).

Salzman, L. F., 'The early heraldry of Pelham', *Sussex Archaeological Collections*, 69 (1928), 53–70.

Samuel, E. R., 'London's Portuguese Jewish community, 1540–1753', in R. Vigne and C. Littleton (eds), *From Strangers to Citizens: Immigrant Communities in Britain, Ireland and Colonial America, 1550–1750* (London, 2001), pp. 239–46.

Saul, A., 'English towns in the late Middle Ages: the case of Great Yarmouth', *Journal of Medieval History*, 8 (1982), 75–97.

Saul, N., *Richard II* (London, 1997).

Saygin, S., *Humphrey, Duke of Gloucester (1390–1447) and the Italian Humanists* (Leiden, 2002).

Scales, L., 'Bread, cheese and genocide: imagining the destruction of peoples in medieval Western Europe', *History*, 92 (2007), 284–300.

Scattergood, J., 'The *Libelle of Englyshe Polycye*: the nation and its place', in H. Cooney (ed.), *New Essays on Fifteenth-Century English Poetry* (Dublin, 2001), pp. 29–48.

Schoeck, R. J., *Erasmus of Europe*, 2 vols (Edinburgh, 1990–3).

Schofield, R., *Taxation under the Early Tudors, 1485–1547* (Oxford, 2004).

Selwood, J., *Diversity and Difference in Early Modern London* (Abingdon, 2016).

Sheely, E. H., 'The persistence of particularism: the county of Ponthieu in the thirteenth and fourteenth centuries', in J. S. Hamilton and P. J. Bradley (eds), *Documenting the Past: Essays in Medieval History Presented to George Peddy Cuttino* (Woodbridge, 1989), pp. 33–52.

Siegmund, S. B., *The Medici State and the Ghetto of Florence: The Construction of an Early Modern Jewish Community* (Stanford, 2006).

Skinner, P., 'Introduction: Jews in medieval Britain and Europe', in P. Skinner (ed.), *The Jews in Medieval Britain: Historical, Literary and Archaeological Perspectives* (Woodbridge, 2003), pp. 1–12.

Slack, P., 'Great and good towns, 1540–1700', in P. Clark (ed.), *The Cambridge Urban History of Britain, II* (Cambridge, 2000), pp. 347–76.

Smith, D. M. (ed.), *Heads of Religious Houses of England and Wales*, 3 vols (Cambridge, 1972–2008).

Smith, T. P., *The Medieval Brickmaking Industry in England 1400–1450*, British Archaeological Reports, British Series, 138 (1985).

Spindler, E., 'Flemings in the Peasants' Revolt, 1381', in H. Skoda, P. Lantschner and R. L. J. Shaw (eds), *Contact and Exchange in Later Medieval Europe: Essays in Honour of Malcolm Vale* (Woodbridge, 2012), pp. 59–78.

Stacey, R. C., 'Anti-semitism and the medieval English state', in J. R. Maddicott and D. M. Palliser (eds), *The Medieval State: Essays Presented to James Campbell* (London, 2000), pp. 163–77.

Stacey, R. C., 'The conversion of Jews to Christianity in thirteenth-century England', *Speculum*, 67 (1992), 263–83.

Strohm, P., 'Trade, treason and the murder of Janus Imperial', *Journal of British Studies*, 35 (1996), 1–23.

Summerson, H. R. T., 'Foreigners and felony: aliens as perpetrators and victims of crime in London, 1272–1327', in M.-L. Heckmann (ed.), *Von Nowgorod bis London: Studien zu Handel, Wirtschaft und Gesellschaft im mittelalterlichen Europa* (Göttingen, 2008), pp. 409–24.

Summerson, H. R. T., *Medieval Carlisle*, 2 vols (Stroud, 1993).

Summerson, H. R. T., 'Responses to war: Carlisle and the West March in the later fourteenth century', in A. Tuck and A. Goodman (eds), *War and Border Societies in the Middle Ages* (London, 1992), pp. 155–77.

Sutton, A. F., 'George Lovekyn, tailor to three kings of England, 1470–1504', *Costume*, 15 (1981), 1–12.

Sutton, A. F., 'Dress and fashions c. 1470', in R. H. Britnell (ed.), *Daily Life in the Late Middle Ages* (Stroud, 1998), pp. 5–26.

Sutton, A. F., 'Marcellus Maures, alias Selis, of Utrecht and London, a goldsmith of the Yorkist kings', *Ricardian*, 17 (2007), 77–82.

Sutton, A. F., *The Mercery of London: Trade, Goods and People* (Aldershot, 2005).

Sutton, A. F., 'Merchants', in V. Gillespie and S. Powell (eds), *A Companion to the Early Printed Book in Britain, 1476–1558* (Cambridge, 2014), pp. 127–33.

Swann, J., 'English and European shoes from 1200–1520', in R. C. Schwinges, R. Schorta and K. Oschema (eds), *Fashion and Clothing in Late Medieval Europe* (Basel, 2010), pp. 15–25.

Swanson, H., *Medieval Artisans: An Urban Class in Late Medieval England* (Oxford, 1989).

Talbot, C. H. and E. A. Hammond, *The Medical Practitioners in Medieval England: A Biographical Register* (London, 1965).

Tanner, N., 'Religious practice', in C. Rawcliffe and R. Wilson (eds), *Medieval Norwich* (London, 2004), pp. 137–55.

Tarbutt, W., 'The ancient cloth trade of Cranbrook', *Archaeologia Cantiana*, 9 (1874), xcvi–civ.

Terpstra, N., *Religious Refugees in the Early Modern World: An Alternative History of the Reformation* (Cambridge, 2015).

Thielemans, M.-R., *Bourgogne et Angleterre: Relations politiques et économiques entre les Pays-Bas bourguignons et l'Angleterre* (Brussels, 1966).

Thoen, E., 'Immigration to Bruges during the late Middle Ages', in S. Cavaciocchi (ed.), *Le migrazioni in Europa secc. XIII–XVIII* (Florence, 1994), pp. 335–53.

Thomas, A., 'Margaret of Teschen's Czech prayer: transnationalism and female literacy in the later Middle Ages', *Huntington Library Quarterly*, 74 (2011), 309–23.

Thomas, A., *Reading Women in Late Medieval Europe: Anne of Bohemia and Chaucer's Female Audience* (London, 2015).

Thomas, H. M., *The English and the Normans: Ethnic Hostility, Assimilation, and Identity, 1066–c. 1220* (Oxford, 2003).

Thompson, B., 'The laity, the alien priories and the redistribution of ecclesiastical property', in N. J. Rogers (ed.), *England in the Fourteenth Century* (Stamford, 1994), pp. 19–41.

Thompson, P., *The History and Antiquities of Boston* (London, 1856).

Thomson, J. A. F., 'Scots in England in the fifteenth century', *Scottish Historical Review*, 79 (2000), 1–16.

Thornton, T., *The Channel Islands, 1370–1640: Between England and Normandy* (Woodbridge, 2012).

Thrupp, S., 'Aliens in and around London in the fifteenth century', in A. E. J. Hollaender and W. Kellaway (eds), *Studies in London History Presented to P. E. Jones* (London, 1969), pp. 251–72.

Thrupp, S., 'A survey of the alien population of England in 1440', *Speculum*, 32 (1957), 262–73.

Tillott, P. M. (ed.), *The Victoria History of the County of York: The City of York* (London, 1961).

Treharne, R. F., *The Baronial Plan of Reform, 1258–1263*, 2nd edn (Manchester, 1971).

Treuherz, J., *Ford Madox Brown: Pre-Raphaelite Pioneer* (Manchester, 2011).

Tuck, J. A., 'The emergence of a northern nobility, 1250–1400', *Northern History*, 22 (1986), 1–17.

Turville-Petre, T., *England the Nation: Language, Literature, and National Identity, 1290–1340* (Oxford, 1996).

Twycross, M., 'Some aliens in York and their overseas connections: up to c. 1470', *Leeds Studies in English*, 29 (1998), 359–79.

Ungerer, G., 'Prostitution in late Elizabethan London: the case of Mary Newborough', *Medieval and Renaissance Drama in England*, 15 (2003), 138–223.

Ungerer, G., 'Recovering a black African's voice in an English law suit', *Medieval and Renaissance Drama in England*, 17 (2005), 255–71.

Vale, M., *The Angevin Legacy and the Hundred Years War, 1250–1340* (Oxford, 1990).

Vale, M., *The Princely Court: Medieval Courts and Culture in North-West Europe, 1270–1380* (Oxford, 2001).

Van Der Wee, H., 'Structural changes and specialization in the industry of the Southern Netherlands, 1100–1600', *Economic History Review*, 2nd series, 28 (1975), 203–21.

Vaughan, R., *Philip the Good: The Apogee of Burgundy* (Woodbridge, 2002).

Wakelin, M. F., *Language and History in Cornwall* (Leicester, 1975).

Wallace, D., 'Constance', in D. Wallace (ed.), *Europe: A Literary History, 1348–1418*, 2 vols (Oxford, 2015), II, 673–5.

Walsham, A., *Charitable Hatred: Tolerance and Intolerance in England, 1500–1700* (Manchester, 2008).

Warneke, S., *Images of the Educational Traveller in Early Modern England* (Leiden, 1995).

Warnicke, R. M., *The Marrying of Anne of Cleves: Royal Protocol in Early Modern England* (Cambridge, 2000).

Watts, J., 'The Plantagenet Empire and the continent: retrospect and prospect', in P. Crooks, D. Green and W. M. Ormrod (eds), *The Plantagenet Empire, 1259–1453* (Donington, 2016), pp. 403–20.

Wedgwood, J. C. (ed.), *History of Parliament: Biographies of the Members of the Commons House, 1439–1509* (London, 1936).

Weiner, A., 'A note on Jewish doctors in England in the reign of Henry IV', *Jewish Quarterly Review*, 18 (1905), 141–5.

Wilson, D., 'Evil May Day 1517', *History Today*, 67:6 (2017), 66–71.

Wilson, R[ichard], 'The textile industry', in C. Rawcliffe, R. Wilson and C. Clark (eds), *Norwich since 1550* (London, 2004), pp. 219–42.

Wilson, R[obert], *Bloody Foreigners: The Story of Immigration to Britain*, rev. edn (London, 2013).

Wright, L., 'Trade between England and the Low Countries: evidence from historical linguistics', in C. M. Barron and N. Saul (eds), *England and the Low Countries in the Late Middle Ages* (Stroud, 1995), pp. 169–79.

Wyatt, T., 'Aliens in England before the Huguenots', *Proceedings of the Huguenot Society of London*, 19 (1953–9), 77, 80–1.

Yungblut, L. H., *Strangers Settled Here Amongst Us: Policies, Perceptions and the Presence of Aliens in Elizabethan England* (London, 1996).

Internet sources

Anglo-Norman Dictionary, www.anglo-norman.net.

Dictionary of Medieval Latin from British Sources, www.dmlbs.ox.ac.uk.

Dizionario Biografico degli Italiani, www.treccani.it/biografico/index.html.

England's Immigrants 1330–1550, www.englandsimmigrants.com.

Middle English Dictionary, http://quod.lib.umich.edu/m/med.

Oxford Dictionary of Family Names in Britain and Ireland, www.oxfordreference.com.

Oxford Dictionary of National Biography, www.odnb.com.

Oxford English Dictionary, www.oed.com.

The Soldier in Later Medieval England, research.reading.ac.uk/medievalsoldier.

A Vision of Britain through Time, www.visionofbritain.org.uk/census/1901.

INDEX

Note: English places are indexed by their historic county; places outside England are indexed by their equivalent modern state.

Aachen (Germany) 108
Aagaard (Denmark) 110
Aartswaarde (Netherlands) 140
Aberdeen (Scotland) 89, 90
Abingdon (Berkshire) 116, 149
abjuration 59
Adriatic and Aegean Seas 120
Africa and Africans 182, 187-91, 193-4
Agen (France) 98
Agincourt, battle of (1415) 166
Ainstable (Cumberland) 64
Aldeburgh (Suffolk) 229
Aldobrandi family 113, 116
Alexandria (Egypt) 189
Alfonso V, king of Portugal 119
alien priories 21-2, 25, 134, 167, 207, 231
alien subsidy 5-7, 9, 30, 32, 42-4, 48-51,
        60-1, 69-70, 74-5, 78, 83, 86,
        99-100, 107, 109-10, 115-16, 118,
        121, 129, 134, 137, 145-6, 149-50,
        158, 161-5, 168-9, 173, 177, 187,
        208-9, 212, 220-1, 226-8, 234
    exemption from 4, 6, 23, 27, 45-8, 83,
        85, 144
    grants and collections
        (1440) 5, 6, 9, 18, 32, 44-51, 53-7,
            59-65, 68-9, 74-6, 78-83, 85-7,
            89-90, 94-8, 103, 106-7, 109,
            111-12, 114-18, 128-30, 134-6,
            140, 144, 146, 149, 159-60, 166-8,
            170, 174, 176, 179 n.69, 191, 219,
            221, 230, 235, 249
        (1441) 45, 51-2, 78, 99, 114, 116, 140,
            144, 158-9, 163, 209, 219, 238-9

        (1442) 46, 51, 166
        (1443) 99, 113-14, 116, 118, 134, 136,
            140, 144, 229
        (1449) 112-13, 146, 187
        (1453) 31, 47, 50, 112
        (1455) 76, 87, 112, 136
        (1456) 51, 116, 144-5
        (1457) 112, 114, 120, 145
        (1458) 75, 106, 112, 115, 146
        (1464) 75, 158
        (1466) 164
        (1468) 49, 115-16, 135, 163-4
        (1469) 145
        (1470) 49, 87, 114
        (1471) 50, 112
        (1483-4) 6-7, 50, 56, 60, 74, 87-8,
            90, 99-100, 103, 109-10, 112-16,
            118-19, 130-2, 138-41, 145-6, 158,
            173, 217, 227-8, 231
        (1487) 5, 7, 9, 50, 87, 128, 130,
            134-6, 144, 149, 159, 166, 170,
            174-6, 195
aliens 3, 12-14
    anti-alien attitudes and policies 17, 21,
        29-37, 47, 51, 88, 109-10, 184-5,
        197, 229, 241, 243-50, 256-7
    householders 6, 32, 34, 36, 42-5, 47-8,
        50, 52-6, 62, 82, 84, 89, 95, 107,
        113, 118, 139, 162, 174-5, 177, 187,
        191, 228
    legal status 1, 4, 5, 8, 12, 16-17, 20-2,
        25-6, 36, 70
    non-householders 89, 107, 158, 163,
        190, 195, 221

Cathedral 136
province 159
Cappadocia (Turkey) 120
cappers 130, 165, 172, 232
Carlisle (Cumberland) 62–4
Carlow (Ireland) 16
Carmarthen (Wales) 76
Carpenter, John and Katherine 35, 176, 229
carpenters 82, 238
Carta Mercatoria (1303) 20, 31
carters 34, 220
carvers 84, 135
Castelyn, Edward and William 121, 197
Castile, kingdom of 4, 118, 188
Castle Hedingham (Essex) 45, 65
Catalans in England 118, 146
Cattaneo family 115–16
cattle-herders 165
Cawood (Yorkshire) 172
Caxton, William 211, 228
Centurione, Galeotto 245, 253 n.94
Centurione family 114
chamberlains 29, 166
chancery and chancery documents 5,
        20–8, 75, 89–90, 161, 196–7, 221,
        243–4, 246
Channel Islanders in England 46, 83–4
Channel Islands 16, 46, 76, 81, 84, 94,
        192, 208
Charles IV, emperor 211
Charles V, emperor 196
Charles VII, king of France 27
Charles the Bold, duke of
        Burgundy 246
Charterhouse, Sheen (Surrey) 134
Chaucer, Geoffrey 173, 211, 214
chefs 137
Chelmsford (Essex) 65, 174
Cheshire, palatinate county of 54, 65,
        104, 106
Chester (Cheshire) 15, 77, 79, 85, 191,
        234, 258
Chios (Greece) 121
Chippenham (Wiltshire) 65, 83, 160
Chipping Camden (Gloucestershire) 163

Christchurch Priory (Hampshire) 167
Cini, Filippo 164, 168, 191
Cini family 116
Cinque Ports (Kent/Sussex) 54, 67,
        80, 84, 99
clergy 29–30, 228
    alien 1, 22, 27, 29–30, 30, 45, 82, 101,
        158–61, 197, 209, 215, 219
    archdeacons 119
    bishops 16, 158–9, 218
    canons 119
    chaplains 89–90, 111, 129, 159–61
    clerks 89, 160, 219, 221
    English clergy abroad 58
    expelled from England 58, 207–8
    Irish 82, 161, 258
    monks 19, 21, 25, 45, 54, 58
    nuns 45, 54
    parish clergy 30, 215–16
Clevelanders in England 145, 149
Cleves, duchy of 105, 107
cloth workers 147–50, 188, 227,
        242, 249
cobblers 130–1, 141, 171
Cobham, George Brooke, Lord 84
coinage 132
Cok, Edmund 118
Cok, Tilman 132, 227
Colchester (Essex) 62–3, 65, 147–50,
        173, 242
Cologne (Germany) 108, 145
Colwich (Staffordshire) 88
comb set makers 115
Coney Weston (Suffolk) 228
Constance (Germany) 203
    Council of (1414–18) 203, 214
Constantinople (modern Istanbul,
        Turkey) 120–1
cooks 84, 118, 137, 144, 210
Cordoba (Spain) 119
cordwainers 130–1, 137, 141–2, 162,
        220, 245
Cork (Ireland) 83
Cornwall 54, 68, 79–80, 83, 87, 96–7, 99,
        104, 106, 117–18, 166, 226